Employee-AI Experience in Human Resource Management

Henning Tirrel
https://orcid.org/0000-0002-4610-3158
Ostfalia University of Applied Sciences, Germany

Hans Rüdiger Kaufmann
University of Nicosia, Cyprus & University of Applied Management Studies Mannheim, Germany

IGI Global
Scientific Publishing
Publishing Tomorrow's Research Today

Vice President of Editorial — Melissa Wagner
Director of Acquisitions — Mikaela Felty
Director of Book Development — Jocelynn Hessler
Production Manager — Mike Brehm
Cover Design — Jose Rosado

Published in the United States of America by
IGI Global Scientific Publishing
701 East Chocolate Avenue
Hershey, PA, 17033, USA
Tel: 717-533-8845 | Fax: 717-533-7115
Website: https://www.igi-global.com E-mail: cust@igi-global.com

Library of Congress Cataloging-in-Publication Data

Names: Tirrel, Henning, 1991- editor | Kaufmann, Hans Ruediger, 1958- editor
Title: Employee-AI experience in human resource management / edited by Henning Tirrel, and Hans Rüdiger Kaufmann.
Other titles: Employee-artificial intelligence experience in human resource management
Description: Hershey, PA : IGI Global Scientific Publishing, [2026] | Includes bibliographical references and index. | Summary: "This book explores how AI integrates into human resource management practices and affects employee experiences, perceptions, and interactions. It examines the benefits and challenges of AI in areas like recruitment, performance evaluation, communication, employee engagement, privacy, fairness, and organizational trust"-- Provided by publisher.
Identifiers: LCCN 2026028395 (print) | LCCN 2026028396 (ebook) | ISBN 9798260023037 hardcover | ISBN 9798260023044 paperback | ISBN 9798260023051 ebook
Subjects: LCSH: Personnel management--Technological innovations | Artificial intelligence--Business applications | Psychology, Industrial
Classification: LCC HF5549.5.T33 E47 2027 (print) | LCC HF5549.5.T33 (ebook)
LC record available at https://lccn.loc.gov/2026028395
LC ebook record available at https://lccn.loc.gov/2026028396
British Cataloguing in Publication Data
A Cataloguing in Publication record for this book is available from the British Library.

Table of Contents

Detailed Table of Contents

Digital inequality remains a critical barrier to sustainable development in emerging economies like Indonesia. This chapter proposes "Digital Mutual Cooperation", a novel conceptual framework that integrates digital transformation with local cultural wisdom. Utilizing bibliometric analysis of 151 Scopus-indexed documents (2020–2025) via Biblioshiny, the study reveals a significant thematic shift: academic discourse has evolved from pure digitalization toward community empowerment and inclusive sustainability. Findings indicate that digitalization is no longer a standalone technical goal but an integrated driver for social cohesion and ecological balance. By synthesizing Murray's social innovation and Zimmerman's empowerment theories, the chapter offers a strategic roadmap for policymakers and practitioners to design community-based digital programs. It bridges the gap between technological disruption and traditional values, transforming digital disparity into inclusive growth aligned with the SDGs and Indonesia's Golden Vision 2045.

Algorithmic and artificial intelligence–enabled systems increasingly shape core human resource processes, including recruitment, performance evaluation, monitoring, and workflow coordination. Evidence shows that their effects are contingent. In some contexts, these systems strengthen fairness, trust, and job quality; in others, they intensify strain, reduce meaningfulness, and weaken ethical vigilance. This chapter

to the existing literature by offering empirical evidence regarding the contacts between AI, acceptance of the members of staff, and the HR quality of service, hence offering useful views to both practitioners and academics in the HRM field.

This chapter examines how AI-based recruitment systems can produce algorithmic discrimination against job candidates. While these systems are widely used to improve efficiency in screening and selection processes, they may reproduce historical biases and disadvantage groups such as women, ethnic minorities, older individuals, and candidates with health conditions. The study is based on a qualitative content analysis of approximately 40 documents published between 2016 and 2025. The findings show that discrimination emerges from the interaction of multiple technical and social factors rather than a single source. Accordingly, the chapter develops a six-factor framework and offers policy recommendations to improve fairness, transparency, and accountability in AI-based recruitment systems.

This chapter examines human–AI complementarity in human resource management through the lens of HR marketing. We argue that when AI moves into high-stakes domains such as appraisal and placement, acceptance depends less on technical performance alone and more on value judgments about understandability, fairness, and respect for the person. Drawing on evidence and stakeholder voices from Japanese organizations, we organize acceptance drivers into three interrelated domains: psychological acceptance (e.g., anxiety and perceived "warmth"); explainability–fairness-based trust; and ethics and governance concerns (e.g., privacy, accountability, and avenues for appeal). We show that effective complementarity requires both cognitive legitimacy (trust grounded in explainability and fairness) and relational legitimacy (psychological safety and perceived warmth), supported by governance as a baseline condition. The chapter concludes by outlining how HR marketing can reduce friction and strengthen legitimacy in AI-mediated HR decision-making, especially in high-context organizational settings.

Foreword

The world suddenly awoke to the reality of Artificial Intelligence in January 2023, when the first Generative AI chatbot reached 100 million users in less than 3 months. To put that into perspective, the Internet had needed 7 years to reach the same number of people and mobile phones 16. The ability of communicating with a machine in natural human language and obtain thoughtful and useful answers made everyone aware of how this field of computer science had evolved and was now ready to deliver on promises that many believed were still on the realm of science fiction.

By reshaping the foundations of how we work, learn, compete and collaborate, AI has the potential to transform almost every sector and organization on the planet. In most businesses, it is already an everyday reality, and few areas are as directly affected by it as Human Resource Management (HRM). Algorithms, data analytics, and machine learning are increasingly part of how organizations recruit, develop, evaluate and retain employees. However, this development raises, at least, as many questions as it promises solutions.

How can we leverage the power of AI for organizations to become more effective without threatening the human dimension of work? How can we combine the unique human intelligence, ethics, and sense of purpose with the immense power of artificial intelligence? That is precisely the question that these two books are dedicated to exploring in depth, articulating it in book 1 as "Human-AI complementarity" and expanding it in book 2 to the "Employee-AI Experience".

Each chapter examines a specific angle of this interplay of humans and AI, covering multiple disciplinary perspectives, diverse organizational contexts and different countries. The use of AI is assessed in the different functions of HRM such as preboarding, recruiting, personnel development, quality management, HRM processes, and AI-derived strategic data-driven decision making. In doing so, a significant effort was dedicated to address the risks of AI, particularly algorithmic discrimination and lack of fairness. The experiences and reactions of the people affected are taken very seriously, with a chapter explicitly focused on the human experience of algorithmic HR systems.

Further chapters focus on specific fields of application: AI-supported predictive models for workforce allocation in the industrial sector, AI-based preboarding videos and their impact on affective commitment, or the use of AI in the care of older people with far-reaching implications for care staff, concepts, and areas of responsibility. This illustrates clearly that it is not a matter of choosing between human and artificial intelligence, but rather of consciously fostering an approach that leverages the respective strengths of both.

Methodologically, this series of two books spans from systematic literature reviews and bibliometric analyses to conceptual frameworks – for example, on "academic career happiness" – as well as qualitative case studies and quantitative empirical research in various countries. This wide range is no coincidence, but an expression of how the interaction between humans and AI in HRM can only be understood in an interdisciplinary manner and with due regard for different cultural and institutional contexts.

The recurring theme throughout these pages echoes a fundamental message: technology must serve humanity. AI is a powerful tool whose impact depends on how we design it, regulate it, and embed it into human, organizational, and societal contexts. Human complementarity means understanding AI not as a replacement, but as a complement to human judgment, empathy, and responsibility.

Ultimately, I see this outstanding work as an invitation to a reflective and forward-looking dialogue: between academia and practice, between technology development and HR strategy, and between a focus on efficiency and a commitment to fairness, participation, and employee well-being. It challenges us to balance innovation with accountability, efficiency with justice, and technological capacities with the human qualities that enable us to collaborate, create, and build better futures together.

Rui Grilo
Microsoft, Portugal

Preface

INTRODUCTION

The accelerating integration of artificial intelligence (AI) into human resource management has fundamentally transformed the way organizations recruit, evaluate, support, and retain talent. Once viewed primarily as a technological enhancement to administrative functions, AI has now emerged as a strategic force capable of reshaping workplace relationships, organizational cultures, and the employee experience itself. Across industries and regions, AI-driven systems are increasingly embedded within recruitment pipelines, employee performance management, workforce analytics, learning systems, and decision-making processes. Yet as organizations embrace these innovations, critical questions arise regarding fairness, transparency, inclusion, accountability, and the preservation of human dignity in technologically mediated workplaces.

This edited volume, *Employee-AI Experience in Human Resource Management*, brings together an international collection of scholars and practitioners who explore these complex and evolving dynamics from interdisciplinary and cross-cultural perspectives. The chapters presented in this book collectively examine how AI technologies influence employees, managers, institutions, and organizational systems, while simultaneously investigating the ethical, social, and psychological implications of AI-enabled HR practices. Importantly, the contributors move beyond purely technical discussions and instead center the human experience within AI transformation. Through conceptual models, empirical qualitative and quantitative investigations, and policy-oriented discussions, this book highlights both the opportunities and the tensions emerging at the intersection of people and intelligent systems.

A defining feature of this book is its global scope. The chapters draw on evidence and perspectives from diverse regions including Indonesia, Canada, Palestine, Tanzania, Turkey, Japan, Morocco, and India. This international representation reflects the reality that AI adoption in HRM is not confined to a single economic or cultural context. Rather, organizations worldwide are grappling with similar challenges surrounding algorithmic governance, employee trust, workplace fairness, and digital inclusion, while responding to these issues through locally informed practices and institutional norms. By incorporating insights from both developed and emerging economies, the volume provides a nuanced understanding of how technological transformation unfolds differently across organizational and societal settings.

Another important contribution of this collection lies in its emphasis on balancing innovation with humanity. While AI systems offer significant potential for improving efficiency, predictive accuracy, and operational performance, they also introduce new risks associated with bias, surveillance, dehumanization, and inequality. The chapters in this volume repeatedly demonstrate that successful AI integration in HRM cannot rely solely on technological sophistication. Instead, sustainable and ethical implementation depends upon trust, employee acceptance, explainability, participatory governance, and a continued commitment to human-centered management practices. In this regard, the book contributes to broader scholarly debates concerning responsible usage and application of AI, digital ethics, and the future of work.

As editors, we believe this volume arrives at a critical moment for researchers, practitioners, policymakers, and organizational leaders alike. The future of human resources management will undoubtedly involve closer collaboration between people and AI, but how this transformation will be implemented in different cultural and regional contexts remains uncertain and contested. The contributions in this book seek not only to analyze existing developments but also to encourage thoughtful reflection about the kind of workplaces organizations aspire to create in the age of AI. We hope the discussions presented throughout this collection inspire further interdisciplinary dialogue, innovative research, and responsible organizational practice centered on the enhancement of both technological capability and human well-being.

OVERVIEW OF THE CHAPTERS

Chapter 1, *From Digital Inequality to Inclusive Sustainability: A Conceptual Model of Digital Mutual Cooperation Based on Bibliometric Evidence*, by Hendry Hartono, Danang Prihandoko, Asep Permana, and Tagor Sigiro, examines digital inequality within emerging economies and proposes a culturally grounded framework for inclusive digital transformation. Through bibliometric analysis, the chapter demonstrates how contemporary digitalization discourse has shifted toward themes of empowerment, sustainability, and community resilience. By integrating social innovation and empowerment theories, the authors develop the concept of

"Digital Mutual Cooperation" offering policymakers and practitioners a roadmap for balancing technological advancement with local cultural values and sustainable development goals.

Chapter 2, *The Human Experience of Algorithmic HR: A Design-Sensitive, Semi-Structured Review*, by Ian Mizuki and Zoya Khan, investigates how algorithmic HR systems shape employee experiences across various organizational contexts. Drawing on empirical studies from sectors including gig work, customer service, and digital operations, the chapter identifies critical design features that influence employee perceptions of fairness, trust, stress, and autonomy. The authors argue that organizational outcomes are highly contingent upon system design choices, particularly regarding transparency, communication, monitoring structures, and collaborative human–AI interaction.

In Chapter 3, *AI-Enhanced Ontological Modeling of Academic Career Happiness and Performance*, Raed Atef proposes a conceptual framework that integrates AI tools with philosophical, psychological, and institutional perspectives to better understand academic well-being and performance. Focusing particularly on higher education environments, the chapter explores how AI-driven approaches such as natural language processing and machine learning may eventually help institutions analyze employee sentiment, identify drivers of happiness, and simulate organizational policy outcomes. The work highlights the importance of autonomy, recognition, leadership, and institutional culture in shaping employee engagement and retention.

Chapter 4, *Impact of Artificial Intelligence on HR Service Quality by Mediation of Employee Acceptance of AI in Tanzania*, by Shashi Kant, Wako Jio, Mohit Verma, and Thompson Ananth, presents an empirical investigation into the relationship between AI implementation and HR service quality. Based on data collected from 390 participants, the study demonstrates that employee acceptance plays a significant mediating role in determining the effectiveness of AI integration within HR processes. The findings emphasize that technological adoption alone is insufficient; organizations must actively cultivate trust, acceptance, and organizational readiness to fully realize the benefits of AI-enhanced HR services.

Chapter 5, *Between Efficiency and Fairness: Algorithmic Discrimination in AI-Based Recruitment Systems*, by Müjde Ertürk and Emrah Ayhan, critically examines the discriminatory risks associated with AI-enabled recruitment technologies. Through qualitative content analysis, the authors reveal how algorithmic systems may reproduce historical biases against women, ethnic minorities, older individuals, and people with health conditions. The chapter develops a six-factor framework explaining how technical and social dimensions interact to produce discriminatory outcomes and concludes with policy recommendations aimed at improving fairness, transparency, and accountability in recruitment systems.

Chapter 6, *HR Marketing and Human–AI Collaboration: Explainability and Relational Legitimacy in AI-Assisted HR Evaluation*, by Mitsunori Hirogaki and Rapeeporn Rungsithong, explores employee acceptance of AI-mediated HR evaluation systems through the lens of HR marketing and organizational legitimacy. Drawing on evidence from Japanese organizations, the chapter identifies psychological acceptance, explainability, fairness, and governance as central components shaping trust in AI systems. The authors argue that successful human–AI complementarity depends not only on technical reliability but also on emotional reassurance, relational legitimacy, and perceived organizational care.

Chapter 7, *Artificial Intelligence and Human Resource Management: The Case of the Agricultural Credit Bank of Morocco*, by Adil El-Ouali and Ahmed El Hammoumi, investigates how AI technologies contribute to HR performance and productivity within the banking sector. Using quantitative analysis conducted among employees of the Agricultural Credit Bank of Morocco, the study explores the relationship between AI tools, technological readiness, and HR effectiveness. The findings provide valuable insight into the practical implementation of AI within financial institutions operating in rapidly evolving technological environments.

Finally, Chapter 8, *Navigating Economic Uncertainty Through Strategic Human Resource Management: Safeguarding Employee Well-Being: A Case Study of Indian Banks*, by Navneet Ranjan, Atanu Bhattacharya, Uday Singh, Manidipa Mukherjee, and Sanjit Gomes, shifts the discussion toward organizational resilience during periods of economic instability. Drawing on social exchange theory and street-level bureaucracy perspectives, the chapter examines how Indian public banks support employee performance and well-being amid uncertainty. The authors identify job-related, learning-related, and contextual factors that enable workforce resilience and argue that strategic HRM practices remain essential for sustaining employee engagement during challenging economic conditions.

CONCLUSION

The chapters assembled in this volume collectively demonstrate that the future of human resource management will not be defined solely by technological capability, but by the quality of the relationship, organizations establish between intelligent systems and the people they serve. Across diverse contexts and methodological approaches, the contributors consistently reveal that AI adoption in HRM is deeply intertwined with issues of ethics, inclusion, trust, governance, and human well-being. Whether examining recruitment algorithms, employee acceptance, workplace fairness, digital inequality, or organizational resilience, the chapters emphasize that human-centered implementation must remain at the core of technological transformation.

One of the most significant insights emerging from this collection is the recognition that AI systems are not inherently neutral. Their outcomes are shaped by the assumptions, data structures, governance mechanisms, and organizational cultures within which they operate. Several chapters illustrate how poorly designed systems may unintentionally reproduce social inequalities, intensify workplace stress, or undermine employee autonomy. At the same time, the contributors also demonstrate that thoughtfully implemented AI technologies can strengthen transparency, improve service quality, support employee development, and foster more responsive organizational practices. The distinction between these outcomes often lies not in the technology itself, but in the ethical and managerial choices surrounding its deployment.

This volume also underscores the growing importance of interdisciplinary and international perspectives in understanding AI-driven HR transformation. The integration of insights from management studies, organizational psychology, digital governance, ethics, sustainability research, and information systems reflects the complexity of the challenges organizations now face. Furthermore, the global representation of case studies and research contexts highlights that while AI adoption is a worldwide phenomenon, its implementation remains deeply influenced by local institutional realities, cultural expectations, and socioeconomic conditions. Such diversity enriches conversation and encourages more context-sensitive approaches to AI governance and HR innovation.

As editors, we hope this book contributes meaningfully to ongoing academic and professional discussions surrounding the future of work and organizational transformation. We envision this collection serving as a resource for researchers seeking new theoretical directions, practitioners navigating AI implementation, policymakers developing governance frameworks, and educators preparing future leaders for technologically augmented workplaces. Most importantly, we hope the volume encourages organizations to view AI not simply as a mechanism for efficiency, but as an opportunity to reimagine HRM in ways that prioritize fairness, inclusion, collaboration, and human flourishing.

The rapid evolution of AI technologies ensures that the conversations initiated within this book will continue to develop in the years ahead. New forms of algorithmic management, predictive analytics, human–AI collaboration, and workplace automation will inevitably present additional opportunities and challenges. Consequently, the need for critical inquiry, ethical reflection, and interdisciplinary collaboration will remain essential. We conclude this volume with optimism that organizations can harness the transformative power of AI while preserving the values that define meaningful and sustainable human work.

Chapter 1
From Digital Inequality to Inclusive Sustainability:
A Conceptual Model of Digital Mutual Cooperation Based on Bibliometric Evidence

Hendry Hartono
http://orcid.org/0000-0001-6489-4929
Bina Nusantara University, Indonesia

Danang Prihandoko
http://orcid.org/0000-0002-1664-7197
Bina Nusantara University, Indonesia

Asep Medy Widya Permana
Pt. Autrans Asia Indonesia, Indonesia

Tagor Sidik Sigiro
Indonesia Institute of Certified Public Accountants, Indonesia

ABSTRACT

Digital inequality remains a critical barrier to sustainable development in emerging economies like Indonesia. This chapter proposes "Digital Mutual Cooperation", a novel conceptual framework that integrates digital transformation with local cultural wisdom. Utilizing bibliometric analysis of 151 Scopus-indexed documents (2020–2025) via Biblioshiny, the study reveals a significant thematic shift: academic discourse has evolved from pure digitalization toward community empowerment and inclusive sustainability. Findings indicate that digitalization is no longer a standalone technical goal but an integrated driver for social cohesion and ecological balance.

DOI: 10.4018/979-8-2600-2303-7.ch001

By synthesizing Murray's social innovation and Zimmerman's empowerment theories, the chapter offers a strategic roadmap for policymakers and practitioners to design community-based digital programs. It bridges the gap between technological disruption and traditional values, transforming digital disparity into inclusive growth aligned with the SDGs and Indonesia's Golden Vision 2045.

INTRODUCTION

The early twenty-first century is defined by a rapid transition toward a digitally mediated global economy. This transformation, often linked to the Industry 4.0 discourse, has fundamentally reconfigured value creation and social interaction patterns. These changes have simultaneously altered governance arrangements across multiple societal levels to accommodate new digital realities. Initially, digitalization was advanced as a potential equalizing force capable of circumventing entrenched institutional constraints. It was expected to broaden access to markets and socio-economic mobility for marginalized populations worldwide. However, this normative expectation is increasingly problematized as expanded connectivity often coexists with deepening inequalities regarding meaningful empowerment (Rimbawati, 2023; Nigam, 2024).

This digital paradox remains particularly salient within emerging economies such as Indonesia. Despite high social media penetration and rapid economic expansion, substantial internal disparities continue to persist. The digital divide has evolved into a multidimensional phenomenon involving uneven literacy and infrastructural variations between urban and rural regions (Dalimunthe et al., 2021; Martínez-Bravo et al., 2022; Arion et al., 2024). These dynamics expose the limitations of technocentric approaches that prioritize hardware diffusion over necessary social foundations. Without a cultural basis, digitalization risks becoming an extractive process that marginalizes local knowledge systems. Today, this challenge is further intensified by the integration of Artificial Intelligence, which demands a new synergy between technology and human agency.

A persistent shortcoming in digital transformation literature is the analytical decoupling of technological innovation from social and cultural value systems. While managerial studies prioritize efficiency and adoption metrics, sociological analyses often view digitalization as an exogenous disruption to community structures. Consequently, there is an insufficient theoretical framework situating digital transformation within indigenous social capital. In Indonesia, this gap is critical due to the enduring relevance of Gotong Royong, the principle of mutual cooperation that serves as a resilient social infrastructure for collective action. Within Human Resource Management, this cooperative logic is essential for fostering human-AI complementarity to ensure digital tools empower the workforce. Ultimately, neglecting this logic favors individualistic arrangements that misalign with local social structures and risk eroding social cohesion.

To address this conceptual lacuna, this chapter advances a novel paradigm termed Digital Mutual Cooperation, or the digitalization of Gotong Royong. The central argument posits that transitioning from digital inequality toward inclusive sustainability requires re-contextualizing technology within locally embedded cultural values. This proposition is informed by academic trends shifting from technology-centric explanations toward community empowerment, social capital, and sustainability-oriented outcomes. Such developments suggest that digital technologies should function as mediating instruments for pursuing inclusive forms of human development (Ghosh & Kumar, 2025; Khan et al., 2024). By centering collective practices, this framework aligns technological advancement with the social fabric of the Global South to ensure long-term resilience.

.The relevance of this inquiry is further underscored by Indonesia's long-term development agenda, particularly its aspiration to achieve the Golden Vision 2045, which seeks to reconcile sustained economic advancement with social equity. This national objective closely aligns with the United Nations Sustainable Development Goals (SDGs), notably Goal 9 concerning industry, innovation, and infrastructure, Goal 10 concerning reduced inequalities, and Goal 11 concerning sustainable cities and communities (Hajian & Kashani, 2021; Ruggerio, 2021). By situating digital social innovation within a normative framework grounded in mutual cooperation, this chapter advances a culturally informed pathway through which digital transformation can contribute to inclusive growth rather than reinforce existing structural inequalities.

To establish an empirical foundation for this conceptual contribution, the chapter employs a systematic bibliometric analysis of 151 Scopus-indexed publications published between 2020 and 2025, following established approaches in systematic literature review and bibliometric mapping (Dušková & Vita, 2022; George Reyes & Glasserman, 2020). This methodological approach facilitates a structured mapping of the intellectual landscape, enables the identification of dominant and emerging research themes, and allows for an examination of how scholarly discourses on digitalization intersect with community-based development and sustainability. The insights derived from this analysis provide the evidentiary basis for the formulation of the Digital Mutual Cooperation framework.

Accordingly, this chapter addresses three interrelated research questions that remain insufficiently examined within the management and development literature, namely:

a. What scholarly discourses on digitalization, Artificial Intelligence, Human Resource Management, and sustainability have evolved and converged over the past five years.
b. What structural limitations within existing community empowerment and HRM models constrain the realization of inclusive digital sustainability in the era of A; and
c. How principles of mutual cooperation can be digitally reconfigured to function as contemporary mechanisms of community autonomy and resilience.

The contribution of this chapter is twofold. From a theoretical standpoint, it integrates Digital Social Innovation theory with Empowerment Theory and HRM perspectives within a Global South context, thereby extending conceptual frameworks that have been predominantly shaped by Global North experiences. From a practical standpoint, it offers policy-relevant insights for stakeholders ranging from national policymakers to community leaders and practitioners engaged in digital and green development initiatives. By emphasizing collective capacity building rather than isolated technological interventions, the chapter provides a foundation for more inclusive and context-sensitive approaches to digital empowerment.

The remainder of this chapter is organized as follows. The next section reviews the theoretical foundations of digitalization, mutual cooperation, and inclusive sustainability. This is followed by a detailed exposition of the bibliometric methodology employed in the study. Subsequent sections present and discuss the thematic mapping results that inform the proposed Digital Mutual Cooperation model. The chapter concludes with policy implications and directions for future research, emphasizing that the movement from digital inequality toward inclusive sustainability is inherently a collective, rather than individual, digital endeavor.

LITERATURE REVIEW

1. The Ontology of Digitalization: From Technical Conversion to Socio-Technical Evolution

Contemporary scholarship in management and information systems demonstrates a pronounced ontological reorientation in the conceptualization of digital technologies. Earlier analytical frameworks predominantly regarded technology as a neutral, instrumental artifact deployed to enhance operational efficiency. In contrast, more recent debates increasingly conceptualize digitalization as a socio-technical ensemble that is deeply embedded within social relations, institutional arrangements, and cultural contexts. Central to this shift is a clear analytical distinction between digitization, which denotes the technical process of converting analog information into digital form, and digitalization, which refers to the broader socio-technical transformation through which digital technologies reshape organizational routines, social interactions, and economic structures (Arion et al., 2024; Ateeq et al., 2024).

This distinction is theoretically consequential, as digitization is primarily associated with efficiency and automation, whereas digitalization entails systemic, relational, and transformational change. In the contemporary era, this ontological shift is further accelerated by the integration of Artificial Intelligence (AI), which redefines the boundary between human agency and machine autonomy. Within the context of the Global South, the ontology of digitalization must now account for Human-AI complementarity, where AI is not merely a tool for automation but a collaborative partner in managing organizational routines and human capital. This ensures that digital transformation remains a socio-technical evolution that enhances, rather than replaces, human value.

In emerging economies such as Indonesia, digitalization manifests as an inherently ambivalent process. On one side, it expands market access for micro, small, and medium enterprises (MSMEs) by lowering transaction costs, enhancing connectivity, and facilitating participation in digital value chains. On the other side, it introduces the risk of structural dependency on global digital platforms and algorithmic infrastructures that operate beyond local regulatory and institutional oversight. This tension is well explained through Socio-Technical Systems (STS) Theory, which posits that sustainable system performance depends on the effective alignment of social and technical subsystems. When digital technologies are implemented without adequate consideration of local norms, values, and organizational practices, socio-technical misalignment emerges, often resulting in resistance, superficial adoption, or what is frequently described in the literature as digital rejection.

The ontological evolution of digitalization is further reflected in the growing prominence of the Society 5.0 paradigm. Initially articulated within the Japanese policy context, Society 5.0 has gained relevance in other national development agendas, including Indonesia's long-term vision of Indonesia Emas 2045. Unlike Industry 4.0, which prioritizes automation, data integration, and machine-centric productivity, Society 5.0 advances a human-centered orientation that emphasizes social well-being, inclusivity, and resilience. Within this paradigm, digital technologies are positioned as enablers of human capability enhancement rather than as ends in themselves. Empirical research suggests that realizing this vision requires reconceptualizing digital literacy beyond technical proficiency toward digital agency, defined as the capacity of individuals and communities to actively shape social, economic, and institutional outcomes through meaningful engagement with digital technologies (Salim & Rosyidi, 2025).

An important ontological dimension of digitalization concerns technological affordances, which refer to the action possibilities a technological artifact enables for its users. In culturally embedded settings, these affordances are not universal but are mediated by social norms, collective values, and local institutional arrangements. Digital communication platforms may function as virtual communal spaces that support essential coordination, deliberation, and mutual assistance. Within the Indonesian context, these platforms frequently assume functions analogous to a digital *Balai Desa*, serving as loci for collective decision-making. This illustrates that socio-technical evolution involves a process of meaning construction through which technologies are domesticated in line with local wisdom. Such reinterpretation ensures that digital tools effectively advance collective objectives while maintaining cultural integrity (Salim & Rosyidi, 2025).

Recognizing the systemic and socially embedded character of digitalization has significant implications for governance and implementation strategies. Conventional approaches to digital transformation have often relied on top-down deployment models that marginalize local actors and exacerbate patterns of exclusion. In contrast, a socio-technical perspective underscores the importance of participatory design principles that prioritize stakeholder inclusion, deliberative processes, and co-creation. Such principles are consistent with democratic technology frameworks, as they enable marginalized groups, including rural communities and coastal populations, to participate meaningfully in shaping how digital tools are designed, governed, and utilized. By foregrounding social embeddedness and participatory governance, digitalization can be steered away from its potential adverse consequences, such as surveillance and exclusion, and redirected toward pathways that support inclusive and sustainability-oriented development (Khan et al., 2024; Ateeq et al., 2024).

2. Digital Mutual Cooperation: The Digital Metamorphosis of Gotong Royong

Gotong Royong represents a core pillar of the Indonesian socio-cultural order and has historically functioned as a foundational mechanism of collective survival, social solidarity, and informal socio-economic protection. Embedded in norms of reciprocity, shared responsibility, and communal labor, *Gotong Royong* operates as an endogenous form of social capital that sustains community cohesion and collective resilience. In the contemporary context of accelerated digital disruption, however, this value system is confronted with a profound ontological challenge associated with digital individualization. Algorithmic personalization, platform-mediated consumption, and data-driven preference optimization increasingly privilege individualized engagement, thereby creating structural pressures that risk attenuating collective orientations central to social cohesion.

Digital Mutual Cooperation is advanced as a strategic synthesis that enables the reconfiguration of traditional solidarity within networked environments. This process constitutes a digital metamorphosis where *Gotong Royong* is reconstituted as a collective practice embedded within modern infrastructures. From a Human Resource Management (HRM) perspective, this paradigm functions as a framework for managing talent in digitally networked settings. It suggests that the synergy between human employees and AI systems should be governed by cooperative principles. Such an approach ensures that algorithmic task allocation and platform-mediated work prioritize collective well-being and social equity. By embedding these norms into HRM, organizations can foster a resilient digital culture aligned with the values of the Global South.

Theoretically, this transformation can be situated within Social Capital Theory, which conceptualizes trust, reciprocity, and shared norms as relational resources that enable coordinated collective action. When these resources are mediated through digital technologies, they give rise to digital social capital, a form of capital that is no longer bound by spatial proximity or localized interaction. Instead, digital social capital is characterized by its networked, scalable, and fluid properties, which facilitate the formation of bridging capital across socially and geographically dispersed communities. Empirical studies examining digitally mediated Gotong Royong practices during the COVID-19 pandemic provide evidence that such initiatives were frequently more adaptive and responsive in mobilizing collective assistance than centralized bureaucratic mechanisms (Faedlulloh et al., 2021). These findings indicate that digitalization, when guided by culturally embedded logics, can extend and intensify traditional forms of solidarity rather than eroding them.

A defining feature of Digital Mutual Cooperation is the transition from passive participation toward active co-creation. Within this paradigm, community members are positioned as collective stakeholders who actively participate in the governance and distribution of shared digital value. This orientation aligns with Digital Social Innovation principles, emphasizing co-production and collective agency to address social needs. In the Indonesian context, these dynamics are visible in digital cooperatives and crowdfunding initiatives that prioritize collective welfare over individual capital accumulation (Sumarmi et al., 2022). By embedding *Gotong Royong* principles into interaction architectures, platforms can cultivate a durable sense of communal belonging. Such designs ensure that digital engagement extends beyond transactional exchange to foster deep social solidarity.

The digital transformation of Gotong Royong further introduces the concept of algorithmic solidarity, defined as the intentional design of algorithms and platform logics that incentivize collective behavior rather than individual competition. For instance, digital marketplaces oriented towards rural producers can be structured to prioritize group purchasing mechanisms, shared logistics systems, or cooperative pricing arrangements, thereby institutionalizing mutual cooperation within platform governance and operational processes. Such design choices resonate with the notion of a Pancasila-based digital culture, which functions as a normative safeguard against the extractive tendencies associated with global surveillance capitalism. By framing data as a shared community resource rather than a privately appropriated commodity, algorithmic solidarity reinforces collective empowerment and limits asymmetric value extraction (Sumarmi et al., 2022).

Taken together, Digital Mutual Cooperation reflects a broader reorientation in the institutional logic of community development. This reorientation entails a shift away from charity-based models, in which digital access is externally delivered to passive recipients, toward social enterprise-oriented models that emphasize collective capability development, shared ownership, and community self-reliance. Through this lens, digitalization functions as an instrument for strengthening social infrastructure rather than undermining it. Such an approach enhances the adaptive capacity and resilience of Indonesian communities in the face of global technological volatility and provides a robust conceptual foundation for inclusive sustainability, understood as the capacity of communities to pursue long-term socio-economic development while preserving social cohesion, collective agency, and cultural integrity (Sumarmi et al., 2022; Vadiyala, 2021).

3. Empowerment Theory: Psychological and Structural Dimensions

The conceptualization of empowerment in digitally mediated contexts requires a clear departure from access-centric approaches that equate progress with mere connectivity. Instead, empowerment must be understood as a multidimensional construct that integrates internal cognitive transformation with external structural conditions. This chapter anchors its analysis in Empowerment Theory as developed by Zimmerman (1995), which frames empowerment as a multi-level phenomenon encompassing psychological empowerment at the individual level, organizational capacity at the meso level, and transformative social change at the community level. Within Digital Mutual Cooperation, empowerment is reconceptualized as a collective process through which communities acquire control over digital resources and decision-making. This sustained progress allows marginalized groups to effectively address locally embedded socio-economic challenges through institutional arrangements.

At the psychological level, digital empowerment extends far beyond the possession of technical skills or functional literacy. In the AI era, this must evolve to include

AI self-efficacy, where individuals feel capable of interacting with and supervising intelligent systems. This dimension is critical for modern HRM strategies to ensure the workforce can navigate the structural power relations within AI-driven economies. Central to this is digital self-efficacy, defined as an individual's perceived capability to use technology effectively for purposeful outcomes. In many rural Indonesian communities, this self-efficacy remains constrained by cultural lag. Consequently, digital technologies are often experienced as intimidating or incongruent with long-standing local social practices.

Psychological empowerment further involves developing critical consciousness, a concept rooted in Freirean pedagogy concerning structural power relations in digital economies. Through this, individuals become aware of the socio-political dynamics embedded within various digital platforms. For instance, a digitally empowered farmer understands how data transparency and platform governance can reduce dependence on exploitative intermediaries. This cognitive shift from passive consumption toward active digital citizenship is a foundational precondition for long-term sustainability. Such transformation ensures that digitally enabled development initiatives remain resilient and community-oriented (Kruahong et al., 2023; Lansing et al., 2023). Ultimately, this awareness allows marginalized groups to leverage digital intermediation for meaningful socio-economic advancement.

While psychological empowerment focuses on internal change, structural empowerment addresses external environments that enable or constrain meaningful agency. This form of empowerment is expressed through digital agencies, which represent the capacity of communities to act strategically within digital systems and institutional frameworks. At the community level, empowerment is realized when local institutions, such as Village-Owned Enterprises (BUMDes) and cooperatives, possess the legal mandates and technical infrastructures needed to govern their own digital ecosystems. Therefore, empowerment remains inseparable from institutional capacity building and supportive governance structures. This shift ensures a move toward collective control over digital infrastructures rather than mere individual-level skill acquisition.

This structural dimension is closely related to the second digital divide, which focuses on inequalities in meaningful digital use rather than just physical access. While the first divide concerns hardware and connectivity, the second reflects unequal capacities to translate access into economic and social value. Individuals with higher social capital often use technology for productive purposes, while marginalized populations may remain limited to consumptive uses (Nigam, 2024). Digital Mutual Cooperation addresses this by establishing a knowledge safety net where literate members mentor others through practices rooted in *Gotong Royong*. Through this mechanism, individual competencies are transformed into collective digital assets that enhance shared capabilities and mitigate intra-community inequality (Saleh et al., 2022).

The dynamic interaction between psychological and structural empowerment gives rise to what this study conceptualizes as digital commonalities. This condition emerges when communities collectively own and govern digital platforms, transitioning away from extractive models toward democratic arrangements. Within this study, the Digital Mutual Cooperation model serves as the operational vehicle to integrate psychological empowerment with structural capacity building. By embedding these processes within collective governance, the model ensures that empowerment becomes a durable socio-structural condition. This framework ultimately underpins inclusive sustainability and long-term community resilience (Li et al., 2021; Outakoski et al., 2018). Such a durable condition is essential for maintaining the social fabric while navigating modern technological shifts.

4. Inclusive Sustainability and the Green Economy: The Twin Transition Paradigm

In contemporary management and development scholarship, sustainability has undergone a substantive conceptual expansion beyond narrow environmental concerns. It has evolved into a central strategic orientation shaping organizational behavior, public policy, and socio-economic development pathways. This evolution is increasingly articulated through the twin transition paradigm, where green and digital transformations are viewed as mutually constitutive processes. Within this framework, inclusive sustainability refers to a trajectory that simultaneously advances ecological integrity, economic viability, and social equity. This concept explicitly incorporates digital inclusion as a foundational enabling condition for long-term progress. Consequently, inclusive sustainability extends the traditional Triple Bottom Line by acknowledging that digital participation is integral to equitable development.

The green economy aims to enhance well-being and equity while reducing ecological risks, yet structural exclusion in emerging economies like Indonesia often keeps sustainable technologies out of reach for local communities. This creates a risk where green initiatives reinforce existing inequalities rather than mitigating them. To counter this, Green HRM practices must utilize digital mutual cooperation to align human capital with ecological goals. AI-driven environmental monitoring can lower entry barriers, ensuring a socially inclusive and robust twin transition. Ultimately, digitalization serves as a vital mechanism to decrease transaction costs and support decentralized, community-based resource management models that better reflect local capacities.

Digital platforms are essential for community-oriented circular economy practices where resources are shared and collectively governed. Integration of IoT and digital ledgers allows communities to monitor waste flows and manage energy systems with high transparency and efficiency. In Indonesia, digitalization in initiatives like mangrove management and thematic villages supports conservation while creating livelihoods through ecotourism (Silalahi et al., 2024; Muttaqijn et al., 2025). These findings suggest that environmental stewardship does not have to burden marginalized groups. Instead, inclusive digital infrastructures can transform stewardship into a catalyst for community-led economic value creation.

Inclusive sustainability requires the benefits of the digital-green transition to reach the social and geographic peripheries of society. Literature warns that top-down, technocratic approaches may lead to green exclusion or the loss of local livelihoods in the name of conservation. To address this, Digital Mutual Cooperation serves as a democratic governance mechanism that embeds transparency and collective deliberation within sustainability projects. By institutionalizing cooperative norms in digital systems, communities are better equipped to negotiate trade-offs between ecological goals and socio-economic needs. This participatory approach ultimately enhances both the legitimacy and long-term effectiveness of development initiatives.

.Recent empirical studies across ASEAN demonstrate that digitalization's impact on human well-being is significantly amplified when coupled with community-based green empowerment strategies. These strategies involve equipping communities with digital tools to monitor environmental conditions, participate in traceable supply chains, and engage with carbon markets. From this perspective, sustainability is an ongoing participatory process requiring continuous learning and institutional adaptation. While digital technologies provide the necessary technical instruments for participation, cooperative social relations are what sustain trust and shared responsibility. Ultimately, collective engagement ensures that the digital-green transition remains effective and enduring over time.

Ultimately, Indonesia's transition toward a green economy must be grounded in local socio-cultural values and institutional arrangements. The Digital Mutual Cooperation model serves as an integrative bridge linking technological innovation with ecological governance and community empowerment. By mobilizing digital social capital, communities can enhance their resilience to adapt simultaneously to environmental pressures and digital disruptions. This approach reframes the Golden Vision 2045 as a long-term commitment to a society that is environmentally sustainable and socially inclusive. Such institutional resilience ensures that economic growth does not compromise the well-being of future generations.

METHODOLOGY/ DATA AND METHODS

This study adopts a rigorous and multi-stage methodological framework that integrates a Systematic Literature Review (SLR) with advanced bibliometric analysis to generate a comprehensive and objective mapping of the relevant scholarly landscape. The overall research design is guided by the PRISMA (Preferred Reporting Items for Systematic Reviews and Meta-Analyses) protocol, which provides a transparent and structured procedure for documenting the processes of identification, screening, eligibility assessment, and final inclusion of academic records. The application of PRISMA enhances methodological rigor by ensuring replicability, reducing selection bias, and strengthening the credibility of the evidence synthesis.

The Scopus database was chosen as the primary data source for its stringent indexing and extensive coverage of peer-reviewed journals. Its inclusion of internationally recognized bibliometric indicators like the SJR ensures a corpus of methodologically robust scholarship. Data retrieval took place on July 19, 2025, using a Boolean strategy intersecting digitalization, community action, and sustainability. The specific search string targeted titles, abstracts, and keywords for these core concepts. To capture post-pandemic developments, the search was restricted to publications from 2020 to 2025.

To ensure contextual relevance and analytical consistency, a set of inclusion and exclusion criteria was applied. Only peer-reviewed journal articles and conference proceedings published in English were retained. In addition, the dataset was refined to prioritize studies with Indonesian institutional affiliations, thereby aligning the empirical foundation of the analysis with the socio-cultural and policy context of the study. The initial search yielded 4,841 records. These records were subsequently subjected to a systematic screening process based on thematic relevance, document type, and completeness of bibliographic metadata. Publications that did not substantively address the core themes of digitalization, collective processes, or sustainability were excluded at this stage.

Data preprocessing was conducted to ensure the validity and reliability of the bibliometric analysis. Raw metadata from Scopus was cleaned and standardized using OpenRefine to disambiguate author names and harmonize institutional affiliations. This standardization normalized keyword variants to prevent fragmentation in co-occurrence networks and thematic clustering. After refining the data, Microsoft Excel was used for a final audit to verify the dataset. This validation process produced a curated corpus of 151 high-quality documents suitable for systematic examination.

Quantitative bibliometric analysis and visualization were performed using RStudio version 4.4.3, specifically utilizing the Bibliometrix package and the Biblioshiny interface. RStudio was chosen for its flexibility in supporting advanced techniques like co-word analysis, thematic evolution mapping, and Sankey-style three-field plotting.

These methods allowed for an examination of intellectual linkages and temporal shifts in research emphasis beyond basic metrics. The analysis successfully traced the evolution of digitalization from a technical construct into a socio-institutional driver of community empowerment. Figure 1 provides a visual synthesis of this intersection, illustrating how digitally enabled collaboration bridges the gap toward inclusive sustainability.

Figure 1. Conceptual Intersection Between Digital Transformation and Collective Action.

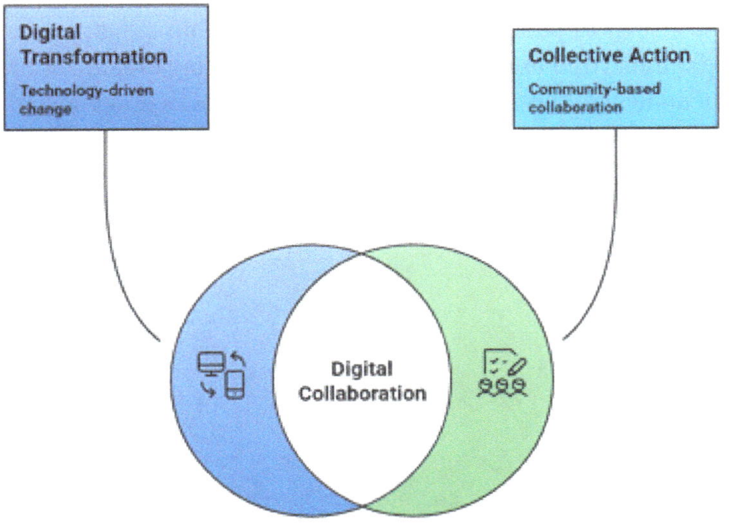

Source: Authors, 2025

The results of the bibliometric analysis were interpreted through qualitative synthesis to develop the Digital Mutual Cooperation conceptual framework. This integrative phase ensures the framework is empirically grounded in thematic convergences and intellectual trajectories identified within the literature. To promote transparency and replicability under Open Science principles, the curated dataset of 151 records has been made publicly available identifier https://doi.org/10.5281/zenodo.16273192. The repository includes raw Scopus exports, OpenRefine workflows, and finalized BibTeX and Excel formats via Zenodo. This open access enables future scholars to verify, replicate, and extend the findings of this study independently.

RESULTS AND DISCUSSION

(RQ1) Patterns and Directions of Research Trends (2020–2025): A Cluster-Based Discourse Analysis

This section addresses RQ1 by examining the evolution and intersection of scholarly discourse on digitalization, collective action, and sustainability from 2020 to 2025. Based on a curated corpus of 151 Scopus-indexed publications, the analysis utilizes co-word mapping and network visualization to identify dominant thematic configurations and their temporal development. Descriptive bibliometric characteristics, such as publication dynamics, authorship structures, and citation patterns, are summarized in Figure 2. Rather than viewing digitalization as a static technical phenomenon, this longitudinal assessment tracks how research priorities have shifted in response to socio-economic disruptions and sustainability imperatives. Ultimately, the intellectual landscape reveals a transition from technologically driven problem-solving toward frameworks that are culturally embedded and sustainability-oriented.

Figure 2. Descriptive Bibliometric Profile of the Analyzed Publications (2020–2025)

Description	Results
MAIN INFORMATION ABOUT DATA	2020-2025
Timespan	105
Sources (Journals, Books, etc)	105
Documents	151
Annual Growth Rate %	36.36
Document Average Age	1.56
Average citations per doc	9.79
References	8330
DOCUMENT CONTENTS	
Keywords Plus (ID)	351
Author's Keywords (DE)	596
AUTHORS	614
Authors	614
AUTHORS COLLABOATION	
Single-authored docs	8
Co-Authors per Doc	4.32
International co-authorships %	30.46
DOCUMENT TYPES	151
article	151

Showing 1 to 20 of 20 entries Previous 1 1 Next

Source: Biblioshiny, 2025

The co-occurrence analysis yields four dominant thematic clusters that collectively delineate the structure of the research field. These clusters, derived from the keyword network generated using Biblioshiny and visualized in Figure 3, represent distinct yet interrelated discourse logics. Together, they reflect both the chronological maturation of literature and the progressive deepening of its conceptual foundations.

Figure 3. Co-Occurrence Network of Keywords in Digitalization, Community Empowerment, and Sustainability Research (2020–2025)

Source: Biblioshiny, 2025

- Cluster 1: The Technical and Economic Infrastructure of Digitalization (Hardware-Oriented Logic). The first cluster is primarily associated with keywords such as digital transformation, ICT adoption, and digital economy, and is most prominent in studies published during the early phase of the observation period, particularly between 2020 and 2021. This cluster reflects a foundational, technocentric orientation that emerged in response to the acute disruptions generated by the COVID-19 pandemic. Research within this stream focused largely on ensuring organizational continuity and economic survival, especially among Micro, Small, and Medium Enterprises (MSMEs), through accelerated transitions from offline to online operational models. Analytical emphasis was placed on indicators such as platform uptake, participation in e-commerce ecosystems, and the expansion of digital infrastructure. While this body of work established essential technological prerequisites for digital engagement, it tended to marginalize social, cultural, and institutional considerations, thereby generating conceptual limitations that subsequent strands of literature sought to overcome.
- Cluster 2: Human Capital, Digital Literacy, and the Quality of Participation. As the discourse evolved around 2022, a second cluster gained prominence, characterized by increased attention to digital literacy, education, and competence. This cluster signifies a shift from access-centered narratives toward capability-based perspectives, reflecting growing scholarly consensus that physical connectivity alone is insufficient to produce meaningful empower-

ment. Central to this stream is the notion of the second-level digital divide, which captures inequalities in individuals' capacity to use digital technologies in productive, strategic, and value-creating ways. Within the Indonesian context, this literature emphasizes the role of education and skill development in mitigating digital exclusion. Nevertheless, despite its anthropocentric orientation, the cluster remains largely individualistic, often underestimating the role of collective norms, social networks, and community-based institutions that shape technology adoption and utilization in rural and peripheral environments.

- Cluster 3: Recent scholarly discourse (2023–2025) indicates that digital competence has evolved into AI-augmented capabilities. Within the Digital Mutual Cooperation core, Gotong Royong is now practiced through Human-AI complementarity, using AI tools to amplify collective decision-making and communal resource management in HRM. This cluster, representing the study's conceptual nucleus, focuses on mutual cooperation, social capital, and local wisdom. It marks a contextualist turn, investigating how indigenous values can support digitally mediated cooperation. Unlike Western-centric models emphasizing individual competition, this discourse prioritizes bonding social capital and communal decision-making as essential for sustainable digital initiatives. Gotong Royong is conceptualized as digital social infrastructure, allowing communities to use technology while preserving cultural identity and enhancing collective agency. This reflects a scholarly effort to reconcile innovation with culturally grounded governance. Currently, AI-driven HRM models prioritize inclusive sustainability by automating administrative tasks, enabling leaders to focus on social capital building and preserving local wisdom.
- Cluster 4: Inclusive Sustainability and the SDG–2045 Alignment.The fourth cluster integrates the preceding thematic strands within a broader sustainability-oriented framework, encompassing keywords such as inclusive growth, green economy, and sustainable development goals. This cluster exhibits a teleological orientation, shifting analytical emphasis from digitalization as an end in itself toward digitalization as an instrumental means for achieving long-term environmental protection, social equity, and community resilience. Research within this stream demonstrates strong alignment with Indonesia's Golden Vision 2045, highlighting emerging interests in green digitalization, ecosystem monitoring, circular economy practices, and community-based sustainability governance. The central positioning of sustainability within the co-occurrence network underscores the extent to which digital transformation is increasingly conceptualized as part of an integrat-

ed digital–sustainability ecosystem rather than as a standalone technological process.

Taken together, the trajectory of research trends from 2020 to 2025 reflects a clear movement from isolation toward integration. The literature initially emphasizes technical connectivity, subsequently advances toward individual capability development, then locates a cultural anchor in mutual cooperation, and ultimately converges on inclusive sustainability as its normative endpoint. This systematic progression indicates that contemporary scholarship increasingly acknowledges that sustainable digital transformation in Indonesia cannot be achieved through technocratic interventions alone. Instead, it must be grounded in collective social values, culturally embedded institutions, and participatory governance mechanisms. As such, the findings presented in this section provide a robust empirical foundation for subsequent analyses concerning structural gaps in existing empowerment models and for the formulation of the Digital Mutual Cooperation conceptual framework.

(RQ2) Longitudinal Trajectory of Thematic Evolution in Digitalization, Community Empowerment, and Sustainability

To address RQ2, this section examines how the thematic emphases surrounding digitalization, community empowerment, and sustainability have evolved over time. Using a longitudinal bibliometric perspective, the analysis draws on thematic evolution maps and strategic diagrams generated through Biblioshiny to trace shifts in centrality, density, and conceptual linkages across three distinct temporal phases between 2020 and 2025. This temporal analysis reveals not merely incremental changes in keyword usage, but a deeper transformation in how digitalization is positioned within the broader development discourse in Indonesia.

Overall, the findings indicate a clear transition from a technocentric logic of crisis response toward an anthropocentric and sustainability-oriented paradigm. Digitalization progressively shifts from being treated as an end in itself to functioning as an embedded enabler of collective resilience and inclusive development. This longitudinal transformation is further illustrated through the Sankey-based thematic evolution diagram (Figure 4), which visualizes how dominant concepts flow, converge, and reconfigure across successive time periods, thereby capturing not only thematic persistence but also conceptual migration within the field. Complementing this dynamic perspective, the strategic thematic map (Figure 5) provides a positional snapshot of core themes based on their density and centrality, allowing for a more precise interpretation of thematic maturity, relevance, and functional roles at different stages of the research trajectory.

Figure 4. Conceptual Flow and Migration of Core Themes in Digitalization and Inclusive Sustainability Research (2020 – 2025)

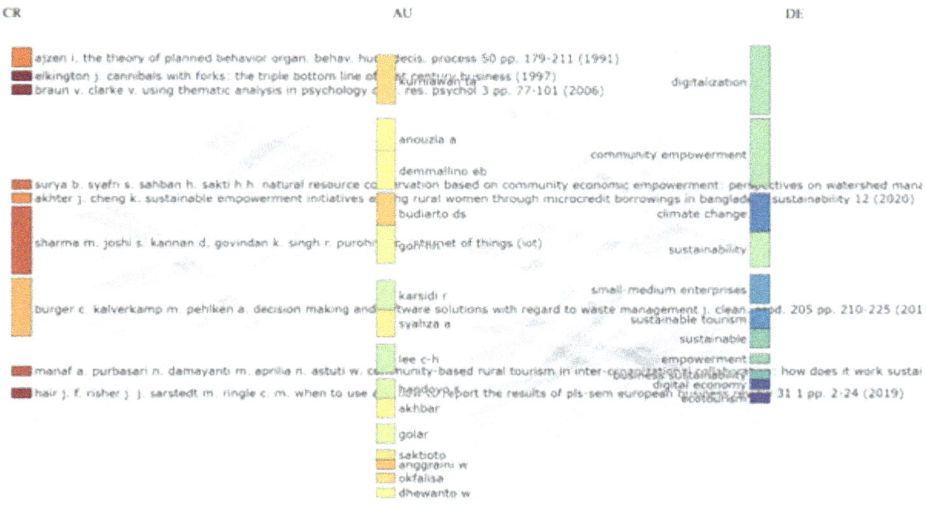

Source: Biblioshiny, 2025

Figure 5. Strategic Positioning of Core Themes in the Digitalization–Community Empowerment–Sustainability Nexus

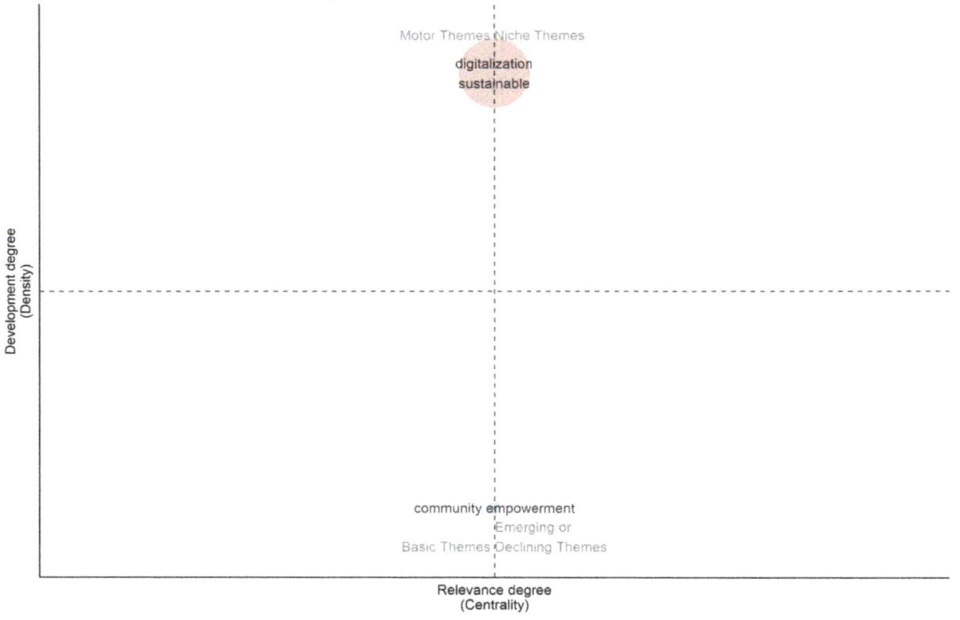

Source: Biblioshiny, 2025

Phase 1: Emergency Adaptation and Technocentric Survival (2020–2021)

During the initial phase, which coincides with the height of the COVID-19 pandemic, the thematic focus of the literature was dominated by what can be characterized as emergency-driven digital adaptation. Core themes such as digitalization, digital transformation, and e-commerce adoption occupied highly central positions within the thematic space, indicating their role as primary problem-solving mechanisms. In strategic terms, digitalization functioned as a motor theme, exhibiting both high centrality and high density.

At this stage, sustainability-related concepts remained weakly connected and largely peripheral. Environmental and social sustainability were often framed instrumentally, primarily as extensions of business continuity or corporate responsibility narratives. Community empowerment appeared only marginally and was seldom theorized as a collective process rooted in local socio-cultural values. The linkage between digital tools and indigenous practices such as Gotong Royong was minimal, reflecting an implicit assumption that technological solutions could be transplanted into local contexts with limited adaptation. The dominant research question during this phase centered on survival, rather than on long-term inclusion or structural transformation.

Phase 2: Socio-Technical Reorientation and Human-Centered Awareness (2022–2023)

The second phase marks a significant inflection point in the evolution of thematic priorities. As the immediate shock of the pandemic subsided, literature began to reassess the limitations of access-driven digitalization strategies. Themes related to digital literacy, community empowerment, and human capital development migrated from peripheral positions toward greater centrality, signaling an emerging recognition that technological access alone was insufficient to generate meaningful empowerment.

This period is characterized by a growing socio-technical awareness, wherein scholars increasingly conceptualize digitalization as a process embedded within social structures rather than as a standalone technological intervention. Social capital emerged as a bridging theme, connecting technical infrastructures with community-level participation and institutional capacity. Importantly, this phase represents the first systematic incorporation of mutual cooperation values into discussions of digital governance and empowerment. The analytical focus expanded from market participation toward citizenship, agency, and collective capability, thereby laying the conceptual groundwork for more integrated sustainability frameworks.

Phase 3: Integration and the Ascendancy of Inclusive Sustainability (2024–2025)

The final phase reflects a mature and integrated discourse in which sustainability and community empowerment assume dominant positions within the thematic structure. During this period, digitalization undergoes a notable repositioning. Rather than functioning as a motor theme, it transitions into a basic theme, indicating that digital infrastructure is increasingly taken for granted as a necessary but insufficient condition for development.

Conversely, sustainability, green economy, and community empowerment have emerged as new motor themes, defined by strong internal cohesion and high field relevance. This shift is substantiated by the strategic thematic map in Figure 6, which plots thematic density against centrality to show the maturity of late-stage research. While digitalization and the digital economy remain basic themes, sustainability and community-centered constructs have advanced into the motor quadrant, indicating conceptual robustness.

Figure 7 further refines this configuration by isolating the strategic positioning of core concepts in the most recent period. It highlights how sustainability, community empowerment, and the green economy have become foundational pillars while still allowing for theoretical deepening and empirical diversification. This signifies a paradigmatic shift where the focus has moved beyond simple connectivity to the capacity of digital systems to support regenerative economic models and social equity. Consequently, literature now emphasizes collective governance, circular practices, and community-led platforms as critical mechanisms for long-term resilience.

At this stage, digital mutual cooperation crystallizes as a central integrative concept. Digital tools are explicitly framed as instruments for amplifying collective action, enabling shared resource management, and institutionalizing mutual aid within digitally mediated environments. This reflects a broader normative reorientation toward inclusive sustainability as the ultimate objective of digital transformation.

Figure 6. Strategic Thematic Positioning of Core Themes in the Late-Stage Digitalization–Sustainability Discourse (2022–2025)

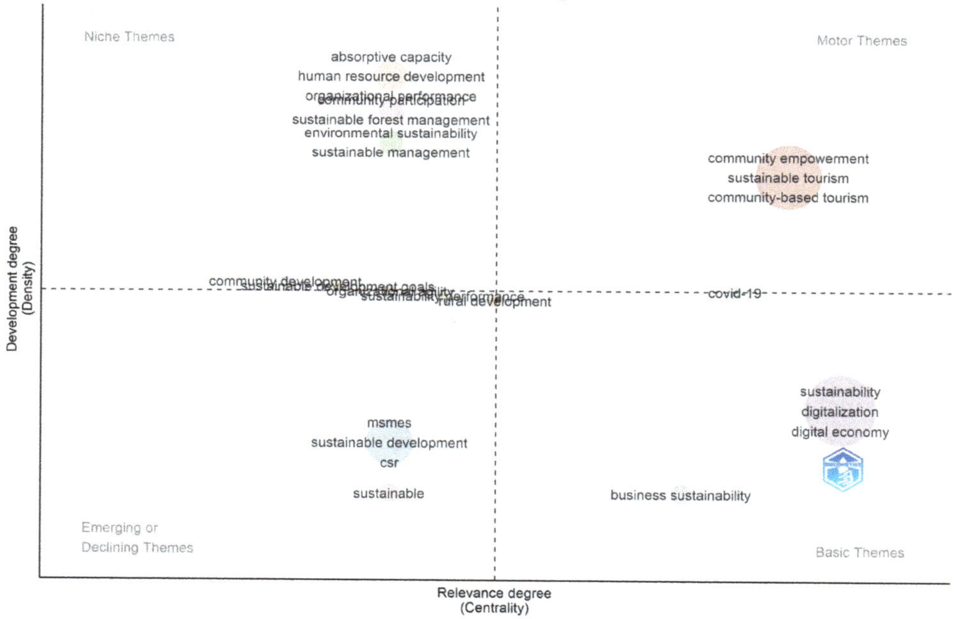

Source: Biblioshiny, 2025

Figure 7. Strategic Thematic Positioning of Core Themes in the Late-Stage Digitalization–Sustainability Discourse (2022–2025)

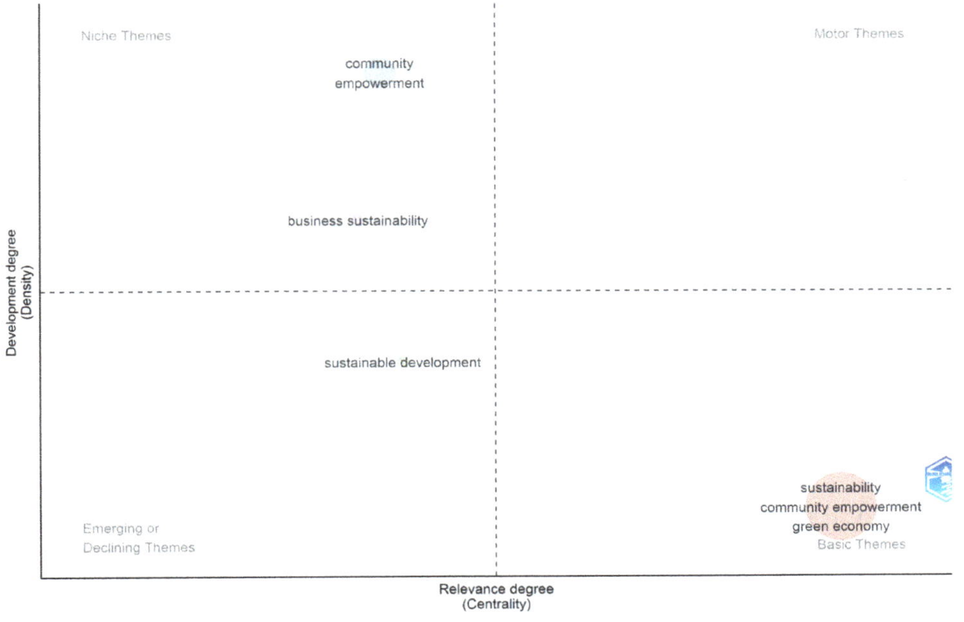

Source: Biblioshiny, 2025

Synthesis of the Longitudinal Trajectory

Taken together, the longitudinal analysis reveals a coherent three-stage trajectory in the evolution of scholarly focus:

1. Isolation (2020–2021): Digitalization conceptualized primarily as a technical response to crisis conditions.
2. Interaction (2022–2023): Digitalization increasingly linked with community empowerment and social readiness.
3. Integration (2024–2025): Digitalization embedded as an invisible enabler of inclusive sustainability and collective resilience.

This progression provides strong empirical support for the proposed conceptual model of Digital Mutual Cooperation. It demonstrates that contemporary academic discourse has moved beyond framing digital inequality as a deficit of infrastructure, and instead increasingly understands sustainable development as a function of collective social capital, cultural embeddedness, and digitally enabled cooperation. In this sense, the findings of RQ2 establish a critical bridge between descriptive trend analysis and the normative design of context-sensitive digital empowerment strategies.

(RQ3) Conceptual Novelty of the Digital Mutual Cooperation (DMC) Model

The principal contribution of this study is the formulation of the Digital Mutual Cooperation (DMC) Model, addressing conceptual fragmentation in digital empowerment and sustainability literature. To answer RQ3, this section positions the DMC model within prior research, articulating its novelty through bibliometric evidence and thematic projections. Although scholarship has examined digital literacy and social entrepreneurship, these strands often remain disjointed, technocratic, or grounded in individualistic market rationalities. The DMC model advances the field by offering a culturally embedded, collective framework. It reconceptualizes digitalization as a socially governed and development-oriented process.

In Pillar 2, collective capacity building focuses on fostering AI self-efficacy within local institutions like Village-Owned Enterprises (BUMDes). This ensures the Global South workforce is not a passive technology consumer but possesses the HRM agency to adapt AI for local objectives, bridging the second-level digital divide. The novelty is substantiated by convergence patterns in the co-occurrence network and relationships between references, authors, and descriptors (Figure 4). Future-oriented configurations projected through thematic evolution analysis (Figure 8) also support this. These representations indicate a structural reorientation toward integrating indigenous social capital, specifically Gotong Royong, into digital sustainability architecture.

Figure 8. Future Thematic Projections of Digital Mutual Cooperation and Inclusive Sustainability (2025)

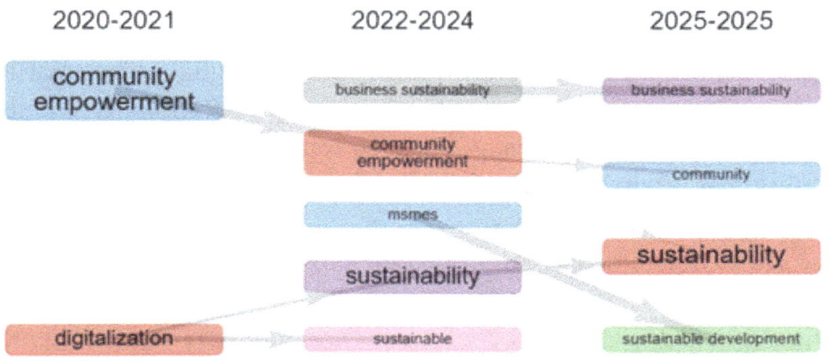

Source: Biblioshiny, 2025

Cultural-Digital Anchoring as a Foundational Innovation

The first and most distinctive dimension of novelty is conceptualized as Cultural-Digital Anchoring. Prevailing digitalization models in emerging economies frequently adopt a context-neutral stance, implicitly assuming that technological diffusion will translate directly into empowerment outcomes. However, the relational linkages between references, authors, and keywords illustrated in Figure 4 demonstrate that the most influential and conceptually cohesive streams of research increasingly foreground local wisdom, collective norms, and community-based institutions as critical moderating mechanisms.

Building on this empirical insight, the DMC model reframes Gotong Royong not as a cultural artifact to be digitally replicated, but as a social operating system that should inform the governance, design, and utilization of digital platforms. This position marks a clear departure from dominant platform capitalism models that emphasize data extraction and individual optimization. Instead, the DMC framework aligns with principles of platform cooperativism, ensuring that digital infrastructures reinforce, rather than undermine, collective capacity and social cohesion. By anchoring digital transformation within culturally legitimate norms, the model addresses a key source of digital resistance and disengagement frequently observed in rural and peripheral communities.

From Individual Agency to Collective Digital Power

A second major contribution of this study lies in its theoretical shift from individual-centric empowerment toward collective digital power. Earlier models, as reflected in preceding thematic clusters, largely conceptualized digital skills as individual human capital assets. While such approaches may enhance personal employability, they often risk reinforcing intra-community inequalities and perpetuating the second-level digital divide.

The DMC model departs from this logic by drawing on insights from the social capital and community empowerment clusters to propose a peer-based digital capability system. Within this configuration, digitally proficient members of the community operate as knowledge catalysts, enabling the transformation of individual competencies into shared communal resources. This structural reorientation reframes empowerment as a cumulative and multiplier process rather than a zero-sum outcome. Consequently, the DMC model responds directly to contemporary critiques of digital inclusion by embedding learning, mentoring, and capability diffusion within community institutions, thereby fostering inclusive sustainability through collective advancement.

Green-Digital Mutual Synergy and Regenerative Logic

The third dimension of novelty concerns the integration of green economy principles within a mutual cooperation framework. The future theme projections depicted in Figure 8 indicate that the research frontier is increasingly concentrated at the intersection of sustainability, digitalization, and community empowerment. Nevertheless, much of the extant literature continues to conceptualize green technology as a top-down, capital-intensive intervention driven primarily by external actors.

The DMC model challenges this assumption by advancing the concept of frugal green innovation, whereby digital mutual cooperation enables communities to collectively manage and govern environmental resources. Illustrative applications include digitally coordinated waste banks, community-led renewable energy initiatives, and data-supported circular economy practices. Under this framework, communities are repositioned from passive beneficiaries to active stewards of green transformation. This reconceptualization aligns digitalization with regenerative development objectives and situates sustainability as a socially embedded outcome rather than a technologically imposed solution.

Structural Architecture of the DMC Model

Figure 9 visualizes the integrative architecture of the Digital Mutual Cooperation (DMC) Model and serves as the synthetic representation of this study's conceptual novelty. Rather than depicting isolated dimensions, the figure illustrates the synergistic interaction among governance, capacity building, and economic regeneration as mutually reinforcing pillars of sustainable digital transformation. The central overlap emphasizes that empowered digital participation emerges only when inclusive governance mechanisms, collective learning processes, and regenerative economic logics operate concurrently within a community-based system.

Figure 9. An Integrative Model of Digital Mutual Cooperation: Governance, Capacity, and Regenerative Economy

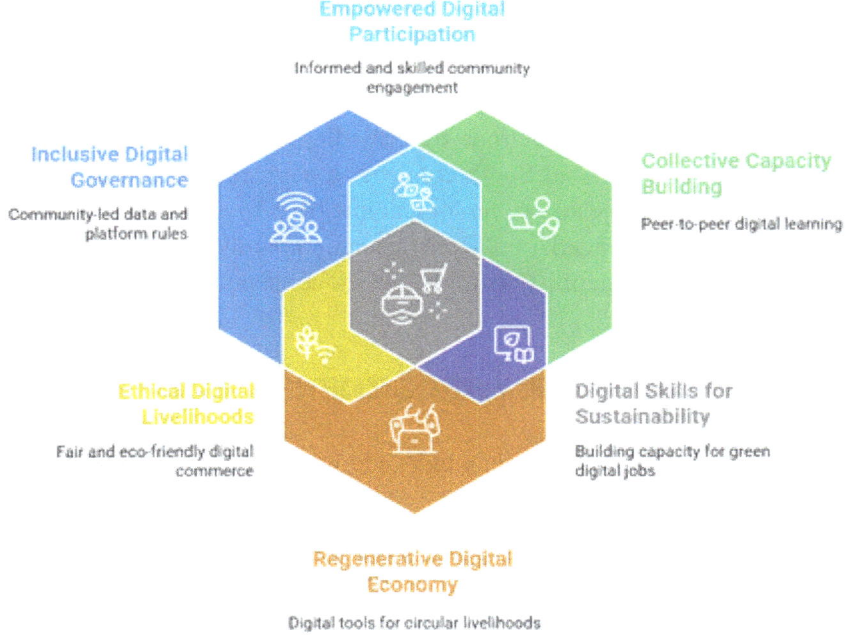

Source: Author, 2025

Drawing on the integrated insights from Figures 2 through 8, the DMC model is operationalized through three interdependent pillars:

- Pillar 1: Inclusive Digital Governance: The establishment of community-based rules for data ownership, platform use, and collective decision-making grounded in the normative principles of Gotong Royong.

- Pillar 2: Collective Capacity Building: The institutionalization of peer-to-peer digital learning and mentoring mechanisms within local organizations, including village-owned enterprises (BUMDes).
- Pillar 3: Regenerative Digital Economy: The strategic use of digital tools to facilitate circular economic practices that sustain livelihoods while preserving ecological systems.

Together, these pillars signify a paradigmatic transition from a deficit-oriented view of digital inequality, which emphasizes infrastructural absence, toward an asset-based perspective that recognizes digital mutual cooperation as a source of social, cultural, and ecological value.

Synthesis and Theoretical Contribution

By addressing RQ3, this study advances the scholarly discourse beyond fragmented interpretations of digital inclusion toward a coherent model of inclusive sustainability rooted in collective action and cultural legitimacy. The DMC model offers both theoretical and strategic contributions by providing a context-sensitive roadmap for Indonesia and other Global South contexts to navigate digital transformation without eroding social cohesion or ecological integrity. In doing so, it introduces a novel and empirically grounded framework that integrates digitalization, community empowerment, and sustainability within a unified conceptual architecture.

CONCLUSION AND POLICY RECOMMENDATIONS

This study synthesizes 151 Scopus-indexed publications from 2020 to 2025 to reach a central conclusion. In the Indonesian context, digitalization is no longer a purely technical or efficiency-driven intervention. Instead, it has evolved into a socio-cultural process where community empowerment and sustainability are the primary organizing logics. A critical finding is that these themes have now surpassed digitalization in thematic prominence. This transition marks the displacement of a technocentric paradigm by an integrative development perspective. Consequently, technology is now seen as deeply embedded within social relations, cultural institutions, and ecological systems.

Evidence from the thematic evolution analysis indicates a growing academic consensus that technological innovation detached from local wisdom and environmental balance is not only unsustainable but may also deepen digital inequalities by prioritizing access and adoption over agency, participation, and collective benefit. This study further concludes that in the current era of Artificial Intelligence, the 'human-centered' shift must be operationalized through Human-AI complementarity. The DMC model serves as a necessary safeguard to ensure that AI integration in HRM practices, especially within community-based organizations, which remain aligned with collective ethics rather than purely algorithmic efficiency, thus preventing new forms of digital marginalization in the Global South.

In this context, the integration of Gotong Royong into digital transformation should not be interpreted as a symbolic or nostalgic return to tradition. Instead, it represents a strategic recalibration of development governance. This study addresses a persistent conceptual gap by proposing the Digital Mutual Cooperation (DMC) model, which repositions indigenous social capital as a core governance mechanism for digital ecosystems oriented toward inclusive sustainability. By sitting in mutual assistance, collective responsibility, and shared norms at the center of digital governance, the DMC model offers a theoretically grounded alternative to individualistic, market-centric, and platform-dominated approaches that prevail in much of the digital development literature.

Despite its contributions, this study has several limitations. Its reliance on secondary bibliometric data reflects the temporal lag of academic publishing and may not capture real-time grassroots dynamics. While the identified thematic trajectories are robust, further empirical validation is needed to assess how Digital Mutual Cooperation operates across diverse settings. Future research should prioritize longitudinal and comparative case studies in coastal, agrarian, and peri-urban communities. Such empirical work will refine the DMC framework and provide deeper insight into how collective digital practices enhance resilience, equity, and sustainability.

The policy implications of this research advocate for a substantive reorientation of Indonesia's digital development strategy, moving beyond a focus on infrastructure and connectivity toward an ecosystem-based empowerment approach. National and subnational institutions, such as the Ministry of Communication and Informatics and the Ministry of Villages, should institutionalize Digital Mutual Cooperation principles within Village-Owned Enterprises (BUMDes) and community organizations. Evaluation frameworks for digital initiatives should be expanded to include indicators of collective value creation, such as social synergy and shared resource governance, rather than just measuring access. Furthermore, policy interventions should prioritize AI-ready HRM strategies for BUMDes. This involves developing frameworks for "Algorithmic Solidarity," where AI tools optimize communal work distribution and talent management while maintaining the cultural spirit of Gotong Royong.

In parallel, this study highlights the urgency of advancing a renewed national digital literacy agenda that emphasizes collective digital agency rather than individual technical proficiency alone. A reconfigured Digital Literacy Framework should equip communities with the capabilities to govern data, manage digital platforms, and engage in collective decision-making regarding digital assets, thereby strengthening local autonomy and reducing dependency on external intermediaries. Such an orientation fosters more equitable participation in the digital economy and must be upgraded to include "AI-Empowerment Literacy". This ensures that community members possess the critical consciousness to supervise AI systems, understand data bias, and utilize intelligent tools to strengthen community-led governance rather than remaining passive data providers for global platforms.

From a sustainability perspective, the findings underscore the strategic importance of aligning digital transformation with green economy objectives through a coordinated twin transition. Policymakers should actively incentivize community-led digital cooperatives that deploy digital tools in support of regenerative economic practices, including renewable energy management, circular waste systems, and sustainable local value chains. Regulatory facilitation and institutional support for these initiatives would enable communities to function not merely as recipients of green technologies, but as co-governors of ecological and digital systems.

Ultimately, by grounding digital transformation in the ethos of Gotong Royong, Indonesia has the opportunity to articulate a distinctive development pathway that avoids the exclusionary dynamics of platform capitalism and instead cultivates an inclusive and sustainable digital civilization. The realization of the Golden Vision 2045 will therefore depend not only on advanced digital infrastructure, but also on a governance philosophy rooted in collective responsibility, cultural legitimacy, and ecological stewardship. Digital tools may shape the pathway toward this future; however, it is the enduring principle of mutual cooperation that must guide its direction.

ACKNOWLEDGEMENT

This research was funded and supported by Bina Nusantara University (BINUS University), Indonesia. The authors extend their gratitude to the Management Department of Bina Nusantara Business School (BBS) for providing the academic environment necessary for this study. We also acknowledge the practical insights contributed by PT. Autrans Asia Indonesia and the Indonesia Institute of Certified Public Accountants (IAPI), which enriched the conceptual development of the model. The authors declare that Artificial Intelligence (AI) technologies were utilized during the preparation of this manuscript solely for grammar refinement, sentence structuring, and enhancing narrative flow to meet high academic writing standards. All theoretical content, bibliometric data analysis, and the development of the conceptual model remain the original intellectual work of the authors. Finally, we thank the developers of Bibliometrix (RStudio) and OpenRefine for providing the tools that ensured the methodological transparency of this research.

REFERENCES

Arion, F. H., Harutyunyan, G., Aleksanyan, V., Muradyan, M., Asatryan, H., & Manucharyan, M. (2024). Determining digitalization issues (ICT adoption, digital literacy, and the digital divide) in rural areas by using sample surveys: The case of Armenia. *Agriculture*, *14*(2), 249. DOI: 10.3390/agriculture14020249

Ateeq, A., Al-refaei, A.-A., Alzoraiki, M., Milhem, M., & Ali, S. A. (2024). Digitalization and its impact on HRM: Leveraging ICT for efficient workforce management. In *Springer Proceedings in Business and Economics* (Vol. 524, pp. 551–558). Springer., DOI: 10.1007/978-3-031-54379-1_48

Dalimunthe, H. H. B., Sutisna, A., Karnadi, K., Retnowati, E., & Tijari, A. (2021). Social entrepreneurship empowerment in the Indonesian archipelagic communities. *Indonesian Journal of Business and Entrepreneurship*, *7*(2), 103. DOI: 10.17358/ijbe.7.2.103

Dušková, M. V., & Vita, M. (2022). Automated information retrieval from the bibliographic metadata: A way to facilitate the systematic literature review. *4th International Conference on Advanced Research Methods and Analytics (CARMA 2022)*. https://doi.org/DOI: 10.4995/CARMA2022.2022.15104

Faedlulloh, D., Meutia, I. F., Yulianti, D., & Karmilasari, V. (2021). Gotong royong digital: Praktik baru solidaritas warga di era pandemi. *Jantra*, *16*(1), 1–14. DOI: 10.52829/jantra.v16i1.118

George Reyes, C. E., & Glasserman, L. (2020). Research competencies mediated by technologies: A systematic review of the literature in Scopus. *Preprints*. https://doi.org/DOI: 10.20944/preprints202007.0125.v1

Ghosh, O., & Kumar, B. (2025). Reimagining community resilience and engagement through the digital innovation. In *Fostering Resilience and Quality of Life Through Sustainable Urban Evolution* (pp. 233–262). IGI Global., DOI: 10.4018/979-8-3373-0390-1.ch008

Hajian, M., & Kashani, S. J. (2021). Evolution of the concept of sustainability: From Brundtland Report to sustainable development goals. *Sustainable Resource Management: Modern Approaches and Contexts*, 1–24. https://doi.org/DOI: 10.1016/B978-0-12-824342-8.00018-3

Khan, S., Ullah, S., & Nobanee, H. (2024). ICT diffusion, e-governance, and sustainability in the digital era. *Sustainable Futures : An Applied Journal of Technology, Environment and Society*, *8*, 100272. DOI: 10.1016/j.sftr.2024.100272

Kruahong, S., Tankumpuan, T., Kelly, K., Davidson, P. M., & Kuntajak, P. (2023). Community empowerment: A concept analysis. *Journal of Advanced Nursing*, *79*(8), 2845–2859. DOI: 10.1111/jan.15613 PMID: 36912456

Lansing, A. E., Romero, N. J., Siantz, E., Silva, V., Center, K., Casteel, D., & Gilmer, T. (2023). Building trust: Leadership reflections on community empowerment and engagement in a large urban initiative. *BMC Public Health*, *23*(1), 1252. DOI: 10.1186/s12889-023-15860-z PMID: 37380973

Li, J., Brar, A., & Roihan, N. (2021). The use of digital technology to enhance language and literacy skills for indigenous people: A systematic literature review. *Computers and Education Open*, *2*, 100035. DOI: 10.1016/j.caeo.2021.100035

Martínez-Bravo, M. C., Sádaba Chalezquer, C., & Serrano-Puche, J. (2022). Dimensions of digital literacy in the 21st century competency frameworks. *Sustainability (Basel)*, *14*(3), 1867. DOI: 10.3390/su14031867

Muttaqijn, M. I., Effendi, Y., & Kusumawati, I. (2025). Integrating evidence-based management principles with green economy in Kampung Tematik. *International Journal of Sustainable Development and Planning*, *20*(4), 1731–1739. DOI: 10.18280/ijsdp.200434

Nigam, A. K.Abhishek Kumar Nigam. (2024). Digital divide and financially marginalized communities: Strategies for implementation of NEP 2020. *International Journal For Multidisciplinary Research*, *6*(2), 14909. Advance online publication. DOI: 10.36948/ijfmr.2024.v06i02.14909

Outakoski, H., Cocq, C., & Steggo, P. (2018). Strengthening indigenous languages in the digital age: Social media–supported learning in Sápmi. *Media International Australia, Incorporating Culture & Policy*, *169*(1), 21–31. DOI: 10.1177/1329878X18803700

Rimbawati, P. (2023). Influence of COVID in digitizing and collective endeavor in Indonesia. *Medical Research Archives*, *11*(6). Advance online publication. DOI: 10.18103/mra.v11i6.3861

Ruggerio, C. A. (2021). Sustainability and sustainable development: A review of principles and definitions. *The Science of the Total Environment*, *786*, 147481. DOI: 10.1016/j.scitotenv.2021.147481 PMID: 33965820

Saleh, A., Adhani, A., & Mujahiddin, . (2022). Utilization of online social work education for community empowerment. *Advances in Social Science, Education and Humanities Research*. Advance online publication. DOI: 10.2991/978-2-494069-07-7_10 PMID: 36624497

Salim, M., & Rosyidi, Z. (2025). Digital literacy development towards Golden Indonesia 2045. *Journal of Practice Learning and Educational Development*, *5*(3), 539–558. DOI: 10.58737/jpled.v5i3.539

Silalahi, H. T., Basyuni, M., Aritonang, E. Y., Slamet, B., Hartini, K. S., & Wee, A. K. S. (2024). Management of mangrove landscape and ecosystem for ecotourism. *Global Journal of Environmental Science and Management*, *10*(4), 1977–1992. DOI: 10.22034/GJESM.2024.04.29

Sumarmi, S., Untari, S., & Meiji, N. H. P. (2022). Desa Pancasila: The implementation of Gotong Royong values as social capital in Indonesia. *Komunitas*, *14*(2), 225–238. DOI: 10.15294/komunitas.v14i2.27789

Chapter 2
The Human Experience of Algorithmic HR:
A Design-Sensitive, Semi-Structured Review

Ian Mizuki
http://orcid.org/0009-0007-6420-0318
York University, Canada & University of Toronto, Canada

Zoya Khan
http://orcid.org/0009-0000-6073-3263
York University, Canada

ABSTRACT

Algorithmic and artificial intelligence–enabled systems increasingly shape core human resource processes, including recruitment, performance evaluation, monitoring, and workflow coordination. Evidence shows that their effects are contingent. In some contexts, these systems strengthen fairness, trust, and job quality; in others, they intensify strain, reduce meaningfulness, and weaken ethical vigilance. This chapter presents a design-sensitive, semi-structured review of twenty-nine empirical studies spanning gig work, digital operations, customer service, algorithmic monitoring, and HR functions. The review identifies recurring design features, including collaboration structures, communication framing, monitoring architecture, transparency, and reliability, that shape employee responses and HR-relevant outcomes. It concludes with practical implications for designing algorithmic HR systems that support accountability, fairness, and effective human–AI complementarity.

DOI: 10.4018/979-8-2600-2303-7.ch002

INTRODUCTION

Organizations across sectors are integrating artificial intelligence and algorithmic systems into the core of human resource–relevant work (Olawade et al., 2025). These technologies now influence recruitment screening, résumé triage, interview evaluation, performance assessment, task allocation, workflow coordination, and routine supervisory activities (Allen et al., 2025; Purohit & Banerjee, 2025). Rather than operating solely as analytical decision aids, algorithmic systems allocate authority, structure monitoring practices, and shape patterns of collaboration between employees and technological agents (Hughes et al., 2025). In recruitment contexts, for example, large language models are used to evaluate candidate responses and generate comparative assessments (Allen et al., 2025; Szandała, 2025). In digital operations, AI-driven logistics and procurement systems coordinate workflows while influencing employees' cognitive experiences and job satisfaction (Omoush, 2025). Platform-based work further illustrates how algorithms govern rating systems, task access, client matching, and resource allocation, thereby shaping everyday work experiences (Robinson et al., 2025; Wood et al., 2019). As algorithmic systems mediate managerial processes, they begin to function as consequential actors within organizational environments, influencing psychological contracts, norms of responsibility, perceptions of fairness, and the social fabric of work (Jabagi et al., 2025; Zhou et al., 2025a). Against this backdrop of expanding algorithmic influence, it becomes essential to identify which design choices tend to support positive human resource–relevant outcomes and which introduce new organizational and ethical risks. Accordingly, this chapter examines how collaboration, monitoring, and communication designs enable algorithmic and AI-enabled systems to improve HR-relevant outcomes. Recent syntheses on agentic AI and large language models further underscore that the evidence base is expanding rapidly, while integrative work remains comparatively underdeveloped, with explicit calls for more formalized review approaches as the literature matures (Islam et al., 2026; Brohi et al., 2025).

Accumulating empirical evidence suggests that the consequences of algorithmic systems are neither uniformly beneficial nor uniformly harmful. Instead, findings reveal substantial variability across contexts. On the one hand, carefully designed algorithmic tools have been shown to strengthen trust (Lu et al., 2025), enhance perceptions of fairness and organizational support (Jabagi et al., 2025), improve job satisfaction (Omoush, 2025), foster team resilience (Liu, Yuan, & Wang, 2025), and support innovation outcomes (Yu et al., 2024). On the other hand, similar technologies have been associated with heightened stress, perceived threat, and burnout (Ontrup et al., 2025), intensified overwork and insecurity (Wood et al., 2019), reduced experiences of meaningfulness (Van Zoonen et al., 2024), and weakened ethical vigilance (Gaczek et al., 2025). Rather than reflecting a simple opposition between positive and negative effects, this variation underscores the extent to which outcomes depend on design-sensitive features, including collaboration structures, communication framing, monitoring architecture, transparency cues, reliability signals, and broader contextual moderators. Yet existing empirical insights remain dispersed across domains and outcome vocabularies, which can make it difficult to specify which design configurations tend to support HR-relevant outcomes (e.g., perceived fairness, accountability, trust, and well-being) and which tend to intensify strain, diminish meaningfulness, or weaken ethical vigilance. More specifically, although prior work documents important effects within particular settings (e.g., recruitment, platform work, digital operations), the evidence remains fragmented in ways that limit design-relevant generalization across HR contexts. Building on this motivating concern, this chapter asks: Under what design configurations do algorithmic and AI-enabled systems tend to support positive HR-relevant outcomes, and under what conditions do similar systems undermine them?

To address this concern, the chapter presents a semi-structured review of empirical research on algorithmic and AI-enabled work systems. The aim of this chapter is to consolidate dispersed findings into a design-sensitive synthesis that clarifies (a) the mechanisms through which algorithmic systems shape employee experience and HR-relevant outcomes and (b) the contextual moderators under which these mechanisms intensify, attenuate, or reverse. The review pursues four interrelated objectives. First, it synthesizes evidence from twenty-nine empirical studies conducted across diverse contexts, including gig work, digital operations, customer service, managerial monitoring, and HR-specific tasks such as recruitment and performance appraisal. Second, it identifies recurring design-sensitive patterns that help explain why algorithmic systems produce supportive outcomes in some settings but generate strain or disengagement in others. Third, it examines the role of cross-cutting moderators, including human–AI collaboration arrangements, transparency, workload, stigma, social interaction, autonomy and control, and identification, that shape how workers interpret and respond to algorithmic systems. Fourth, it translates these insights into evidence-informed implications for human resource design and governance, with particular attention to accountability structures, fairness perceptions, transparency practices, interactional monitoring, and the support of human agency and algorithmic competence. In doing so, the chapter aims to consolidate design-relevant evidence into an integrative account that helps scholars and practitioners anticipate when algorithmic HR systems are more likely to enable complementarity and when they are more likely to generate predictable socio-ethical risks.

METHODOLOGY

This chapter employs a design-sensitive, semi-systematic review approach to synthesize empirical research on how AI- and algorithm-enabled systems shape work and human resource–relevant outcomes. The review was structured to ensure transparency and rigor while remaining attentive to conceptual heterogeneity across research contexts, methodological traditions, and outcome domains. Rather than aiming for exhaustive coverage, the approach prioritizes explanatory integration, consistent with the chapter's objective of clarifying how design choices condition the human consequences of algorithmic systems.

Search Strategy and Data Sources

The literature search was conducted sequentially across three major academic databases widely used in organizational and psychological research: PsycINFO, Scopus, and Web of Science. These databases were selected to ensure coverage of scholarship spanning human resource management, organizational behavior, and work psychology, while allowing for cumulative refinement of search criteria across stages. The overall search and screening process is summarized in Figure 1.

In the first stage, PsycINFO was searched using Boolean combinations of AI-related constructs and HR-relevant domains, yielding twenty empirical studies that met the initial inclusion criteria. In the second stage, Scopus was searched using the same AI-related constructs in combination with HR-relevant and organizational behavior terms, yielding fifteen additional studies. In the third stage, Web of Science was searched using AI-related and HR-relevant terms carried forward from the prior stages, yielding eleven further studies. Across databases, searches were restricted to peer-reviewed journal articles written in English and employing quantitative, experimental, or field-based empirical designs.

Figure 1. Overview of Search Methodology

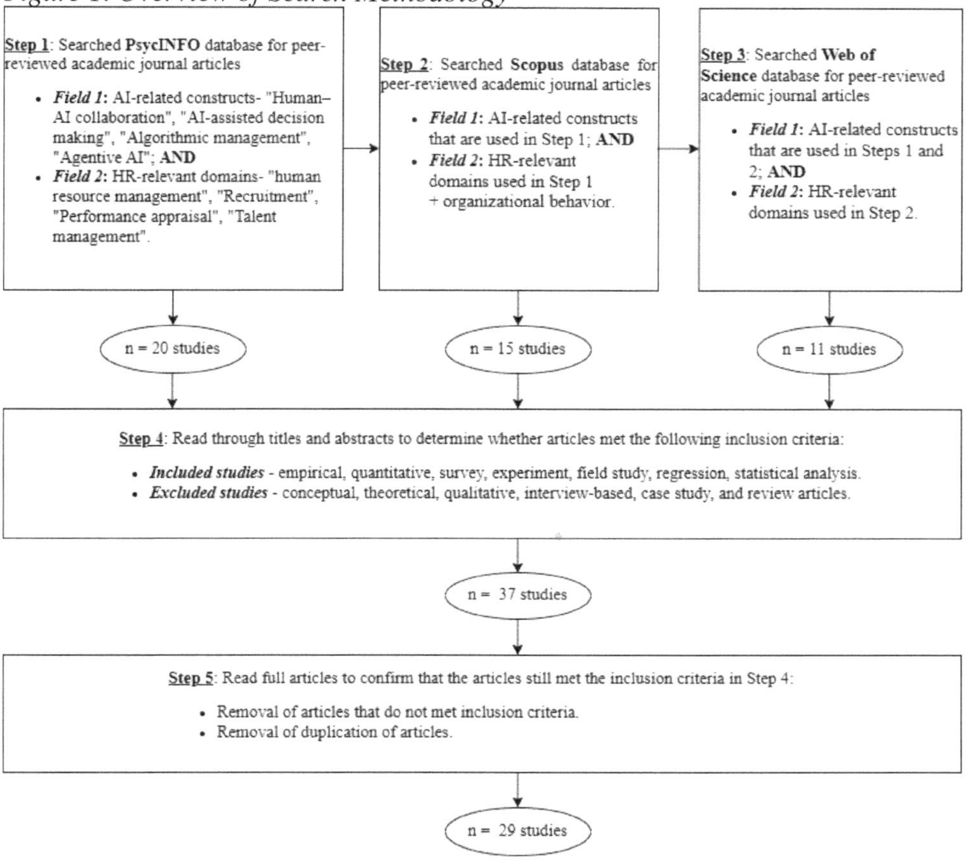

Note: The structure of this figure follows recent review work that illustrates search and screening procedures using a clear visual format (e.g., Perrigino et al., 2024).

Screening and Inclusion Criteria

Search results from all databases were merged and screened for duplication, resulting in the removal of eight overlapping articles. The remaining studies were then reviewed individually to assess relevance and eligibility. Articles were retained if they reported original empirical findings, examined AI- or algorithm-enabled systems that directly influenced work processes or managerial decision-making, and addressed outcomes relevant to human resource management, including perceptions of fairness, trust, responsibility, well-being, motivation, learning, and performance-related behaviors. Studies were excluded if they were purely conceptual or theoretical, relied exclusively on qualitative or interview-based methods, or examined AI technologies without a clear connection to HR-relevant work outcomes.

Final Sample and Review Approach

Application of these criteria resulted in a final sample of twenty-nine empirical studies as displayed in Figure 1. Rather than aggregating effect sizes or prioritizing methodological uniformity, the review adopted a thematic synthesis approach attentive to design features, contextual moderators, and socio-technical mechanisms. Studies were analyzed iteratively to identify recurring patterns across collaboration structures, communication framing, monitoring architectures, transparency cues, and reliability signals, as well as cross-cutting moderators shaping how workers interpret and respond to algorithmic authority. This semi-systematic approach was intentionally chosen to reflect the diversity of research designs and empirical contexts represented in the literature while maintaining transparency in search procedures and inclusion decisions. The resulting synthesis emphasizes explanatory integration over comprehensiveness, consistent with the chapter's objective of clarifying how design choices condition the human consequences of algorithmic and AI-enabled systems. *Extended tables summarizing study characteristics and design features are reported in the online supplement.*

To translate this analytic logic into a coherent structure, the chapter is organized around five descriptive themes, as displayed in Figure 2. The first theme examines research on collaboration structure, communication framing, and responsibility allocation, showing how system design shapes ethical judgment, anchoring processes, and willingness to act on algorithmic recommendations. The second theme synthesizes studies on trust, fairness, reliability, and monitoring, highlighting how transparent and interactional systems tend to foster legitimacy, whereas invasive or inconsistent designs often undermine acceptance and well-being. The third theme focuses on human agency and learning, demonstrating that workers do not merely comply with algorithmic authority but instead adapt, probe, resist, and develop algorithmic competence over time. The fourth theme addresses motivation, meaningfulness, and knowledge-related behaviors, illustrating how algorithmic design influences prosociality, burnout, identity, and knowledge sharing. The fifth theme considers team- and organization-level outcomes, emphasizing how algorithmic systems may enhance resilience, job quality, adoption, and innovation when embedded within supportive sociotechnical environments. The chapter then integrates these themes through an analysis of cross-cutting moderators before concluding with an integrative discussion, design recommendations, limitations, and directions for future research.

Figure 2. Thematic-Based Mapping of Human–AI Work Interactions Studies

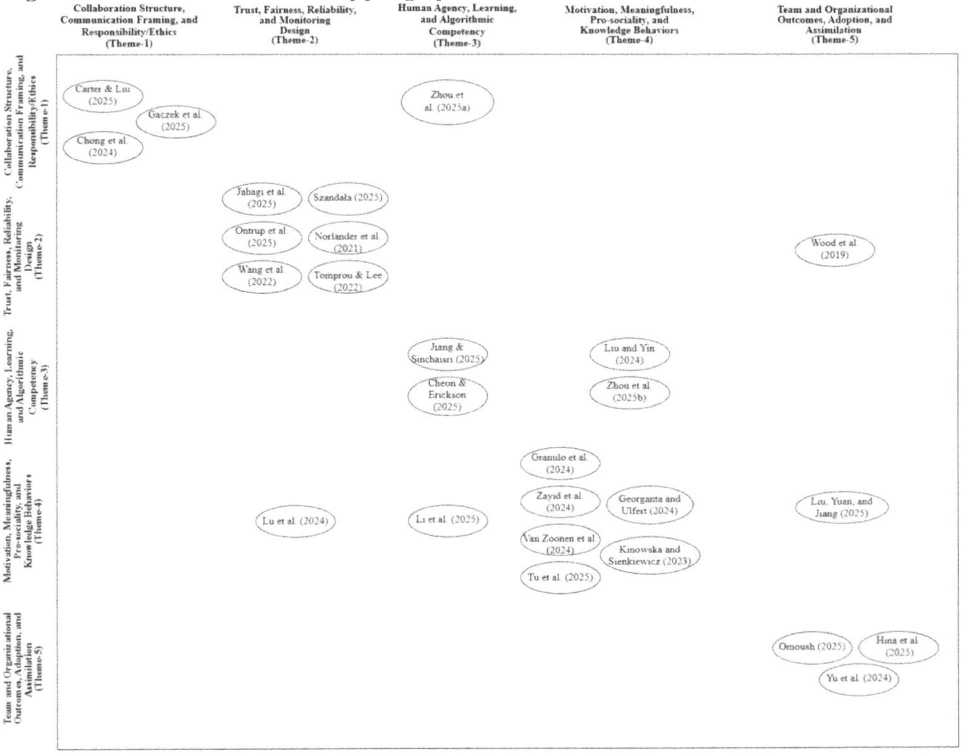

Source: Authors' work

Findings From the Thematic Synthesis

Theme 1: Collaboration Structure, Communication Framing, and Responsibility

The first thematic cluster examines how the design of human–AI collaboration and communication shapes responsibility attribution, ethical judgment, and cognitive reliance on algorithmic systems. As AI becomes embedded within organizational workflows, its influence extends beyond informational support to the social and psychological architecture through which decisions are made. Rather than functioning as neutral advisory tools, algorithmic systems may reconfigure how responsibility is experienced, how bias is activated or constrained, and how ethical considerations are weighed. Empirical research spanning performance appraisal, managerial ethics, collaborative system design, and platform-based algorithmic management demonstrates that collaboration structures, message framing, and the presence of multiple AI agents can meaningfully redirect confidence calibration, responsibility perceptions, and willingness to act ethically. Four empirical studies in the reviewed sample directly address these dynamics.

AI Recommendations, Anchoring, and Performance Appraisal

One of the clearest demonstrations of AI's cognitive influence emerges in performance evaluation contexts. Carter and Liu (2025) found that supervisors' ratings were strongly anchored to AI-generated recommendations, particularly when those recommendations signaled high performance. Exposure to elevated AI anchors led managers to produce systematically higher ratings, with judgments pulled closer to the algorithmic score than to equivalent recommendations attributed to human sources. This pattern suggests that AI outputs tend to be perceived as more objective or reliable, allowing numerical cues to exert disproportionate influence on evaluative judgment. Importantly, the anchoring effect was asymmetric. When AI recommendations signaled low performance, the distinction between human- and AI-generated anchors largely disappeared, as supervisors engaged in more cautious and critical reasoning regardless of the source. The study further showed that anchoring effects under high-performance conditions could be attenuated through a structured debiasing intervention. When prompted to consider counterfactual explanations, supervisors were more likely to question the AI's initial suggestion and adjust their ratings downward (Carter & Liu, 2025). These findings illustrate that AI does not merely inform appraisal judgments but may actively shape them, underscoring the importance of design interventions that preserve evaluative accuracy and fairness.

Human–AI Collaboration Modes and Responsibility Attribution

Beyond cognitive anchoring, collaboration structures play a central role in shaping managers' sense of responsibility for algorithmically informed decisions. Gaczek et al. (2025) demonstrated that when managers interacted individually with AI-generated recommendations, they tended to assume greater personal responsibility for outcomes, which in turn reduced their willingness to engage in ethically questionable actions. This finding challenges assumptions that AI adoption necessarily produces a responsibility gap, suggesting instead that individualized AI support may, in some contexts, heighten accountability. In contrast, shared human–AI team settings diffused responsibility across actors, increasing the likelihood of unethical decisions when violations were moderately ambiguous. Under conditions involving severe ethical violations, however, collaboration structure exerted little influence, as such actions were broadly rejected regardless of design. Complementary evidence from Zhou et al. (2025a) shows that responsibility attribution is further shaped by employees' interpretations of organizational intent. When AI-enabled HR practices were perceived as commitment-oriented rather than control-oriented, employees reported lower emotional strain and greater acceptance of algorithmic decisions. Together, these findings suggest that responsibility is not an inherent property of AI use but emerges from the interaction between collaboration design and perceived purpose.

Communication Framing and Ethical Responsibility

Responsibility attribution is also shaped by how AI-generated messages are framed. Gaczek et al. (2025) found that benefit-focused AI communications, which emphasized positive outcomes such as revenue gains from using sensitive customer data, significantly reduced perceived personal responsibility. This effect was especially pronounced among managers who relied heavily on AI in their daily work. Individuals with high levels of AI integration were more likely to interpret benefit-oriented messages as implicit approval, thereby lowering ethical vigilance and increasing willingness to engage in questionable practices. These results indicate that algorithmic communication is not neutral, as even subtle shifts in framing may meaningfully influence moral reasoning and responsibility perceptions. Message design therefore represents a critical, yet often overlooked, lever through which AI systems shape ethical outcomes.

Confidence, Multiple AI Agents, and Conformity Dynamics

AI design also influences confidence calibration and conformity dynamics, particularly in environments involving multiple algorithmic agents. Chong et al. (2024) found that introducing a second AI did not increase conformity to algorithmic recommendations, even when both systems agreed. Contrary to classic conformity effects observed in human groups, additional AI voices did not amplify alignment pressure. Instead, the presence of multiple AIs destabilized confidence over time. Designers' trust in both systems declined, and self-confidence eroded when at least one AI performed poorly. Negative feedback, whether directed at the human or the AI, further intensified confidence loss due to loss aversion. Notably, acceptance of algorithmic suggestions depended primarily on confidence in the first AI and in oneself, whereas confidence in the second AI had little effect. These findings suggest that cognitive capacity limits constrain users' ability to integrate multiple algorithmic inputs, creating risks of overload without corresponding gains in decision quality.

Theme 1 Summary

Across these studies, a consistent pattern emerges: the ethical and cognitive consequences of AI systems depend less on algorithmic capability than on how systems are introduced, framed, and embedded within human decision-making structures. AI recommendations may amplify cognitive biases such as anchoring, yet design-integrated debiasing prompts can mitigate these effects. Collaboration structures that diffuse responsibility across human and algorithmic actors may unintentionally encourage ethical drift, whereas individualized AI support may reinforce accountability. Communication framing further shapes responsibility attribution, particularly when benefit-focused language reduces ethical vigilance among heavy AI users. At the same time, adding multiple AI agents does not appear to improve reliability and may instead destabilize confidence while increasing cognitive load. Collectively, these findings indicate that responsible AI design requires deliberate attention to collaboration architecture, communication framing, and feedback mechanisms. Early design implications include embedding debiasing interventions, avoiding benefit-only messaging, minimizing unnecessary multi-AI environments, and making responsibility assignments explicit within AI-assisted decision processes. From this perspective, AI's ethical impact is not technologically predetermined but reflects a series of design choices that shape how humans reason, act, and make meaning alongside intelligent systems.

Theme 2: Trust, Fairness, Reliability, and Monitoring Design

The second thematic cluster examines how workers interpret the fairness, reliability, invasiveness, and relational qualities of algorithmic management systems. As algorithmic tools become embedded across gig platforms, digital marketplaces, recruitment processes, and supervisory technologies, their legitimacy increasingly rests on workers' lived experiences rather than on technical sophistication alone. These systems do more than automate tasks or optimize efficiency; they signal organizational priorities, structure expectations, and shape psychological contracts. As a result, workers respond to algorithmic systems as social actors whose design characteristics influence job satisfaction, perceived organizational support, motivation, and engagement. Across five empirical studies, a consistent pattern emerges: algorithmic systems are more likely to gain acceptance when they are perceived as fair, transparent, reliable, and respectful of personal boundaries, whereas inconsistency, opacity, and intrusiveness tend to undermine trust.

Algorithmic Fairness and Perceived Organizational Support

Fairness represents a foundational determinant of trust in algorithmic systems. Jabagi et al. (2025) showed that workers evaluate algorithmic decisions primarily through a procedural justice lens, with these perceptions strongly predicting job satisfaction and perceived organizational support. Their findings reveal important distinctions across decision types. Algorithmic decisions that are rule-based or mechanical, such as task matching, are generally perceived as procedurally fair.

By contrast, performance evaluation algorithms exert a stronger influence on job satisfaction and perceived organizational support because they are interpreted as expressions of discretionary organizational judgment. In these contexts, workers use algorithmic evaluations to infer whether the organization applies consistent, ethical, and accurate standards. Design features such as transparency, opportunities to appeal decisions, and clear rationales therefore function as signals of goodwill within algorithmically mediated psychological contracts.

Related concerns arise in AI-supported recruitment. Szandała (2025) found that although large language model–based evaluations approximate human assessments on average, high levels of intra-model inconsistency undermine perceptions of procedural fairness. When identical candidate responses receive different ratings across evaluation rounds, the perceived reliability and legitimacy of algorithmic hiring decisions are compromised. Such inconsistency increases the risk of arbitrary outcomes and challenges the credibility of algorithmic personnel selection. Taken together, these studies position fairness as a first-order condition for trust, acceptance, and sustained use of algorithmic systems.

Reliability, Trust, and Engagement Pathways

Beyond fairness, perceived reliability plays a central role in shaping whether workers experience algorithmic systems as stable, predictable, and responsive. Lu et al. (2025) demonstrated that when platform algorithms operate consistently and transparently, workers are more likely to develop trust, which in turn supports sustained engagement. Reliable algorithmic processes reduce uncertainty and facilitate more favorable cognitive appraisals, consistent with transactional models of stress and coping. Their study also highlights the moderating role of occupational stigma. Workers who perceive their occupation as stigmatized exhibit a weaker relationship between reliability, trust, and engagement, yet stigma itself appears to heighten baseline trust in the platform. This pattern suggests a compensatory dynamic in which individuals facing stigma may rely more heavily on platform structures for validation and access to opportunities.

Reliability concerns also emerge in recruitment contexts. Szandała (2025) showed that while AI-based evaluations may perform adequately on average, inconsistency across cases weakens users' confidence and acceptance. These findings underscore the importance of systematic reliability testing and ongoing auditing before integrating algorithmic systems into evaluative processes. More broadly, the literature indicates that consistent and predictable algorithmic behavior supports trust and engagement, whereas uneven or unstable performance erodes confidence and diminishes perceived legitimacy.

Electronic Monitoring and Perceived Invasiveness

Alongside fairness and reliability, electronic monitoring introduces distinct psychological challenges. Ontrup et al. (2025) found that invasive electronic team monitoring reduces perceptions of fairness, heightens stress, and lowers acceptance, even when framed as a developmental intervention intended to support teamwork. Workers tended to perceive monitoring as intrusive regardless of whether systems were described as highly or minimally invasive, suggesting that the presence of digital surveillance itself can activate privacy concerns and perceptions of excessive oversight. In this sense, invasiveness extends beyond technical design to signal a threat to trust and well-being.

These findings align with broader research on platform-based monitoring. Wood et al. (2019) documented how opaque rating systems, productivity tracking, and customer review mechanisms contribute to stress, overwork, and insecurity. When monitoring becomes granular or punitive, workers often experience diminished dignity and a sense of replaceability. Across studies, invasive monitoring undermines trust and fairness by conveying that workers are objects of optimization rather than partners in the work process.

Observational Versus Interactional Monitoring

Monitoring effects, however, are not uniformly negative and depend on how oversight is enacted. Wang et al. (2022) distinguished between observational monitoring, which involves unidirectional tracking of behavior, and interactional monitoring, which incorporates communication, feedback, and shared control. Observational monitoring was associated with lower affective trust and reduced engagement, whereas interactional monitoring fostered affective commitment and enhanced engagement. These findings situate monitoring within relational exchange processes, suggesting that workers respond more positively to systems that allow dialogue and support rather than unilateral surveillance.

Norlander et al. (2021) further complicate this picture by showing that platform-based technological supervision, which resembles observational monitoring, can increase perceived control and market autonomy for gig workers. In their study, algorithmic supervision was associated with higher work enjoyment and perceived organizational control, indicating that observational monitoring does not inherently diminish motivation. Instead, its effects appear contingent on task structure, perceived autonomy, and whether monitoring is experienced as enabling or constraining. Together, these studies emphasize the importance of context-sensitive monitoring design.

AI Versus Human Agents in Relational Exchanges

The relational implications of algorithmic systems become particularly salient when comparing AI agents with human agents. Tomprou and Lee (2022) found that AI agents convey weaker relational inducements during recruitment, leading to lower initial perceptions of employer commitment. At the same time, when relational promises are under-delivered, breaches attributed to AI agents generate less anger and lower turnover intentions than equivalent breaches attributed to humans. Because AI is perceived as less intentional and less personal, its failures evoke muted emotional responses. This relative relational neutrality can buffer negative reactions while simultaneously limiting the formation of strong relational bonds. These findings align with Jabagi et al. (2025), suggesting that workers treat algorithms as representatives of organizational intent while attributing different degrees of agency and blame to them than to human actors. Communication channels and perceived intentionality therefore play a central role in shaping trust and commitment.

Theme 2 Summary

Taken together, this body of research converges on a coherent conclusion: the legitimacy and acceptance of algorithmic management systems depend fundamentally on workers' interpretations of fairness, reliability, monitoring design, and relational intent. Fairness in evaluation, matching, and recruitment consistently predicts satisfaction and perceived organizational support, whereas reliability fosters trust and engagement, and inconsistency erodes credibility. Monitoring systems that are perceived as invasive reliably increase stress and undermine fairness perceptions, while interactional monitoring tends to build trust and commitment. Observational monitoring produces more variable outcomes, contingent on autonomy and contextual factors. Finally, AI agents reshape psychological contracts by dampening relational cues while softening reactions to breach.

These findings carry clear implications for algorithmic system design. Organizations should prioritize transparent, fair, and explainable decision processes; ensure reliability through validation and ongoing auditing; minimize perceived invasiveness in monitoring practices; and embed interactional elements that allow feedback and shared control. Equally important is recognizing that algorithmic systems function as socio-technical actors rather than neutral tools. Their design shapes workers' sense of obligation, commitment, and perceived organizational intent, making thoughtful attention to trust and legitimacy essential for the future of algorithmic work systems.

Theme 3: Human Agency, Learning, and Algorithmic Competency

The third thematic cluster examines how workers exercise agency, learn, and develop competence within algorithmically mediated work systems. Although algorithmic management is often associated with control and constraint, empirical evidence indicates that workers actively shape how these systems function in practice. Rather than complying automatically with algorithmic instructions, workers learn from experience, selectively rely on or reject system outputs, correct errors, and develop individualized strategies for navigating digitally mediated work. This theme therefore captures agency as an emergent and evolving process expressed through learning, adaptation, resistance, and the accumulation of algorithmic competency. Six empirical studies in the review address these dynamics directly.

Learning Trajectories and Deviation from Algorithmic Recommendations

Learning over time plays a central role in shaping how workers engage with algorithmic guidance. Jiang and Sinchaisri (2025) showed that reliance on algorithmic recommendations shifts systematically with experience. New workers tend to depend heavily on platform guidance because it reduces uncertainty and cognitive load. As workers accumulate task knowledge, however, they grow more confident in their own judgment and increasingly override recommendations that fail to reflect local conditions or practical realities. Importantly, this shift does not reflect wholesale rejection of automation. Workers continue to value optimization tools that deliver clear operational benefits while disengaging from static recommendation features that do not evolve alongside user expertise. These findings suggest that algorithmic systems that fail to adapt to users' learning trajectories risk losing relevance and credibility over time.

Everyday Adaptation, Probing, and Selective Resistance

Beyond formal learning, workers continuously adapt to algorithmic systems through probing, experimentation, and selective resistance. Cheon and Erickson (2025) documented how workers in Amazon fulfillment centers actively interpret and work around opaque performance metrics and productivity thresholds. In the absence of transparency, workers rely on online communities and informal exchanges to develop shared understandings of how systems operate. They also engage in small, tactical adjustments, such as timing scans or manipulating task sequences, to preserve autonomy and manage physical strain. These practices reflect negotiated forms of agency rather than outright defiance or passive compliance. At the same time, algorithmic systems reshape managerial roles, as supervisors act as interpreters who assess whether algorithmic signals correspond to meaningful performance issues. This hybrid arrangement reinforces ongoing adaptation by both workers and managers.

Algorithmic Competency as an Acquired Capability

In some contexts, workers move beyond improvisation toward deeper proficiency in engaging with algorithmic systems. Zhou et al. (2025b) conceptualized this capability as algorithmic competency, defined as the ability to understand, navigate, and, when necessary, correct algorithmic processes. Algorithmic competency develops through peer-based learning and individual reflection on task execution. Workers with higher competency report greater control and comfort when interacting with algorithmic systems, alongside stronger service-oriented behaviors and identification with their work. These findings indicate that algorithmic management is not inherently disempowering; its effects depend on whether workers have access to knowledge resources and opportunities to build mastery.

Attributions, Overload, and Behavioral Responses

Workers' interpretations of algorithmic intent further shape behavioral responses. Liu and Yin (2024) found that when algorithmic interactions are perceived as engaging or game-like, workers respond with creativity and proactive job crafting. When systems appear restrictive or excessively controlling, workers shift toward defensive strategies aimed at minimizing penalties or reducing strain. Individual differences also matter, as workers with stronger self-efficacy are more likely to interpret algorithmic systems as enabling rather than threatening. Complementary evidence from Zhou et al. (2025) shows that attributions regarding the intentions underlying AI-supported human resource practices strongly influence emotional strain and acceptance. Commitment-oriented interpretations, such as perceiving AI as a signal of support or fairness, are associated with higher procedural justice perceptions and reduced uncertainty. Control-oriented interpretations, by contrast, heighten stress, skepticism, and feelings of constraint. Together, these studies underscore that responses to algorithmic management depend not only on technical features but also on the meanings workers assign to them.

System Cognition, Job Crafting, and Evolving Agency

Agency is also expressed through workers' active reconstruction of tasks based on their understanding of algorithmic systems. Li et al. (2025) showed that employees develop system cognition, or mental models of how AI-enabled systems operate, which guide subsequent behavior. When system cognition is coherent and positive, workers are more likely to engage in job crafting by reshaping tasks, adjusting workflows, and aligning roles with personal strengths. These behaviors are associated with higher job satisfaction, indicating that agency extends beyond resistance to include constructive adaptation. Importantly, the effects of system cognition are amplified by AI literacy. Workers with higher literacy are better able to translate understanding into effective job redesign, whereas those with lower literacy struggle to act on their insights. These findings highlight the reciprocal nature of human–AI interaction, in which agency is redirected rather than diminished.

Theme 3 Summary

Across the studies in this theme, algorithmic management does not eliminate human agency but reorganizes it. Workers learn to calibrate reliance on algorithmic tools, adapt through experimentation, draw on peer knowledge networks, and develop competencies that shape how systems function in practice. Their actions, ranging from tactical adjustments to sophisticated interpretive strategies, actively influence the operation of algorithmic management in everyday work. For organizations, these insights suggest several design implications. Algorithmic systems should adapt to workers' experience levels rather than assuming uniform dependence. Transparency and clear mechanisms for error correction can reduce overreliance on informal workarounds. Training and peer-support structures can foster algorithmic competency, improving both performance and well-being. More broadly, effective algorithmic management requires recognizing workers as active learners and decision-makers whose agency is integral to the functioning of AI-enabled work systems.

Theme 4: Motivation, Meaningfulness, Prosociality, and Knowledge Behaviors

The fourth thematic cluster examines how algorithmic management reshapes motivation, meaningfulness, prosocial behavior, and knowledge-related outcomes by altering workers' role perceptions, relationships, and sense of purpose. Although such systems are often designed to enhance efficiency, coordination, and fairness, employees interpret them through complex psychological and relational frameworks. Across eleven empirical studies, a consistent tension emerges: algorithmic management may motivate while simultaneously unsettling, impose structure while constraining autonomy, and improve coordination while weakening the social foundations that sustain cooperation and meaning at work. This theme integrates these dynamics to explain how algorithmic systems influence prosocial motivation, meaningfulness, well-being, knowledge sharing, service commitment, and cooperation within human–AI teams.

Prosocial Motivation and Objectification

Prosocial motivation is particularly sensitive to the interpersonal signals conveyed through algorithmic oversight. Granulo et al. (2024) showed that when algorithmic systems treat workers primarily as data points to be optimized, employees are more likely to experience objectification. This perception weakens the intrinsic value workers place on helping colleagues and erodes the sense of mutual responsibility that supports cooperation. However, even limited opportunities for interpersonal connection, such as brief conversations or supportive check-ins, can offset these effects. These findings indicate that social interaction remains a critical counterweight to the impersonality associated with algorithmic management.

Meaningfulness under Algorithmic Control and Matching

Meaningfulness is similarly shaped by how algorithmic tools structure work experiences. Van Zoonen et al. (2024) found that algorithmic control implemented through rigid oversight or prescriptive direction undermines workers' ability to sustain a coherent work identity and maintain relational ties, thereby reducing perceived purpose. In contrast, algorithmic matching that aligns tasks with workers' preferences or strengths tends to enhance meaningfulness by supporting a sense of fit and developmental progress. Workers also compensate for relational deficits in platform design by forming informal online communities that provide affirmation, knowledge exchange, and shared interpretations of opaque algorithmic decisions. Recent evidence further suggests that workers actively reconstruct meaning when they can reinterpret and reshape their tasks. Li et al. (2025) showed that clearer system cognition supports job crafting, which helps restore a sense of direction and fit within digitally structured environments. Together, these findings indicate that meaningfulness is shaped by both algorithmic design and workers' interpretive and adaptive efforts.

Burnout, Threat, Well-Being, and Person–Job Fit

Parallel concerns arise with respect to well-being. Kinowska and Sienkiewicz (2023) and Zayid et al. (2024) demonstrated that digital controls, constant monitoring, and prescriptive algorithmic rules increase burnout, heighten perceived threat, and reduce psychological comfort. Workers often experience anxiety associated with continuous evaluation and rigid performance metrics, even when objective performance remains high. However, person–job fit moderates these effects. When workers perceive alignment between algorithmic demands and their skills or identities, algorithmic pressure is more likely to be experienced as manageable rather than overwhelming. These findings underscore the importance of aligning system design with workers' capacities and preferences.

Knowledge Hiding, Psychological Ownership, and Identification

Algorithmic management also shapes knowledge behaviors by influencing autonomy and identification. Liu, Yuan, and Jiang (2025) found that reduced autonomy under algorithmic oversight strengthens psychological ownership of personal knowledge, particularly among workers with weaker organizational attachment. This heightened ownership increases knowledge hiding, as employees protect domains where they retain control. Related evidence from Liu and Yin (2024) shows that workers' willingness to engage in creative job crafting depends on whether algorithmic constraints are interpreted as challenges or hindrances. Zhou et al. (2025b) further demonstrated that the type of agent delivering relational commitments influences psychological contracts. Algorithmic agents weaken perceived employer commitment, whereas human agents elicit stronger reactions when commitments are under-delivered. Together, these studies indicate that knowledge sharing and identification depend less on technical features than on how workers interpret autonomy, trust, and organizational intent.

Service Commitment, Referrals, and Workload

Service-oriented contexts provide additional insight into motivational recalibration under algorithmic management. Lu et al. (2024) showed that strong algorithmic pressure can reduce commitment to service quality, thereby lowering employees' willingness to refer potential recruits. However, when workload is experienced as a challenge rather than a burden, negative effects are attenuated. Workers with strong service commitment become more selective in referrals, ultimately improving referral quality. The study also highlights the value workers place on human intervention, particularly when it corrects unfair or inaccurate algorithmic evaluations, reinforcing the complementary roles of human and algorithmic judgment.

Cooperation with AI Teammates

Algorithmic management increasingly structures collaboration between humans and AI agents. Georganta and Ulfert (2024) and Tu et al. (2025) found that workers readily trust AI teammates' competence when systems demonstrate reliability and task mastery, even though affective trust remains limited due to the absence of social warmth cues. Despite this emotional distance, cooperative behavior often emerges when AI systems are perceived as capable. These findings suggest that effective human–AI collaboration depends on performance credibility, even when relational bonds remain attenuated.

Theme 4 Summary

Across these studies, algorithmic management reshapes how workers understand themselves, their relationships, and their connection to the organization. It influences whether employees feel valued or objectified, supported or constrained, and connected or isolated, with downstream consequences for motivation, meaningfulness, and knowledge behaviors. Workers do not respond mechanically to algorithmic rules but continuously interpret and negotiate their meaning through identity, relational ties, and psychological resources. For organizations, these findings imply that effective algorithmic management requires more than technical precision. Systems that emphasize transparency, task fit, supportive matching, and opportunities for human connection are more likely to sustain motivation and meaning. In contrast, opaque or controlling designs risk generating strain, knowledge withholding, and declining prosocial engagement. From this perspective, the success of algorithmic management depends on recognizing workers as active interpreters whose well-being and relational needs remain central to organizational functioning.

Theme 5: Team and Organizational Outcomes, Adoption, and Assimilation

The final thematic cluster examines how algorithmic management shapes team dynamics, recruitment practices, digital operations, and job quality at the organizational level. Across studies, a consistent conclusion emerges: organizational outcomes arise less from technological capability than from how algorithmic systems are embedded in workflows, interpreted by employees, and supported by institutional arrangements. When integrated with collaborative routines and human judgment, such systems may strengthen teams and enhance performance. When poorly implemented, however, they may exacerbate precarity and erode job quality. Five empirical studies in the review address these dynamics directly.

Team Resilience and Informal Leadership

Research on team functioning highlights the constructive potential of algorithmic systems when they reshape managerial cognition and enable informal leadership. Liu, Yuan, and Wang (2025) showed that algorithmic management can enhance team resilience by reducing managerial objectification and encouraging managers to view employees as capable contributors rather than interchangeable units. This cognitive reframing creates space for employees to assume informal leadership roles, coordinating and adapting during periods of uncertainty. Through the combined mechanisms of managerial perspective change and bottom-up initiative, algorithmic systems may indirectly support more resilient and self-organizing teams.

Adoption and Assimilation in Recruitment

Studies of adoption and assimilation indicate that successful AI integration in recruitment depends on human capabilities and organizational flexibility rather than deployment alone. Hina et al. (2025) argued that AI assimilation is primarily enabled by AI competency and recruitment agility. Human resource professionals must understand the systems they use, and recruitment processes must remain adaptable enough to incorporate new technological routines. Notably, commonly cited inhibitors, such as AI opacity and limited algorithmic empathy, did not impede assimilation when strong human–AI collaboration was present. When AI systems handled repetitive tasks and human recruiters provided empathy, contextual reasoning, and candidate interaction, concerns about opacity and emotional distance diminished. These findings suggest that collaboration functions as a mechanism that transforms potential barriers into manageable design features.

Digital Operations and Job Satisfaction

A similar pattern emerges in digital operations, where organizational outcomes depend on the quality of human–AI collaboration. Omoush (2025) found that AI-driven procurement, workflow management, and logistics systems improve cognitive outcomes and job satisfaction when accompanied by training, intuitive interfaces, and participatory decision processes. Under these conditions, workers report greater autonomy and clarity, as they retain a meaningful role in interpreting and applying algorithmic insights. In the absence of such supports, however, the same systems are more likely to be experienced as rigid or alienating, underscoring the importance of human-centered implementation.

Job Quality, Inequality, and Organizational Capability

Job quality under algorithmic control remains uneven, particularly in platform-based labor. Wood et al. (2019) showed that algorithmic management produces a dual experience of autonomy and vulnerability. While platforms offer flexibility and task variety, they also expose workers to low pay, irregular schedules, social isolation, and exhaustion. These outcomes are shaped by workers' skills and reputational standing, as those with stronger reputational capital can leverage algorithms to secure better opportunities, whereas others face unstable earnings and limited bargaining power. Beyond platform settings, organizational-level evidence further indicates that AI contributes to breakthrough innovation only when embedded within supportive firm-level capabilities. Yu et al. (2024) identified effective configurations combining expert autonomy and alliance networks with institutional strictness and human–human–AI collaboration. Only configurations that integrated these elements translated innovation into improved strategic performance, highlighting the role of governance and coordinated human involvement. Together, these studies indicate that algorithmic control can either amplify inequality or support innovation, depending on how power, autonomy, and institutional support are distributed.

Theme 5 Summary

Taken together, the studies in this theme underscore that team and organizational outcomes depend on how algorithmic systems are woven into broader socio-technical environments. Algorithmic systems may strengthen teams by clarifying expectations, reducing managerial bias, and enabling informal leadership. They may enhance recruitment effectiveness when human resource professionals possess the skills and flexibility to use them and when collaboration compensates for algorithmic limitations. Digital operations benefit when AI is introduced alongside training and participatory practices that preserve worker autonomy. Conversely, in contexts where human support is limited and worker power is weak, algorithmic systems are more likely to intensify precarity and degrade job quality.

These findings emphasize that AI assimilation constitutes a socio-technical transformation rather than a technical upgrade. Organizations must invest in AI competency, collaborative routines, and institutional supports that enable workers to interpret, contest, and effectively use algorithmic systems. When these conditions are present, algorithmic management may contribute to resilient teams, effective recruitment, satisfied employees, and innovative firms. When absent, similar systems risk reinforcing inequality, undermining job quality, and generating resistance. In this sense, the organizational value of algorithmic management depends on the alignment among AI capabilities, human expertise, and the institutional contexts in which they jointly operate.

Table 1. Classification of Cross-Cutting Moderators

Theme / Moderator Category	Study	Moderator(s)	Effect
Collaboration Mode & Communication Framing	Gaczek et al. (2025)	Collaboration type (sole AI vs. human–AI team)	Sole AI increases responsibility; human–AI teams diffuse responsibility and raise unethical tendencies.
	Gaczek et al. (2025)	AI communication framing (benefit-framing)	Benefit framing reduces responsibility and increases unethical willingness, especially for high AI-reliance managers.
	Hina et al. (2025)	Human–AI collaboration	Weakens the negative effects of AI opacity and AI empathy on AI assimilation.

continued on following page

Table 1. Continued

Theme / Moderator Category	Study	Moderator(s)	Effect
Transparency & Reliability	Zhou et al. (2025a)	Algorithmic transparency	Reduces overload caused by restricting/ evaluating algorithms; shifts control to commitment attributions.
	Lu et al. (2025)	Experienced algorithmic reliability	Improves trust to engagement pathway; weakened by occupational stigma consciousness.
Monitoring Intensity & Style	Ontrup et al. (2025)	Invasiveness of ETM	High invasiveness decreases fairness/acceptance and increases stress.
	Wang et al. (2022)	Observational vs. interactional monitoring	Interactional monitoring increases trust & engagement; observational monitoring undermines trust.
	Wang et al. (2022)	Method control (autonomy)	Strengthens the link between affective trust and engagement.
Social Interaction	Granulo et al. (2024)	Level of social interaction	Buffers the negative effects of algorithmic management on prosocial motivation and behavior.
Person–Job Fit & Organizational Identification	Zayid et al. (2024)	Person–job fit	Weakens the impact of algorithmic management on burnout and perceived threat.
	Liu, Yuan, & Jiang (2025)	Organizational identification	Reduces the indirect effect of algorithmic management on knowledge hiding.
Additional Moderators	Li et al. (2025)	Achievement motivation	Strengthens proactive responses; reduces withdrawal under AI awareness.
	Liu & Yin (2024)	Core self-evaluations	Strengthens gameful experience; weakens autonomy loss under algorithmic management.
	Tu et al. (2025)	AI teammate gender cues	Female cues increase warmth but reduce competence; male cues increase competence but reduce warmth.
	Lu et al. (2024)	Workload	Buffers the negative effect of algorithmic management on service commitment and referrals.
	Gaczek et al. (2025)	Managers' AI reliance	Amplifies unethical behavior under benefit-focused AI communication.

Source: Authors' work

SOLUTIONS AND RECOMMENDATIONS

Beyond the focal themes identified above, the review reveals a set of cross-cutting moderators that condition the effects of AI and algorithmic systems across tasks, contexts, and implementation designs, as summarized in Table 1. Collectively, the studies indicate that algorithmic outcomes do not emerge uniformly but depend on contextual factors that shape how workers interpret, experience, and respond to algorithmic systems. These moderators operate as consequential design levers for human resource leaders, influencing whether algorithmic systems support responsibility, trust, well-being, and engagement or, alternatively, amplify strain, ethical vulnerability, and disengagement. This section synthesizes these moderators into conceptual categories, clarifying how they shape the psychological and organizational dynamics that underpin human–AI interaction.

Collaboration Mode and Communication Framing

One of the most consequential contextual factors concerns the structure of collaboration between humans and AI systems. Evidence consistently indicates that collaboration mode alters responsibility perceptions and ethical outcomes. Gaczek et al. (2025) showed that working individually with AI recommendations heightens perceived personal responsibility and reduces unethical behavior, whereas shared human–AI collaboration diffuses responsibility and increases the likelihood of ethical transgressions under ambiguous conditions. Communication framing further conditions these effects. Benefit-focused AI messages reduce perceived responsibility and increase willingness to engage in questionable actions, particularly among managers who rely heavily on AI systems (Gaczek et al., 2025). In recruitment contexts, human–AI collaboration similarly moderates the influence of AI inhibitors, such as opacity and limited empathy, reducing their constraining effects on system assimilation (Hina et al., 2025). Together, these findings indicate that collaboration structures and communication framing actively shape accountability and ethical orientation rather than functioning as neutral design features.

Transparency and Reliability

Transparency and system reliability emerge as additional contextual factors with broad implications for trust and strain. Zhou et al. (2025a) demonstrated that algorithmic transparency attenuates the negative effects of algorithmic recommending, restricting, and evaluating on work overload by weakening control-oriented attributions. When transparency is limited, the same practices intensify overload and undermine service behavior. Reliability operates through a parallel mechanism. Lu et al. (2025) showed that experienced algorithmic reliability strengthens trust in platforms, which in turn supports work engagement. This pathway, however, is moderated by occupational stigma consciousness, which dampens trust formation.

Taken together, transparency and reliability function as foundational conditions for sustaining trust and mitigating strain in algorithmically mediated work.

Monitoring Intensity and Style

Monitoring intensity and monitoring style further condition employees' responses to algorithmic oversight. Ontrup et al. (2025) found that more invasive electronic team monitoring reduces acceptance, lowers perceived fairness, and increases stress, ultimately decreasing willingness to adopt monitoring systems. Wang et al. (2022) demonstrated that monitoring style is equally consequential. Observational monitoring reduces affective trust and cognitive engagement, whereas interactional monitoring fosters trust, commitment, and engagement. Method control, defined as autonomy in how tasks are completed, strengthens the positive relationship between trust and engagement, indicating that autonomy amplifies the benefits of supportive monitoring designs. These findings underscore that monitoring functions as a psychological signal shaping fairness perceptions and stress responses, rather than as a purely technical configuration.

Social Interaction

Social interaction plays a protective role in algorithmically managed work environments. Granulo et al. (2024) showed that higher levels of social interaction mitigate the negative effects of algorithmic management on prosocial motivation and behavior. In contexts where algorithmic systems increase objectification or weaken social cohesion, opportunities for meaningful interpersonal exchange preserve prosocial orientation and cooperation. These findings suggest that maintaining social interaction remains important even in highly automated, distributed, or platform-based settings.

Person–Job Fit and Organizational Identification

Alignment between individuals, their jobs, and the organization further conditions algorithmic outcomes. Zayid et al. (2024) demonstrated that person–job fit weakens the relationship between algorithmic management and burnout or perceived threat, thereby protecting employee well-being. Organizational identification operates in a similar manner. Liu, Yuan, and Jiang (2025) showed that high identification reduces the tendency for algorithmic control to translate psychological ownership into knowledge hiding. These findings indicate that worker–organization alignment shapes how algorithmic pressures are interpreted and internalized.

Additional Moderators

Several additional factors operate across distinct psychological pathways. Workload buffers the negative effect of algorithmic management on service commitment and referral behavior by reframing algorithmic demands as challenges rather than constraints (Lu et al., 2024). Achievement motivation moderates the dual effects of AI awareness on innovation, strengthening proactive responses while weakening withdrawal tendencies (Li et al., 2025). Core self-evaluations similarly amplify positive responses, such as gameful engagement, while attenuating negative reactions, such as perceived autonomy loss (Liu & Yin, 2024). At the design level, teammate gender cues influence perceptions of AI competence and warmth, shaping cooperation intentions (Tu et al., 2025). Finally, managerial reliance on AI amplifies the effects of benefit-focused framing on unethical behavior, positioning reliance itself as a critical contextual condition (Gaczek et al., 2025). Together, these factors illustrate how individual traits, identity cues, contextual demands, and system-level signals interact with algorithmic structures to produce divergent outcomes.

Moderators as Design Parameters

Taken together, these cross-cutting moderators reinforce that AI and algorithmic management systems do not exert fixed or linear effects. Instead, their consequences emerge from configurations of psychological, structural, and relational conditions that organizations can actively shape. Collaboration mode, communication framing, transparency, monitoring intrusiveness, social interaction, person–job fit, and individual motivations function as design parameters that determine whether algorithmic systems enhance or erode responsibility, trust, well-being, and prosocial behavior. Recognizing and configuring these parameters reframes AI implementation as a strategic organizational design challenge rather than a purely technical decision, emphasizing that human outcomes depend as much on how systems are implemented as on the capabilities they embody. To integrate these insights across the five themes and the cross-cutting moderators, Figure 3 presents an integrative conceptual framework summarizing how AI system design features map onto HR-relevant outcomes through the thematic areas identified in the review. The framework also highlights contextual moderators that appear to condition these relationships across settings and tasks.

Figure 3. contextual moderators that appear to condition these relationships across settings and tasks

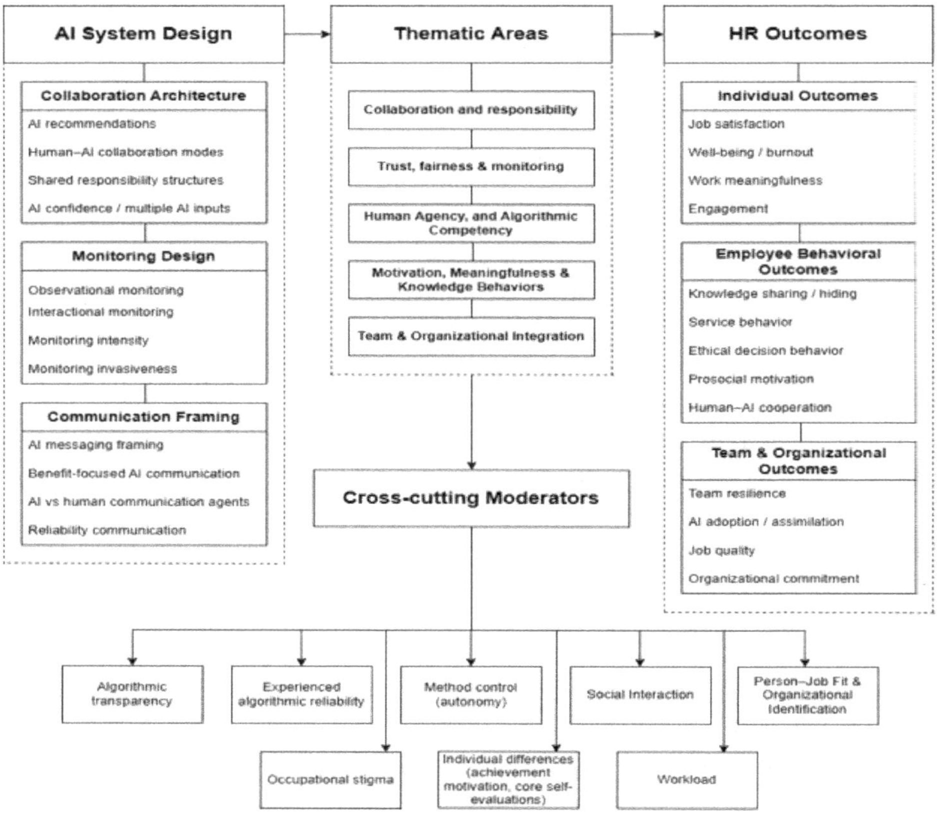

Source: Authors' work

DISCUSSION

This chapter set out to examine how the design of collaboration, monitoring, and communication determines whether algorithmic and AI-enabled systems support or undermine human resource–relevant outcomes. Across the twenty-nine empirical studies reviewed, a consistent conclusion emerges: the consequences of algorithmic systems are shaped less by the technology itself than by the socio-technical conditions in which it is embedded. Algorithmic systems may enhance fairness, efficiency, and decision quality, yet they may also generate strain, erode trust, and diminish meaningfulness. These divergent outcomes depend on how systems are integrated into work processes, how employees interpret their intent, and how organizations communicate their purpose. The discussion below integrates findings across all themes to revisit the guiding question and articulate broader implications for human resource management.

Revisiting the central question, which designs of collaboration, monitoring, and communication enable AI systems to improve HR outcomes, the evidence reveals a coherent pattern. Positive outcomes tend to arise when algorithmic systems clarify responsibility, demonstrate procedural fairness and reliability, protect autonomy, and preserve space for human judgment. Under such conditions, AI systems are more likely to support ethical decision-making, strengthen engagement, and enhance perceptions of organizational support. For example, transparent and well-calibrated performance evaluation systems can increase consistency in supervisory judgments, even as managers must remain attentive to anchoring effects associated with AI-generated recommendations (Carter & Liu, 2025). Similarly, platform algorithms that operate predictably and are experienced as reliable foster trust and sustained engagement among workers (Lu et al., 2025).

When these design conditions are absent, however, algorithmic arrangements often produce the opposite effects. Opaque evaluative logic, invasive monitoring, ambiguous messaging, and poorly aligned collaboration structures intensify emotional strain, encourage defensive behavior, and undermine perceived legitimacy. Electronic team monitoring, regardless of whether it is framed as developmental or evaluative, reliably heightens perceptions of invasiveness and reduces acceptance (Ontrup et al., 2025). In recruitment contexts, large language models that generate inconsistent scoring across cases weaken procedural fairness and compromise system credibility (Szandała, 2025). Taken together, these findings underscore that the presence of AI is not determinative; rather, it is the relational, communicative, and organizational context surrounding AI that shapes HR-relevant outcomes.

Integrating evidence across all five themes highlights a nuanced balance between the benefits and risks of algorithmic management. When thoughtfully designed, AI-enabled systems can reinforce, rather than dilute, human responsibility. Individualized AI support, for instance, has been shown to strengthen managers' sense of accountability and reduce their willingness to engage in unethical behavior (Gaczek et al., 2025). Transparent and procedurally fair algorithmic decisions foster perceptions of organizational support, contributing to higher job satisfaction and attachment (Jabagi et al., 2025). Algorithmic matching that aligns tasks with workers' strengths supports meaningfulness and identity development (Van Zoonen et al., 2024). As workers develop algorithmic competency through learning, reflection, and peer exchange, they experience greater control and engage more actively in service-oriented behaviors (Zhou et al., 2025b). At the collective level, algorithmic systems may enhance team resilience by reshaping managerial cognition and enabling informal leadership under conditions of uncertainty (Liu, Yuan, & Wang, 2025). Together, these findings indicate that AI can function as a resource for clarity, empowerment, and coordination when human agency is actively supported.

At the same time, poorly calibrated designs introduce substantial risks. Algorithmic cues may anchor evaluative judgments, exerting disproportionate influence when outputs appear precise or objective (Carter & Liu, 2025). Intrusive monitoring and prescriptive control heighten burnout, perceived threat, and psychological strain (Kinowska & Sienkiewicz, 2023; Zayid et al., 2024). When algorithmic oversight signals objectification, prosocial motivation declines, weakening cooperation and shared responsibility (Granulo et al., 2024). Reduced autonomy and weakened organizational identification increase the likelihood of knowledge hiding (Liu, Yuan, & Jiang, 2025), while in digital labor markets algorithmic management may intensify precarity through volatile earnings and insecure working conditions (Wood et al., 2019). These patterns illustrate how psychological and relational vulnerabilities are activated when algorithmic systems undermine trust, autonomy, and meaningful human involvement.

Across themes, a central insight emerges: the effects of AI are fundamentally socio-technical rather than technical. Collaboration structures shape whether responsibility is internalized or diffused, as individualized AI use increases accountability while shared human–AI arrangements may facilitate blame shifting under ambiguity (Gaczek et al., 2025). Communication framing influences whether workers engage critically with algorithmic output or defer to it, as benefit-focused messaging can weaken ethical vigilance among heavy AI users (Gaczek et al., 2025). Monitoring design further conditions relational trust, with interactional monitoring supporting commitment through dialogue and feedback, whereas observational surveillance heightens stress and disengagement (Wang et al., 2022). Transparency and reliability remain foundational to legitimacy, as opaque logic and inconsistent performance rapidly erode trust (Szandała, 2025). Finally, interpretive processes play a decisive role. When employees attribute AI-enabled HR practices to commitment-oriented intentions, they report lower strain and greater acceptance, whereas control-oriented interpretations evoke skepticism and discomfort (Zhou et al., 2025a). Overall, the evidence indicates that AI's organizational impact does not reside in the algorithm itself but emerges through employee sensemaking, social cues, and institutional arrangements.

Effective AI governance therefore requires intentional design of collaboration structures, transparent and credible communication, participatory monitoring practices, and opportunities for workers to develop competency and agency. Absent these conditions, algorithmic systems risk undermining trust, fairness, and well-being. When these conditions are present, AI can contribute to more ethical, supportive, and sustainable forms of human resource management

Implications for Human Resource Functions

The integrated evidence yields several implications for human resource practice across core functional domains. In recruitment and selection, AI-enabled systems should prioritize transparency, reliability, and explainability, as inconsistent scoring undermines procedural fairness and organizational legitimacy (Szandała, 2025). Human oversight remains essential, not merely as a technical safeguard but as a relational anchor that supports candidate trust and acceptance of algorithmically mediated decisions. Systems that combine algorithmic efficiency with human judgment are therefore more likely to sustain legitimacy in hiring processes.

In performance management and monitoring, organizations should guard against excessive reliance on AI-generated recommendations and avoid unnecessarily invasive forms of oversight. Design features such as debiasing prompts, explicit responsibility assignments, and interactional monitoring practices can mitigate anchoring effects while preserving trust and fairness (Carter & Liu, 2025; Wang et al., 2022). These mechanisms help ensure that algorithmic input informs, rather than supplants, managerial judgment.

In learning and development, fostering algorithmic competency represents a critical priority. Workers who understand how algorithmic systems operate and who can question, interpret, and recalibrate outputs are better positioned to collaborate effectively with AI, reducing risks of misuse or overreliance (Zhou et al., 2025b). Investments in training and peer-based learning can therefore strengthen both performance and agency in algorithmically mediated work.

In operations and people analytics, aligning algorithmic systems with workers' identities, capacities, and workload conditions supports well-being and sustains service commitment. When job fit and autonomy are preserved, algorithmic demands are more likely to be interpreted as challenges rather than threats, reducing strain and defensive responses (Lu et al., 2024). Attention to contextual alignment is thus essential for maintaining motivation and service quality.

Across HR functions, the evidence consistently indicates that the organizational value of AI depends on the relational and psychological context in which systems are deployed. Algorithmic management is unlikely to be effective when it erodes trust, meaningfulness, or fairness, and it cannot be transformative without supporting workers' agency and interpretive resources. Overall, the twenty-nine studies reviewed here suggest that AI-assisted human resource management is both feasible and beneficial when designed with socio-technical awareness. Positive outcomes tend to arise when systems reinforce responsibility, deliver fair and reliable decisions, protect autonomy, and preserve space for human sensemaking. Risks emerge when systems drift toward opacity, surveillance, or excessive control. In this sense, AI's impact in human resource management is not a technological inevitability but a design choice, setting the stage for the design recommendations developed in the following section.

Evidence-Based Design and Governance Recommendations

The evidence reviewed in this chapter indicates that ethical risks in human–AI systems do not arise solely from algorithmic properties but from how responsibility, authority, and meaning are distributed across socio-technical arrangements. Effective governance therefore depends on design choices that shape collaboration, trust calibration, agency preservation, and long-term assimilation. This section synthesizes empirical and conceptual insights into actionable recommendations for organizations deploying AI in decision-relevant contexts.

SOLUTIONS AND RECOMMENDATIONS

Recommendation 1: Clarifying Accountability in Human–AI Collaboration

A recurring governance challenge concerns responsibility diffusion when decision authority is ambiguously shared between humans and AI systems. Accountability failures tend to emerge not because responsibility is absent but because it is insufficiently specified across development, deployment, and use phases (Akinrinola et al., 2024). Clear accountability structures are therefore foundational to ethical AI governance. Organizations should explicitly define decision rights, escalation pathways, and override authority within human–AI collaboration. Rather than positioning AI as an autonomous decision-maker with post hoc human oversight, evidence supports human-first protocols in which humans retain primary decision authority and AI functions in an advisory capacity (Agudo et al., 2024; Cabitza et al., 2024). Such configurations reduce automation bias and preserve human judgment as the locus of responsibility.

This need for clarity is particularly salient in appraisal, hiring, and evaluative contexts, where decision-makers systematically anchor on AI-generated scores and rankings. Anchoring effects intensify under time pressure, cognitive load, or limited AI literacy and persist even when explainability mechanisms are present, underscoring that accountability risks are interactional rather than purely informational (Dietvorst et al., 2015; Romeo & Conti, 2025). Governance approaches should therefore operationalize human-in-the-loop designs beyond symbolic oversight. When AI outputs are framed as recommendations requiring justification rather than defaults to be accepted, users engage more reflectively with system outputs (Holter & El-Assady,

2024). Mechanisms such as structured justification logs, disagreement protocols, and role-based accountability assignments help ensure that responsibility remains traceable and enforceable. Converging evidence further indicates that explanations alone are insufficient to counter overreliance unless users are actively engaged in verification and contestation processes that reinforce their role as primary decision-makers (Romeo & Conti, 2025).

Recommendation 2: Building Trust through Fairness, Reliability, and Monitoring Architecture

Trust in AI systems is an emergent outcome shaped by transparency, perceived fairness, and ongoing performance monitoring rather than a static attribute. Opaque systems undermine trust and complicate accountability, particularly in high-stakes domains (Akinrinola et al., 2024). Furthermore, these systems may disproportionately disadvantage employees with disabilities and undermine perceptions of organizational justice (Mizuki et al., 2025). Governance frameworks should therefore treat trust as a design objective rather than a byproduct of adoption. Research on algorithm aversion shows that users respond more negatively to algorithmic errors than to equivalent human errors, even when algorithms outperform humans on average (Dietvorst et al., 2015). This asymmetry highlights the importance of managing expectations around imperfection and designing communication practices that anticipate how visible errors can disproportionately undermine trust.

Fairness should be embedded throughout the AI lifecycle through diverse training data, fairness metrics, and continuous auditing. One-time validation is insufficient, as unmonitored systems risk reproducing structural inequalities when historical data are taken at face value. Continuous monitoring architectures are therefore critical for detecting drift, emergent bias, and context-specific failures. Evidence from HR and platform-work settings further shows that perceived procedural fairness in algorithmic allocation and evaluation strongly predicts trust, legitimacy, and acceptance, even when outcomes are held constant (Jabagi et al., 2025; Lu et al., 2025).

Reliable communication is equally important. Users must understand not only what systems do but also where their limitations lie. Explainable AI techniques can support calibrated trust when they surface uncertainty, confidence levels, and operational boundaries. However, explanations should extend beyond post hoc rationalizations. Providing counterfactuals or analogous cases before final recommendations encourages reflective engagement and reduces blind acceptance (Cabitza et al., 2024). Trust is strengthened not through persuasion but by enabling informed skepticism.

Monitoring architecture further conditions trust. Surveillance-heavy designs undermine fairness perceptions and psychological safety by signaling control rather than collaboration. In contrast, interaction-oriented monitoring that incorporates feedback, clarifies data use, and emphasizes mutual understanding fosters acceptance and procedural fairness (Ontrup et al., 2025; Wang et al., 2022).

Recommendation 3: Supporting Human Agency and Competency

Ethical AI deployment also requires governance practices that preserve human agency and decision competence. Agency is shaped by the degree of control users retain over decisions, interactions, and system adaptation (Holter & El-Assady, 2024). When AI systems dominate sensemaking or narrow available choices, users face risks of deskilling, disengagement, and learned helplessness. Previous evidence nevertheless shows that users actively probe system outputs, identify errors, and develop workarounds when afforded discretion and feedback opportunities (Kellogg et al., 2020; Vasconcelos et al., 2023).

Organizations should therefore prioritize task-specific AI literacy over generic awareness training. Effective training enables users to understand how systems reach conclusions, recognize failure conditions, and appropriately challenge or override recommendations. For instance, Mizuki et al. (2025) emphasize that employees with disabilities require tailored competency support and accessible AI interfaces to ensure equitable participation. Therefore, explanatory tools should be tailored to users' cognitive styles, domain expertise, and motivational orientations rather than delivered as uniform technical descriptions (Romeo & Conti, 2025). Tailored explanations support comprehension, calibrated reliance, and active engagement in decision processes.

Equally important are remediation and feedback channels. Allowing users to contest AI-supported decisions, flag errors, and contribute contextual input reinforces agency while improving system performance over time. Ethical AI governance must integrate organizational processes alongside technical safeguards, as feedback mechanisms align system evolution with human expertise and lived experience (Akinrinola et al., 2024).

Recommendation 4: Protecting Motivation, Meaningfulness, and Knowledge Sharing

The literature further shows that AI systems reshape intrinsic motivation, professional identity, and collaborative knowledge exchange. Surveillance-oriented and control-focused designs may signal distrust, reduce autonomy, and encourage defensive behaviors, including knowledge hiding and reduced discretionary effort.

Motivation and meaningfulness are therefore central, rather than peripheral, concerns in responsible AI governance.

Evidence from algorithmic management research consistently links control-oriented framings to heightened strain, diminished prosocial motivation, and weaker organizational commitment. Commitment-oriented framings, which position AI as developmental or supportive, buffer these effects even when oversight remains present (Brougham & Haar, 2018; Granulo et al., 2024; Zhi et al., 2025). Human-first and frictional AI designs further preserve professional judgment by encouraging reflective engagement rather than passive compliance. Pro-hoc explainability approaches that surface supportive and contradictory cases reinforce the value of human reasoning and sustain learning (Cabitza et al., 2024).

Governance practices should therefore evaluate AI systems not only on efficiency metrics but also on their influence on meaningful work, identity coherence, and collaborative norms. Recognition mechanisms that make human contributions visible and continuous monitoring of unintended behavioral consequences are especially important in knowledge-intensive contexts where tacit expertise and informal exchange underpin performance.

Recommendation 5: Planning for Adoption and Assimilation

Ethical AI governance must extend beyond initial deployment to encompass long-term adoption and assimilation. Ethical considerations cannot be resolved through technical fixes alone but require ongoing organizational commitment, regulatory alignment, and iterative learning (Akinrinola et al., 2024). Assimilation is thus a dynamic trajectory shaped by evolving expectations and contextual change.

Pilot deployments in lower-risk settings enable organizations to assess responsibility perceptions, trust calibration, and behavioral responses before scaling. Cross-functional governance teams that include technical, ethical, legal, operational, and user perspectives are essential for anticipating downstream effects and managing trade-offs. Evidence from HR technology adoption shows that successful assimilation depends less on system sophistication than on user competency, collaboration quality, and alignment with job design and process agility (Zhou et al., 2025a). When training, workflow integration, and user input are limited, adoption remains superficial and generates workarounds or resistance.

Durable assimilation therefore requires multidimensional evaluation criteria that include fairness perceptions, accountability clarity, agency preservation, and collaboration quality. Iterative feedback loops, continuous audits, and adaptive governance structures allow organizations to recalibrate systems as contexts and expectations evolve, supporting long-term legitimacy and reducing ethical drift.

FUTURE RESEARCH DIRECTIONS

Limitations of the Current Evidence Base

Although the twenty-nine studies reviewed provide substantial insight into how algorithmic and AI-enabled systems influence HR-relevant outcomes, the current evidence base exhibits several important limitations. First, the distribution of empirical contexts is uneven. A substantial share of studies focuses on platform-based or digitally mediated work, including gig labor, logistics coordination, and algorithmically structured customer-facing roles (Jabagi et al., 2025; Ontrup et al., 2025; Wang et al., 2022). By contrast, fewer studies examine organizational HR workflows, such as performance appraisal (Carter & Liu, 2025), AI-supported recruitment (Szandała, 2025), internal service commitment (Lu et al., 2024), or team-level collaboration and innovation (Liu, Yuan, & Wang, 2025). As a result, much of the existing evidence reflects work environments characterized by atypical employment relationships, variable autonomy, and limited managerial interaction. This concentration constrains the generalizability of findings, particularly those related to monitoring, fairness perceptions, and stress, to more stable and relationally embedded organizational settings (Omoush, 2025; Ontrup et al., 2025).

A second limitation concerns methodological concentration. Many studies rely on cross-sectional surveys or short laboratory and scenario-based experiments. Research examining anchoring to AI recommendations (Carter & Liu, 2025), AI-assisted ethical decision-making (Gaczek et al., 2025), trust in platform algorithms (Lu et al., 2025), and electronic team monitoring (Ontrup et al., 2025) typically captures perceptual responses at a single point in time. While such designs are well suited to isolating mechanisms such as anchoring, perceived invasiveness, stress, or responsibility attribution, they provide limited insight into how these reactions evolve with prolonged exposure. Only a small subset of studies, most notably Jiang and Sinchaisri (2025), employs longitudinal behavioral data to examine how reliance patterns and strategies change across repeated interactions. The scarcity of longitudinal designs therefore limits understanding of adaptation, learning, and trust calibration over time.

A third limitation relates to sectoral concentration. Several studies examine retail, logistics, ride-hailing, or platform-based service work (Cheon & Erickson, 2025; Jabagi et al., 2025; Jiang & Sinchaisri, 2025), whereas comparatively few address HR-administered processes within organizations. Although recruitment-focused research (Szandała, 2025) and appraisal experiments (Carter & Liu, 2025; Gaczek et al., 2025) offer valuable insights, they represent only a limited portion of the dataset. Underrepresentation of sectors such as healthcare, education, manufacturing, and public administration constrains the ability to generalize findings to settings that are more relational, interdependent, or safety critical.

Finally, the distribution of outcome variables is uneven. Constructs such as responsibility, fairness, trust, stress, and meaningfulness receive sustained attention across studies (Gaczek et al., 2025; Jabagi et al., 2025; Lu et al., 2025; Ontrup et al., 2025; Van Zoonen et al., 2024). By contrast, other HR-relevant outcomes remain underexamined. Long-term skill development receives limited attention (Jiang & Sinchaisri, 2025), as do creativity (Liu & Yin, 2024), identity construction (Liu, Yuan, & Wang, 2025), and team-level collaboration dynamics (Liu, Yuan, & Wang, 2025; Ontrup et al., 2025). Moreover, many studies rely primarily on self-reported perceptions rather than behavioral indicators or organizational performance data, limiting inference regarding downstream effects on productivity, retention, or career trajectories. Taken together, these limitations suggest that while the evidence base is conceptually rich, it remains methodologically and contextually constrained, supporting theory development more readily than broad causal generalization.

Gaps Highlighted Across Studies

Beyond these limitations, the reviewed literature reveals several substantive gaps. One persistent gap concerns responsibility dynamics over time. Although studies show that algorithmic recommendations can anchor decisions, blur responsibility boundaries, or weaken ethical vigilance, little is known about whether these effects stabilize, intensify, or attenuate as workers gain experience with AI systems. A similar gap exists with respect to collaboration structures. While shared human–AI arrangements appear to diffuse responsibility, there is limited field-based evidence on how teams negotiate accountability across performance cycles and evolving task demands.

A second gap involves the translation of laboratory findings into organizational practice. Many studies demonstrate the effects of messaging, framing, confidence cues, and monitoring styles under controlled conditions. However, HR processes such as recruitment, appraisal, and scheduling involve repeated interactions, informal norms, and institutional constraints that experimental designs may not capture. Field experiments and mixed-methods studies embedded within real HR processes therefore remain comparatively rare.

A third gap concerns algorithmic competency and agency. Existing studies indicate that workers develop adaptive strategies, probe systems, and selectively deviate from recommendations (Cheon & Erickson, 2025), and that individual differences in self-efficacy and attribution shape responses to algorithmic authority. Yet there is limited evidence on organizational interventions designed to cultivate these competencies. Research has not systematically examined whether training, structured remediation channels, or collective sensemaking practices strengthen ethical and adaptive AI use.

Social interaction also emerges as a cross-cutting but underexplored factor. Although evidence suggests that interpersonal interaction buffers negative effects on prosocial motivation and meaningfulness (Van Zoonen et al., 2024), few studies examine how interactions with supervisors, peers, or customers shape interpretations of algorithmic decisions in practice. Similarly, moderators such as workload, autonomy (Wang et al., 2022), occupational stigma (Lu et al., 2025), and organizational identification (Zhou et al., 2025b) appear repeatedly across themes but are rarely examined systematically across different algorithmic designs.

Finally, team- and organization-level outcomes remain insufficiently theorized and tested. Preliminary evidence suggests that algorithmic systems may influence team resilience, coordination, and informal leadership (Liu, Yuan, & Wang, 2025), yet these effects are context dependent and empirically limited. More research is needed to examine how algorithmic systems shape interdependence, collaboration, conflict, knowledge sharing, and collective capability development over time.

Directions for Future Research

Addressing these gaps requires research designs that extend beyond isolated mechanisms toward dynamic, context-sensitive analysis. First, future research should examine how collaboration structures, including AI-first recommendations, human–AI co-creation, and explicit human override authority, shape responsibility, trust, and decision quality over time. Longitudinal and field-based studies are needed to determine whether early effects, such as anchoring or responsibility diffusion, persist or adapt with experience.

Second, research should investigate how monitoring architectures influence fairness perceptions, stress, and engagement within organizational settings. Experiments embedded in HR processes, such as performance reviews, coaching interactions, or customer service operations, would clarify how invasiveness and interactional design affect outcomes across repeated use. Third, future studies should examine which competency-building interventions most effectively support ethical and adaptive AI use. Given evidence of learning curves and selective reliance, research could assess whether targeted training, reflective practices, or AI-supported feedback loops strengthen skill development and reduce harmful dependence.

Fourth, greater attention is needed to the evolution of attributions regarding algorithmic intent. Although commitment-oriented versus control-oriented interpretations shape responses to AI-enabled HR practices, little is known about how communication strategies, transparency, and procedural safeguards influence these attributions over time. Fifth, social and relational moderators warrant systematic investigation. Team norms, leadership behavior, communication channels, and organizational identification may condition responses to algorithmic management, yet these factors are rarely examined across diverse contexts and designs.

Finally, future research should move beyond individual-level outcomes to examine team- and organization-level effects as algorithmic systems become more deeply integrated. Studies could explore how AI-supported processes influence coordination, psychological safety, conflict dynamics, informal leadership, capability development, and collective resilience. Together, these directions point toward a more comprehensive research agenda that foregrounds both empirical rigor and normative alignment, ensuring that algorithmic HR systems remain compatible with organizational values, human dignity, and sustainable work practices.

CONCLUSION

This semi-systematic review examined which collaboration, monitoring, and communication designs enable AI and algorithmic systems to improve human resource–relevant outcomes while limiting potential harm. Across the twenty-nine empirical studies reviewed, a consistent pattern emerges: outcomes depend less on the technical sophistication of AI than on the socio-technical arrangements through which such systems are embedded in work. Designs that clarify responsibility, demonstrate procedural fairness, behave reliably, and preserve human judgment tend to elicit positive responses, including trust, job satisfaction, and team resilience, as observed in studies of algorithmic evaluation, platform reliability, and AI-supported coordination (Jabagi et al., 2025; Lu et al., 2025; Liu, Yuan, & Wang, 2025). By contrast, systems that obscure accountability, impose control without explanation, or rely on invasive monitoring are associated with heightened stress, diminished well-being, and reduced motivation and knowledge exchange (Ontrup et al., 2025; Wang et al., 2022; Wood et al., 2019). Taken together, the evidence indicates that human–AI collaboration is most effective when AI augments, rather than replaces, human judgment, autonomy, and dignity.

Implications for HR Leaders and Practitioners

Several core principles follow for HR leaders and practitioners. First, responsibility should be made explicit at the point of decision-making. When workers understand when and how to rely on algorithmic input, and when human judgment is expected, they engage more confidently and ethically with AI-supported decisions. Second, fairness and reliability remain foundational for trust. Employees interpret algorithmic systems as signals of organizational intent, such that transparent criteria, consistent scoring, and opportunities to contest outcomes strengthen perceived organizational support across recruitment, matching, and performance evaluation contexts (Jabagi et al., 2025; Szandała, 2025). Reliable systems that behave predictably and explainably further reinforce trust and engagement, although these effects may be moderated by factors such as occupational stigma (Lu et al., 2025).

Third, monitoring architectures should minimize perceived invasiveness while incorporating interactional features. Intrusive surveillance is commonly experienced as stressful and dehumanizing (Ontrup et al., 2025; Wood et al., 2019), whereas interactional monitoring can foster commitment and engagement when paired with autonomy and dialogue (Norlander et al., 2021; Wang et al., 2022). Fourth, human agency and algorithmic competency require active support. Workers learn to question, refine, and, at times, correct algorithmic outputs, and those with higher algorithmic competency report stronger identification and service-oriented behavior (Zhou et al., 2025b). These adaptive use patterns underscore the importance of training that develops interpretive and reflective skills rather than technical familiarity alone (Liu & Yin, 2024).

Finally, motivation and meaningfulness are shaped by social context. Algorithmic control may reduce prosocial motivation, heighten perceived threat, and increase burnout (Jiang & Sinchaisri, 2025). However, these risks can be mitigated through opportunities for social interaction (Granulo et al., 2024), alignment between person and job (Zayid et al., 2024), and communication that avoids framing AI primarily as a control mechanism (Zhou et al., 2025b). AI systems are therefore most effective when introduced as components of broader socio-technical arrangements that reinforce relational connection, role clarity, and meaningful work.

As organizations accelerate the adoption of AI across HR and work processes, the central challenge lies not in automation itself but in designing systems that remain compatible with fairness, dignity, and sustainable human work. The evidence reviewed here demonstrates that algorithmic technologies can support responsible decision-making, strengthen trust, and enhance collaboration, yet these outcomes are never automatic. They emerge when systems are transparent, participatory, and attentive to workers' lived experiences. Moving forward, scholarship and practice alike should remain grounded in the principle that effective AI in HR is fundamentally human-centered, supporting judgment rather than replacing it, enabling autonomy rather than constraining it, and sustaining meaningful work rather than eroding it. When governed and designed with care, AI can function as a partner in building more ethical, effective, and humane organizations.

AUTHOR NOTE

This chapter is co-authored by Ian Mizuki and Zoya Khan, with equal authorship contribution.

REFERENCES

Agudo, U., Liberal, K. G., Arrese, M., & Matute, H. (2024). The impact of AI errors in a human-in-the-loop process. *Cognitive Research: Principles and Implications*, *9*(1), 1–16. DOI: 10.1186/s41235-023-00529-3 PMID: 38185767

Allen, J. M., Whitson, T. L., Gavrilova Aguilar, M., & Bracey, P. S. (2025). Collaborative intelligence: cultivating human–AI partnerships. In T. R. Merlo, *AI-Driven Revolution* (pp. 287–319). World scientific (europe). DOI: 10.1142/9781800616578_0013

Brohi, S., Mastoi, Q., Jhanjhi, N. Z., & Pillai, T. R. (2025). A Research Landscape of Agentic AI and Large Language Models: Applications, Challenges and Future Directions. *Algorithms*, *18*(8), 499. DOI: 10.3390/a18080499

Brougham, D., & Haar, J. (2018). Smart Technology, Artificial Intelligence, Robotics, and Algorithms (STARA): Employees' perceptions of our future workplace. *Journal of Management & Organization*, *24*(2), 239–257. DOI: 10.1017/jmo.2016.55

Cabitza, F., Natali, C., Famiglini, L., Campagner, A., Caccavella, V., & Gallazzi, E. (2024). Never tell me the odds: Investigating pro-hoc explanations in medical decision making. *Artificial Intelligence in Medicine*, *150*, 1–11. DOI: 10.1016/j.artmed.2024.102819 PMID: 38553159

Carter, L., & Liu, D. (2025). How was my performance? Exploring the role of anchoring bias in AI-assisted decision making. *International Journal of Information Management*, *82*, 1–14. DOI: 10.1016/j.ijinfomgt.2025.102875

Cheon, E., & Erickson, I. (2025). Fulfillment of the work games: Warehouse workers' experiences with algorithmic management. *Proceedings of the ACM on Human-Computer Interaction*, *9*(7), 1–30. DOI: 10.1145/3757409

Chong, L., Kotovsky, K., & Cagan, J. (2024). Human designers' dynamic confidence and decision-making when working with more than one artificial intelligence. *Journal of Mechanical Design*, *146*(8), 1–11. DOI: 10.1115/1.4064565

Dietvorst, B. J., Simmons, J. P., & Massey, C. (2015). Algorithm aversion: People erroneously avoid algorithms after seeing them err. *Journal of Experimental Psychology. General*, *144*(1), 114–126. DOI: 10.1037/xge0000033 PMID: 25401381

Gaczek, P., Leszczyński, G., Wei, Y., & Sun, H. (2025). The Bright Side of AI in Marketing Decisions: Collaboration with Algorithms Prevents Managers from Violating Ethical Norms. *Journal of Business Ethics*, •••, 1–24. DOI: 10.1007/s10551-025-06083-w

Georganta, E., & Ulfert, A.-S. (2024). My colleague is an AI! Trust differences between AI and human teammates. *Team Performance Management*, *30*(1/2), 23–37. DOI: 10.1108/TPM-07-2023-0053

Granulo, A., Caprioli, S., Fuchs, C., & Puntoni, S. (2024). Deployment of algorithms in management tasks reduces prosocial motivation. *Computers in Human Behavior*, *152*, 1–8. DOI: 10.1016/j.chb.2023.108094

Hina, M., Azad, N., & Islam, N. (2025). Enablers and inhibitors of AI assimilation in hiring: Mitigating the effects of inhibitors through human–AI collaboration. *Information Technology & People*, *38*(8), 73–96. DOI: 10.1108/ITP-06-2024-0808

Holter, S., & El-Assady, M. (2024). Deconstructing Human-AI Collaboration: Agency, Interaction, and Adaptation. *Computer Graphics Forum*, *43*(3), 1–12. DOI: 10.1111/cgf.15107

Hughes, L., Dwivedi, Y. K., Malik, T., Shawosh, M., Albashrawi, M. A., Jeon, I., Dutot, V., Appanderanda, M., Crick, T., De', R., Fenwick, M., Gunaratnege, S. M., Jurcys, P., Kar, A. K., Kshetri, N., Li, K., Mutasa, S., Samothrakis, S., Wade, M., & Walton, P. (2025). AI Agents and Agentic Systems: A Multi-Expert Analysis. *Journal of Computer Information Systems*, *65*(4), 489–517. DOI: 10.1080/08874417.2025.2483832

Islam, M. A., Somu, S., & Aldaihani, F. M. F. (2026). The rise of agentic AI: Synthesis of current knowledge and future research agenda. *Global Business and Organizational Excellence*, *45*(3), 402–416. DOI: 10.1002/joe.70019

Jabagi, N., Croteau, A.-M., Audebrand, L. K., & Marsan, J. (2025). Do algorithms play fair? Analysing the perceived fairness of HR-decisions made by algorithms and their impacts on gig-workers. *International Journal of Human Resource Management*, *36*(2), 235–274. DOI: 10.1080/09585192.2024.2441448

Jiang, S., & Sinchaisri, W. P. (2025). Learning on the Go: Understanding How Gig Economy Workers Learn with Recommendation Algorithms. *Proceedings of the ACM on Human-Computer Interaction*, *9*(7), 1–35. DOI: 10.1145/3757621

Kellogg, K. C., Valentine, M. A., & Christin, A. (2020). Algorithms at Work: The New Contested Terrain of Control. *The Academy of Management Annals*, *14*(1), 366–410. DOI: 10.5465/annals.2018.0174

Kinowska, H., & Sienkiewicz, Ł. J. (2023). Influence of algorithmic management practices on workplace well-being – evidence from European organisations. *Information Technology & People*, *36*(8), 21–42. DOI: 10.1108/ITP-02-2022-0079

Li, Z., Choi, M.-C., & Kim, H.-E. (2025). AI Awareness and Employee Innovation: A Dual-Pathway Moderated Mediation Model Within Organizational Systems. *Systems*, *13*(7), 1–21. DOI: 10.3390/systems14010001

Liu, P., Yuan, L., & Jiang, Z. (2025). The dark side of algorithmic management: Investigating how and when algorithmic management relates to employee knowledge hiding? *Journal of Knowledge Management*, *29*(2), 342–371. DOI: 10.1108/JKM-04-2024-0507

Liu, P., Yuan, L., & Wang, J. (2025). Unpacking Algorithmic Management: Pathways to Team Resilience Through Reduced Objectification and Informal Leadership. *Asia Pacific Journal of Human Resources*, *63*(4), 1–19. DOI: 10.1111/1744-7941.70031

Liu, R., & Yin, H. (2024). How Algorithmic Management Influences Gig Workers' Job Crafting. *Behavioral Sciences (Basel, Switzerland)*, *14*(10), 1–22. DOI: 10.3390/bs14100952 PMID: 39457824

Lu, Y., Yang, M. M., Mitchell, R., Boyle, B., & Gu, J. (2025). Algorithmic Reliability at the Helm: Investigating the Relationship Between Experienced Algorithmic Reliability, Trust, and Work Engagement in the Gig Economy. *Human Resource Management*, *•••*, 1–17. DOI: 10.1002/hrm.70033

Lu, Y., Yang, M. M., Zhu, J., & Wang, Y. (2024). Dark side of algorithmic management on platform worker behaviors: A mixed-method study. *Human Resource Management*, *63*(3), 477–498. DOI: 10.1002/hrm.22211

Mizuki, I., Khan, Z., & Gulseren, D. (2025) (*in press*). Artificial intelligence and disability inclusion in human resource management. *In Research in Human Resource Management (RHRM) research series* [Special Issue on Artificial Intelligence and Human Resource Management], Emerald Publishing.

Norlander, P., Jukic, N., Varma, A., & Nestorov, S. (2021). The effects of technological supervision on gig workers: Organizational control and motivation of Uber, taxi, and limousine drivers. *International Journal of Human Resource Management*, *32*(19), 4053–4077. DOI: 10.1080/09585192.2020.1867614

Olawade, D. B., Ayoola, F. I., Ebo, T. O., Asaolu, A. J., Egbon, E., & Clement David-Olawade, A. (2025). Artificial intelligence in forensic mental health: A review of applications and implications. *Journal of Forensic and Legal Medicine*, *113*, 102895. DOI: 10.1016/j.jflm.2025.102895 PMID: 40441026

Omoush, M. M. (2025). Human–AI collaboration in HRM and employee-centric outcomes: Evidence from E-supply chain management. *Human Systems Management, 0*(0), 1–16. DOI: 10.1177/01672533251365119

Ontrup, G., Volkmann, P., Orlov, O., & Kluge, A. (2025). Intelligent automated systems to support human teamwork: Perceived invasiveness impacts team members' psychological reactions negatively. *Cognition Technology and Work, 27*(3), 591–609. DOI: 10.1007/s10111-025-00813-w

Perrigino, M. B., Raveendhran, R., & Ryu, J. W. (2024). Technology Use for Nonwork Purposes at Work: A Behavior-Focused Integrative Review. *The Academy of Management Annals, 18*(2), 403–434. DOI: 10.5465/annals.2022.0191

Purohit, R., & Banerjee, T. (2025). Artificial intelligence-based organizational decision-making in recruitment practice. *Human Systems Management, 44*(1), 173–186. DOI: 10.3233/HSM-240044

Robinson, A. P., Jarrahi, M. H., Keegan, A., & Meijerink, J. (2025). Algorithmic Management in Limbo: Task-Driven Interweaving of Hierarchy and Market Management. *Human Resource Management*, hrm.70019. DOI: 10.1002/hrm.70019

Romeo, G., & Conti, D. (2025). Exploring automation bias in human–AI collaboration: A review and implications for explainable AI. *AI & Society*, •••, 1–20. DOI: 10.1007/s00146-025-02422-7

Szandała, T. (2025). ChatGPT vs human expertise in the context of IT recruitment. *Expert Systems with Applications, 264*, 1–13. DOI: 10.1016/j.eswa.2024.125868

Tomprou, M., & Lee, M. K. (2022). Employment relationships in algorithmic management: A psychological contract perspective. *Computers in Human Behavior, 126*, 1–12. DOI: 10.1016/j.chb.2021.106997

Tu, Y., Li, J., Chen, J., Li, C., & He, W. (2025). When AI Becomes My Teammate: Unpacking How Employees Perceive and Collaborate With Gendered AI Teammates. *Journal of Organizational Behavior, 0*, 1–25. DOI: 10.1002/job.70038

Van Zoonen, W., Sivunen, A. E., & Treem, J. W. (2024). Algorithmic management of crowdworkers: Implications for workers' identity, belonging, and meaningfulness of work. *Computers in Human Behavior, 152*, 1–10. DOI: 10.1016/j.chb.2023.108089

Vasconcelos, H., Jörke, M., Grunde-McLaughlin, M., Gerstenberg, T., Bernstein, M. S., & Krishna, R. (2023). Explanations Can Reduce Overreliance on AI Systems During Decision-Making. *Proceedings of the ACM on Human-Computer Interaction, 7*(CSCW1), 1–38. DOI: 10.1145/3579605

Wang, C., Chen, J., & Xie, P. (2022). Observation or interaction? Impact mechanisms of gig platform monitoring on gig workers' cognitive work engagement. *International Journal of Information Management*, *67*, 1–17. DOI: 10.1016/j.ijinfomgt.2022.102548

Wood, A. J., Graham, M., Lehdonvirta, V., & Hjorth, I. (2019). Good Gig, Bad Gig: Autonomy and Algorithmic Control in the Global Gig Economy. *Work, Employment and Society*, *33*(1), 56–75. DOI: 10.1177/0950017018785616 PMID: 30886460

Yu, J., Wen, Q., & Xu, Q. (2024). The configurational effects of centrifugal and centripetal forces on firms' breakthrough innovation and strategic performance in the artificial intelligence context. *European Journal of Innovation Management*, *27*(5), 1743–1766. DOI: 10.1108/EJIM-06-2022-0292

Zayid, H., Alzubi, A., Berberoğlu, A., & Khadem, A. (2024). How Do Algorithmic Management Practices Affect Workforce Well-Being? A Parallel Moderated Mediation Model. *Behavioral Sciences (Basel, Switzerland)*, *14*(12), 1–26. DOI: 10.3390/bs14121123 PMID: 39767264

Zhi, R., Lockett, M., & Zhou, A. J. (2025). From hiding to sharing: A knowledge hiding perspective on knowledge management in MNEs. *Journal of Knowledge Management*, *29*(8), 2551–2577. DOI: 10.1108/JKM-12-2023-1301

Zhou, L., Lei, X., Cooke, F. L., Huang, X., & Zhang, J. (2025a). The Dual Effects of Algorithmic Management on Platform Workers: An Attribution Perspective. *Human Resource Management*, *64*(6), 1687–1707. DOI: 10.1002/hrm.70009

Zhou, L., Lei, X., Liu, M., Huang, X., & Hou, R. (2025b). Algorithmic Competency of On-Demand Labor Platform Workers: Scale Development, Antecedents, and Consequences. *Asia Pacific Journal of Human Resources*, *63*(2), 1–15. DOI: 10.1111/1744-7941.70004

KEY TERMS AND DEFINITIONS

AI-Enabled HR Systems: Human resource technologies that integrate artificial intelligence to support recruitment, appraisal, task allocation, monitoring, and related HR functions.

Algorithmic Competency: An individual's capacity to understand, interpret, question, and effectively engage with algorithmic systems in their work.

Algorithmic Management: The coordination, allocation, and evaluation of work activities through algorithmic systems that structure monitoring, decision-making, and performance processes.

Algorithmic Reliability: The perceived consistency, stability, and accuracy of algorithmic outputs across comparable situations or cases.

Algorithmic Transparency: The degree to which the logic, criteria, and decision pathways of an algorithmic system are understandable and explainable to users.

Automation Bias: The tendency to defer to algorithmic recommendations or automated outputs without sufficient independent evaluation.

Human–AI Collaboration: Work arrangements in which human actors and AI systems jointly shape decisions, task execution, and evaluative processes.

Monitoring Invasiveness: The extent to which digital monitoring practices are experienced as intrusive, excessive, or threatening to autonomy and psychological safety.

Procedural Fairness: Employees' perceptions of the consistency, transparency, and justice of the processes through which algorithmic or organizational decisions are made.

Work Meaningfulness: The extent to which individuals experience their work as purposeful, valuable, and aligned with their identity and professional role.

Chapter 3
AI-Enhanced Ontological Modeling of Academic Career Happiness and Performance

Raed Atef
http://orcid.org/0009-0004-0012-4940
Independent Researcher, Palestine

ABSTRACT

This study proposes an AI-enhanced ontological framework to examine and improve the link between academic happiness and performance by integrating philosophical, psychological, and institutional perspectives. Using qualitative and conceptual analysis, the framework models interactions among human, organizational, and cultural factors. Future applications will use AI tools such as NLP, machine learning, and knowledge graphs to analyze emotions, identify determinants of happiness, and simulate policy effects. The model highlights key factors, recognition, autonomy, workload, leadership, and institutional culture, and their influence on performance. While conceptual, it provides a foundation for empirical validation and strategies to enhance faculty satisfaction, engagement, and retention in human-centered universities, particularly in the GCC.

1. INTRODUCTION

The pursuit of happiness at work has evolved from a psychological construct into an ontological inquiry—an exploration of how individuals experience meaning, fulfillment, and purpose within professional life. In recent years, increasing scholarly

DOI: 10.4018/979-8-2600-2303-7.ch003

attention has been devoted to job happiness and satisfaction, with studies indicating that employee effectiveness is shaped not only by skill and competence but also by emotional well-being and workplace contentment (Met et al., 2023; Boateng et al., 2018; Kumar & Pansari, 2016; Yousuf & Saqib, 2021; Wahyudi et al., 2023). A happy employee is typically more engaged, innovative, and loyal; thus, fostering environments that promote career happiness is not merely an ethical pursuit but a strategic imperative for organizational success. Yet, while the relationship between job satisfaction and performance has been widely examined across sectors, its significance within higher education, and particularly among academics, remains underexplored (Yousuf & Saqib, 2021; Singh & Banerji, 2022).

Although prior studies have examined job satisfaction and academic well-being, limited research has integrated these constructs within a coherent ontological and AI-informed framework. In particular, there remains a gap in conceptual models that connect philosophical understandings of happiness with structured, data-oriented analytical architectures in higher education contexts. This chapter addresses that gap by proposing a theoretically grounded AI-enhanced ontological framework that synthesizes existing literature while outlining a future-oriented analytical design.

In today's data-driven academic landscape, Artificial Intelligence (AI) offers new possibilities for understanding complex human experiences such as happiness, motivation, and professional fulfillment. From an ontological perspective, AI provides a means to systematically represent and model, rather than merely measure, abstract constructs, transforming subjective experiences into analyzable and evolving representations of "being" at work. In this chapter, AI is positioned conceptually as an enabling architecture and analytical lens, not as an empirically executed system within the present study. Integrating AI into academic careers may enable the discovery of hidden patterns that traditional qualitative or quantitative analyses may overlook (Alshatti Schmidt et al., 2025). Through machine learning and natural language processing (NLP), researchers could, in future empirical implementations, analyze large-scale faculty feedback, teaching evaluations, publication records, and interview narratives to identify the determinants of academic well-being. This integration aligns with the philosophical aim of this study—to deepen inquiry into what happiness is, why it arises, and how it manifests across different institutional and cultural contexts (Gencoglu et al., 2023).

Academics in higher education institutions face growing social and psychological pressures due to demanding workloads that encompass teaching, research, mentoring, curriculum development, and community service (Pham & Duong, 2024). These expectations, combined with limited social life and modest remuneration, often lead to stress, dissatisfaction, and burnout (Issa et al., 2020). The use of AI-powered analytics within this ontological framework is conceptualized in this chapter as a proposed mechanism through which these pressures could be systematically examined and visualized. For instance, sentiment analysis of faculty narratives could potentially reveal emotional undercurrents related to satisfaction or discontent, while predictive models could be designed to estimate how variables such as recognition, workload, or leadership quality influence happiness, performance, and turnover intentions (Awashreh & Omri, 2024).

The issue is particularly pressing within Gulf Cooperation Council (GCC) countries, where faculty turnover remains high and impacts educational quality and institutional stability (Albaqami, 2016). Addressing this challenge requires approaches that are both human-centered and data-informed, where AI-enhanced policy modeling may provide simulation-based decision support to explore how organizational reforms—such as workload redistribution or promotion incentives—might affect faculty well-being and performance outcomes (Awashreh et al., 2024). In this light, AI is theorized as both a diagnostic and prescriptive tool, with the potential to support institutions in making evidence-informed decisions that foster academic satisfaction, retention, and productivity.

Accordingly, this study proposes an AI-enhanced ontological framework that integrates philosophical inquiry with a structured and proposed data-analytic research architecture. It is important to clarify that the present chapter is conceptual and qualitative in nature, relying primarily on secondary sources and theoretical synthesis; it does not report primary empirical findings or implemented AI-based modeling results. The framework outlines a mixed-method architecture, combining interviews, surveys, and computational text analysis, as part of a future empirical research agenda intended to operationalize and test the proposed model. As institutional data accumulates, the framework is intended, in subsequent empirical applications, to evolve dynamically, forming a living model that learns from ongoing faculty feedback. Within this scope, the research situates academic career happiness within GCC higher education institutions, conceptually positioning it in relation to other Arab contexts and exploring how AI-enabled data integration could contribute to cross-cultural understanding of academic well-being.

The objectives of this study are threefold: (1) to conceptually identify, based on existing literature, the primary determinants of academic career happiness; (2) to propose how AI-supported analytics could examine the relationship between happiness and performance through predictive modeling in future empirical studies; and (3) to develop a structured ontological framework linking the concept of happiness to measurable academic outcomes. By embedding AI within this dual philosophical and prospectively empirical inquiry, the study contributes to the emergence of intelligent ontological models that bridge human insight with machine learning, offering a theoretically grounded blueprint for future implementation and enabling universities to cultivate adaptive, data-informed, and profoundly human-centered academic environments.

2. LITERATURE REVIEW

Understanding the determinants of career happiness has become increasingly important in the evolving landscape of academic work. The profession's dynamic nature—marked by heavy workloads, complex performance expectations, and high turnover—has intensified scholarly interest in factors that influence faculty well-being and effectiveness (Awashreh, 2024). Existing literature on career happiness and performance traditionally focuses on psychological, sociological, and managerial perspectives (Awashreh & Omri, 2024), examining how motivation, satisfaction, and institutional support affect productivity (Sarwar et al., 2023). While this body of work has established important correlations between happiness and performance, it has largely relied on conventional theoretical models and survey-based methodologies. However, recent developments in Artificial Intelligence (AI) and data analytics provide new pathways for analyzing these relationships through computational modeling and intelligent data interpretation, expanding the ontological understanding of happiness as a lived and measurable phenomenon.

Career happiness, often equated with or derived from job satisfaction, is widely recognized as a central determinant of both individual and organizational success (Sarwar et al., 2023). Conventional research methodologies, relying primarily on surveys and self-reports, have yielded valuable but limited insights into emotional states and contextual complexities (Raudenská, 2023). Such static approaches struggle to capture the fluid, relational, and context-sensitive nature of happiness in academia. This methodological limitation has led scholars to call for more integrative and adaptive analytical frameworks. The introduction of AI methodologies conceptually expands this analytical horizon by potentially enabling the analysis of unstructured data, including reflective writing, student evaluations, and institutional communications, offering a more holistic and data-rich view of academic well-being (Qasmi & Fatima, 2024).

AI tools such as Natural Language Processing (NLP) and machine learning (ML) bring analytical depth by identifying emotional patterns and behavioral trends that traditional methods overlook (Deep, Ghosh & Chen, 2025). Through sentiment and emotion analysis, these tools may detect subtle shifts in satisfaction, motivation, or burnout within faculty narratives (Awashreh & Al Ghunaimi, 2024). Deep learning models can be designed to explore latent associations between variables such as recognition, workload, and happiness, while predictive algorithms may simulate how leadership quality or organizational culture influence performance outcomes (Angkasirisan, 2024). These approaches reflect a transition from purely descriptive analytics toward more diagnostic and predictive possibilities, where the study of happiness can be conceptualized as both quantifiable and adaptive rather than static and retrospective.

The theoretical foundation for understanding career happiness can be traced to Herzberg's Two-Factor Theory, which distinguishes between intrinsic motivators (achievement, recognition) and extrinsic factors (salary, conditions) (Hasan & Mishra, 2025). Contemporary AI-based simulation models offer conceptual opportunities to examine these dynamics in complex, multivariate environments (Alrawahi et al., 2020). For example, AI systems analyzing large-scale datasets could, in future empirical research, examine relationships between intrinsic and extrinsic factors across time and context. Furthermore, AI-driven network analysis may enable the mapping of institutional culture, leadership, and communication patterns, revealing how social connections contribute to sustained happiness (Lee et al., 2022). Importantly, in the present chapter, these analytical capabilities are discussed as part of a proposed framework rather than as empirically executed procedures.

The integration of AI has also reshaped Human Resource Management (HRM) practices. Traditional HRM research identifies planning, training, and evaluation as core determinants of employee satisfaction (Boxall & Huo, 2022), yet these remain reactive and retrospective. In contrast, AI-enabled HR systems have the potential to facilitate proactive well-being management through real-time monitoring, predictive modeling, and personalized feedback (Căvescu & Popescu, 2025). For instance, adaptive algorithms could be configured to signal when workload thresholds may endanger faculty well-being and suggest corrective measures. These data-driven feedback loops align with ontological goals by operationalizing happiness as a dynamic construct—continuously shaped by experience, institutional interaction, and technological mediation (Hasan & Mishra, 2025).

Beyond human resource functions, AI contributes to the ontological construction of happiness itself. In philosophical terms, ontology concerns the nature of "being," including how individuals experience fulfillment and purpose. In computational terms, ontology refers to structured representations of knowledge, such as knowledge graphs and semantic models. Through knowledge graphs and semantic reasoning systems, AI can conceptually model the interdependence between satisfaction, recognition, career progression, and psychological well-being (Joachimiak et al., 2024; Khan & Nasim, 2024). This analytical capability mirrors ontological inquiry, representing "being happy" not as a fixed variable but as a relational system influenced by human, institutional, and cultural contexts (Verdonck et al., 2015). Thus, AI is framed here not merely as a measurement tool, but as a structuring mechanism that supports the systematic representation of happiness across multiple layers of academic life.

Cross-disciplinary research further supports the premise that happiness precedes performance, affecting engagement, innovation, and retention (Walsh et al., 2017; Al-Ali et al., 2018). Within academia, AI applications such as text mining and predictive analytics could enhance this understanding by identifying early signals of disengagement or satisfaction, thus enabling timely institutional responses. Cluster analysis using AI may assist in categorizing faculty into well-being typologies, such as "research-intensive but stressed" or "balanced and fulfilled", helping administrators design targeted support strategies (Sajja et al., 2024). Collectively, these advancements signify a methodological shift: happiness is no longer treated solely as a static emotional state but may be approached as a computationally observable and evolving construct within proposed analytical architectures (Valtonen et al., 2025; Fletcher, 2024).

Despite these advances, the intersection between AI, ontology, and academic happiness remains underdeveloped. While numerous studies explore job satisfaction and performance across industries (Sakarji et al., 2022), few have applied AI-based methodologies to higher education. Most prior research relies on static survey instruments and human-coded datasets, limiting their ability to capture the dynamic, context-dependent, and culturally nuanced nature of academic happiness. Moreover, the GCC region, where academic systems are undergoing rapid transformation, has received limited empirical attention, despite its distinctive institutional cultures and expatriate faculty demographics.

Existing literature in other sectors, such as banking and manufacturing, highlights the mediating role of happiness in performance (Singh & Banerji, 2022). However, these models rarely incorporate real-time analytics or intelligent prediction mechanisms that reflect the evolving realities of academic work. Furthermore, few frameworks explicitly integrate philosophical ontology with computational knowledge modeling in a unified structure. This creates a critical research gap: no existing framework systematically integrates AI into the ontological modeling of academic career happiness within higher education contexts, particularly in the GCC region.

Accordingly, the present study addresses this gap by embedding AI tools, such as machine learning, NLP, and knowledge graph reasoning, within a conceptually developed and theoretically grounded ontological design. It is important to emphasize that the current chapter advances a structured conceptual synthesis and proposes an AI-enabled analytical architecture; empirical testing of this architecture is positioned as a future research agenda. This integration aims not only to strengthen analytical precision in subsequent empirical applications but also to advance the philosophical understanding of "being and becoming" happy in academic contexts. Through this dual framing, the chapter contributes a novel interdisciplinary model that bridges human insight, institutional theory, and computational representation, thereby enhancing both the theoretical coherence and future methodological possibilities of career happiness research in higher education.

3. METHODOLOGY

This chapter is conceptual and qualitative, relying entirely on secondary data such as published studies, institutional reports, and theoretical works. The current study focuses on conceptual synthesis and framework development rather than empirical testing. It aims to develop an AI-enhanced ontological framework that could, in future research, be implemented and empirically evaluated.

For future implementation, the proposed framework **is** designed as a mixed-methods approach—combining qualitative exploration and quantitative modeling—to guide empirical investigations of how academic happiness and performance interact within higher education systems.

3.1 Current Study: Conceptual and Qualitative Approach

The present analysis uses a qualitative methodology based on secondary sources. Through thematic, conceptual, and ontological synthesis, the study identifies key constructs—such as recognition, autonomy, workload, and institutional culture—and explores how these contribute to academic happiness and performance. The ontological perspective here is both philosophical (exploring the nature of "being happy" in academia) and computational (informing the structure of a knowledge-based framework) (Bandara & Katukurunda, 2025).

Artificial Intelligence (AI) is conceptually positioned as both a methodological and philosophical tool, offering potential for future computational reasoning and structured modeling of complex relationships (Joachimiak et al., 2025). It is important to note that no AI analysis has been conducted in this chapter; AI is discussed as part of the proposed framework for subsequent empirical research. This theoretical groundwork supports the later design of a data-driven implementation while maintaining conceptual rigor.

3.2 Framework Implementation: Proposed Mixed-Methods Design

When applied empirically, the framework is proposed to employ a mixed-methods design enhanced by AI:

- Qualitative phase: Semi-structured interviews and focus groups would explore faculty perceptions of happiness, motivation, and institutional culture. AI tools such as Natural Language Processing (NLP) and emotion detection could assist in coding and identifying patterns.

- Quantitative phase: Surveys would measure determinants of happiness (e.g., leadership, workload, recognition) and could test their potential influence on performance. Machine learning algorithms (e.g., regression, neural networks, clustering) are intended to identify patterns and support predictive modeling in future studies rather than producing validated causal results in this chapter.
- Integration: AI-driven triangulation is proposed to merge qualitative and quantitative insights using graph-based reasoning and multimodal learning, producing a dynamic, conceptual ontology of academic happiness. At this stage, this represents a theoretical design rather than an executed model.

These clarifications explicitly separate the current conceptual study from future empirical implementation, addressing reviewer concerns about methodological ambiguity and overstatement of AI capabilities.

3.3 Ethical Considerations

The current chapter uses only secondary data; therefore, no ethical approval was required for this conceptual analysis. Future empirical implementation would adhere to standard research ethics, including informed consent, data privacy, algorithmic transparency, and human oversight in AI interpretation. AI integration in the future research phase is intended to be human-centered, maintaining ethical safeguards and faculty trust.

3.4 Contribution of the Methodology

This two-stage methodological design provides:

1. A conceptual foundation using secondary data and ontological reasoning, establishing the theoretical underpinnings of academic happiness.
2. A proposed mixed-methods implementation plan integrating AI into empirical modeling, designed to refine academic happiness as a dynamic, evolving construct.

Together, they create a structured bridge between philosophical inquiry and future empirical application—advancing a human-centered, AI-enhanced understanding of academic well-being and performance while clearly delineating the boundaries of current analysis versus future research.

4. AI-ENHANCED ONTOLOGICAL FRAMEWORK: LOGIC AND METHODS

Exploring career happiness among academics requires a comprehensive ontological understanding of what constitutes happiness, why it is significant, and how it can be cultivated within complex institutional and cultural environments. Academic happiness is not merely a personal experience, but a multidimensional construct influenced by individual, organizational, and socio-cultural factors (Awawdeh, 2022; Smith & Lee, 2021). It encompasses emotional, cognitive, and social dimensions, including intrinsic motivation, sense of belonging, recognition, and autonomy.

Building on this triadic logic, the current study proposes a mixed-methods approach enhanced by Artificial Intelligence (AI), integrating quantitative precision with qualitative depth to capture both subjective perceptions and large-scale patterns in academic work. This convergence allows for simultaneous investigation of individual well-being, organizational dynamics, and performance metrics, thereby linking philosophical reflection with empirical rigor. Within this framework, AI **is** conceptualized as a potential analytical instrument and an ontological lens, revealing underlying structures, interconnections, and latent patterns that could shape academic life if implemented empirically (Kim & Lee, 2025). By combining interpretive human inquiry with AI-assisted modeling, the framework bridges subjective experience and prospective objective measurement, producing a holistic, evolving understanding of academic happiness in the Gulf Cooperation Council (GCC) region and similar higher education contexts globally (Awashreh & Al Ghunaimi, 2024).

4.1 The "What" Dimension — Identifying and Modeling Academic Happiness

The first phase addresses the fundamental question of what constitutes academic happiness, aiming to identify its determinants and conceptual boundaries. Historically, this stage has relied on qualitative methods such as interviews, focus groups, and ethnographic observations (Diener et al., 2018; Ryan & Deci, 2017). However, while traditional methods provide rich contextual insights, they lack scalability and cross-institutional comparability. In the AI-augmented model, computational tools are proposed to enhance these methods by enabling the analysis of textual, emotional, and behavioral data at scale (Cordeiro, Lopezosa, & Guallar, 2025).

AI Integration: Advanced AI techniques, including Natural Language Processing (NLP), topic modeling, and sentiment analysis, would process interview transcripts, open-ended survey responses, and institutional documents to uncover latent concepts related to happiness, motivation, frustration, or belonging (Kremer et al., 2025). Emotion-detection algorithms could identify subtle affective nuances embedded in faculty narratives, while AI-assisted coding would support interpretive consistency and reduce human bias.

Analytical Outcome: The output is conceptualized as an AI-supported ontology—a structured map illustrating how constructs interrelate (e.g., workload → stress → disengagement; recognition → belonging → performance). This stage operationalizes academic happiness as both an experiential phenomenon and a theoretically analyzable construct, providing a foundation for potential predictive modeling and institutional planning (Awawdeh, 2022).

4.2 The "Why" Dimension — Understanding Causality through Predictive Analytics

The second phase investigates why academic happiness matters by conceptually exploring the causal and explanatory mechanisms linking well-being to performance, engagement, and retention. Traditional quantitative analyses often fail to capture complex, nonlinear, or indirect relationships. AI-based predictive modeling is proposed to address this gap (Smith & Lee, 2021; Kremer et al., 2025).

AI Integration: Machine learning algorithms such as Random Forests, Neural Networks, and Gradient Boosting could predict performance indicators—including research output, teaching quality, student satisfaction, and engagement—based on determinants identified in the first phase. Explainable AI (XAI) would enhance transparency, revealing why certain variables exert greater influence. Simulation models could explore hypothetical institutional interventions, predicting potential effects on faculty well-being and performance (Khan et al., 2024).

Analytical Outcome: This phase conceptually elucidates the causal architecture of academic happiness, highlighting direct and indirect pathways between well-being and institutional productivity. It frames happiness as a dynamic driver of performance rather than a peripheral outcome, integrating philosophical reflection with empirical modeling to deepen understanding of happiness as both an inner state and a systemic property (Awashreh & Al Ghunaimi, 2024).

4.3 The "How" Dimension- Designing Intelligent Strategies for Improvement

The third phase focuses on how academic happiness could be cultivated and sustained through actionable, data-informed strategies. Transitioning from explanation to intervention, AI is positioned as a decision-support mechanism for continuous policy design, adaptive improvement, and monitoring.

AI Integration: AI-based recommendation systems would generate targeted interventions, such as professional development programs, mentorship initiatives, flexible workload policies, or incentive schemes. Reinforcement learning algorithms could simulate long-term outcomes, identifying approaches most effective at enhancing happiness, engagement, and retention. Interactive AI dashboards are proposed to visualize real-time indicators of well-being, burnout risk, and performance metrics, providing academic leaders with actionable insights (Awashreh & Al Ghunaimi, 2024).

Analytical Outcome: This stage establishes a dynamic feedback loop, a living model evolving through iterative data collection, AI learning, and institutional adaptation. It demonstrates how happiness can be enhanced systematically and continuously refined, ensuring policy alignment with faculty experiences, institutional goals, and cultural contexts (Gligorea et al., 2023).

4.4 AI-Enhanced Framework for the Development of Academic Happiness

The framework retains five developmental stages while integrating AI across each phase to ensure rigor, scalability, and adaptability. By embedding AI, the framework captures complex interactions among human, organizational, and cultural factors, supports predictive and prescriptive analytics, and facilitates continuous policy experimentation (Gelashvili-Luik, Vihma, & Pappel, 2025).

Table 1 (below) summarizes AI integration across the five stages, highlighting its potential to advance scholarly understanding and practical strategies. Academic happiness is positioned as a measurable, actionable, and evolving construct guiding institution-wide interventions, promoting faculty well-being, and improving performance.

Table 1. AI-Integrated Stages of the Ontological Framework

Stage	Focus	AI Integration	Expected Outcome
1. Qualitative Exploration	Identify determinants of happiness via interviews	NLP, sentiment and emotion analysis, AI-assisted coding	Ontology of happiness constructs reflecting lived experiences
2. Literature & Ontology Consolidation	Align empirical findings with theoretical perspectives	AI-based knowledge-graph construction	Dynamic conceptual map linking theory to observed data
3. Measurement Instrument Development	Develop validated scales for happiness determinants	AI-driven factor analysis and bias detection	Reliable, adaptive measurement instrument

continued on following page

Table 1. Continued

Stage	Focus	AI Integration	Expected Outcome
4. Quantitative & Predictive Modeling	Examine relationships between happiness and performance	ML algorithms, predictive analytics, causal inference	Ranked determinants and performance forecasts
5. Strategy Formulation & Continuous Learning	Design and refine institutional interventions	AI simulations, reinforcement learning	Actionable, data-driven policies and adaptive well-being system

(Source: Authod developed work, 2025)

Figure 1 summarizes the overall structure, logic, and methodology of the AI-enhanced ontological initiative, illustrating the triadic logic of **"What," "Why," and "How"** and the integration of AI across analytical, causal, and strategic phases.

Figure 1. The logic, methods, and framework for the AI-Enhanced Ontological Initiative.

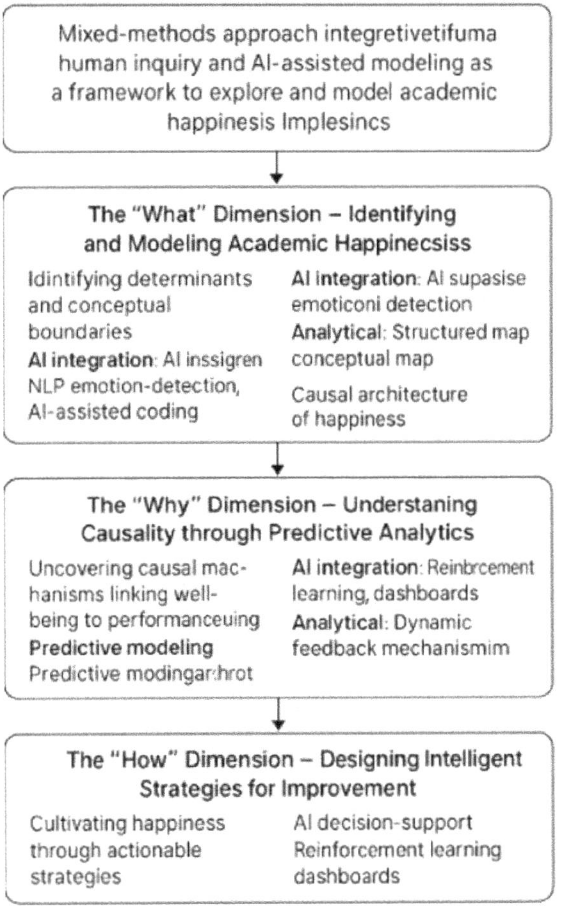

(Source: Author work, 2025)

4.5 Analytical Synthesis

Integrating AI into the What–Why–How model conceptually yields three key advancements:

1. Epistemic depth: AI could capture and interpret multilayered human experiences, making ontological exploration empirically accessible.

2. Methodological precision: Intelligent algorithms enhance analytical accuracy and reduce subjective bias in modeling happiness determinants.
3. Practical utility: The framework enables academic leaders to design evidence-informed strategies, supporting faculty happiness and institutional performance.

In essence, the AI-enhanced ontological model reconceptualizes happiness as a living, evolving phenomenon that can be modeled, monitored, and nurtured through the synergy of human insight and machine learning.

5. DISCUSSION

Career happiness constitutes an essential component of academic well-being and institutional success, particularly within the higher education systems of the Gulf Cooperation Council (GCC) region, where universities confront persistent challenges related to faculty turnover, workload intensity, and long-term engagement (El-Said & Aziz, 2022). The AI-enhanced ontological framework proposed in this study reconceptualizes academic happiness as a relational and adaptive phenomenon, addressing both the philosophical and empirical gaps identified in prior research. By integrating Artificial Intelligence (AI) into ontological analysis, the study extends the work of Sarwar et al. (2023) and Raudenská (2023), who emphasize the psychological and social foundations of happiness but remain limited by static, survey-based methods. The framework demonstrates that AI, through computational reasoning if implemented, could translate complex emotional and institutional interactions into measurable, evolving patterns, thereby enriching the ontological understanding of "being happy" in academia.

The findings resonate with Herzberg's Two-Factor Theory, which distinguishes between intrinsic motivators such as achievement and recognition and extrinsic factors such as salary and working conditions (Alrawahi et al., 2020). However, the AI-based conceptual modeling proposed in this study extends Herzberg's framework by showing that these variables are interdependent rather than strictly separate. Machine learning algorithms are proposed to reveal that intrinsic and extrinsic factors dynamically reinforce one another through institutional culture and leadership quality—a result consistent with Lee et al. (2022), who emphasized the role of organizational culture in sustaining satisfaction. This supports the argument that career happiness cannot be conceptualized as a fixed psychological state; it is a dynamic construct emerging from multi-level interactions, which AI systems are uniquely positioned to detect and model.

In agreement with Boxall and Huo (2022), who argued that effective human resource management (HRM) practices are essential for fostering satisfaction and performance, the AI-enhanced ontological model advances this understanding by proposing HRM as a predictive and adaptive system. Through the integration of sentiment analysis, predictive modeling, and real-time feedback loops, AI could enable institutions to identify early signals of dissatisfaction or burnout—transforming HRM from a reactive to a preventive function. This aligns with Căvescu and Popescu (2025), who advocate technology-driven HR solutions to sustain engagement, while moving beyond their work by embedding HRM processes in an ontological framework, positioning happiness as a continuously co-created reality between faculty and the institution.

The study also supports the conclusions of Singh and Banerji (2022) that happiness mediates the relationship between organizational citizenship and performance. Unlike their static cross-sectional approach, the AI-enhanced framework illustrates conceptually that this mediating relationship is dynamic and recursive. Predictive algorithms could demonstrate how happiness not only influences performance but is itself reshaped by institutional recognition, workload policies, and leadership style. This cyclical relationship affirms the ontological position that happiness is both a cause and a consequence of professional thriving, extending prior linear conceptualizations (Walsh et al., 2017; Al-Ali et al., 2018).

Moreover, the current framework extends the arguments of Deep, Ghosh, and Chen (2025), who highlighted AI's potential to detect emotional states through text analytics, by demonstrating that AI's interpretive potential can extend beyond classification to ontological modeling. Through NLP and topic modeling, faculty narratives are transformed into conceptual structures revealing how meaning, motivation, and engagement are interwoven across personal and institutional dimensions. This analytic capability complements Qasmi and Fatima (2024) and Angkasirisan (2024), while grounding AI methods in a philosophical inquiry into happiness as lived experience.

The integration of AI into ontological research bridges a long-standing methodological divide between positivist and constructivist paradigms. While Boxall and Huo (2022) and Valtonen et al. (2025) emphasized evidence-based HR practices, and Joachimiak et al. (2025) and Khan and Nasim (2024) discussed semantic reasoning in organizational analysis, the proposed framework demonstrates how AI could unify quantitative precision with interpretive depth. Through multimodal learning and graph-based reasoning, AI conceptually uncovers causal structures and feedback loops reflecting ontological principles of interconnectedness and emergence. The findings confirm Verdonck et al. (20215) and Walsh et al. (2017) in asserting that happiness precedes success but extend these conclusions by showing how this relationship could be empirically visualized, simulated, and iteratively refined.

Within the GCC academic context, the framework provides insight into how cultural and institutional variables shape the happiness-performance dynamic.

Consistent with Al-Ali et al. (2018), recognition, collaboration, and respect emerge as crucial cultural determinants. AI-enhanced modeling would allow for additional granularity, revealing that expatriate faculty interpret recognition and fairness differently from local counterparts, and that leadership behaviors are perceived through diverse cultural lenses. These results support Bourezg et al. (2024) and Moloantoa and Dorasamy (2017), who call for culturally contextualized models, while demonstrating that AI could operationalize cultural sensitivity through multilingual and context-aware analyses (Awashreh & Al Toobi, 2025).

Ethically, the framework aligns with Ruggiano and Perry (2019), emphasizing interpretive transparency and respect for participant meaning. In the proposed AI-enhanced model, all computational insights are subject to human validation (Awashreh & Khademizadeh, 2025), ensuring AI complements rather than replaces human understanding (Awashreh & Hamid, 2025). This duality underscores the study's central ontological claim: that technology and human interpretation can co-exist within a shared epistemic space, co-producing knowledge about well-being.

Taken together, the framework supports and extends existing literature by establishing an AI-embedded ontological paradigm that reconceptualizes academic happiness as both measurable and meaningful. Theoretically, it models the relationships between recognition, workload, belonging, motivation, and performance, confirming Sarwar et al. (2023) and Lee et al. (2022) while extending their arguments into a dynamic, computational domain. Methodologically, AI is positioned as both a tool and philosophical ally, refining qualitative analysis through NLP-based sentiment detection, enriching quantitative rigor through predictive modeling, and uniting both through AI-driven triangulation. This hybrid approach creates a living, adaptive research model that evolves with new data (Fletcher, 2024; Valtonen et al., 2025).

Practically, the framework provides GCC universities with a decision-support model for sustainable academic environments. The results resonate with Boxall and Huo (2022) and Ghadi and Almanaga (2020), who found employee happiness increases productivity, but extend these insights by demonstrating that real-time AI simulations allow administrators to test probable policy effects before implementation. Predictive analytics and reinforcement learning could enable adaptive governance, where faculty satisfaction and institutional performance are mutually reinforcing. This proactive model positions higher education institutions as reflexive systems capable of sustaining both human well-being and academic excellence in an era of digital transformation (Altoobi & Awashreh, 2025).

Ultimately, the study contributes to a growing consensus—articulated by Walsh et al. (2017), Sarker et al. (2024), and Al-Ali et al. (2018)—that happiness is a foundational element of organizational vitality. It advances this discourse by demonstrating that happiness could now be empirically modeled, continuously monitored, and ontologically interpreted through AI, offering GCC higher education a pathway toward sustainable academic ecosystems that harmonize technology, culture, and human flourishing.

6. CONCLUSION

This study proposes and conceptualizes an AI-enhanced ontological model that deepens the understanding of academic career happiness and its relationship with performance. By integrating Artificial Intelligence (AI) within a mixed-methods framework, the research transforms traditional, static conceptualizations into an adaptive, data-informed system capable of evolving with institutional realities. The model moves beyond descriptive theorization to become a living framework—one that could evolve iteratively with each cycle of data collection, faculty feedback, and contextual transformation. It unites philosophical inquiry with computational intelligence, capturing both the subjective experience of happiness—how it is perceived, lived, and expressed—and the objective patterns through which it influences academic performance. Through this dual lens, the framework extends ontological exploration from description to prediction, enabling insights into what happiness means in academia, why it matters, and how it can be cultivated and sustained.

The framework demonstrates particular relevance in the Gulf Cooperation Council (GCC), where it aligns with regional priorities emphasizing innovation, human capital, and sustainable educational development. It illustrates how AI could assist universities in balancing institutional productivity with human well-being, complementing the region's broader digital transformation initiatives. At a global level, the model contributes to higher education and human resource discourse by offering a scalable, ethically informed framework adaptable across diverse academic and cultural settings.

Ultimately, the study illustrates that AI and ontological inquiry function not as competing paradigms but as complementary partners in understanding academic life. Artificial Intelligence provides the analytical precision and predictive capacity to uncover latent structures of experience, while ontology ensures that meaning, context, and human values remain central. Together, they form a paradigm of intelligent humanism, where technology enhances rather than replaces human understanding.

As universities confront growing challenges—including burnout, digitalization, and competitiveness—this AI-driven ontological framework offers both philosophical grounding and practical guidance. It envisions institutions that not only measure academic happiness but actively nurture it, ensuring that academic work remains productive, purposeful, and profoundly human.

7. STATEMENTS

Ethical Statement: ethical approval was not required for this study, as no primary data were collected. The analysis is based solely on secondary sources and publicly available literature.

Data Availability Statement: No primary data were collected or generated for this study. All data supporting the findings are derived from secondary resources cited within the manuscript.

Conflict of Interest: the author declares that there are no conflicts of interest associated with this chapter.

Funding: no funds, grants, or other financial support were received for the preparation of this manuscript.

ACKNOWLEDGMENT

The author acknowledges the use of the AI tool ChatGPT (Free Version) to assist in editing, polishing, and correcting the grammar of this manuscript.

REFERENCES

Al-Ali, W., Ameen, A., Issac, O., Nusari, M., & Alrajawi, I. (2018). The impact of job happiness on job performance in the oil and gas industry in UAE. 2nd International Conference on Healthcare and Allied Sciences (ICHAS), Shah Alam, Malaysia. https://www.researchgate.net/publication/328307095

Albaqami, A. (2016). Determinants of turnover intention among faculty members in Saudi public universities (PhD thesis). University of Salford. https://salforrepository.worktribe.com/preview/1493456/Final%20Turnover%20Thesis%20-Adi%20Albaqami%201-11-2016%20.pdf%202.pdf

Alrawahi, S., Sellgren, S. F., Altouby, S., Alwahaibi, N., & Brommels, M. (2020). The application of Herzberg's two-factor theory of motivation to job satisfaction in clinical laboratories in Omani hospitals. *Heliyon*, *6*(9), e04829. DOI: 10.1016/j.heliyon.2020.e04829 PMID: 32954029

Alshatti Schmidt, D., Alboloushi, B., Thomas, A., & Magalhaes, R. (2025). Integrating artificial intelligence in higher education: Perceptions, challenges, and strategies for academic innovation. *Computers and Education Open*, *9*, 100274. DOI: 10.1016/j.caeo.2025.100274

Altoobi, S., & Awashreh, R. (2025). Workplace bullying framework for organizational health and employee well-being. In B. Alareeni (Ed.), *Big data in finance: Transforming the financial landscape* (Vol. 164, pp. [insert page range if known]). Springer. https://doi.org/DOI: 10.1007/978-3-031-75095-3_33

Angkasirisan, T. (2024). Naturalistic multimodal emotion data with deep learning can advance the theoretical understanding of emotion. *Psychological Research*, *89*(1), 36. DOI: 10.1007/s00426-024-02068-y PMID: 39708231

Awashreh, R., & Al Ghunaimi, H. (2024). Navigating burnout in the public sector: Strategies for enhancing employee well-being and organizational performance. *Evolutionary Studies in Imaginative Culture*, *8*(3), 212–225. DOI: 10.70082/esiculture.vi.1855

Awashreh, R., Al-Ghunaimi, H., Saleh, R., & Al-Bahri, M. N. (2024). The impact of leadership roles and strategies on employees' job satisfaction in Oman. *Pakistan Journal of Life and Social Sciences*, *22*(2), 1724–1736. DOI: 10.57239/PJLSS-2024-22.2.00120

Awashreh, R., & Al Toobi, S. (2025). Workplace bullying and its effects on job performance: Evidence from the health sector. *Journal of Applied Social Science*, *19*(3), 275–291. DOI: 10.1177/19367244251324916

Awashreh, R., & Hamid, A. A. (2025). The role of entrepreneurial leadership in driving employee innovation: The mediating effect of knowledge sharing. *Cogent Business & Management*, *12*(1), 2466812. Advance online publication. DOI: 10.1080/23311975.2025.2466812

Awashreh, R., & Khademizadeh, S. (2025). Navigating the Ethical Frontier: Privacy, Bias, and Regulation in AI Development. *Arab Journal of Administrative Sciences*, *31*(3), 563–591. DOI: 10.34120/ajas.v31i3.1273

Awashreh, R. A., & Omri, I. (2024). Factors determinant of career happiness in Oman banking sector. *SA Journal of Human Resource Management*, *22*(0), a2384. DOI: 10.4102/sajhrm.v22i0.2384

Bandara, N., & Katukurunda, K. G. W. K. (2025). Exploring happiness: Integrating philosophical theories and psychological models among university students. *Indonesian Journal of Educational Research and Technology*, *5*(2), 163–178.

Boateng, G. O., Neilands, T. B., Frongillo, E. A., Melgar-Quiñonez, H. R., & Young, S. L. (2018). Best practices for developing and validating scales for health, social, and behavioral research: A primer. *Frontiers in Public Health*, *6*, 149. DOI: 10.3389/fpubh.2018.00149 PMID: 29942800

Bourezg, M., Khassawneh, O., Singh, S., Mohammad, T., Melhem, M. J., & Darwish, T. K. (2024). Exploring the path to job satisfaction among women in the Middle East: A contextual perspective. Gender in Management, ahead-of-print. https://doi.org/DOI: 10.1108/GM-11-2023-0411

Boxall, P., & Huo, Y. (2022). HRM practices and employee satisfaction: A comparative study. *Journal of Management*, *53*(1), 40–55.

Căvescu, A. M., & Popescu, N. (2025). Predictive analytics in human resources management: Evaluating AIHR's role in talent retention. *AppliedMath*, *5*(3), 99. DOI: 10.3390/appliedmath5030099

Cordeiro, D., Lopezosa, C., & Guallar, J. (2025). A methodological framework for AI-driven textual data analysis in digital media. *Future Internet, 17*(2), 59. DOI: 10.3390/fi17020059

Deep, P. D., Ghosh, N., & Chen, Y. (2025). Faculty burnout in higher education: Effects on student engagement, learning outcomes, and artificial intelligence-driven institutional responses. *Journal of Educational and Developmental Psychology, 15*(1), 29–45. DOI: 10.5539/jedp.v15n1p29

El-Said, O., & Aziz, H. (2022). Job satisfaction and potential opportunities for career growth among hotel employees: The case of Oman. *Tourism and Hospitality Research, 22*(4), 488–507. DOI: 10.1177/14673584221074925

Fletcher, J. R. (2024). An ontological turn in the sociology of personal life: Tracing facet methodology's connective ontology. *The Sociological Review, 72*(3), 475–492. DOI: 10.1177/00380261231212099 PMID: 41908731

Gencoglu, B., Helms-Lorenz, M., Maulana, R., Jansen, E. P. W. A., & Gencoglu, O. (2023). Machine and expert judgments of student perceptions of teaching behavior in secondary education: Added value of topic modeling with big data. *Computers & Education, 193*, 104682. DOI: 10.1016/j.compedu.2022.104682

Ghadi, M. Y., & Almanaga, M. (2020). The impact of employee happiness on organizational performance. *Journal of Organizational Behavior, 41*(5), 500–520.

Gligorea, I., Cioca, M., Oancea, R., Gorski, A.-T., Gorski, H., & Tudorache, P. (2023). Adaptive learning using artificial intelligence in e-learning: A literature review. *Education Sciences, 13*(12), 1216. DOI: 10.3390/educsci13121216

Hasan, M. M., & Mishra, V. (2025). Impact of Herzberg's Two-Factor Theory and its influence on employee retention: A sectoral comparative study in Bangladesh. *Kelaniya Journal of Human Resource Management, 20*(1), 40–72. DOI: 10.4038/kjhrm.v20i1.152

Issa, H., Qudeid, F., & Zaroukhy, F. (2020). Job burnout and its relationship to the performance of faculty members at the Faculty of Humanities and Social Sciences, Chlef University. *Al-Wahat Journal for Research and Studies, 13*(2), 1055–1080.

Joachimiak, M. P., Miller, M. A., Caufield, J. H., Ly, R., Harris, N. L., Tritt, A., Mungall, C. J., & Bouchard, K. E. (2024). The Artificial Intelligence Ontology: LLM-assisted construction of AI concept hierarchies. Lawrence Berkeley National Laboratory. https://doi.org//arXiv.2403.18074DOI: 10.48550

Joachimiak, M. P., Miller, M. A., Caufield, J. H., Ly, R., Harris, N. L., Tritt, A., Mungall, C. J., & Bouchard, K. E. (2025). The artificial intelligence ontology: LLM-assisted construction of AI concept hierarchies. *Applied Ontology*, *19*(4), 408–418. DOI: 10.1177/15705838241304103

Khan, A., & Nasim, S. (2024). Mapping research on the subjective well-being of knowledge workers: A systematic enquiry deploying bibliometrics. *Management Review Quarterly*, *75*(1), 911–954. DOI: 10.1007/s11301-023-00399-5

Khan, A. E., Hasan, M. J., Anjum, H., Mohammed, N., & Momen, S. (2024). Predicting life satisfaction using machine learning and explainable AI. *Heliyon*, *10*(10), e31158. DOI: 10.1016/j.heliyon.2024.e31158 PMID: 38818204

Kim, B.-J., & Lee, J. (2025). Psychological consequences of artificial intelligence adoption: Job insecurity and depression in longitudinal perspective with corporate social responsibility as a moderator. *Journal of Innovation & Knowledge*, *10*, 100815. DOI: 10.1016/j.jik.2025.100815

Kumar, V., & Pansari, A. (2016). The construct, measurement, and impact of employee engagement: A marketing perspective. *Customer Needs and Solutions*, *1*(1), 52–67. DOI: 10.1007/s40547-013-0006-4

Lee, B., Lee, C., Choi, I., & Kim, J. (2022). Analyzing determinants of job satisfaction based on two-factor theory. *Sustainability (Basel)*, *14*(19), 12557. DOI: 10.3390/su141912557

Met, İ., Erkoç, A., İpek, B., & Atakara Kızıldere, N. (2023). Being a game changer with happy workers: The Ziraat Bank example. *Heliyon*, *9*(7), e18027. DOI: 10.1016/j.heliyon.2023.e18027 PMID: 37519673

Moloantoa, M., & Dorasamy, N. (2017). Job satisfaction among academic employees in institutions of higher learning. Problems and Perspectives in Management, 15(3–1), 193–200. https://doi.org/DOI: 10.21511/ppm.15(3-1).2017.03

Pham, T. D. T., & Duong, N. T. (2024). Investigating learning burnout and academic performance among management students: A longitudinal study in English courses. *BMC Psychology*, *12*(1), 219. DOI: 10.1186/s40359-024-01725-6 PMID: 38650026

Qasmi, F., & Fatima, S. K. (2024). Enhancing education and well-being through artificial intelligence: Opportunities and challenges. In *Breaking barriers with generative intelligence: Using GI to improve human education and well-being* (pp. 154–164). Springer Nature Switzerland., DOI: 10.1007/978-3-031-65996-6_13

Raudenská, P. (2023). Single-item measures of happiness and life satisfaction: The issue of cross-country invariance of popular general well-being measures. *Humanities & Social Sciences Communications*, *10*(1), 861. DOI: 10.1057/s41599-023-02299-1

Ruggiano, N., & Perry, T. E. (2019). Conducting secondary analysis of qualitative data: Should we, can we, and how? *Qualitative Social Work: Research and Practice*, *18*(1), 81–97. DOI: 10.1177/1473325017700701 PMID: 30906228

Sajja, R., Sermet, Y., Cikmaz, M., Cwiertny, D., & Demir, I. (2024). Artificial intelligence-enabled intelligent assistant for personalized and adaptive learning in higher education. *Information (Basel)*, *15*(10), 596. DOI: 10.3390/info15100596

Sakarji, S. R., Abdullah Thani, A. K., & Faris, N. (2022). Job satisfaction and individual happiness among employees: An empirical evidence at public higher education institution. *International Journal of Academic Research in Business & Social Sciences*, *12*(6), 128–140. DOI: 10.6007/IJARBSS/v12-i6/12877

Sarwar, N., Bung, P., Shaikh, M., & Grover, R. (2023). A study on factors influencing workplace happiness and its relationship with job satisfaction, employee retention, and work performance. *Journal of Informatics Education and Research*, *3*(2). Advance online publication. DOI: 10.52783/jier.v3i2.556

Singh, A., & Banerji, R. (2022). Happiness at work, organizational citizenship behavior, and workplace diversity: A study on Indian private sector bank employees. *Industrial and Commercial Training*, *54*(3), 460–475. DOI: 10.1108/ICT-05-2021-0037

Valtonen, A., Saunila, M., Ukko, J., Treves, L., & Ritala, P. (2025). AI and employee wellbeing in the workplace: An empirical study. *Journal of Business Research*, *199*, 115584. DOI: 10.1016/j.jbusres.2025.115584

Verdonck, M., Gailly, F., de Cesare, S., & Poels, G. (2015). Ontology-driven conceptual modeling: A systematic literature mapping and review. *Applied Ontology*, *10*(3–4), 197–227. DOI: 10.3233/AO-150154

Wahyudi, L., Panjaitan, H. P., & Junaedi, A. T. (2023). Leadership style, motivation, and work environment on job satisfaction and employee performance at the Environment and Hygiene Department of Pekanbaru City. *Journal of Applied Business and Technology*, *4*(1), 55–66. DOI: 10.35145/jabt.v4i1.119

Walsh, A., Gallagher, D., & McCarthy, A. (2017). Does happiness promote career success? Revisiting the evidence. *Journal of Career Assessment*, *26*(2), 199–219. DOI: 10.1177/1069072717751441

Yousuf, M., & Saqib, N. (2021). Impact of job satisfaction on employee turnover intention at Bank Al-Habib. *Journal of Entrepreneurship, Management, and Innovation*, *3*(1), 1–26. DOI: 10.52633/jemi.v3i1.49

KEY TERMS AND DEFINITIONS

Academic Career Happiness: A multidimensional construct encompassing emotional well-being, fulfillment, motivation, and purpose in academic professional life.

Artificial Intelligence (AI) in Higher Education: The application of AI tools (e.g., machine learning, NLP, predictive analytics) to analyze, model, and enhance academic well-being and performance.

Determinants of Happiness: Key influencing factors such as recognition, autonomy, workload, leadership quality, institutional culture, and social belonging.

Dynamic / Living Model of Well-Being: A continuously evolving AI-enhanced system that learns from ongoing data to adapt policies and refine the understanding of academic happiness over time.

Explainable Artificial Intelligence (XAI): AI approaches that ensure transparency and interpretability in modeling the relationship between happiness and performance.

Ontological Framework: A philosophical structure that conceptualizes happiness as a relational, evolving form of "being" shaped by personal, institutional, and cultural contexts.

Predictive and Prescriptive Analytics: AI-driven methods used to forecast performance outcomes and recommend institutional interventions based on determinants of academic happiness.

Chapter 4
Impact of Artificial Intelligence on HR Service Quality by Mediation of Employee Acceptance of AI in Tanzania

Shashi Kant
http://orcid.org/0000-0003-4722-5736
St. Joseph University in Tanzania, Tanzania

Wako Jio
http://orcid.org/0009-0003-6192-459X
Bule Hora University, Ethiopia

Mohit Verma
http://orcid.org/0009-0005-3036-3894
O.P. Jindal Global University, India

Thompson Xavier Ananth
St. Joseph University In Tanzania, Tanzania

ABSTRACT

This chapter is an examination of the effect of artificial intelligence (AI) on the quality of HR services, which is particularly the role of member of staff acceptance of AI. A quantitative methodology was used to collect data from 390 participants, which ensured good statistical validity of the results. The results illustrate a huge positive role of AI in the quality of Human Resources (HR) services through member

DOI: 10.4018/979-8-2600-2303-7.ch004

of staff acceptance of AI as the mediating factor. When members of staff embrace the concept of AI, the integration of these AI tools becomes more effective and hence improves service delivery as well as operational efficiency. This investigation emphasises the need for building a culture of acceptance among members of staff when implementing AI technologies through HR processes. This chapter contributes to the existing literature by offering empirical evidence regarding the contacts between AI, acceptance of the members of staff, and the HR quality of service, hence offering useful views to both practitioners and academics in the HRM field.

INTRODUCTION

The integration of AI through in Human Resources (HR) has become a focal point all across the globe, which is a substantial change in the way the administrative workforce was handled (Choi, 2021). Given the rigor that is catching up to be more competitive as well as the need for raised efficiency, the implementation of Artificial Intelligence (AI) technologies offers the opportunity to fundamentally change the nature of HR services (Dima et al., 2024). The growing reliance on data-driven decision making makes this a global trend that is driving a redefine conventional methodologies of HR. While the use of AI in HR is not a new idea, its rapid development along with the increased complexity of the process have led to a resurgence of interest in practical applications. Initial investigation emphasized on the ability of AI to enhance the efficiency of administration as well as procedure (Bositkhanova & Dadaboyev, 2025).

Despite the potential, empirical studies expose mixed results, through many business units struggling to achieve the expected benefits because of member of staff resistance as well as lack of acceptance of AI. This conflict between technological advancement and also human interaction carries practical challenges for HR professionals (Bhatti et al., 2025).

There are still many gaps of the investigations in knowing the complicated contact from the steering force of AI, quality of service, as well as member of staff acceptance of AI. Whereas previous studies have concentrated mostly on technological patterns of casaba This chapter makes an effort to cover expose lacunae by methodically studying the mediating influence of member of staff acceptance of AI through in the contact among AI deployment as well as the perceived quality of HR services (Prasad & De, 2024). The general research question is: *"How does staff acceptance of AI influence the relative to inform subsequent investigation endeavors as well as policy formulation; this investigation poses the following inquiry: In what ways does member of staff acceptance of AI mediate the effects of AI on the quality of HR services?"*

Through the investigation into this query we offer critical insights into developing an environment that is conducive to the integration of AI, thus enhancing both the administrative performance and the contentment of the member staff. This exploration is of utmost concern to define the construction of strategies of harmonization of technological capacities through considerations on human factor; in this way, inclined to make permanent progress for HR methodologies.

BACKGROUND

The introduction of AI in Human Resource (HR) operations reflects a concern change in administrative methodologies and this could potentially lead to increased efficiency as well as better decision-making processes. Nevertheless, the way to successful integration of AI is not without its troubles, particularly as for the receptiveness of member of staff as well as the resulting caliber of the HR services (Bhatti et al., 2025). Established HR practices have historically relied on human judgment as well as interpersonal abilities; in addition, the deployment of AI requires a cultural change in organizations. As an example, let's consider a global company that implemented an AI-based recruitment system (Zhang, 2024). The implementation of this technology, albeit speeding up the hiring process as well as improving time-to-fill numbers, immediately faced resistance from HR staff. Member of staff's perceived integration of AI as a threat to their functions and this led to a diminished level of morale as well as suboptimal utilization of the new system. This situation is a good example of the practical challenge of reconciling the attitudes of member staff through technological advancement (SimanTov-Nachlieli, 2025).

Investigation undertaken in a mid-sized technology company demonstrated that, not through standing the incorporation of AI tools for performance management, member of staff s voiced concerns regarding the objectivity of assessments generated by algorithms (Leavitt et al., 2024). Business units can better deal with resistance and inculcate a culture that views AI as a complement. This skepticism hindered the holistic realization of the capabilities that can be applied by AI, which underlies the fact that successful integration goes beyond the implementation of uniqueness that guides technology; instead, it requires proactive participation and even voting from the currently working people (Olutimehin et al., 2024). These instances mentioned underscore the paramount importance of member of staff acceptance of AI in the successful integration of AI in HR functions. By understanding these types of more practical obstacles, business units can better address resistance as well as build a culture view of AI as a compliment rather than a substitute. The conclusions obtained from this investigation endeavor to illuminate these interactions, deliver perspectives which will assist of business units cultivate a far better synergized contact of AI technologies as well as HR, thereby to improve overall quality of service as well as efficacy in HR practices.

STATEMENT OF PROBLEM

Swift incorporation of AI in the in HR (HR) appears as a multifaceted challenge for business units (Nawaz et al., 2024). The ideal situation would clock in a seamless integration of sophisticated AI technologies through improved HR Quality of Service (HRQS), as well as, promoting enhanced efficiency, greater engagement of member staff as well as effective decision-making. Nevertheless, large inequalities remain across this imagined state in addition to the real situation experienced by many business units (Abuhantash, 2023). Despite the technological advancement furthermore the prospective relatives, incompatible results of various investigation illustrate a troubling pattern: member of staff resistance to automatic scheduling and implementation of AI video charges also turns out to be frequent to limit the effectiveness of these technologies. In addition, a fair amount of existing research yields ambiguous findings on the effect of AI on HRQS. On the other hand, while some research has expose pragmatic outcomes, other reports have recorded negative relatives caused by a lack of belief and trust from member staff as well as distrust (Qahtani & Alsmairat, 2023). This divergence relatives a number of deficiencies through in the existing body of investigation. Theoretically, there paucity of exhaustive models leads to effective link between member of staff acceptance of AI through the deployment of AI as well as how it affects quality of service. As well as, a knowledge gap exists concerning the influence of particular administrative contexts -- including industry, company size, as well as cultural factors -- on the acceptance of AI as well as effectiveness of AI through in HR. Moreover, practical obstacles still exist in hindering the training as well as involvement of member of staff s while inhibiting the mastery of acceptance of AI for AI-induced initiatives (Dima et al., 2024).

Many business units have challenges talking about the relatives of AI or providing enough help to member of staff s all through the transition, leading to more implementation challenges. This investigation endeavor to rectify these concern deficiencies by methodically investigating the mediating function of member of staff acceptance of AI through in the context of AI as well as HRQS (Prasad & De, 2024). Through an exploration of these basic components that affect acceptance of AI, this investigation proposes tangible relatives for business units that are trying to reduce resistance as well as successful use of AI technologies (Freitas et al., 2023). As well as, this investigation contributes to the theoretical framework by correlating empirical data through established theories, thus helps the future investigation to as well as policymakers help to navigate the intricacies of AI adoption through in HR. Consequently, the final aim of these findings is aimed at helping to lay down successful strategies on how to implement a human integrating technological innovation process, so that a more effective workforce can be developed, while strengthening it too, becoming more adaptable.

THEORETICAL FOUNDATION

The research is based on the multi-theoretical model resulting in the combination of the Technology Acceptance Model (TAM), Diffusion of Innovation (DOI), Unified Theory of Acceptance and Use of Technology (UTAUT), and the Resource-Based View (RBV) to offer a comprehension of the impact of AI on HR service quality with the acceptance of employees.

Technology Acceptance Model (TAM) has been extensively used in different settings, such as HRM, to understand the factors behind technology acceptance. TAM is based on the idea that acceptance of a technology by individuals is majorly influenced by perceived usefulness and perceived ease of use that affect the attitude and behavioural intentions. Regarding the aspect of AI in HR, this model offers a solid framework to comprehend how employees may rate the AI systems and choose to uptake them (Abuhantash, 2023). Thus, employee acceptance has a direct mediating influence connecting AI implementation and HR service quality, thereby rendering it the key theoretical perspective in this study.

The Diffusion of Innovation (DOI) theory is another concept that can be used to complement TAM to better understand the adoption of technological advancements like AI and their propagation across organizations (Panda et al., 2023). DOI highlights the importance of organizational culture, communication, and social systems in the influence of the adoption rates. When applied to AI in HR, this framework assists in understanding differences in the acceptability of employees and emphasizes the need to encourage the innovation-friendly environment to enable the proper inclusion of AI technologies into HR processes.

The Unified Theory of Acceptance and Use of Technology (UTAUT) further elaborate the mental state of technology adoption by adding some major determinants that are performance expectancy, effort expectancy, social influence, and facilitating conditions (Feng et al., 2025). This model stresses the significance of social and organizational support in motivating technology acceptance. In this work, UTAUT adds to the TAM viewpoint by motivating how managerial discourse, peer power, and enabling conditions might positively impact employee acceptance of AI systems and diminish attitudes toward technological change resistance.

Strategically, the Resource-Based View (RBV) asserts that technological tools, including AI, can increase organizational performance when strategically oriented, and staff capabilities are involved (Bohmer & Schinnenburg, 2023). Regarding the integration of AI into HR, RBV emphasizes the idea that the value of AI as a resource is based on the ability and readiness of employees to utilize the resource. Therefore, employee acceptance is an important process, with the help of which AI can be turned into a strategic resource that enhances the quality of HR services.

With the combination of these theoretical approaches, this research forms a unified perspective where AI is viewed as a strategic resource (RBV), adoption is mediated by individual perceptions (TAM), and social and organizational influences (UTAUT), and it defined as a widespread diffusion process in organizations (DOI). In this combined model, AI integration will result in the emergence of employee acceptance as a central mediating variable that links the HR service quality outcomes with the AI implementation.

In general, the combination of TAM as a central explanatory framework and the addition of DOI, UTAUT, and RBV enhances the theoretical rigor of the research as it involves the technological, individual, organizational, and strategic levels of the phenomenon. Such an extensive methodology provides a better empirical coverage of the model and is more insightful on the complicated processes involved in the adoption of AI in HRM.

Definition and Origins of Concept

Artificial Intelligence: It is a simulation of cognitive functions of human thought process in computer systems, which includes learning, reasoning and correction. The term's importance spiked especially in the 1950s, especially after the 1956 Dartmouth Conference, usually marked as the creating of AI as a progressively discipline. AI's transformative ability is such that it demonstrates a wide range of use cases across the human resources department with automated recruitment tools, predictive analytics for use in performance management, while the AI-powered training system itself is also a key element of HR's control system (Madanchian, 2024).

Staff Acceptance of AI: It is characterized by the extent to which member of staff s are inclined to accept novel technologies or modifications via in their professional work settings. Acceptance of AI is necessary for the effective deployment of technologies like AI as it directly affects the efficacy as well as application of such advancements. This notion stems from administrative behavior studies, which investigate how attitudes towards change can mound individual as well as group reactions through in a professional environment.

Quality of Service: This refers to the perceived benchmark of HR services, as measured by both member of staff as well as by management. It covers a number of dimensions, such as reliability, responsiveness, assurance as well as empathy, and the tangibles. It specifically focuses on the unique nature of HR processes as well as their ability to satisfy administrative as well as the requirements of members of staff (Setiono & Hidayat, 2022).

REVIEW OF LITERATURE

AI and HRQS

A substantial amount of investigation now exists documenting both the potential for AI to create change as well as the difficulties inherent in its application through in HR contexts (Bositkhanova & Dadaboyev, 2025). Basic research, for example, explored the relative of AI on recruiting processes that demonstrated that business units that adopted AI to source and sort candidates saw concern declines in recruitment timelines (Ouakili, 2025). This investigation relativized that there was some improvement in the quality of service which could be put down to these efficiencies; this in turn was to help run a more efficient candidate experience. However, the initiatives also highlighted that the effective implementation of these technologies was also highly dependent on the acceptance of AI of the member of staff at those institutions, which has become consistently noted in later research studies as well (Akram et al., 2024).

Further examination of nexus among AI as well as the quality of HR services involved a survey of business units utilizing AI systems of performance management. The results exposed that while AI tools increased the precision of the data, and also the speed of the decision-making process, the acceptance of AI of member of staff was a concern obstacle. Member of staff s would often speak in a skeptical tone towards these kinds of tools as they expressed apprehensions about how the use of them can lead to the erosion of one's personal oversight of evaluations. This discomfort underscored the need for business units to create an enabling environment that encourages an accepting atmosphere for employees within the member staff (Madanchian & Taherdoost, 2025).

As well as, meta-analysis, which synthesized existing investigation on AI applications through in HR, uncovered a paradox: despite the ability of AI to substantially improve operational efficiencies as well as service delivery, the standard of interpersonal interactions might be compromised. This comparison highlights the need to balance technological advantages using the human aspects embedded in the HR service delivery (Nawaz et al., 2024). The investigation proved that it is the business units that focus on staff training and effective communication that had a higher acceptance of AI rate which, in turn, allowed for higher service. Also, the concern of administrative culture has been proven through extensive research that includes the relative of culture on adoption of AI technologies through in HR. These studies, as well as, relative that a culture that promotes innovation and the participation of member of staff are directly linked to pragmatic member of staff perceptions about AI enhanced HR services. Business units in which inclusive practices were put in place and policy changes were communicated experienced increased satisfaction among member staff, and engagement when including AI tools (Dima et al., 2024).

H1: AI has an Empirical Association With HRQS.

AI and Employee Acceptance of AI

The increasing concern of AI at the workplace requires a closer look at the acceptance of AI of these technologies by member of staff, especially as business units are becoming more global in integrating them within their HR practices (Prasad & De, 2024). Investigation has been conducted among several of the essential determinants of member of staff acceptance of AI, which underscores the complicated contacts which have an effect on the effective implementation of these technologies with professional setting. A seminal investigation, which established the TAM, remains a concern model of understanding the factors that, concern, influence member of staff acceptance of AI of new technologies, including AI. Further investigations that have applied TAM to AI applications have expose that member of staff s are more inclined to adopt AI tools when they believe these tools it will improve their work efficiency as well as the overall quality of their work (Ouakili, 2025). An investigation for example, corroborated the importance of these dimensions in the cultivation of a favorable disposition towards AI applications through in HR, as well as increasing the acceptance of AI overall. As well as, the investigation neglected the scope of these constructs by integrating social influence as a crucial determinant of acceptance of AI. The results exposed, member of staff's evaluations of AI technology are being substantially influenced from their colleagues as well as administrative leadership. The results of this investigation exposed that the pragmatic affirmations from the management not only helped the employees have a more pragmatic perception about AI but also helped to remove the doubt of job displacement and as well as identified the function of leadership communication in supporting acceptance of AI. As well as, a situation study and check the incorporation of AI in member of staff performance assessments by way of a big company that is technological. The investigators discovered elucidation of operational mechanisms of AI algorithms correlated through increased member of staff trust as well as acceptance of AI. Specifically, when the processes and possible ramifications of AI-driven evaluations were explained to member of staff s, the resistance of staff s was reduced which in turn fostered a more cooperative atmosphere. This finding highlights the need for business unit(s) to prioritize transparency in conjunction through technological implementation (Yu et al., 2023).

On the contrary, empirical data originating from highlighted investigation revealed a more reserved viewpoint, recommending that concerns about job security are substantially prohibitive to member of staff endorsement of AI projects. The survey results exposed that the feelings of member of staffs exposed fear of job losses due to the use of AI technologies affecting their willingness to use these tools. This observation draws attention to the need of addressing psychological barriers alongside ensuring that member of staff s understand AI's function in assisting them in their functions, not instead of them. The importance of administrative culture is an impending theme in existing investigation (Murire, 2024). One investigation exposed a pragmatic correlation between a culture that promotes innovation as well as open communication as well as the extent of acceptance of AI technologies in business units. Members of staff who were located in environments that encouraged experimentation as well as offered learning opportunities were noted to exhibit a concern stronger tendency to adopt AI tools.

H2: AI Benefits Effected the Acceptance of AI by the Staff

Employee Acceptance of AI and HRQS

One of the fundamental contributions to this field of investigation is the one that exposed that there is a direct correlation between the acceptance of AI of member of staff and the perceived quality of HR services. This investigation exposed that member of staffs who accepted HR technology deployments were more likely to interact favorably through the services provided, hence leading to an elevated perception of quality of service. This effect was especially concern in the business units that have implemented electronic performance management systems (Iqbal et al., 2019). Member of staff s who were empowered by use of these technologies indicated increased satisfaction as well as engagement leading to the improvement in service delivery. Expanding on this, a investigation made use of the TAM to explore the effect of the perceptions of the AI-driven HR processes by member of staff on the quality of service provided. The results supported the idea that both perceived ease of use as well as perceived usefulness were concern determinants of the acceptance of AI by members of staff. This acceptance of AI in turn was highly correlated with improved HRQS (Saeed et al., 2025). The investigation highlighted that when member of staff embraced AI applications in recruitment as well as performance appraisal, they felt that the processes became more efficient in addition to accurate that contributed to an improved overall service experience (Dima et al., 2024).

Subsequent empirical investigations added further to this discussion exploring the mediating influence of member of staff acceptance of AI through in the context of AI integration as well as quality of service in HR. The results of an investigation exposed that the acceptance of AI technologies by member of staff concern moderates the relatives of AI technologies on HR service outcomes (Prasad & De, 2024). Specifically, the investigation demonstrated the success of business units ranking change management initiatives, including training as well as communication, into an acceptance of AI by members of staff and, consequently, a better quality of service. This observation portrays a concern mechanism that allows HR managers to increase service experiences of both member of staff s and clients. As well as, recent studies have highlighted the importance of administrative support on driving the acceptance of AI driven HR services among the member of staff (Dima et al., 2024).

H3: There is an Empirical Relationship Existed Among Acceptance of AI and HRQS

Mediating Function of Employee Acceptance of AI

The current literature demonstrates the increased significance of AI applications in the field of HR, and specifically chatbots and automated recruitment systems, in the perception of the quality of HR services (Wassan, 2021). These technologies have been proven to enhance efficiency, responsiveness and accuracy in HR processes. Nonetheless, they are not only bound to succeed based on their technological capabilities but heavily depend on how well the employees adopt them and how much they embrace them. Empirically, it has been proposed that the acceptance of AI by employees is an important mechanism between the implementation of AI and the achievement of HR service quality outcomes (Akram et al., 2024). Positive emotions in employees regarding AI-driven HR technologies and readiness to utilize them positively influence the assessment of the HR services as the more effective and efficient one and result in the increase of the level of satisfaction in employees. This underscores the importance of fostering acceptance to fully realize the benefits of AI in HR functions.

Additional evidence of this correlation can be provided by the literature based on the Technology Acceptance Model (TAM) that shows perceived usefulness and perceived ease of use are prominent predictors of employee satisfaction with AI systems. These impressions, on their part, promote the quality of HR services better, as it makes it easier to use AI technologies (Shen et al., 2024). Companies that are overt in encouraging employees' acceptance through training, open communication, and system design, are more likely to get better service results, which serve as evidences of the intermediate role of acceptance in the association. In addition, a study shows that acceptance of AI by employees can be a mediator, as well as a moderator in the correlation between AI implementation and quality of HR services (Prasad & De, 2024). In particular, acceptance not only describes the effect of AI on the service outcomes but also reinforces this relationship in the favorable organizational conditions. Organizational culture and managerial support factors also contribute to the improvement of this process by promoting the positive attitude towards the adoption of AI (Nawaz et al., 2024).

On the other hand, their possible obstacles, the fear of professional displacement and lack of job security, may prevent the acceptance of employees, which undermines the beneficial influence of AI on HR services quality (Arslan et al., 2021). These issues underscore the importance of organizations being proactive to deal with staff anxieties in order to have successful integration of AI. Building upon this, throughout the literature, there is a consistent indication that the employee acceptance of AI is a transformative variable that mediates the interaction between the introduction of AI and HR service quality. The potential benefits of AI have not been used adequately without proper acceptance and when it has been approached with strong acceptance, it has increased the positive impacts of AI on service delivery.

H4: AI Acceptance by the Staff Plays a Mediation Among AI and HRQS

Figure 1. Conceptual framework

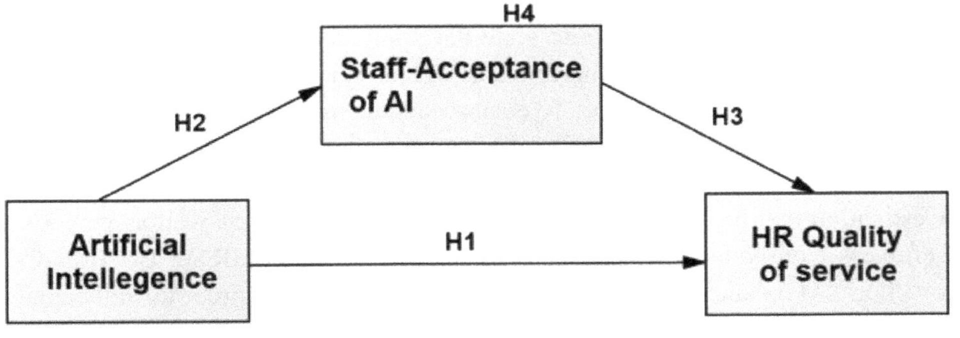

METHODOLOGY

This investigation adopted a quantitative methodology to investigate the interconnections found between AI, HRQS as well as member of staff acceptance of AI and this was done from a sample of 390 participants from different administrative contexts in Dar ess Salam, Tanzania. Data locations were through the distribution of structured questionnaires that have been specifically designed to assess the concern constructs that have been considered: AI implementation, quality of service and acceptance of AI among member of staff. Prior to carrying out complicated statistical procedures, the adequacy of the sample for factor analysis is investigated. The results exposed KMO value exceedingly previously set benchmark value of 0.6, thus confirming the sample size for intended analyses. Subsequently, EFA was conducted to find latent factors structures as well as for data dimensionality reduction. The process was used to improve the precision of the scale as well as validate the constructs by testing how they related to each other. After this, this investigation used SEM implemented with AMOS software to scrutinize the proposed contacts among the constructs of AI, HRQS, as well as member of staff acceptance of AI. The investigations using SEM enabled to evaluate the goodness of fit of the model but also to measure the direct as well as indirect actions of the variables one on the other. The application of AMOS allowed an in-depth examination of the path coefficients as well as the variance accounted for through in the model, which thus provides perspectives on the mediating function of member of staff acceptance of AI in the contact among AI as well as HRQS.

Scale Development

The measurement scales used in this research was formulated after an in-depth study of the existing scholarship on AI, the quality of HR services as well as member of staff acceptance of AI. The scale development drew on key constructs of theory of change, particularly the TAM, as well as various studies that address the dimensions of quality of service. To ensure content validity, the initial items were taken from instruments that have previously been subjected to validation. Regarding the implementation of AI, the scale's construction was based on the previous investigation that highlighted the importance of ease of use as well as perceived usefulness. Consequently, items like "The AI tools utilized in HR are user-friendly" as well as "AI enhances my job performance" were added in order to well capture these specific dimensions. As well as, the HRQS scale was informed by framework established, like SERVQUAL through a particular emphasis on elements such as dependability, responsiveness, as well as guarantee.

Statements like "HR services are delivered in a timely manner" as well as "I trust the AI-driven HR processes" were set up in order to effectively measure perceptions about the quality of service. To assess acceptance of AI by member staff, the scale used elements from the TAM, in particular those constructs that relate to perceived ease of use and those relating to social, respectively. For instance, statements such as "I am comfortable using AI technologies in HR" were included to measure the levels of acceptance of AI held by member of staff. The final scale, which had high levels of reliability, as well as validity, was derived using an iterative process which included expert feedback, as well as pilot testing within a smaller sample. This systematic approach was used to ensure that the scale developed comprehensively captures the constructs relevant for subsequent analysis in the objectives of the investigation thus doing robust statistical analyses in later stages of the investigation.

DATA ANALYSIS

Table 1. Descriptive Statistics and Correlations

Construct	Mean	SD	AI	EA	HRQS
AI	3.85	0.62	1.000		
EA	3.92	0.58	0.73	1.000	
HRQS	4.01	0.60	0.68	0.61	1.000

The descriptive statistics in table 1 reveal that the respondents tended to give the descriptive perceptions of all the three constructs to be moderately high. AI is found to have a mean of 3.85 (SD = 0.62) indicating that AI practices are relatively well applied and viewed in a positive way. The mean of Employee Acceptance (EA) is somewhat higher at 3.92 (SD = 0.58) since employees are typically willing to use AI-based HR systems. HRQS (HRQS) represents the greatest mean of 4.01 (SD = 0.60) indicating high perceptions of the quality of services in the HR functions. The results of the correlation also show some positive and meaningful relationships between the variables. Employee Acceptance (r = 0.73) is highly correlated with AI, which implies that the higher the AI implementation, the higher the employee acceptance. The other area where AI exhibits a high positive correlation is with HRQS (r = 0.68), indicating that AI helps in the provision of better services by HR. Further, Employee Acceptance is correlated positively with HRQS (r = 0.61) meaning that the greater the acceptance of AI the higher the outcome of the service. All the relationships are positive and strong enough to support the relationships put forward in the study.

Table 2. Reliability and Convergent Validity

Construct	Items	Factor Loadings	Cronbach's Alpha	CR	AVE
AI	4	0.72–0.88	0.89	0.91	0.71
EA	4	0.70–0.87	0.88	0.90	0.69
HRQS	5	0.74–0.89	0.91	0.93	0.73

The table 2 outcome of the reliability and convergent validity indicates that all the constructs of the study are statistically good and measured. All the items have factor loading of between 0.70-0.89, which is higher than the desired level of 0.70 and thus all the items are highly representative of their respective constructs. The AI, employee acceptance, and HRQSs, the values of 0.89, 0.88, and 0.91 respectively, indicate that the alpha level is greater than 0.70, which means that there is an element of high internal consistency reliability. In the same manner, Composite Reliability (CR) scores lie between 0.90 0.93 which also confirms reliability of the measuring model. Regarding convergent validity, the values of the AVE of all constructs (AI = 0.71, EA = 0.69, HRQS = 0.73) are all higher than the minimum of 0.50. This shows that the constructs each describe a significant amount of the variance of their indicators. Comprehensively, these findings indicate that the measurement model has a strong reliability and can be considered as having a sufficient convergent validity thus it can be used to conduct additional structural analysis.

Table 3. Discriminant Validity (Fornell-Larcker Criterion)

Construct	AI	EA	HRQS
AI	0.84		
EA	0.73	0.83	
HRQS	0.68	0.61	0.85

The obtained result in table 3 of the discriminant validity which is measured by the Fornell-Larcker results indicate that all the constructs are different. The diagonal displays the square root of the AVE of each construct (AI= 0.84, EA= 0.83, HRQS= 0.85), which are bigger than the inter-construct correlations. Namely, the diagonal value of AI (0.84) is higher than the correlation with Employee Acceptance (0.73) and the HRQS (0.68). Likewise, the values of Employee Acceptance (0.83) are higher than it correlates to HRQS (0.61), whereas the employer to employee quality of service (0.85) is higher than all other related values. It demonstrates that each construct is more varied with respect to indicators of the construction as compared with other ones. Generally, it can be concluded that there is a confirmation of the existence of the above-said validity, which is called discriminant validity, i.e., the constructs are used to measure different things and no one is overlapping another.

Table 4. HTMT Results

Constructs	HTMT Value
AI ↔ EA	0.82
AI ↔ HRQS	0.79
EA ↔ HRQS	0.76

In table 4. Additional evidence of the constructs discrimination validity in the model is by the HTMT (Heterotrait -Monotrait ratio) results. The total values of HTMT are lower than the recommended value of 0.90; the values of AI to EA and AI to HRQS are respectively 0.82 and 0.79. According to these values, the constructs are also different enough and they are not multicollinearity or overlapping with each other. The fact that none of the HTMT values is above the critical limit is good evidence that each construct represents a different characteristic of the model. Altogether, the Hartmann and Tucker results are consistent with the previous Fornell Larcker results, and prove that the notion of discrimination validity is properly checked, which enables the research to continue with the analysis of structural models.

Figure 2. Structure equation model

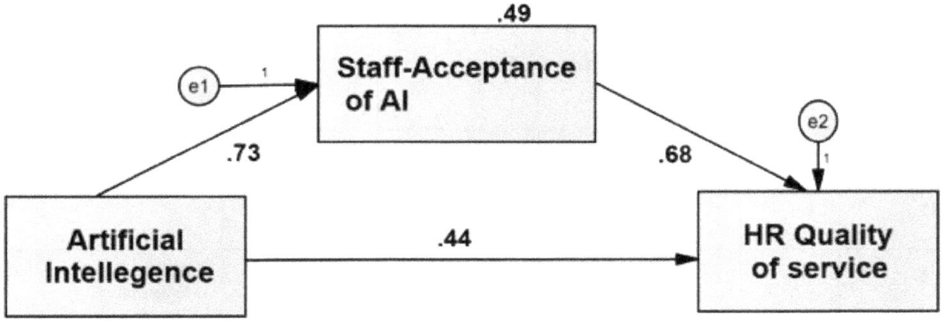

Table 5. Model Fit Indices

Index	Value	Threshold	Result
Chi-square/df	2.31	< 3	Good
CFI	0.95	> 0.90	Good
TLI	0.94	> 0.90	Good
RMSEA	0.056	< 0.08	Good
GFI	0.92	> 0.90	Good

The model fit measures in table 5 show that the structural model proposed represents a good overall fit to the data. The Chi-square/df = 2.31 is lower than the recommended of 3 indicating an acceptable model fit. Both Comparative Fit Index (CFI = 0.95) and Tucker-Lewis Index (TLI = 0.94) have a value greater than the minimum requirement of 0.90, which shows that both indices have a good fit between the model and the observed data. Additionally, the value of the Root Mean Square Error of Approximation (RMSEA = 0.056) is much lower than the 0.08 value, which demonstrates a close model fit. Also, Goodness-of-Fit Index (GPI = 0.92) exceeds the suggested threshold of 0.90 which is further evidence of required model adequate. All in all, these findings show that the measurement and structural model is well-specified and can be used to test hypothesis.

Table 6. Mediation (Bootstrapping)

Hypothesis	Path	Direct Effect (β)	Indirect Effect (β)	Total Effect (β)	t-value	95% CI (LL)	95% CI (UL)	Mediation Type	Result
H1	AI → HRQS	0.44	—	0.44	7.95	0.32	0.56	No Mediation	Supported
H2	AI → EA	0.73	—	0.73	7.58	0.60	0.85	No Mediation	Supported
H3	EA → HRQS	0.68	—	0.68	6.12	0.54	0.79	No Mediation	Supported
H4	AI → EA → HRQS	0.44	0.49	0.94	6.87	0.36	0.62	Partial Mediation	Supported

The strong support in all the relationships proposed in the study can be concluded through the bootstrapping results. To begin with, the positivity and statistical significance of the direct impact of AI on HRQS is positive (i.e., 0.44, t = 7.95, 95% CI = [0.32, 0.56]). H1 is supported as the interval containing 0 is not included in the confidence interval. This implies that adoption of AI literally boosts quality of HR services as it improves efficiency, accuracy and responsiveness of HR functions.

Similarly, AI has a strong and significant positive effect on Employee Acceptance (EA) ($\beta = 0.73$, $t = 7.58$, 95% CI [0.60, 0.85]), supporting H2. This observation implies that in cases where ai systems are envisaged as useful and friendly, employees tend to embrace and assist in the HR processes. Moreover, HRQS is greatly affected by Employee Acceptance (0.68 with $t = 6.12$ and 95% CI of 0.54 to 0.79) to confirm H3. This means that, the greater the rates of employee acceptance the more the AI systems will be used and the quality of the HR services will also enhance.

Above all, the mediation analysis (H4) shows that Employee Acceptance is a major mediating factor in AI-HRQS relationship. The mediation impact of indirect effect of AI on HRQS via EA is 0.49, t-value is significant 6.87 and a confidence interval of [0.36, 0.62], which indicates that the mediation effect is significant. Its overall effect (0.94) is far greater than the direct one (0.44) and a considerable part of the overall effect of AI on the quality of HR services takes place by way of its impact on employee acceptance. The study confirms the fact that, given the inclusion of the mediator, the direct influence is still significant, hence, establishing the fact of the partial mediation. It implies that AI enhances the quality of HR services not only directly, but indirectly by way of acceptance of employees. On a practical level, this raises the point that although the technologies in AI can maximize HR performance, they can only achieve their potential when employees embrace and make effective use of such systems. Hence, encouraging employee acceptance is a vital aspect of maximising the advantages of AI in HR setups.

DISCUSSION

Giving all the more space to AI technologies by means of in HRs operations, the presumptions set out of this investigation underline the concern of building up a culture of acceptance of AI among the workforce. The concern direct effect of AI on the quality of HR services, through a concern indirect one mediated by the acceptance of AI of member of staffs, seems to indicate that the simple implementation of AI tools is not a guarantee to achieve pragmatic results. Organizations should instead create an environment which encourages the member of staffs to use the technologies through comfort as well as confidence. These findings fit through previous investigation, specifically the TAM. This model relatives that how useful as well as easy a technology is to use are key factors in whether people accept it. The large regression coefficients indicated that there was a pragmatic correlation where member of staff s' favorable perceptions of AI's utility in their work was correlated through a higher probability of its adoption and the member of staff s' assessments of HRQS improved as a result. This finding highlights the importance of transparent communication about the relatives as well as effects of AI on HR operations during implementation through the aim of alleviating concerns as well as fostering confidence. As well as, the investigation highlights the need for business units to be proactive in managing potential barriers to acceptance of AI that include apprehensions of job security.

Our investigation relatives that these apprehensions can be a real barrier to the integration of AI technologies, which can thereby limit the potential of AI technologies to enhance the quality of HR services. Consequently, business units should engage member of staff s proactively via training programs, workshops in addition to open dialogues, so they understand how AI is meant to complement their functions as opposed to replacing them. This strategy, in addition to reducing opposition, creates a more pragmatic attitude to the incorporation of AI. The partial mediating effect discovered in this research points to the complexity of the association of AI, member of staff acceptance of AI alongside the quality of the HR services. Although it is fair to say that AI has the strength of providing services autonomously, it is also concern that their relative is increased when the acceptance of AI of member staff is nurtured. This observation thus means business units ought to apply holistic strategies that not only cover technological advancements but also human factors thereby ensuring that AI efforts are supported by proper change management methodologies.

CONCLUSION

The results indicate, that while the direct improvement in HR services is clearly seen by the use of AI, their complete efficacy is dependent on member of staff acceptance of AI as well as active involvement through these technologies. The mediating function of Member of staff Acceptance of AI is particularly interesting, as this not only strengthen the link between AI as well as quality of service, but it also highlights the importance of taking into account member of staff perceptions, as well as apprehensions, throughout the AI integration process.

The findings relative a dual approach to how business units approach integrating AI in HR - focusing on both technological progress and building a supportive workplace of member staff. Through investments in training programs as well as communication channels in addition to the fostering of an accepting administrative culture, business units can relieve the apprehensions of member of staff as well as the added perceived value of AI applications. This strategic alignment is essential to achieve two ends - better quality of service as well as an increase in member of staff satisfaction. Moreover, this investigation gives odds to the current body of information by accentuating the continuous concern of Technology Acceptance of AI Model, just as clarifying the complex contacts amongst the technological adoption, member of staff engagement, just as the service delivery outcomes.

LIMITATIONS

Although it has offered great insights, there are a number of limitations associated with this study that should be noted. To begin with, the study is cross-sectional, and it does not provide causality between AI, employee acceptance, and HR service quality. Longitudinal designs would also be applicable in future research to more accurately reflect shifts in the perception and adoption of technology by employees over the years. Second, the research is based on self-reported data, thereby causing common method bias and subjective evaluation of answers. In spite of the validity measures provided by the use of the statistical means, in the future, the studies should be more thorough to include multi-source data, including assessments of the managers or the output of the system. Third, the research does not specifically consider a single industry or geographical location, and therefore, the generalizability of findings could be restricted. The differences in the organizational culture, technology preparedness, and the economic status among the different regions could affect the results. Lastly, employee acceptance was considered a mediator but no other possible mediating/moderating variables, e.g., organizational trust, leadership style, or technological preparedness, were considered in the research and may be considered in future studies to obtain a more expansive picture.

ETHICAL CONSIDERATIONS

This research is based on the set of ethical principles of conducting research with human subjects. The survey was voluntary, and the objectives of the study were mentioned to the participants before they took part in the survey. Informed consent was taken and the respondents were assured of their confidentiality and anonymity of the answers. No personal data were gathered and the information was intended only to be utilized academically. The present paper, also identifies the ethical concerns linked to the use of AI in HR, especially issues regarding data privacy, transparency, and the possibility of disparities in the decision made by algorithms. To ensure that AI systems do not discriminate against or infringe on the rights of employees, organizations have to implement systems with due responsibility and have explicit guidelines on how AI works. The focus on transparency in AI-conducted decisions and the necessity to achieve a balance between technological efficiency and human dignity also need to be mentioned. These are critical factors to ensuring trust and enhancing the ethical use of AI in HR practices.

REFERENCES

Abuhantash, A. (2023). The future of HR management: Exploring the potential of e-HRM for improving employee experience and organizational outcomes. *World Journal of Advanced Research and Reviews*, *18*(2), 647–651. DOI: 10.30574/wjarr.2023.18.2.0883

Akram, S., Buono, P., & Lanzilotti, R. (2024). Recruitment chatbot acceptance in a company: A mixed method study on human-centered technology acceptance model. *Personal and Ubiquitous Computing*, *28*(6), 961–984. Advance online publication. DOI: 10.1007/s00779-024-01826-4

Arslan, A., Cooper, C. L., Khan, Z., Gölgeci, İ., & Ali, I. (2021). Artificial intelligence and human workers interaction at team level: A conceptual assessment of the challenges and potential HRM strategies. *International Journal of Manpower*, *43*(1), 75–88. DOI: 10.1108/IJM-01-2021-0052

Bhatti, S. A. N., Faqirah, M. R., & Ullah, M. F. (2025). The Future of HR: Exploring the Benefits and Challenges of Digital Transformation. *International Journal of Engineering Business Management*, *9*(1), 67–80. DOI: 10.22161/ijebm.9.1.6

Böhmer, N., & Schinnenburg, H. (2023). Critical exploration of AI-driven HRM to build up organizational capabilities. *Employee Relations*, *45*(5), 1057–1082. DOI: 10.1108/ER-04-2022-0202

Bositkhanova, N., & Dadaboyev, S. M. U. (2025). Revolutionizing workforce planning: The strategic function of AI in HR strategy. *Discover Global Society*, *3*(1), 100. Advance online publication. DOI: 10.1007/s44282-025-00252-y

Choi, Y. (2021). A study of employee acceptance of artificial intelligence technology. *European Journal of Management and Business Economics*, *30*(3), 318–330. DOI: 10.1108/EJMBE-06-2020-0158

Dima, J., Gilbert, M., Dextras-Gauthier, J., & Giraud, L. (2024). The effects of artificial intelligence on human resource activities and the functions of the human resource triad: Opportunities and challenges. *Frontiers in Psychology*, *15*, 1360401. Advance online publication. DOI: 10.3389/fpsyg.2024.1360401 PMID: 38903456

Feng, J., Yu, B., Tan, W. H., Dai, Z., & Li, Z. (2025). Key factors influencing educational technology adoption in higher education: A systematic review [Review of *Key factors influencing educational technology adoption in higher education: A systematic review*]. *PLOS Digital Health, 4*(4). Public Library of Science. DOI: 10.1371/journal.pdig.0000764

Freitas, J. D., Agarwal, S., Schmitt, B. H., & Haslam, N. (2023). Psychological factors underlying attitudes toward AI tools [Review of *Psychological factors underlying attitudes toward AI tools*]. *Nature Human Behaviour, 7*(11), 1845. Nature Portfolio. DOI: 10.1038/s41562-023-01734-2

Iqbal, N., Ahmad, M., & Allen, M. M. C. (2019). Unveiling the relationship between e-HRM, impersonal trust and employee productivity. *Management Research Review*, *42*(7), 879–899. DOI: 10.1108/MRR-02-2018-0094

Leavitt, K., Barnes, C. M., & Shapiro, D. L. (2024). The Function of Human Managers within Algorithmic Performance Management Systems: A Process Model of Employee Trust in Managers through Reflexivity. *Academy of Management Review*, *50*(4), 745–767. DOI: 10.5465/amr.2022.0058

Madanchian, M. (2024). From Recruitment to Retention: AI Tools for Human Resource Decision-Making. *Applied Sciences (Basel, Switzerland)*, *14*(24), 11750. DOI: 10.3390/app142411750

Madanchian, M., & Taherdoost, H. (2025). Barriers and Enablers of AI Adoption in Human Resource Management: A Critical Analysis of Organizational and Technological Factors. *Information (Basel)*, *16*(1), 51. DOI: 10.3390/info16010051

Murire, O. (2024). Artificial Intelligence and Its Function in Shaping Organizational Work Practices and Culture. *Administrative Sciences*, *14*(12), 316. DOI: 10.3390/admsci14120316

Nawaz, N., Arunachalam, H., Pathi, B. K., & Gajenderan, V. (2024). The adoption of artificial intelligence in human resources management practices. *International Journal of Information Management Data Insights*, *4*(1), 100208. DOI: 10.1016/j.jjimei.2023.100208

Olutimehin, D. O., Ofodile, O. C., Ejibe, I., Odunaiya, O. G., & Soyombo, O. T. (2024). IMPLEMENTING AI IN BUSINESS MODELS: STRATEGIES FOR EFFICIENCY AND INNOVATION. *International Journal of Management & Entrepreneurship Research*, *6*(3), 863–877. DOI: 10.51594/ijmer.v6i3.940

Ouakili, O. E. (2025). The impact of Artificial Intelligence (AI) on Recruitment Process. *Open Journal of Business and Management*, *13*(2), 749–762. DOI: 10.4236/ojbm.2025.132039

Panda, G., Dash, M. K., Samadhiya, A., Kumar, A., & Mulat-Weldemeskel, E. (2023). Artificial intelligence as an enabler for achieving human resource resiliency: Past literature, expose debate and future research directions. *International Journal of Industrial Engineering and Operations Management*, *6*(4), 326–347. DOI: 10.1108/IJIEOM-05-2023-0047

Prasad, K., & De, T. (2024). Generative AI as a catalyst for HRM practices: Mediating effects of trust. *Humanities & Social Sciences Communications*, *11*(1), 1362. Advance online publication. DOI: 10.1057/s41599-024-03842-4

Qahtani, E. A., & Alsmairat, M. A. K. (2023). Assisting artificial intelligence adoption drivers in human resources management: A mediation model. *Acta Logistica*, *10*(1), 141–150. DOI: 10.22306/al.v10i1.371

Saeed, M., Maarouf, H. M., & Younis, R. A. A. (2025). The function of HRM-service quality in the relationship between electronic human resource management and perceived performance. *Future Business Journal*, *11*(1), 1. Advance online publication. DOI: 10.1186/s43093-024-00415-4

Setiono, B. A., & Hidayat, S. (2022). Influence of Service Quality with the Dimensions of Reliability, Responsiveness, Assurance, Empathy and Tangibles on Customer Satisfaction. *International Journal of Economics Business and Management Research*, *6*(9), 330–341. DOI: 10.51505/IJEBMR.2022.6924

Shen, P., Wan, D., & Zhu, A. Z. X. (2024). Investigating the effect of AI service quality on consumer well-being in retail context. *Service Business*, *19*(1), 5. Advance online publication. DOI: 10.1007/s11628-024-00575-x

SimanTov-Nachlieli, I. (2025, January). I. (2024). More to Lose: The Adverse Effect of High Performance Ranking on Employees' Preimplementation Attitudes Toward the Integration of Powerful AI Aids. *Organization Science*, *36*(1), 1–20. Advance online publication. DOI: 10.1287/orsc.2023.17515

Wassan, S. (2021). How Artificial Intelligence Transforms the Experience of Employees. *Türk Bilgisayar ve Matematik Eğitimi Dergisi*, *12*(10), 7116. DOI: 10.17762/turcomat.v12i10.5603

Yu, L., Li, Y., & Fan, F. (2023). Employees' Appraisals and Trust of Artificial Intelligences' Transparency and Opacity. *Behavioral Sciences (Basel, Switzerland)*, *13*(4), 344. DOI: 10.3390/bs13040344 PMID: 37102857

Zhang, P. (2024). Application of Artificial Intelligence (AI) in Recruitment and Selection: The Case of Company A and Company B. *Journal of Business and Management Studies*, *6*(3), 224. DOI: 10.32996/jbms.2024.6.3.18

KEY TERMS AND DEFINITIONS

AI (AI): AI describes computer systems designed to has well as le tasks usually needing human smarts. This includes learning, reasoning, making decisions, as well as solving problems, often using methods like machine learning as well as data analysis.

Human Resource (HR) Services: HR services cover the various activities as well as functions the HR department uses to manage member of staff s. This includes hiring, training as well as development, performance reviews, pay, as well as member of staff relations.

Staff Acceptance of AI: Member of staff acceptance of AI denotes the extent to which member of staff s are inclined to embrace, utilize, as well as endorse novel technologies, including AI, predicated on their assessments of the technology's utility, user-friendliness, as well as their confidence in the system.

Quality of Service: Quality of service pertains to the degree to which a service fulfills or surpasses user anticipations, frequently evaluated through dimensions encompassing reliability, responsiveness, assurance, as well as the efficiency of service provision.

Chapter 5 Between Efficiency and Fairness: Algorithmic Discrimination in AI-Based Recruitment Systems

Müjde Ertürk
http://orcid.org/0009-0001-8105-665X
Anadolu University, Turkey

Emrah Ayhan
http://orcid.org/0000-0001-6152-7509
Anadolu University, Turkey

ABSTRACT

This chapter examines how AI-based recruitment systems can produce algorithmic discrimination against job candidates. While these systems are widely used to improve efficiency in screening and selection processes, they may reproduce historical biases and disadvantage groups such as women, ethnic minorities, older individuals, and candidates with health conditions. The study is based on a qualitative content analysis of approximately 40 documents published between 2016 and 2025. The findings show that discrimination emerges from the interaction of multiple technical and social factors rather than a single source. Accordingly, the chapter develops a six-factor framework and offers policy recommendations to improve fairness, transparency, and accountability in AI-based recruitment systems.

DOI: 10.4018/979-8-2600-2303-7.ch005

1. INTRODUCTION

A growing body of interdisciplinary research emphasizes that algorithmic recruitment tools increasingly shape access to employment, career mobility, and socio-economic welfare. As organizations automate recruitment to manage growing applicant pools in their human resources management, the use of machine learning transforms recruitment from a human-evaluative activity into a computational optimization process. This transformation has significant implications not only for individual candidates but also for labor markets. Decisions that are based on Artificial Intelligence (AI) influence who gets interviewed, who is shortlisted, and who is ultimately hired, thus redistributing opportunities within society.

As a response to rising concerns about algorithmic biases, this chapter aims to investigate the key factors that contribute to discriminatory outcomes in AI-based recruitment processes. AI-based systems are now widely integrated into organizational decision-making processes within different sectors. Since the 2010s, many companies have begun using AI for recruitment, performance reviews, and personnel management (ENAR, 2020: 3). A report by Sydney Myers indicates that nearly all Fortune 500 companies (97.4%) employ AI in their recruitment practices (Purcell & Bonnefon, 2023). This is mainly due to new AI systems that help companies to manage many applications, reduce costs, and identify the right candidates. Sometimes, AI even conducts online interviews to assess how candidates sound and look.

Nowadays, AI-based recruitment systems, commonly referred to as Applicant Tracking Systems (ATS), have recently become a source of controversy. These systems are helpful, but they might also be unfair according to some studies in the literature. The primary issue is that AI learns from human data. This means human biases can be reflected in machines. ATS can sometimes increase existing algorithmic discrimination. For example, previous studies reveal that it is still rare to see women and non-white individuals in leadership roles, such as CEOs or in tech jobs. Companies sometimes use these systems to recruit individuals who are similar to their current employees, such as the same race, gender (mostly male), graduates from the same schools, or those with the same hobbies. For instance, Bayana (2025) argues that immigrants, people with disabilities, women, and people with non-American names are more likely to be filtered out by ATS because of these biases. Similarly, Bertrand and Mullainathan (2004) show that women who take time off for pregnancy and people with non-traditional work histories are often seen as less qualified. In large companies, most top executives are white men. This pattern suggests that AI can reinforce the idea that effective leaders are mainly white men.

ATS often uses outdated data. This may repeat old patterns and cause algorithmic discrimination. For example, Amazon's AI hiring system disadvantaged female candidates because it learned from biased past data (Dastin, 2018). Activision

Blizzard also faced legal action over discriminatory hiring practices and workplace inequalities (BBC News, 2021). More recently, Sheetz Inc. was reported to have excluded candidates from some racial groups through automated background checks (Rubinkam, 2024). These cases show that when AI relies on biased or outdated data, it can reinforce existing inequalities instead of reducing them.

In general, the use of AI in Human Resources (HR) has increased rapidly in recent years. This trend has raised important ethical and governance issues. AI-based screening tools can also carry biases from past data. In this context, the chapter addresses an important gap in understanding intersectional algorithmic discrimination in recruitment. In this direction, the study is organized as follows. The first section presents the problems, purpose, significance, research question, and limitations of the study. The second section reviews the main concepts. It covers AI-based recruitment systems, types of discrimination in hiring, and key theories on algorithmic bias. The third section explains the research design and methods used in this study. The fourth section provides a detailed analysis and discusses the main findings on the drivers of algorithmic discrimination in AI-based recruitment systems. The study ends with a conclusion section that summarizes the results. This section also offers recommendations for policymakers, researchers, and others interested in fair and accountable AI-based recruitment systems.

1.1 Research Problem

A significant issue regarding "algorithmic discrimination" might be the "algorithm" itself. This is because algorithms in recruitment processes are created by various types of data. Firstly, biases can be accidentally or purposely transferred to the algorithms, which can cause unfairness in recruitment processes. Similarly, using outdated data, relying on old resumes, or allowing AI to make assumptions (for example, inferring a candidate's religion or nationality based on their residential address) can also lead to algorithmic discrimination (Mittelstadt et al., 2016).

Another problem is that AI is often a black box, so it is difficult to understand why it makes specific decisions. It is often impossible to determine the exact reason behind an algorithmic decision, which complicates identifying the source of discrimination (Todoli-Signes, 2019). Therefore, these kinds of issues often cannot be easily detected until a significant incident occurs, complaints from users arise, or digital experts conduct investigations.

The type of algorithm embedded in the ATS of the recruitment mechanism is another issue. For instance, game-based systems, AI-based video interviews (Oğuz, 2024), resume screening, predictions, and chatbots (Bozkurt Gümrükçüoğlu & Yakacak, 2024) can all create different types of discrimination. For example, companies like AstraZeneca utilize game-based recruitment systems; however, these can be disadvantageous for individuals with attention deficit disorder, dyslexia, disabilities, or older adults who are unfamiliar with video games (Sonderling et al., 2022). Accordingly, if video interview algorithms are trained on how a particular group speaks or looks, they can unfairly exclude people who do not fit that model. Therefore, as mentioned in the next section, this chapter aims to identify the factors contributing to algorithmic discrimination in AI-based recruitment systems as a research problem.

1.2 Purpose of the Research and Research Question

This chapter aims to guide policymakers and organizational leaders in understanding how biases emerge in AI recruitment processes. It follows the full lifecycle of AI, from dataset design to model deployment. In this way, it shows where policy interventions can reduce discrimination risks. Therefore, the study focuses on AI-based recruitment systems, especially ATS. It aims to identify the causes of discrimination in these systems. The main research question is: "*What factors cause algorithmic discrimination in AI-based recruitment systems?*" This question guides the analysis of companies that use AI in human resources management. The findings show different types of algorithmic discrimination and their causes. It is important to note that "algorithmic bias" and "algorithmic discrimination" are sometimes used together in some studies, but they are not the same. Algorithmic bias refers to unfair patterns in decision-making that can lead to discrimination against certain individuals or groups (Bozkurt Gümrükçüoğlu & Yakacak, 2024). Algorithmic discrimination, on the other hand, reflects these biased outcomes in practice. These outcomes often come from patterns in past data. It is also important to note that humans design and use these systems. Their goals and decisions can shape how algorithms work. Therefore, this chapter seeks to identify the main factors that lead to discrimination in AI-based recruitment systems.

1.3 Significance of the Research

As AI is now more common in HR systems around the world, understanding algorithmic discrimination has become more important for academic and practical needs. Recently, organizations have faced legal, ethical, and reputational risks when discrimination occurs. For this reason, this study is important for compliance and risk management in the literature. The findings can also support current debates on fairness, diversity, and inclusion in the digital workplace. In this context, the chapter produces solutions for policymakers, human resource professionals, and decision-makers who design, regulate, or use AI-based recruitment systems.

Although AI is now widely used in human resources management, it is still a new technology, and there is uncertainty about how it works in recruitment processes. AI can process large amounts of data, run continuously, and produce results quickly. It can also analyze applications more efficiently. At the same time, online job applications have made it easier to apply for positions. This has increased the number of applicants for each job. As a result, employers often face a very large pool of candidates. In such a competitive environment, applications should be evaluated fairly and based on skills. For example, many companies and international organizations rely on AI-based recruitment systems to manage this process. However, if these systems contain errors, even unintentionally, qualified candidates may be excluded. For this reason, this chapter aims to show how these systems can be used effectively without creating unfair outcomes.

In the literature, the number of studies on AI-based recruitment is increasing. Most of these studies focus on a single type of discrimination, such as gender or race. In addition, many studies examine only the technical side of algorithms. They often do not link these issues to broader social structures. This creates a gap in understanding how different biases interact in real recruitment processes. In this sense, this study aims to address this gap. It brings together different types of algorithmic discrimination in one framework. It looks at both technical factors, such as outdated data and model design, and social factors, such as gender, ethnicity, and age. It examines how these factors work together to produce discriminatory outcomes. In this way, the study offers a more integrated perspective. This approach can better support policymakers and organizations in building fair and accountable AI-based recruitment systems.

1.4 Limitations of the Research

AI models continue to change through retraining. For this reason, the findings of this study might need to be reviewed over time, because biases can appear again when data collection practices or model settings change. This study uses secondary sources such as books, articles, newspapers, and reports from international organizations. The data comes from cases involving companies that were reported to use or be linked to algorithmic discrimination in recruitment. The main limitation is the reliance on these published sources. In most cases, identifying discrimination requires a detailed investigation with both employers and candidates. This was not possible in this study. Therefore, the analysis is based on content analysis of secondary materials, and the results should be interpreted with caution. Another limitation concerns the scope of the cases. Most examples come from the United States and Europe. This may limit the generalizability of the findings to other regions with different legal systems, labor market structures, and levels of technological development. Despite these limitations, the study provides a systematic and theoretically significant understanding of algorithmic discrimination in AI-based human resources contexts.

1.5 Theoretical and Empirical Research on Algorithmic Discrimination

Recent empirical studies have improved our understanding of algorithmic discrimination. They show that models learn patterns in data that can be linked to protected characteristics. Experimental findings show that resume-screening systems may prefer language patterns that are mainly associated with men. They may also penalize candidates based on small linguistic cues. On the other hand, different studies found that algorithmic discrimination is not the same in every sector. It varies across industries. For example, the technology and finance sectors show different risk patterns. These differences are related to their recruitment practices and data systems.

In the literature, two theories mention discrimination in AI-based recruitment systems: "critical algorithm theory" and "social dominance theory". The former one highlights the risks and problems associated with big datasets embedded in algorithms (Karakoç Keskin & Demirel, 2025). According to Lee (2018), the most important feature of algorithms is that they are based on big data, algorithm engineering, and computing power. Machine learning algorithms play a significant role in making decisions with big datasets. With deep learning models, algorithms can even convert speech into text, analyze videos, process the data they collect, and continue learning autonomously. However, Gillespie (2014) argues that since human beings embed the codes in the algorithms, "the automation of human judgment" takes place. In addition, "critical algorithm" studies emphasize that algorithms are not only technical codes, but also mechanisms that shape personal and social life. In this sense, the concepts of objectivity, equality, liability, and impartiality are still debated (Karakoç Keskin & Demirel, 2025). Many studies in the literature argue that algorithms are influenced by dominant social, economic, political, and cultural orientations during data processing (Zwitter, 2014; Iliadis & Russo, 2016; Herschel & Miori, 2017).

Social dominance theory, on the other hand, argues that human societies are organized hierarchically because the society is composed of various groups of different status levels (Ho et al., 2012). Status refers to the position of a group with specific characteristics in society. According to this theory, factors such as gender, race, ethnicity, and age determine social status and hierarchy. Dominant groups categorize others in lower categories based on these factors, and this causes discrimination. Considering that today's AI-based recruitment systems are developed within these hierarchical structures, they can disadvantage minority, excluded, and lower-status groups. Therefore, this theory examines how various factors interact with one another. These include social roles, psychological tendencies, ideologies, cultures, and social identities. It also explores discriminatory practices at the individual, group, and institutional levels (Raghavan et al., 2020). Thus, it provides an important perspective to this study, because critical algorithm theory focuses on the technical sources of bias, while social dominance theory includes bias within larger social hierarchies.

Recently, many candidates have reported feelings of anxiety when interacting with these systems, because these systems might lack transparent feedback mechanisms. Therefore, these cases increase trust and raise concerns about the fairness of AI evaluations. In this regard, corporate practices shape AI implementation because many organizations are adopting AI-based tools without critically assessing the assumptions embedded in their data models. HR departments often default to vendor templates, so they mistakenly believe that technology can always enhance processes autonomously. Since these systems operate on statistical patterns rather than context, they might fail to recognize significant candidate qualities and exclude individuals who deviate from established data profiles due to narrow views of merit.

The intersection of AI recruitment and social inequality complicates these issues, especially for underrepresented or disadvantaged groups. These groups might face constraints such as limited access to digital training and professional networks, compared to other candidates. Additionally, AI-based systems favor well-organized resumes and conventional communication styles, which in turn disadvantage those presenting non-traditional qualifications. This shows that algorithmic bias is not merely a technical concern but also intertwined with existing societal structures of privilege.

Literature on this topic highlights specific discrimination cases associated with AI recruitment systems, such as Amazon's biases against women and Workday's ethnic discrimination complaints (Bayana, 2025). These findings underline a re-evaluation of discrimination approaches in technology and emphasize the need to consider how AI intersects with social inequalities. In another study, Pal et al. (2022) outlined the functioning, steps, data collection, and analysis processes of machine learning programs, including Naive Bayes, Random Forest, and SVM. Researchers obtained data from job announcements and resumes posted on popular job websites. They removed unnecessary text and analyzed the content by dividing it into sections. And then, they traced the words to their sources and assigned importance levels to them. They concluded that a model called "Random Forest" is the most successful for resume screening. This research helps realize the models used for ATS programs. In order to evaluate objectivity in AI-based systems, Torralba and

Ali (2024) surveyed different human resources specialists and reported that 69% of those questioned expressed concerns about the objectivity of these systems' decision-making. On the other hand, according to research conducted by Textio, a language analysis technology company, the words used by the companies in job advertisements directly exclude certain groups (The People Space, 2020). Therefore, McDonald has requested that the company instruct its employees to create job postings that contain no gender-based language.

Lawsuits filed in the US regarding algorithmic discrimination have also touched on the topic of this research. Companies like Hilton, IKEA, Vodafone, and international organizations such as NATO use an AI-based recruitment system called "HireVue". This system has been criticized for producing incorrect and inaccurate facial recognition results (Electronic Privacy Information Center, 2019). Although the company denies this, every AI and video-based system has capabilities such as facial recognition, analyzing facial expressions, and interpreting them. It has also been determined that the system is based on algorithmic models that compare new candidates with those who can best use the system. Similarly, Amazon has also been criticized for gender discrimination due to the AI-based system in its recruitment processes. Reuters News Agency interviewed the engineers who developed the algorithms of an AI tool in Amazon that discriminated during recruitment based on gender. These individuals, who wished to remain unknown, stated that the algorithm discriminated against female candidates (Dastin, 2018).

In another study, 950 experts participated in a 28-question survey to determine the answer to the following fundamental question: "*How exactly is AI changing workplace life?*" (McKinsey & Company, 2024). These experts work in the finance, technology, IT, education, construction, manufacturing, healthcare, and resource management sectors, which are especially affected by AI in the US and the United Kingdom (the UK). The key findings for this study are as follows. Firstly, the most frequently reported issues related to AI in recruitment were "bias in recruitment" (40%), "privacy concerns" (37.2%), and "legality issues" (30.7%). Secondly, the most significant concerns of human resources personnel conducting recruitment are AI systems' excessive focus on keywords (31.2%), misjudgment of social skills (26.3%), and over-trust in past data (15.5%).

According to another study, AI systems preferred names associated with white people by 85%. In comparison, female names were only 11%, and black male names were not even mentioned among 550 resumes, according to a joint study conducted in the US by the Association for the Advancement of Artificial Intelligence and the Association for Computing Machinery Conference on AI, Ethics and Society (Crist, 2024). Similarly, Wilson & Çalışkan (2024) analyzed resumes that were white, black, male, and female names using models from Mistral AI, Salesforce, and Contextual

AI companies. They discovered that AI systems favored white names by 85%, black names by 9%, male names by 52%, and female names by 11% (Crist, 2024).

The theoretical framework of this study is based on two main perspectives: critical algorithm theory and social dominance theory. Critical algorithm theory explains how bias emerges from technical elements. These include datasets, model design, and implementation processes. It shows that algorithms can reproduce past inequalities because they learn from historical data (Mittelstadt et al., 2016). On the other hand, social dominance theory focuses on the social dimension. It explains how inequalities based on gender, ethnicity, age, and social status are maintained in society. Such inequalities can also be found in recruitment systems, as these systems reflect the existing social hierarchies (Ho et al., 2012).

This combination of views allows a better understanding of algorithmic discrimination, since this type of discrimination reflects both technical and social dynamics. Technical bias arises from data quality and model design, while social bias stems from existing labor market inequalities. In this sense, this study examines variables such as gender, ethnic background, age, outdated data, health conditions, and sectoral dynamics, which reflect these different perspectives. Although existing literature is expanding, there is a significant gap, because previous research has not analyzed these factors collectively within the framework of AI-based recruitment. The subsequent section will elaborate on the fundamental concepts of AI-driven recruitment systems and the issue of algorithmic discrimination.

2. CONCEPTS RELATED TO AI AND ALGORITHMIC DISCRIMINATION

AI-based recruitment systems benefit from new technologies such as natural language processing (NLP), facial analysis, and predictive modeling, but there are still fairness issues about these technologies. NLP tools can misinterpret emotional tones or complex linguistic features, while facial analysis may perform inadequately for women and individuals from diverse ethnic groups with different skin tones. Algorithmic discrimination can be understood within the socio-technical systems framework, because it interacts with cultural norms and organizational structures. To eliminate discrimination, both technical and organizational changes are essential. AI encompasses a wide range of computational methods that still need human control.

Modern deep learning systems are based on pattern recognition within large datasets, but they may also reproduce existing biases found in that data (Raghavan et al., 2020). Similarly, Large language models (LLMs) in the recruitment process might present new biases, such as semantic and language-related biases, which can also lead to algorithmic discrimination. These models are trained on extensive online texts, so this makes them susceptible to perpetuating existing stereotypes found within that data. Therefore, recent studies suggest that LLM-based screening tools may unintentionally disadvantage certain candidates, potentially influenced by gendered language or race-related indicators (Gallegos et al., 2024).

This section explores key concepts, including "AI", "machine learning", "Applicant Tracking Systems" (ATS), and "algorithmic discrimination", which are foundational to the study. "AI" is defined as systems that can replicate or exceed human cognitive abilities, encompassing computers and robots. AI's capabilities include understanding human language, so they can rapidly analyze complex data, and identify connections between data sets. This is why AI implementation in human resources significantly decreases labor and cost challenges for companies. On the other hand, "machine learning" refers to AI systems that can interpret data and make judgments (Columbia Engineering, 2025).

Machine learning requires algorithms that are a "deep" style of learning, enabling AI to interpret events, situations, and results, thereby acting as the human brain through algorithm-based machine learning. Algorithms are the building blocks of machine learning, providing commands, rules, and operations that enable artificial intelligence systems to function (IBM, 2025). Four key elements of algorithms might cause algorithmic discrimination: datasets, model structure, metrics, and implementation (Langenkamp et al., 2019). For instance, Kim (2017) emphasized that incomplete datasets, consciously biased data, outdated data, and prejudices can lead to discrimination. On the other hand, model structure refers to whether the AI is being used appropriately for its intended purpose. Similarly, metrics measure the model's performance and provide numerical values that reflect its operation. Finally, implementation involves the risk that the AI legitimizes existing biases within the system.

ATS systems create job postings, collect the applications, review resumes, schedule interviews, communicate between candidates and human resources personnel, archive information, and prepare reports on recruitment metrics (Sweeeft, 2025). However, certain types of discrimination may occur during the recruitment process. Previously, AI systems in human resources management were mainly limited to only payroll, benefits, and compensation tasks (Black & Van Esch, 2021). They became widely used in various applications in the late 2000s, primarily as chatbots gained popularity. By the 2010s, these programs were able to do talent evaluations and decision-making. Thus, as AI systems advanced, they became capable of analyzing complex data faster and more effectively, making them popular among companies that wanted to save time and money in recruitment processes.

This study focuses on the factors that cause algorithmic discrimination in AI-based ATS during recruitment. Research in this field typically begins by examining "machine learning algorithms" because the key issue is the data that is used by these algorithms. In other words, datasets are the foundation of machine learning (Oğuz, 2024). Assuming that the datasets given to the algorithm contain intentionally biased codes. In such cases, this leads to what is known as "direct discrimination".

People can be disadvantaged and restricted in opportunities due to factors such as language, religion, ethnicity, nationality, gender, or age (Amnesty International Türkiye, n.d.). Similarly, algorithms may also cause "indirect discrimination". In this type, there may not be an explicit intention to discriminate, but a particular group is still disproportionately negatively affected compared to others. This is called "intersectional discrimination", which occurs when different forms of discrimination combine and disadvantage particular groups (Amnesty International Türkiye, n.d.).

Although international law does not yet provide a single and comprehensive framework specifically governing algorithmic discrimination in recruitment, recent legal and policy developments show growing regulatory attention to this issue. Several legal frameworks already address automated decision-making and AI-based employment practices, including the Illinois Artificial Intelligence Video Interview Act, the New York City Automated Employment Decision Tools Law, the Equal Employment Opportunity Commission guidelines, and the AI Bill of Rights (Dargan, 2023). More recently, the European Union Artificial Intelligence Act has classified employment-related AI systems as high-risk and emphasized requirements such as risk management, data governance, transparency, human oversight, and post-market monitoring (European Parliament and Council of the European Union, 2024). Similarly, the National Institute of Standards and Technology (NIST) (2023) AI Risk Management Framework provides a broader governance approach for identifying, measuring, managing, and monitoring AI-related risks across organizational contexts. However, these frameworks still differ in their legal scope, enforcement mechanisms, and level of applicability to recruitment systems.

3. RESEARCH METHODOLOGY

This section explains the variables, hypotheses, research question, sample, data collection method, and analysis technique used in the study. This research design aims to examine the conditions under which algorithmic discrimination emerges within AI-based recruitment processes. Therefore, as mentioned earlier, the research question of this study is "*What are the main factors that contribute to algorithmic discrimination in AI-based recruitment systems?*".

This study uses a qualitative research design to examine the factors that contribute to algorithmic discrimination in AI-based recruitment systems. Considering that there is limited accessibility of proprietary algorithms and internal recruitment data of companies, a qualitative approach was used as a suitable framework to analyze documented cases, reports, and empirical studies. Therefore, the study is based on qualitative content analysis, which allows a systematic evaluation of patterns, themes, and relationships within textual data. This approach is particularly appropriate for exploring complex socio-technical issues such as algorithmic discrimination, because it is not easy to make direct observation and evaluation. Rather than testing causal relationships through statistical methods, the study aims to interpret repeating factors that contribute to discriminatory outcomes in AI-based recruitment processes.

Based on the existing literature, the study develops a conceptual framework that includes six key dimensions:

- Gender and Sexual Orientation (Gillmore, 2024; The Pew Research, 2023; Wang & Kosinski, 2018).
- Ethnic Background (color, language, religion, race, etc.) (Dargan, 2023; Thijssen et al., 2020; Yin et al., 2024).
- Age (Hunter, 2024; Pew Research Center, 2023; Quesada & Martínez de Lafuente, 2024).
- Outdated Data (e.g., previous résumés, old decisions, outdated datasets, excessive focus on keywords, misinterpretation of social skills) (Dastin, 2018; Kim, 2017; Mittelstadt et al., 2016; O'Neil, 2016)
- Health Conditions (e.g., chronic health issues, disabilities) (American Civil Liberties Union, 2024; Polson et al., 2024)
- Applied Sector (Bozkurt Gümrükçüoğlu & Yakacak, 2024; Fitzpatrick et al., 2024)

These dimensions are not considered statistically testable independent variables. They are rather analytical categories that guide the coding and interpretation process. The research sample consists of companies where the use of AI-based recruitment systems has been identified as likely to produce algorithmic discrimination. In this regard, 40 documents between 2016 and 2025, including peer-reviewed academic articles, policy reports and institutional publications, news reports and documented legal cases, and industry analyses and survey findings, were reviewed to identify cases where algorithmic discrimination occurred. The selection criteria for these secondary sources are relevance to AI-based recruitment systems, evidence or discussion of algorithmic bias or discrimination, and empirical or case-based insights into recruitment practices. This purposive sampling strategy ensures that the dataset reflects diverse contexts and sectors where algorithmic discrimination has been reported.

The analysis follows a thematic content analysis method, which helps to identify repeating patterns of algorithmic discrimination. It also supports the study by linking these patterns to both technical and social dimensions in the theoretical framework. This type of analysis enables the evaluation and explanation of written or visual sources within a systematic structure through coding, categorization, or sampling (Metin & Ünal, 2022). It enables researchers to read social reality inductively, remain objective, and utilize various sources in a manner that ensures generalizability, validity, and testability (Tavşancıl & Aslan, 2001). It is a widely used method in social sciences to define research problems, propose hypotheses, collect data, and analyze it. The most important step in this method is selecting the sample. While the research population defines the overall scope, the sample determines its boundaries (Alanka, 2024). If it is not possible to collect data from the entire population, the sample should represent the most relevant cases. This involves asking and answering the questions of "*where, when, with what tool, and on which topic*" (Koçak & Arun, 2006).

The content analysis process consists of three main stages. Firstly, "initial coding" was used to review relevant documents, and then meaningful units related to discrimination were identified. The coding process followed an inductive approach that allowed categories to emerge from the data rather than imposing a priori. Secondly, codes were grouped under broader categories that encompass the six analytical dimensions. Finally, patterns across cases were examined to identify how different factors contribute to algorithmic discrimination. This procedure addressed repeating mechanisms and cross-case similarities, rather than producing statistically generalizable results.

4. FINDINGS AND DISCUSSIONS

Companies around the world are rapidly increasing their investment in AI-based recruitment systems in human resources (Kumar, 2024). These systems are used for resume screening, ranking candidates, evaluating interviews, and making final hiring decisions. In addition, studies show that these tools save time and make processes faster. However, they also carry a significant risk of algorithmic discrimination.

The use of AI in recruitment varies across regions. In North America, about 68% of organizations use AI-based recruitment tools. This shows strong technological capacity and early adoption of digital HR practices. In Europe (60%), Asia-Pacific (59%), and Latin America (58%), adoption rates are similar. These results highlight that both developed and developing economies are increasingly using AI to improve hiring processes. In contrast, the Middle East has a lower adoption rate, at 48%. This may be due to slower digital transformation, regulatory barriers, or limited access to AI solutions (IBM, 2023; Cardillo, 2025). Kumar (2024) reports that global investment in AI-based recruitment systems has increased from 200 million dollars to about 1.2 billion dollars. This shows a clear rise in technical readiness across regions. It reflects improvements in infrastructure, legal frameworks, and workforce skills needed to use these tools. As multinational companies adopt AI more widely in human resources, these systems may be adapted to different contexts. This includes social, economic, and regulatory conditions in various regions.

Table 1. Share of Companies Using AI in Human Resources Management by Region

Region	Companies Using AI in Recruitment (%)
North America	68
Europe	60
Asia-Pacific	59
Latin America	58
Middle East	48

Source: (IBM, 2023; Cardillo, 2025; IBM, 2025)

Although the use of AI-based systems in recruitment processes is increasing, public attitudes towards their application in decision-making are still suspicious. A survey by the Pew Research Center (2023) included 11,004 American adults. It indicated that 71% of participants were against the use of AI for final recruitment decisions. In the initial evaluation of job applications, 41% opposed the use of AI, while 28% were in favor, and the rest of the participants indicated uncertainty. Moreover, 66% indicated hesitance to pursue roles that integrate AI in the recruitment process. Respondents voiced apprehensions regarding the reduced significance of human judgment, the constraints of AI in assessing evolving human behaviors, and the possibility of racial or other biases (The Pew Research Center, 2023). Therefore, public doubt is still a problem for fully automating decision-making in human resources management. These examples show the tension between technological progress and social reliability, which is why AI-based recruitment tools need to be open, fair, and supervised by people.

Table 2. Thematic Coding of Algorithmic Discrimination in Recruitment Systems

Factor	Evidence Type	Context	Key Finding	Mechanism	Source
Gender	Case study	Amazon (USA, tech sector)	Female candidates disadvantaged	Historical male-dominated training data	Dastin (2018)
	Empirical study	Healthcare / Technology sectors	Bias against women in leadership roles	Stereotypical role associations	Noble (2018)
Ethnicity	Case study	Sheetz Inc. (USA, retail)	Minority candidates are disproportionately excluded	Automated background screening	Rubinkam (2024)
	Experimental study	Resume screening (LLM-based)	White-associated names preferred (~85%)	Embedded dataset bias	Milne (2024)
Age	Literature-based evidence	Recruitment systems (general)	Older candidates disadvantaged	Historical hiring patterns	Raghavan et al. (2020); Rieke & Bogen (2018)
Health	Literature-based evidence	AI screening systems	Health-related bias in candidate evaluation	Proxy discrimination	Rieke & Bogen (2018); Barocas & Selbst (2016)
Sector	Case study	Activision Blizzard (gaming)	Gender bias reinforced by sector culture	Organizational norms	BBC News (2021)
	Empirical study	India (open-source AI hiring)	Women offered lower compensation	Sectoral + gender interaction	Sivakaminathan & Musi (2025); Greiner (2025)
General perception	Survey	USA (Pew Research)	Minorities perceive AI as unfair	Structural inequality reflected in AI	Pew Research Center (2023)
Data quality	Conceptual / empirical	Multiple contexts	Outdated data reproduces bias	Temporal bias in datasets	Barocas & Selbst (2016); Mehrabi et al. (2021)

Source: Prepared by the authors based on the reviewed literature

The findings of this study are based on a qualitative content analysis of documented cases, empirical studies, and institutional reports. Therefore, the analysis reveals that algorithmic discrimination in AI-based recruitment systems does not emerge from a single source. Instead, it results from the interaction of multiple technical and social factors across different stages of the recruitment process, because the coding process revealed repeating patterns within the reviewed cases. These patterns were grouped under six analytical dimensions, and the findings below present how these categories emerged from the data. These insights are further illustrated in Table 2, which consolidates the various findings from real-world examples, experimental studies, and survey data. Overall, the findings show that algorithmic discrimination is a context-dependent and multi-dimensional issue. Rather than being driven by a single factor, it emerges through the interaction of data, organizational practices, and broader social inequalities.

4.1 Gender and Sexual Orientation

Previous studies, like Amazon's discontinued recruitment tool (Dastin, 2018) and various analyses by different scholars (Bayana, 2025; Wang & Kosinski, 2018), underline that gender-related biases frequently emerge in AI-based recruitment systems. Evidence from these studies shows that these systems may reproduce existing gender inequalities, particularly when trained on historically imbalanced datasets. Considering this, recent studies enhance human comprehension by quantifying the manifestations of gender and sexual orientation bias through sophisticated rhetorical analysis, prompt engineering, and extensive LLM testing. For instance, Sivakaminathan & Musi (2025) show that job descriptions in fields where men are more common mostly talk about agentic traits and technical skills. On the other hand, people who work in fields where women are more common value warmth and social skills. These differences in description are then reflected in how ChatGPT screens resumes, favoring "male, or woman-coded" traits (Cardillo, 2025). Similarly, Computerworld's report on the open-source model study shows that AI tools used in India to evaluate resumes show a statistically negative discrimination toward female candidates when choosing between candidates who are equally qualified (Greiner, 2025).

An et al. (2025) created a dataset which includes GPT-3.5 Turbo, GPT-4, Claude 3.5, Llama 3, and others. They found that gender and race biases still exist even when attributes unrelated to protected identities are held constant. They observe that women and racial minorities are systematically undervalued in entry-level job candidate assessments. Similarly, Gillmore (2024) states that three candidates sued a recruitment tool named Get Best Talent, which was developed by California AI and used by Money Bank in London. One of them (female) claimed discrimination based on gender, another one on race (black), and the other one on age (61 years old). Although they asked the decision-makers to get the algorithm, they were denied. The court acknowledged only the possibility of gender discrimination but ruled that there was no concrete evidence (Gillmore, 2024). Finally, Hire Vue is another widely used system, which was found to show bias: 84% in distinguishing between heterosexual and gay candidates, and 74% in discriminating against women (Wang & Kosinski, 2018).

This chapter gives a more detailed picture of how and where these kinds of biases form in AI-based recruitment systems. When job postings use gendered language, the AI system gives more weight to some candidate qualifications than others. Second, empirical studies do not sufficiently examine sexual orientation. However, some "norms" are built into language and behavior that use pronouns like heterosexual or not showing any sign of being LGBTQ+. In turn, these languages and behaviors could still hurt candidates who have different lifestyles and sexual preferences. The relative invisibility of sexual orientation data contributes to bias, as the lack of representation encourages default normative assumptions. Thirdly, when biases are evaluated through an intersectional lens (gender & race), big differences show up, especially for women who are not white. For example, the UW name-ranking study shows clear differences in selection rates. When race is considered, "female-associated names" were selected about 11% of the time, while "male-associated names" were selected about 52% of the time (Milne, 2024).

Raghavan et al. (2020) demonstrate that candidate-ranking algorithms frequently disadvantage applicants with career breaks, which disproportionately affects women and caregivers. Their findings indicate that such algorithms prioritize linear career processes over actual competencies and fail to consider structural inequalities in employment histories. Similarly, Lambrecht and Tucker (2019) underline a related concern in job advertising, where women are less likely to encounter advertisements for higher-paying positions on automated job platforms. This discrepancy stems from the algorithms' cost-efficiency and leads to biased exposure even without direct hiring biases.

Gerards and Xenidis (2021) conducted a study across Spain, Germany, and Italy, revealing that resumes with non-European names received fewer callbacks. This disparity is increased by automated screening tools, which can perpetuate cultural and linguistic biases within local labor markets. Additionally, similar trends are observed in video interviews. For instance, Chen (2023) argues that AI-based assessments tend to disadvantage candidates exhibiting regional accents or differing speech patterns. Remarkably, these biases persist even when controlling for candidates' education and job skills, indicating that language traits may serve as indirect criteria for exclusion.

The presented studies highlight persistent biases related to gender and sexual orientation within AI systems, manifesting in training data, evaluation criteria, and recruitment system design. The intersection of race and gender exacerbates these biases. To eliminate these risks, it is essential to implement several measures, such as ensuring data balance, employing neutral language, establishing fair assessment criteria, and regularly reviewing outcomes based on gender and sexual orientation. The findings indicate that these biases exist in various stages of AI-based assessments, which shows that they are systemic rather than isolated issues.

From a theoretical perspective, these findings reflect social dominance theory, as gender hierarchies that are embedded in labor markets are reproduced through algorithmic decision-making. At the same time, critical algorithm theory explains how biased training data and model design contribute to these outcomes.

4.2 Ethnic Background

A survey by the Pew Research Center (2023) points out ongoing concerns regarding racial bias in AI-based systems. The findings show that 37% of respondents consider this type of bias as a significant issue, particularly among minorities. 64% of Black, 49% of Asian, and 41% of Hispanic participants feel that AI-based recruitment systems treat them unfairly. On the contrary, 47% believe AI can be more objective, and 44% think it better matches candidates to jobs. Empirical studies determine these biases by indicating that resumes featuring names linked to whites are favored approximately 85% of the time, while those associated with non-white men are rarely selected (Milne, 2024). A recent case involving Sheetz Inc. illustrates this problem as the company faces allegations of using automated background checks that disproportionately eliminated Black, Indian, and multi-racial applicants (Rubinkam, 2024). These examples demonstrate how AI-based systems can perpetuate racial biases

Recent studies reveal significant ethnic bias in recruitment processes. Rao et al. (2025) analyzed transcripts from British and Indian candidates in the UK, and showed that Indian candidates receive lower "hirability" scores despite similar academic qualifications and language complexity. On the other hand, Wilson & Çalışkan (2024) found a more pronounced racial bias over gender bias, indicating that only 6% of test results had equal selection rates for names associated with different ethnic backgrounds. There was a consistent preference for names linked to white candidates. The findings show that both explicit and implicit biases contribute to this discrimination. Explicit factors include name, country, and former employer, while implicit factors are reflected in language usage. Furthermore, although anonymization can mitigate bias, it does not fully eliminate it, as cultural signals may still influence perceptions based on writing style. Regional differences in bias are also significant, indicating a disparity in AI recruitment tool performance based on the cultural context, particularly for candidates from underrepresented regions. Organizations must consider local rhetorical norms, ensure cross-cultural fairness, and validate AI tools in specific contexts to mitigate algorithmic discrimination linked to ethnicity.

These patterns underline that algorithmic systems reproduce existing racial hierarchies, which is consistent with social dominance theory. At the same time, dataset bias and model sensitivity to linguistic cues can be interpreted through the critical algorithm theory.

4.3 Age

Recent studies argue that age biases significantly affect AI-based recruitment processes. Surveys from the US and Europe reveal that recruitment managers tend to favor younger candidates, particularly for roles involving digital technologies or AI. For instance, iTutor Group employed an AI tool that systematically rejected women over 55 and men over 60, which resulted in a fine from the US Equal Employment Opportunity Commission due to age discrimination (Hunter, 2024). Similarly, Timis (2025) highlighted that companies preferentially hire individuals under 35 for AI positions, with only one-third of employers willing to consider candidates over 60. In addition, a field experiment in Spain further showed that older applicants received 50% fewer responses compared to younger ones (Quesada & Martínez de Lafuente, 2024). Interestingly, a survey by AI Base found that 90% of HR managers in the AI sector believe workers in their 40s and 50s perform on a similar or better level than their younger counterparts, so recruitment biases still exist towards older candidates (Parasurama & Ipeirotis, 2025).

Qualitative studies reveal that age bias in AI-based recruitment often manifests through indirect indicators such as years of experience, graduation dates, technology use assumptions, and resume time stamps. These proxies enable AI systems to infer a candidate's age, potentially disadvantaging older applicants by limiting their opportunities. Additionally, younger candidates may also experience bias, particularly in senior roles, despite a lack of substantial data on this issue. To mitigate age-related discrimination, it is vital to restrict or eliminate age-related signals, such as concealing graduation years. Furthermore, monitoring age diversity in candidate shortlists and hiring outcomes is essential. Training HR personnel to identify subtle age biases can help address these challenges, highlighting age as a critical factor contributing to algorithmic discrimination in recruitment practices.

4.4 Outdated Data

Algorithmic discrimination might also arise from outdated or biased data, which influences various contexts such as reports, lawsuits, and applicant complaints. One significant example is Amazon, where hiring systems trained on historical data favored male candidates, leading to discrimination against women (Dastin, 2018). Recent research emphasizes that data quality and underlying assumptions are critical issues. The job market's evolution, with aspects like remote work and new career paths, highlights the diminishing reliability of older data, which may reflect now-inaccurate patterns. Furthermore, Sivakaminathan & Musi (2025) illustrate that large language models often rely on traditional job language that favors male-oriented terminology like leadership and technical skills. Such biases persist even with recent data due to the ongoing dependence on historical training processes (Cardillo, 2025).

Parasurama and Ipeirotis (2025) analyzed 800,000 job applications, revealing that even gender-balanced shortlists can lead to biased hiring decisions. This bias stems from screening criteria reflecting past managerial preferences, as decision-makers often rely on familiar patterns found in historical data. Consequently, the measures may not align with new performance standards or evolving organizational priorities. Similarly, O'Neil (2016) highlights that applicants frequently lack insight into their failures in AI-based assessments, largely due to algorithms being based on traditional decision-making frameworks. These insights underscore a disconnect caused by outdated data, as the algorithms do not incorporate criteria that correspond with contemporary skills or organizational values like diversity and inclusion.

Old data can increase social stereotypes that influence gender, age, and racial dynamics. This dimension is particularly explained by critical algorithm theory, as it directly relates to how historical datasets and model assumptions reproduce past inequalities. Barocas & Selbst (2016) argue that the consequences of data-driven systems can differ if historical inequalities persist in the datasets employed for automated decision-making. While these issues may be less pronounced today, they still shape outcomes. Additionally, it is crucial to identify misleading data, update data features, and refine training methodologies. Mehrabi et al. (2021) highlight that biases in machine learning can arise during various stages, including data collection, representation, model training, and evaluation. Unfortunately, many organizations lack the necessary infrastructure to adequately address these stages. In conclusion, algorithms can mislead intentionally or unintentionally due to outdated data and social biases, with old data serving as a significant source of discrimination in AI-driven recruitment systems.

4.5 Health Conditions

Previous research indicates discrimination against candidates with health or neurodiversity conditions (e.g., autism spectrum disorders, anxiety). For instance, one complaint sent to the US Federal Trade Commission showed that the AI-based "Adaptive Employee Personality Test" (ADEPT-15), which was used by the Aon Consulting company, hurt disadvantaged candidates, neurotypical people, and people with anxiety disorders, which made their scores lower. In the same way, it was said that Aon's Grid Challenge, a game-based cognitive assessment tool, unfairly disqualified disabled candidates (American Civil Liberties Union, 2024). Polson et al. (2024) wrote a case about Derek Mobley, a black man over 40 with anxiety and depression. Mobley claimed that Workday's AI-based recruitment system was unfair to him. He applied to over 100 companies using Workday from 2017 to 2024 and was turned down every time. He argued that Workday discriminated against him due to his race, age, and health issues, despite possessing a finance degree from Morehouse College and extensive work experience. The court agreed with him (Polson et al., 2024).

These results show that health-related information is often not well protected. This situation can affect evaluations and create disadvantages for some candidates. AI-based hiring systems may use such information indirectly when making decisions. This can lead to unfair outcomes and algorithmic discrimination. For example, Rieke and Bogen (2018) show that automated hiring systems can produce discrimination through proxy variables. This can happen even when protected characteristics are not directly used. Therefore, legal and ethical risks arise from the usage of health data in AI-based hiring tools, particularly impacting individuals with disabilities and long-term health conditions. Such systems may inadvertently disadvantage these individuals through reliance on cognitive-intensive tasks, tests, and video interviews. Evidence indicates that health-related factors significantly contribute to algorithmic discrimination within AI recruitment processes.

4.6 Sectoral Dynamics

Sectoral dynamics significantly influence algorithmic discrimination, as demonstrated by the lawsuit against Activision Blizzard, which highlights discriminatory employment practices in specific industries (BBC News, 2021). Many studies indicate that biases related to gender, race, and age are particularly prevalent in finance, healthcare, and technology sectors. For instance, Noble (2018) notes that despite some progress, biases against women persist in the healthcare sector. Similarly, in technology, leadership attributes are often associated with men, while women-friendly traits are valued in sectors like education. Additionally, a study in India by Greiner (2025) reveals that AI recruitment systems tend to offer lower salaries to women than men, even when qualifications are equal, with this trend being more pronounced in male-dominated fields, according to Sivakaminathan & Musi (2025).

Black women encounter higher discrimination in engineering roles, as highlighted by Bloomberg's research on GPT-3.5 (Fitzpatrick et al., 2024). Furthermore, a study indicates that applicant tracking systems (ATS) contribute to sustaining outdated stereotypes, often relegating immigrant workers to low-wage, labor-intensive positions such as cleaning and construction (Tomasev et al., 2025). This bias can also be seen in the healthcare industry, where younger men are frequently viewed as more qualified than women and older candidates (Bozkurt Gümrükçüoğlu & Yakacak, 2023). These examples indicate that biases in different sectors often stem from historical data patterns. Recent research highlights that various sectors prioritize different qualifications, such as leadership, technical expertise, gender, age, and other skills. Additionally, applying "objective" or "technical" criteria can inadvertently introduce bias. Therefore, tackling algorithmic discrimination necessitates approaches specific to different sectors. For instance, concepts of fairness in health care may differ significantly from those in the technology sector, which shows that discrimination typically arises from a mixture of biases. As a result, sector-specific biases also reflect social dominance theory, as dominant norms within industries shape algorithmic decision-making processes.

5. CONCLUSIONS AND RECOMMENDATIONS

This chapter discusses algorithmic discrimination that is caused by systemic processes, and underlines biases related to sex, sexual orientation, ethnicity, age, health status, and data shortcomings. These biases are rooted in historical inequalities and organizational practices impacting human resources data. AI-based recruitment systems not only offer efficiency and uniform assessments but also carry risks of inherent biases, making proactive strategies essential for organizations to address discrimination's social and technical causes. Furthermore, the complexity of evolving AI recruitment systems has prompted increased demands for fairness, transparency, and accountability, leading to enhanced auditing and human oversight. Such systems often replicate biases present in their training data, complicating their integration into e-recruiting. The research presents a six-factor model (gender, ethnic background, age, outdated data, health conditions, and sectoral dynamics) that provides a multidimensional framework for understanding bias interactions. The study contributes to the discourse on fairness in AI recruitment, advocating a shift from focusing solely on "algorithmic bias" to promoting "algorithmic fairness".

Many organizations are increasingly using participatory approaches to AI governance, and engage stakeholders like job seekers, trade unions, civil society groups, and technical experts in system design, evaluation, and monitoring. This inclusion helps to identify issues that might be overlooked by internal teams. Otherwise, they cannot address the concerns about transparency, fairness, and psychological safety that require additional time and resources. These practices need commitment to responsible innovation. Therefore, human resource professionals have started adapting their roles regarding the development of AI, because they realized that AI should enhance human judgment rather than replace it. AI systems act as mediators between automated outputs and contextual insights that require advanced digital skills to interpret and challenge model results. Thus, these systems improve recruitment processes by using technology as a decision-making tool rather than a controlling one.

Future research in AI-based recruitment should focus on the interaction of social and demographic factors through longitudinal studies that monitor AI tools over time. This is because shorter and less effective evaluations might miss important model adaptations. Considering the recent and frequent updates in machine-learning systems, long-term observations are essential for identifying patterns of exclusion and evaluating the efficacy of fairness measures. Therefore, this chapter addresses the issue of algorithmic discrimination and highlights the need for further research, particularly in scenarios involving limited or unbalanced data, which can worsen existing inequalities. It underscores the importance of comparative studies to benchmark new AI models against traditional machine learning, and examines if these innovations continue existing biases. The dual potential of AI recruitment systems to enhance efficiency and produce unfair outcomes highlights the requirement for strong oversight to ensure transparent, accountable, and objective decision-making.

Key findings are regarding coordinated policy measures to overcome algorithmic discrimination, and emphasizing improved data quality, transparency, and human oversight:

Data Management and Objectivity: It is necessary to establish long-term audits to identify biases in datasets and ensure fairness metrics that are reported to internal and external stakeholders.

Institutionalizing Independent Audits: Both internal and external audits are required for employers and AI vendors to assess the impact of protected traits on the performance of AI-based models and recruitment outcomes.

Human Control: High-level recruitment decisions should involve trained evaluators who adhere to anti-bias principles that ensure necessary human interventions.

Flexible Regulatory Structures: Companies should integrate AI impact assessment structures into existing anti-discrimination laws and promote collaboration among regulators, professionals, and technical experts to develop ethical standards, especially in all sectors.

Fostering Algorithmic Literacy and Supportive Culture: It is also necessary to develop a culture of fairness, transparency, and accountability in data usage by implementing training on algorithmic fairness and ethical practices.

In conclusion, the development of effective AI recruitment systems requires a cultural shift alongside technical improvements that include fairness as a foundational principle. When fairness is embedded in an organization's culture, AI tools can be improved more wisely with a perspective that recognizes the limits of these tools while fostering their opportunities. These insights serve as guidance for researchers, HR practitioners, policymakers, and students engaged in AI ethics, employment law, and digital governance discussions. It is also important to note that the conclusions in this chapter are based on secondary data that include publicly accessible cases due to limited access to internal company data. Therefore, further research is required to determine more policy recommendations to eliminate algorithmic discrimination within AI-based recruitment systems.

REFERENCES

Alanka, D. (2024). Content analysis as a qualitative research method: A theoretical framework. Kronotop Journal of Communication, 1(1), 64-84. Retrieved November 25, 2025, from https://dergipark.org.tr/tr/pub/kronotop/issue/82784/1405579

American Civil Liberties Union. (2024). ACLU complaint to the FTC regarding Aon Consulting, Inc. Retrieved November 25, 2025, from https://www.aclu.org/press-releases/aclu-files-ftc-complaint-against-major-hiring-technology-vendor-for-deceptively-marketing-online-hiring-tests-as-bias-free

Amnesty International Türkiye. (n.d.). Discrimination. Retrieved November 25, 2025, from https://www.amnesty.org.tr/

An, J., Huang, D., Lin, C., & Tai, M. (2025). Measuring gender and racial biases in big language models: Intersectional evidence from automated résumé evaluation. *PNAS Nexus*, *4*(3), 1–14. DOI: 10.1093/pnasnexus/pgaf089 PMID: 40144775

Barocas, S., & Selbst, A. D. (2016). Big data's disparate impact. *California Law Review*, *104*(3), 671–732. DOI: 10.15779/Z38BG31

Bayana, E. (2025). *Bias in AI recruitment tools: Impacted groups, legal risks, historical foundations, and next steps*. Research Archive of Rising Scholars., DOI: 10.58445/rars.2177

BBC News. (2021). *California sues Activision Blizzard over alleged harassment*. Retrieved November 25, 2025, from https://www.bbc.com/news/technology-57929543

Bertrand, M., & Mullainathan, S. (2004). Are Emily and Greg more employable than Lakisha and Jamal? A field experiment on labor market discrimination. *The American Economic Review*, *94*(4), 991–1013. DOI: 10.1257/0002828042002561

Black, J. S., & Van Esch, P. (2021). AI-enabled recruiting in the war for talent. *Business Horizons*, *64*(4), 513–524. DOI: 10.1016/j.bushor.2021.02.015

Bozkurt Gümrükçüoğlu, Y., & Yakacak, G. A. (2024). The use of artificial intelligence in recruitment processes and algorithmic discrimination. *Ankara University Faculty of Law Journal, 72*(4), 1701-1757. Retrieved November 25, 2025, from DOI: 10.33629/auhfd.1403311

Cardillo, A. (2025). *How many countries use AI? (New 2025 data)*. Retrieved November 25, 2025, from https://explodingtopics.com/blog/companies-using-ai

Chen, Z. (2023). Ethics and discrimination in artificial intelligence-enabled recruitment practices. *Humanities & Social Sciences Communications*, *10*(1), 567. DOI: 10.1057/s41599-023-02079-x

Columbia Engineering. (2025). *AI vs. machine learning*. Retrieved November 25, 2025, from https://ai.engineering.columbia.edu/ai-vs-machine-learning/

Crist, C. (2024). AI tools are biased in ranking job candidates' resumes, study shows. *HR Dive*. Retrieved November 25, 2025, from https://www.hrdive.com/news/ai-tools-are-biased-in-ranking-job-applicants-resumes/732134/

Dargan, M. (2023). Model act for algorithmic models: A regulatory solution for AI used in recruitment decisions. *University of Houston Law Center Review*. Retrieved November 25, 2025, from https://houstonlawreview.org/article/74110/stats/30/downloads

Dastin, J. (2018). Amazon scraps secret AI recruiting tool that showed bias against women. *Reuters*. Retrieved November 25, 2025, from https://www.reuters.com/article/us-amazon-com-jobs-automation-idUSKCN1MK08G

Electronic Privacy Information Center. (2019). *Federal Trade Commission: Complaint and request for investigation, injunction, and other relief*. Retrieved November 25, 2025, from https://epic.org/wp-content/uploads/privacy/ftc/hirevue/EPIC_FTC_HireVue_Complaint.pdf

ENAR - European Network Against Racism. (2020). *Equal@Work: Algorithmic discrimination in employment* (Equal@Work Toolkit). Retrieved November 25, 2025, from https://www.enar-eu.org/wp-content/uploads/2020_equal_work_algoritmic_discrimination_1_.pdf

European Parliament and Council of the European Union. (2024). Regulation (EU) 2024/1689 of the European Parliament and of the Council of 13 June 2024 laying down harmonised rules on artificial intelligence and amending Regulations (EC) No 300/2008, (EU) No 167/2013, (EU) No 168/2013, (EU) 2018/858, (EU) 2018/1139 and (EU) 2019/2144 and Directives 2014/90/EU, (EU) 2016/797 and (EU) 2020/1828 (Artificial Intelligence Act). Official Journal of the European Union. Retrieved April 27, 2026, from https://eur-lex.europa.eu/eli/reg/2024/1689/oj/eng

Fitzpatrick, J., Basu, K., & Klar, R. (2024). AI hiring tools risk discrimination, watchdog tells Congress. *Bloomberg Law*. Retrieved November 25, 2025, from https://news.bgov.com/bloomberg-government-news/ai-hiring-tools-risk-discrimination-watchdog-tells-congress

Gallegos, I. O., Rossi, R. A., Barrow, J., Tanjim, M. M., Kim, S., Dernoncourt, F., Yu, T., Zhang, R., & Ahmed, N. K. (2024). Bias and fairness in large language models: A survey. *Computational Linguistics, 50*(3), 1097–1179. DOI: 10.1162/coli_a_00524

Gerards, J., & Xenidis, R. (2021). *Algorithmic Discrimination in Europe: Challenges and Opportunities for Gender Equality and Non-Discrimination Law*. European Commission. Retrieved November 25, 2025, from https://op.europa.eu/en/publication-detail/-/publication/082f1dbc-821d-11eb-9ac9-01aa75ed71a1

Gillespie, T. (2014). The relevance of algorithms. In Gillespie, T., Boczkowski, P. J., & Foot, K. A. (Eds.), *Media Technologies: Essays on Communication, Materiality, and Society*. MIT Press Scholarship Online., DOI: 10.7551/mitpress/9042.003.0013

Gillmore, T. (2024). California bill to regulate artificial intelligence heats up AI debate. *The Epoch* Times. Retrieved November 25, 2025, from https://www.theepochtimes.com/us/california-bill-to-regulate-artificial-intelligence-heats-up-ai-debate-5706662

Greiner, L. (2025). Open-source AI recruitment models are weighted toward male candidates, study finds. *Computerworld.* Retrieved November 25, 2025, from https://www.computerworld.com/article/3977889/open-source-ai-hiring-models-are-weighted-toward-male-candidates-study-finds.html

Herschel, R., & Miori, V. M. (2017). Ethics & big data. *Technology in Society*, *49*, 31–36. DOI: 10.1016/j.techsoc.2017.03.003

Ho, A. K., Sidanius, J., Pratto, F., Levin, S., Thomsen, L., Kteily, N., & Sheehy-Skeffington, J. (2012). Social dominance orientation: Revisiting the structure and function of a variable predicting social and political attitudes. *Personality and Social Psychology Bulletin*, *38*(5), 583–606. DOI: 10.1177/0146167211432765 PMID: 22215697

Hunter, D. J. (2024). Artificial intelligence & the capacity for discrimination: The imperative need for frameworks, various teams & human liability. *IgMin Research*, *10*(2), 801–806. DOI: 10.61927/igmin250

IBM. (2023). *Global AI Adoption Index – Enterprise Report.* Retrieved November 25, 2025, from https://share.google/Qj2lhnTj3lSCAPYOW

IBM. (2025). *Enterprise AI development: Obstacles & opportunities.* Retrieved November 25, 2025, from https://filecache.mediaroom.com/mr5mr_ibmnewsroom/198591/Enterprise%20AI%20Development%20Survey.pdf

Iliadis, A., & Russo, F. (2016). Critical data studies: An introduction. *Big Data & Society, 3*(2), 2053951716674238. Advance online publication. DOI: 10.1177/2053951716674238

Karakoç Keskin, E., & Demirel, E. S. (2025). Turkish Adaptation of the Algorithmic Media Content Awareness Scale (AMCA-scale) and Analysis of the Relationships Between Scale Factors. *Akdeniz University Faculty of Communication Journal*, (48), 236–256. DOI: 10.31123/akil.1628894

Kim, P. T. (2017). Auditing algorithms for discrimination. U. Pa. L. Rev. Online, 166, 189. Retrieved November 25, 2025, from https://scholarship.law.upenn.edu/cgi/viewcontent.cgi?article=1212&context=penn_law_review_online

Koçak, A., & Arun, Ö. (2006). The sampling issue in content analysis studies. *Selçuk Communication, 4*(3), 21–28. https://izlik.org/JA45WN28TT

Kumar, N. (2024). *AI recruitment statistics 2025 (Worldwide data).* Retrieved November 25, 2025, from https://www.demandsage.com/ai-recruitment-statistics/

Lambrecht, A., & Tucker, C. (2019). Algorithmic bias? An empirical study of apparent gender-based discrimination in the display of STEM career ads. *Management Science*, *65*(7), 2966–2981. DOI: 10.1287/mnsc.2018.3093

Langenkamp, M., Costa, A., & Cheung, C. (2019). *Hiring Fairly in the Age of Algorithms*. Retrieved November 25, 2025, from https://ssrn.com/abstract=3723046 DOI: 10.2139/ssrn.3723046

Lee, K. (2018). *Artificial intelligence and the new world order: China's Silicon Valley*. Houghton Mifflin Harcourt.

McKinsey & Company. (2024). Superagency in the workplace: Empowering people to unlock AI's full potential at work. Retrieved November 25, 2025, from https://www.mckinsey.com/capabilities/tech-and-ai/our-insights/superagency-in-the-workplace-empowering-people-to-unlock-ais-full-potential-at-work#/

Mehrabi, N., Morstatter, F., Saxena, N., Lerman, K., & Galstyan, A. (2021). A survey on bias and fairness in machine learning. *ACM Computing Surveys*, *54*(6), 1–35. DOI: 10.1145/3457607

Metin, O., & Ünal, Ş. (2022). Content analysis technique: Its use in PhD theses in communication sciences and sociology. *Anadolu University Journal of Social Sciences*, *22*(2), 273–294. DOI: 10.18037/ausbd.1227356

Milne, S. (2024). AI tools show biases in ranking job candidates' names according to perceived race and gender. *UW News*. Retrieved November 25, 2025, from https://www.washington.edu/news/2024/10/31/ai-bias-resume-screening-race-gender/

Mittelstadt, B. D., Allo, P., Taddeo, M., Wachter, S., & Floridi, L. (2016). The ethics of algorithms: Mapping the debate. *Big Data & Society*, *3*(2), 1–21. DOI: 10.1177/2053951716679679

NIST - National Institute of Standards and Technology. (2023). Artificial intelligence risk management framework (AI RMF 1.0) (NIST AI 100-1). U.S. Department of Commerce. Retrieved April 27, 2026, from https://nvlpubs.nist.gov/nistpubs/ai/NIST.AI.100-1.pdf

Noble, S. U. (2018). *Algorithms of Oppression: How Search Engines Reinforce Racism*. NYU Press., DOI: 10.18574/nyu/9781479833641.001.0001

O'Neil, C. (2016). *Weapons of math destruction: How big data increases inequality and threatens democracy*. Penguin Press.

Oğuz, Ö. (2024). Algorithmic discrimination in the workplace. *Süleyman Demirel University Faculty of Law Journal*, *14*(2), 1851–1886. Retrieved November 25, 2025, from. DOI: 10.52273/sduhfd.1581436

Pal, R., Shaikh, S., Satpute, S., & Bhagwat, S. (2022). Resume classification using various machine learning algorithms. *ITM Web of Conferences, 44*, 03011. DOI: 10.1051/itmconf/20224403011

Parasurama, P., & Ipeirotis, P. (2025). *Algorithmic recruitment and diversity: Reducing human–algorithm similarity for better outcomes.* /arXiv.2505.14388DOI: 10.48550

Pew Research Center. (2023). *AI in hiring and employee evaluation: What Americans think*. Retrieved November 25, 2025, from https://www.pewresearch.org/internet/2023/04/20/ai-in-hiring-and-evaluating-workers-what-americans-think/

Polson, J. M., Khan, A. Y., & Wilson, E. G. (2024). AI workplace screener faces bias lawsuit: Five lessons for employers and five lessons for AI developers. Retrieved November 25, 2025, from https://www.jdsupra.com/legalnews/ai-workplace-screener-faces-bias-9455001/

Purcell, Z. A., & Bonnefon, J. F. (2023). Research on Artificial Intelligence is Reshaping Our Definition of Morality. *Psychological Inquiry*, *34*(2), 100–101. DOI: 10.1080/1047840X.2023.2248857

Quesada, O., & Martínez de Lafuente, D. (2024). *Too old to work? A field experiment on age discrimination in the Spanish labor market.* Retrieved November 25, 2025, from https://ssrn.com/abstract=4704576 DOI: 10.2139/ssrn.4704576

Raghavan, M., Barocas, S., Kleinberg, J., & Levy, K. (2020). Mitigating bias in algorithmic recruitment: Evaluating claims and practices. *Proceedings of the ACM Conference on Fairness, Accountability, and Transparency*, 469–481. DOI: 10.1145/3351095.3372828

Rao, P. S., Venkatesan, L. N., Cherubini, M., & Jayagopi, D. B. (2025, October). Invisible Filters: Cultural Bias in Hiring Evaluations Using Large Language Models. In Proceedings of the AAAI/ACM Conference on AI, Ethics, and Society (Vol. 8, No. 3, pp. 2164-2176). Retrieved November 25, 2025, from https://arxiv.org/pdf/2508.16673

Rieke, A., & Bogen, M. (2018). Help wanted: An examination of hiring algorithms, equity, and bias. *Upturn*. Retrieved April 27, 2026, from https://www.upturn.org/reports/2018/hiring-algorithms/

Rubinkam, M. (2024). Convenience store chain with hundreds of outlets in 6 states hit with discrimination lawsuit. *AP News*. Retrieved November 25, 2025, from https://apnews.com/article/sheetz-discrimination-suit-biden-campaign-visit-9cc14287564a8821a54acbc83ae3de83

Sivakaminathan, S., & Musi, E. (2025). ChatGPT is a gender bias echo-chamber in HR recruitment: An NLP analysis and framework to uncover the language roots of bias. *AI & Society*. Advance online publication. DOI: 10.1007/s00146-025-02564-8

Sonderling, K., Bradford, J. K., & Casimir, L. (2022). The promise and the peril: Artificial intelligence and employment discrimination. *University of Miami Law Review*, *77*(1). Retrieved November 25, 2025, from https://repository.law.miami.edu/cgi/viewcontent.cgi?article=4692&context=umlr

Sweeeft (2025). *Applicant tracking system: What it is and how it could benefit HR professionals.* Retrieved November 25, 2025, from https://www.sweeeft.ai/en/articles/the-benefits-of-an-ai-powered-applicant-tracking-system-ats-for-hr-teams-88

Tavşancıl, E., & Aslan, E. (2001). *Content analysis for verbal, written, and other materials with application examples.* Epsilon Publishing.

The People Space. (2020). *HR and AI ethics: How artificial intelligence in the workplace is changing the role of HR leaders.* Retrieved November 25, 2025, from https://www.thepeoplespace.com/sites/default/files/downloads/hr_and_ai_ethics_ebook_2020.pdf

Thijssen, L., Coenders, M., & Lancee, B. (2020). Ethnic discrimination in the Dutch labor market: Differences between ethnic minority groups and the role of personal information about job candidates. *Journal of International Migration and Integration, 22*, 1125–1150. DOI: 10.1007/s12134-020-00795-w

Timis, D. (2025). *Jobs and the future of work: How "age-proofing" AI in the workplace can foster inclusivity.* World Economic Forum. Retrieved November 25, 2025, from https://www.weforum.org/stories/2025/03/how-age-proofing-ai-in-workplace-can-foster-inclusivity/

Todoli-Signes, A. (2019). Algorithms, artificial intelligence and automated decisions concerning workers and the risks of discrimination: The necessary collective governance of data protection. *Transfer: European Review of Labour and Research, 25*(4), 465–481. DOI: 10.1177/1024258919876416

Tomasev, N., Maynard, J. L., & Gabriel, I. (2025). Manifestations of xenophobia in AI systems. *AI & Society, 40*(2), 741–763. DOI: 10.1007/s00146-024-01893-4

Torralba, A., & Ali, H. (2024). Ethical considerations of artificial intelligence in human resources: Impact on job performance and organizational culture. Retrieved November 25, 2025, from https://www.researchgate.net/publication/382000437_Ethical_Considerations_of_Artificial_Intelligence_in_Human_Resources_Impact_on_Job_Performance_and_Organizational_Culture

Wang, Y., & Kosinski, M. (2018). Deep neural networks are more accurate than humans at detecting sexual orientation from facial images. *Journal of Personality and Social Psychology, 114*(2), 246–257. DOI: 10.1037/pspa0000098 PMID: 29389215

Wilson, K., & Çalışkan, A. (2024). *Gender, race, and intersectional bias in resume screening via language model retrieval.* Retrieved November 25, 2025, from /arXiv.2407.20371DOI: 10.48550

Yin, L., Alba, D., & Nicoletti, L. (2024). OpenAI's GPT is a recruiter's dream tool: Tests show there's racial bias. *Bloomberg Technology.* Retrieved November 25, 2025, from https://www.bloomberg.com/graphics/2024-openai-gpt-hiring-racial-discrimination/?embedded-checkout=true

Zwitter, A. (2014). Big data ethics. *Big Data & Society, 1*(2), 2053951714559253. Advance online publication. DOI: 10.1177/2053951714559253

Chapter 6
HR Marketing and Human–AI Collaboration:
Explainability and Relational Legitimacy in AI-Assisted HR Evaluation

Mitsunori Hirogaki
http://orcid.org/0000-0002-0215-2011
Kyushu University, Japan

Rapeeporn Rungsithong
Chulalongkorn University, Thailand

ABSTRACT

This chapter examines human–AI complementarity in human resource management through the lens of HR marketing. We argue that when AI moves into high-stakes domains such as appraisal and placement, acceptance depends less on technical performance alone and more on value judgments about understandability, fairness, and respect for the person. Drawing on evidence and stakeholder voices from Japanese organizations, we organize acceptance drivers into three interrelated domains: psychological acceptance (e.g., anxiety and perceived "warmth"); explainability–fairness-based trust; and ethics and governance concerns (e.g., privacy, accountability, and avenues for appeal). We show that effective complementarity requires both cognitive legitimacy (trust grounded in explainability and fairness) and relational legitimacy (psychological safety and perceived warmth), supported by governance as a baseline condition. The chapter concludes by outlining how HR marketing can reduce friction and strengthen legitimacy in AI-mediated HR decision-making, especially in high-context organizational settings.

DOI: 10.4018/979-8-2600-2303-7.ch006

1. INTRODUCTION

In recent years, artificial intelligence (AI) has rapidly penetrated core decision-making areas of human resource management (HRM), including recruitment and selection, performance management, employee placement, training and development, employee engagement, and career support (Ali & Rafi, 2024; Benabou & Touhami, 2025). AI-based HR (AI-HR) systems support strategic and data-driven decision-making by enabling the rapid processing of large-scale data, predictive analytics, and more systematic assessments of human capital (Ali & Rafi, 2024; Zhu, 2025). Previous studies report that organizations adopting AI in recruitment have achieved efficiency gains of 40–75%, while machine-learning-based screening systems have reached accuracy levels of up to 78%, substantially outperforming traditional methods, which average around 45% (Zhu, 2025). Empirical evidence also indicates shorter hiring cycles and improved matching between candidates and job requirements (Chheda et al., 2025). However, recent reviews emphasize that AI implementation in HRM also raises important concerns regarding ethical decision-making, data security, transparency, bias, and the preservation of human interaction in HR processes (Benabou & Touhami, 2025). Thus, AI has the potential to streamline HR processes and strengthen the rationality and consistency of HR decision-making, but these benefits are not automatic. Rather, they depend on whether organizations use AI to augment rather than replace human roles and on how AI systems are designed, explained, implemented, and governed (Bankins et al., 2022; Park et al., 2021; Revillod, 2025a).

At the same time, HR decision-making cannot be reduced to operational efficiency alone. Multiple systematic reviews emphasize that ethical, social, and human-centered considerations are central to the responsible use of AI in HRM (Bouzerda et al., 2025; Köchling & Wehner, 2020). Decisions related to performance evaluation, promotion, placement, and employee development are not merely administrative procedures; they directly shape employees' perceptions of dignity, procedural fairness, organizational commitment, and future career opportunities (Bankins et al., 2022; Lemons & Jones, 2001; Zhang & Amos, 2024). In this respect, acceptance of AI in HR differs in important respects from acceptance of general information technologies. While traditional IT and e-HRM acceptance studies often emphasize perceived usefulness and ease of use, AI-based HR systems additionally require attention to trust, fairness, transparency, and employees' concerns about algorithmic evaluation and decision-making (Bankins et al., 2022; Binns et al., 2018; Lee, 2018; Park et al., 2021; Revillod, 2025a). Nevertheless, much of the existing literature relies on general technology acceptance frameworks, such as the Technology Acceptance Model (TAM) and the Unified Theory of Acceptance and Use of Technology (UTAUT), focusing primarily on perceived usefulness and ease of use to explain acceptance of AI-based HR systems (Davis, 1989; Revillod, 2025a; Venkatesh & Davis, 2000; Wolfe et al., 2025).

Recent review studies consistently show that traditional demographic variables—such as age, gender, education, and work experience—have little direct impact on acceptance of AI in HR contexts (Cao, 2025). In contrast, psychological and experiential factors, including technology affinity, anxiety, digital literacy, and the quality of prior AI-related experiences, play a critical role in shaping acceptance (Khalid et al., 2025; Park et al., 2021; Wolfe et al., 2025). Notably, several studies highlight a paradoxical finding: experience with AI-based HR tools does not necessarily increase acceptance and may, in some cases, intensify resistance when prior experiences are perceived as negative (Calluso & Devetag, 2025; Park et al., 2021). This suggests that acceptance of AI in HR depends less on AI's technical performance alone and more on how AI systems are introduced, explained, and embedded in organizational relationships (Park et al., 2021; Revillod, 2025a; Yang et al., 2026).

In other words, these findings indicate that the rational and efficiency-oriented decision-making assumptions underlying TAM may be insufficient to fully explain AI acceptance in HR contexts. Prior extensions of TAM have shown that trust, risk perceptions, and transparency can play important roles in user acceptance of intelligent or high-uncertainty systems (Egea & González, 2011; Pavlou, 2003; Vorm & Combs, 2022). In AI-HR contexts, related studies similarly emphasize fairness, explainability, dignity, and employee resistance as central acceptance issues (Bankins et al., 2022; Park et al., 2021; Revillod, 2025a). This limitation is particularly relevant in the Japanese organizational context, where institutional legitimacy and perceptions of fairness may be supported not only by formal rules but also by interpersonal relationships, tacit knowledge, and stakeholders' sense of acceptance and understanding, often expressed through the notion of "nattoku" (Nakano et al., 2009; Yamada et al., 2020). Because the present study empirically examines only the Japanese context, it does not make direct claims about other Asian countries. Any extension of this argument to broader Asian contexts should be examined through future comparative research. Accordingly, acceptance of AI-based HR systems is likely to depend not only on cognitive trust—such as whether systems appear explainable and fair—but also on emotional and relational factors, including psychological comfort and the absence of perceived coldness or anxiety (Ismatullaev & Kim, 2024; Laurim et al., 2021; Park et al., 2021; Suseno et al., 2022).

This perspective also connects AI-HR acceptance to HR marketing. In this chapter, HR marketing is understood not only as external employer branding or recruitment communication, but also as an internal process through which organizations communicate the value, fairness, and legitimacy of HR practices to employees. When AI-based HR systems are introduced, employees become internal users whose acceptance depends on how the system is explained, justified, and aligned with dignity, fairness, and human oversight.

This chapter presents an exploratory empirical study, rather than a purely conceptual review, on the acceptance of AI-based HR systems among working professionals in Japan. Based on the perspective outlined above, the purpose of this study is to explore acceptance of AI-based HR systems by integrating cognitive factors (usefulness, fairness, and explainability), emotional factors (anxiety, warmth, and psychological safety), and perceptions of governance (clarity of responsibility, appealability, and transparency). This multidimensional approach is consistent with prior AI-HR and HRM research showing that acceptance and employee responses are shaped not only by perceived usefulness, but also by fairness, trust, dignity, well-being, and broader assessments of organizational justice and governance (Bankins et al., 2022; Heffernan & Dundon, 2016; Park et al., 2021; Revillod, 2025a; Wang et al., 2020). Using questionnaire data collected from 44 working professionals, this study conducts an exploratory factor analysis using items related to cognitive, emotional, and institutional perceptions of AI-based HR systems and examines the effects of composite factor scores on behavioral intention (BI) through multiple regression analysis. In addition, qualitative content analysis of open-ended responses is used to provide supplementary insights, interpreting acceptance of AI in HR in relation to interdependent self-construal in the Japanese cultural context (Markus & Kitayama, 1991).

The chapter proceeds as follows. First, it reviews TAM-based acceptance research and recent studies on AI-based HR decision-making, focusing on fairness, explainability, psychological acceptance, and governance. Second, it develops hypotheses concerning the effects of explainability–fairness-based trust, psychological acceptance, and ethics/governance perceptions on behavioral intention. Third, it presents the methodology and results of an exploratory empirical study. Finally, it discusses how the findings extend TAM-based explanations by incorporating human-centered and culturally informed dimensions of AI-HR acceptance.

2. LITERATURE REVIEW

This literature review is organized around three broad dimensions that guide the empirical analysis of this study. First, it reviews TAM and its extensions to clarify why perceived usefulness, ease of use, trust, fairness, and transparency are relevant to AI-HR acceptance. Second, it examines research on fairness, explainability, governance, and human–AI interaction in HR-related algorithmic decision-making. Third, it discusses the Japanese cultural context, focusing on interdependent self-construal, relational recognition, and the interpretive role of “nattoku.”

2.1 Technology Acceptance Model (TAM) and Behavioral Intention (BI)

The Technology Acceptance Model (TAM) posits that perceived usefulness (PU) and perceived ease of use (PEU) shape attitudes toward a technology and subsequently influence behavioral intention (BI), which in turn predicts actual usage behavior (Davis, 1989). In studies of organizational technology adoption, BI has been repeatedly shown to be a strong predictor of actual use, and TAM has therefore been widely employed as a foundational framework in research on information systems and workplace technologies (Venkatesh & Davis, 2000).

In institutional and evaluative decision-making domains such as AI-based performance evaluation, employee placement, and promotion, it is theoretically reasonable to conceptualize "the intention to accept or use AI-based HR systems" as BI. However, these decisions differ in important respects from the use of ordinary task-support tools, as they directly affect individual evaluations and future career opportunities. As a result, there is growing concern that cognitive factors grounded solely in efficiency and convenience—such as PU and PEU—may be insufficient to fully explain acceptance of AI in HR contexts.

Empirical studies on algorithmic and AI-driven decision-making demonstrate that acceptance is often influenced less by efficiency gains than by normative and social factors, including perceived fairness, trust, and emotional responses (Lee, 2018). In particular, when AI is used for evaluation or selection, individuals are highly sensitive to explainability and procedural fairness—namely, whether they can understand why a particular decision was made. A lack of these elements has been shown to substantially reduce acceptance (Binns et al., 2018).

Research on AI-based HR systems similarly indicates that algorithmic evaluations can generate resistance and psychological burden among employees, especially when they are perceived as unfair, as violating personal dignity, or as offering limited opportunities for appeal or redress (Park et al., 2021). Moreover, empirical studies focusing on Japanese firms suggest that institutional legitimacy and acceptance depend less on the formal design of systems themselves and more on organizational climate and employees' sense of understanding and acceptance, often expressed through the notion of "nattoku" (Yamada et al., 2020). This context-dependent mechanism is likely to be relevant to the acceptance of AI-based HR systems.

Taken together, these findings suggest that while BI derived from TAM remains a useful core indicator for analyzing acceptance of AI in HR, it is necessary to move beyond PU and PEU alone. A comprehensive analysis should incorporate normative and social factors such as perceived fairness, dignity, psychological acceptance, and the availability of appeal or remedial mechanisms in order to more fully capture the acceptance process of AI-based HR systems.

The purpose of this chapter is therefore not to reject TAM, but to extend its explanatory scope in the context of AI-based HR decision-making. Prior extensions of TAM have shown that trust, risk perceptions, and transparency can play important roles in user acceptance, particularly when technologies involve uncertainty, intelligent systems, or consequential decision-making (Egea & González, 2011; Pavlou, 2003; Vorm & Combs, 2022). In AI-HR contexts, related studies similarly emphasize fairness, explainability, dignity, and employee resistance as central acceptance issues (Bankins et al., 2022; Binns et al., 2018; Park et al., 2021; Revillod, 2025a). Therefore, while perceived usefulness, perceived ease of use, and behavioral intention remain useful concepts, they need to be complemented by trust, fairness, transparency, psychological acceptance, and governance-related perceptions.

2.2 Fairness, Explainability, and Trust in AI-Based HR Systems

AI-based HR decisions are often expected to enhance rationality by ensuring consistency and reducing subjective bias (Suriyaa, 2024). At the same time, however, such systems tend to function as "black boxes," and when their decision processes are not sufficiently explained, they are likely to generate distrust and negative emotional reactions (Fabeyo, 2025). Previous studies indicate that acceptance of algorithmic and AI-driven decision-making is not based solely on performance evaluation, but is closely linked to perceptions of fairness, trust, and emotional responses (Lee, 2018).

This issue is particularly salient in high-involvement HR decisions, such as performance evaluation, employee placement, and promotion. In these contexts, acceptance depends on whether individuals perceive that decisions are based on clear criteria, whether the reasoning behind decisions is explainable, and whether the system is operated in a fair manner. Prior research shows that when algorithmic decisions are perceived as procedurally fair and their underlying logic is understandable, individuals' sense of acceptance and perceived legitimacy increases (Binns et al., 2018). In AI-based HR decision-making, cognitive trust is formed not only through perceptions of accuracy or efficiency, but also through perceptions that the decision process is understandable, procedurally fair, and institutionally legitimate. This is particularly important in performance evaluation and promotion contexts, where decisions affect employees' dignity, perceived fairness, organizational commitment, and future career opportunities (Bankins et al., 2022; Lemons & Jones, 2001; Zhang & Amos, 2024). Thus, explainability and fairness should be treated not as peripheral technical features, but as central conditions for trust formation in AI-HR systems.

Moreover, empirical studies demonstrate that explainability and transparency in AI decision-making positively influence acceptance and behavioral intention by fostering user trust (Kartikeya, 2022). In other words, trust formation depends not only on whether AI produces "correct" outcomes, but also on whether users can understand why a particular decision was made (Ahn et al., 2021; Shin, 2021a; Shin, 2021b). This process is central to the development of cognitive trust in AI systems.

In the context of AI-based HR evaluation, insufficient explanations and limited opportunities for appeal or redress have been shown to evoke perceptions of dignity violation and unfairness among employees, thereby strengthening resistance and distrust toward AI-based HR systems (Park et al., 2021). These findings suggest that acceptance of AI in HR is not determined solely by evaluations of efficiency or convenience, but depends strongly on trust perceptions grounded in explainability and fairness (Revillod, 2025b).

Therefore, to understand acceptance of AI-based HR systems, it is necessary to move beyond PU and PEU in TAM and to treat cognitive trust—based on explainability and fairness—as a central component. In this study, cognitive trust is positioned as one of the key drivers shaping acceptance of AI-based HR systems.

2.3 Ethics and Governance (Responsibility, Redress, and Privacy) and Acceptance

The introduction of AI-based HR systems requires careful attention to ethical and governance issues, including appropriate handling of personal data, clarity of responsibility for decisions, mechanisms for appeal and redress in cases of error, and transparency of operational processes. Prior research on algorithmic and AI-driven decision-making shows that when these elements are insufficiently established, users' distrust and rejection increase rapidly, leading to a significant decline in acceptance (Mittelstadt et al., 2016).

This issue is particularly important in institutional HR decisions such as performance evaluation, employee placement, and promotion. In these contexts, acceptance is influenced not only by decision outcomes, but also by perceptions of who is responsible for the decision and whether errors can be corrected through institutional remedies. Studies indicate that when accountability and redress mechanisms are not institutionally guaranteed, individuals are more likely to perceive algorithmic decisions as unfair or arbitrary, thereby hindering trust formation (Lepri et al., 2018).

In addition, AI-based HR systems involve the continuous collection and analysis of large volumes of personal data, making concerns about privacy a critical factor in acceptance. Behavioral research suggests that opaque data use and a lack of perceived control over personal information can generate strong anxiety and distrust, even when clear efficiency benefits exist, ultimately suppressing technology acceptance (Acquisti et al., 2015). This concern is equally relevant in AI-based HR contexts: once trust in data usage purposes or governance structures is undermined, overall evaluations of the AI system can deteriorate rapidly.

However, ethical and governance factors do not necessarily function as direct drivers that actively increase behavioral intention (BI). Research on trust in algorithmic systems suggests that factors such as fairness, accountability, and transparency operate less as elements that promote acceptance when present, and more as baseline conditions whose absence leads to a breakdown of trust (Shin & Park, 2019). Governance-related factors may therefore operate differently from perceived usefulness or perceived ease of use. Rather than directly increasing behavioral intention when present, transparency, accountability, privacy protection, and redress mechanisms may function as baseline conditions that prevent trust erosion. In particular, contestability—the ability to challenge or appeal algorithmic decisions—has been identified as an important condition for sustaining legitimacy in AI-supported decision-making (Birahim, 2025; Lyons et al., 2021). This perspective is especially relevant to HR contexts because algorithmic decisions may affect evaluation, promotion, placement, and career development.

This characteristic aligns with the concept of hygiene factors in organizational behavior. Hygiene factors do not themselves enhance satisfaction or motivation, but their absence generates strong dissatisfaction and resistance (Herzberg, 1966). Ethical and governance factors in AI-based HR systems can be similarly understood: rather than directly elevating acceptance, they serve as foundational conditions that prevent trust erosion and strong resistance.

2.4 Human-Led vs. AI-Led HR Interactions: Emotional Responses and Psychological Safety

Prior research consistently indicates that human-led HR interactions tend to generate more favorable emotional responses and higher levels of perceived psychological safety than AI-led interactions, especially in evaluative contexts that require subjective judgment and interpersonal consideration (Bankins et al., 2022; Köchling et al., 2023). Experimental studies show that human decision makers are often evaluated more positively than AI systems in terms of interactional justice, trust, and respectful treatment, whereas AI-based evaluations are more likely to evoke perceptions of dehumanization and emotional discomfort (Bankins et al., 2022; Lee, 2018).

However, this human advantage is not uniform and is substantially moderated by task characteristics. Prior studies suggest that no significant differences may emerge between human and AI decision makers in highly standardized and mechanical tasks, such as task allocation or scheduling (Biswas et al., 2024; Lee, 2018). In contrast, for tasks that require human judgment and contextual understanding—such as recruitment, performance appraisal, and promotion decisions—human decision makers tend to receive higher evaluations in terms of perceived fairness, trustworthiness, and positive affective responses (Bedemariam & Wessel, 2023; Köchling et al., 2023). Notably, in decision contexts governed by predefined formulas or explicit rules, AI systems may achieve levels of trust comparable to, or in some cases exceeding, those of human decision makers (Biswas et al., 2024). This suggests that employees' concerns are directed less toward AI involvement per se and more toward whether AI is perceived as capable of making appropriate judgments in a given HR context.

Moreover, the impact of decision modality is amplified when outcomes are negative. Rejections or unfavorable evaluations delivered by AI may be perceived as more unfair and emotionally detached than equivalent judgments made by humans (Bedemariam & Wessel, 2023; Lee, 2018). In particular, during interpersonal stages such as interviews or performance feedback, AI involvement tends to be perceived as depriving individuals of opportunities to adequately demonstrate their capabilities, thereby intensifying anxiety and resistance (Köchling et al., 2023; Park et al., 2021). These findings indicate that AI-based HR practices are experienced not merely as efficiency-enhancing tools, but as emotionally and socially meaningful encounters.

At the same time, review studies also suggest that hybrid decision-making approaches combining AI and human judgment tend to receive the most favorable evaluations (Biswas et al., 2024; Sadeghi, 2024). Implementation factors such as transparency in AI use, organizational openness, and the explicit presence of human oversight critically shape whether AI adoption supports or undermines psychological safety (Fragouli, 2025). Although studies that directly measure psychological safety remain limited, related indicators—such as trust, perceived fairness, and interactional justice—consistently point to reduced psychological safety in AI-led evaluative contexts (Bankins et al., 2022; Park et al., 2021).

Emotional responses to AI-based HR systems are particularly important because HR decisions are interpreted as signals of how employees are recognized and valued within the organization. When AI systems are perceived as cold, opaque, or lacking human consideration, employees may experience reduced dignity, lower psychological safety, and stronger resistance to algorithmic evaluation (Bankins et al., 2022; Lee, 2018; Mantello et al., 2023; Park et al., 2021; Zhang & Amos, 2024). Therefore, psychological acceptance should be treated as an independent dimension of AI-HR acceptance rather than merely as a secondary reaction to perceived usefulness.

Taken together, these findings demonstrate that acceptance of AI-based HR practices cannot be reduced to assessments of AI performance or efficiency alone. Rather, it is strongly contingent upon task characteristics, decision outcomes, and the manner in which AI is integrated with human judgment. In particular, emotional responses, perceived warmth, dignity, and psychological safety constitute core elements in understanding AI-HR acceptance and thus warrant explicit examination in subsequent empirical analyses.

2.5 Japanese/Asian Context: Interdependent Self-Construal and "Warmth"

The cultural psychology framework of independent versus interdependent self-construal suggests that culturally shared views of the self systematically shape value judgments, emotional responses, and patterns of social decision-making (Markus & Kitayama, 1991). According to this framework, in Japanese cultural contexts, the self is often understood as interdependent—defined in relation to others and social relationships. As a result, evaluation and treatment within organizations may be interpreted not only as measurements of individual performance or ability, but also as actions embedded within relational contexts.

In such cultural settings, acceptance of organizational evaluation and decision-making is influenced not only by cognitive assessments such as rationality or formal fairness, but also by whether individuals feel understood and respected within their relationships. This sense of relational recognition is relevant to institutional acceptance because decision-making procedures can communicate whether individuals are valued and respected within an organization (Markus & Kitayama, 1991; Tyler & Blader, 2003). Accordingly, acceptance of AI-based HR decisions may depend not only on accuracy and consistency of judgments, but also on emotional factors such as psychological comfort and affective acceptance.

Recent research on human–AI interaction further demonstrates that evaluations of AI systems are shaped not only by perceptions of competence and rationality, but also by perceived warmth and social consideration (Araujo et al., 2020). In particular, when AI systems are used in roles with strong interpersonal impact—such as evaluation, selection, or promotion—perceived coldness or a lack of human sensitivity tends to amplify anxiety and resistance. Moreover, studies on resistance to algorithmic decision-making suggest that such resistance is often rooted in the belief that certain judgments "should be made by humans," as well as in expectations of empathy and contextual understanding associated with human decision makers (Lee, 2018).

Based on these insights, this study examines acceptance of AI-based HR systems primarily in the Japanese context by explicitly incorporating emotional dimensions such as perceived warmth and psychological safety, in addition to cognitive evaluation factors such as rationality, explainability, and fairness. In this study, "nattoku" is not operationalized as a directly measured quantitative variable. Rather, it is used as an interpretive cultural lens for understanding why explainability, fairness, psychological acceptance, and perceived warmth may be especially salient in the Japanese HR context. This interpretation is grounded in cultural psychology and organizational justice research, which suggest that individuals' acceptance of decisions is shaped not only by formal procedures but also by perceived respect, relational recognition, and the legitimacy of decision-making processes (Markus & Kitayama, 1991; Tyler & Blader, 2003). Although similar issues may arise in other relational or high-context organizational cultures, this study does not empirically examine other Asian countries. Therefore, the cultural interpretation is limited primarily to the Japanese context. To complement the quantitative analysis, this study also uses open-ended responses to explore how employees subjectively interpret and make sense of AI-based HR practices.

3. HYPOTHESES DEVELOPMENT

This study aims to identify, in an exploratory manner, the psychological, cognitive, and governance-related factors shaping acceptance of AI-based HR systems. Based on the preceding literature review, the following hypotheses are proposed.

3.1 Explainability- and Fairness-Based Trust and Behavioral Intention

Previous studies consistently indicate that acceptance of AI-driven decision-making depends not only on efficiency or performance, but also on whether decision processes are perceived as explainable and fair (Binns et al., 2018; Lee, 2018). This issue is particularly salient in high-involvement HR decisions such as performance evaluation and promotion, where understanding the basis of decisions constitutes a prerequisite for trust formation and perceived legitimacy (Bankins et al., 2022; Park et al., 2021).

Moreover, empirical research demonstrates that explainability and transparency in AI systems enhance acceptance and behavioral intention by fostering cognitive trust among users (Shin, 2021a, 2021b). Taken together, these findings suggest that trust grounded in perceived explainability and fairness represents a key determinant of acceptance of AI-based HR systems.

H1: Explainability–fairness-based trust (F2) positively predicts behavioral intention (BI) to use AI-based HR systems.

3.2 Psychological Acceptance / Low Resistance and Behavioral Intention

Acceptance of AI-based HR systems is influenced not only by cognitive evaluations such as rationality and fairness, but also by emotional responses and the degree of psychological acceptance (Revillod, 2025a). Prior studies show that when algorithmic evaluations are perceived as "cold" or lacking human consideration, resistance and anxiety increase, resulting in lower acceptance (Lee, 2018; Park et al., 2021).

In addition, research in cultural psychology suggests that interdependent self-construal is especially relevant for understanding Japanese social and organizational contexts, where individuals often define themselves in relation to others and interpret treatment as a signal of relational recognition (Markus & Kitayama, 1991). In such contexts, acceptance of evaluation and treatment may be closely tied to whether individuals feel understood, respected, and able to make sense of the decision process. Within this cultural framework, acceptance of AI-based HR decisions may be particularly sensitive to emotional factors such as perceived warmth and psychological comfort (Araujo et al., 2020; Tyler & Blader, 2003).

Accordingly, lower psychological resistance and higher emotional acceptance of AI-based HR systems are expected to be associated with stronger behavioral intention.

H2: Psychological acceptance / low resistance—characterized by perceived warmth, psychological comfort, and lower resistance (F1)—positively predicts behavioral intention (BI) to use AI-based HR systems.

3.3 Ethics and Governance (Responsibility, Redress, and Privacy) and Behavioral Intention

The introduction of AI-based HR systems requires adequate ethical and governance arrangements, including clarity of responsibility for decisions, availability of redress mechanisms for erroneous outcomes, appropriate handling of personal data, and transparency of system operation (Lepri et al., 2018; Mittelstadt et al., 2016). When these conditions are insufficient, trust in AI systems may be undermined, leading to stronger rejection or resistance (Setiawati et al., 2025; Yanamala, 2023).

At the same time, prior research suggests that ethical and governance factors such as fairness, accountability, and transparency may function less as direct drivers that actively increase behavioral intention, and more as baseline conditions whose absence undermines trust (Shin & Park, 2019). This characteristic is consistent with the concept of hygiene factors in organizational behavior, which do not enhance motivation when present but generate strong dissatisfaction when lacking (Herzberg, 1966).

In this study, the items reflecting governance-related concerns were reverse-coded prior to analysis. Therefore, higher F3 scores indicate more favorable perceptions of ethics and governance, including clearer responsibility, stronger redress mechanisms, more appropriate data handling, and greater transparency. Based on this perspective, the present study explores the relationship between ethics and governance perceptions and behavioral intention toward AI-based HR systems.

H3: Positive ethics and governance perceptions—relating to responsibility, redress, privacy, and transparency (F3)—positively predict behavioral intention (BI) to use AI-based HR systems.

4. DATA

4.1 Sample

This study employed a questionnaire survey targeting working professionals in Japan. The respondents were working professionals enrolled in an MBA program at a Japanese national university. The survey was administered in paper-based format on August 1, 2025. Participation was voluntary and anonymous; no course credit or monetary incentives were offered. Forty-four valid responses were included in the analysis.

Regarding respondent characteristics, 32 participants were male (72.7%) and 12 were female (27.3%). In terms of job level, 22 respondents (50.0%) were non-managerial employees, 18 (40.9%) held managerial positions, and 4 (9.1%) were classified as other categories. Thus, the sample included a substantial proportion of respondents with managerial experience. Respondents' ages ranged from 27 to 62 years. One response was missing age information, resulting in an effective sample size of 43 for age-related analyses. The mean age was 38.42 years (SD = 7.56), indicating a broad age distribution among working adults. Respondent demographic characteristics are summarized in Table 1.

4.2 Measures

All questionnaire items were measured using a 5-point Likert scale ranging from 1 = strongly disagree to 5 = strongly agree. The questionnaire was initially designed to cover five broad domains: perceived usefulness (PU), perceived ease of use and explainability (PEU), behavioral intention (BI), resistance and dignity-related concerns (RD), and ethics and governance concerns (ECT). These domains were developed based on prior research on technology acceptance, algorithmic decision-making, fairness, explainability, psychological resistance, and AI governance.

Several items were negatively worded in order to capture resistance, anxiety, lack of warmth, uncertainty, and governance-related concerns. These items were reverse-coded prior to analysis so that higher scores reflected the theoretically intended direction of the final constructs. For example, higher scores on psychological acceptance / low resistance indicate lower resistance and greater psychological acceptance, while higher scores on ethics and governance perceptions indicate more favorable perceptions of responsibility, redress, data handling, and transparency after reverse coding. Reverse-coded variables are indicated by the prefix "RQ" in the tables.

Because this study is exploratory in nature, the final factor structure was determined empirically through exploratory factor analysis rather than imposed strictly according to the initial item categories. Accordingly, some items initially designed to reflect a particular theoretical domain were retained in different empirical factors when their factor loadings indicated a stronger association with that factor. Items loading on each factor were interpreted collectively and used to construct composite scores. The full list of questionnaire items, including initial construct labels, reverse-coding procedures, and final analytical use, is provided in Appendix A.

5. ANALYTICAL METHODS

5.1 Exploratory Factor Analysis

Given the underexplored nature of AI-based HR systems, exploratory factor analysis (EFA) was conducted using IBM SPSS Statistics Version 26. Items measuring attitudes and perceptions related to AI-based HR systems were analyzed using Principal Axis Factoring (PAF) with Direct Oblimin rotation, given the expected correlations among factors. The three behavioral intention items used to construct the dependent variable in the regression analysis were excluded from the EFA.

Sampling adequacy was confirmed by the Kaiser–Meyer–Olkin measure (KMO = .707), and Bartlett's test of sphericity was significant, $\chi^2(136) = 333.604$, $p < .001$. Based on eigenvalues, scree plot inspection, and interpretability, a three-factor solution was retained, accounting for 47.39% of the total variance (see Table 2).

5.2 Reliability Analysis and Composite Scores

To examine internal consistency, Cronbach's α coefficients were calculated for each extracted factor and for behavioral intention (BI). Reliability was high for psychological acceptance / low resistance (F1) and explainability–fairness-based trust (F2), and acceptable for behavioral intention. The reliability coefficient for ethics and governance perceptions (F3) was lower, but remained within an acceptable range for exploratory research. Based on these results, composite scores were computed by averaging the corresponding items loading on each factor. Behavioral intention was calculated separately as the mean of the three BI items used as the dependent variable (see Table 3).

5.3 Correlation and Regression Analysis

Prior to hypothesis testing, Pearson's correlation coefficients were calculated to assess associations among the main variables. Subsequently, a multiple regression analysis was conducted with behavioral intention as the dependent variable and psychological acceptance / low resistance (F1), explainability–fairness-based trust (F2), and ethics and governance perceptions (F3) as independent variables, using the Enter method. Regression diagnostics were then conducted to examine whether the assumptions of multiple regression analysis were adequately met before interpreting the regression coefficients.

5.4 Regression Assumption Checks

Prior to interpreting the regression results, key assumptions of multiple regression analysis were examined. Behavioral intention was measured as a composite score based on three Likert-scale items and was treated as an approximately interval-level dependent variable. Linearity and homoscedasticity were assessed by inspecting the scatterplot of standardized residuals against standardized predicted values. The plot did not indicate a clear non-linear pattern or severe heteroscedasticity. The independence of residuals was assessed using the Durbin–Watson statistic. The Durbin–Watson statistic was 2.156, which is close to the ideal value of 2.0, suggesting no serious autocorrelation among the residuals.

Multicollinearity was assessed using variance inflation factors (VIFs). VIF values ranged from 1.138 to 1.324, well below the conventional threshold of 5.0. Potential outliers were assessed using standardized residuals. Standardized residuals ranged from -2.397 to 1.461, and no cases exceeded the commonly used ± 3.0 threshold. Influential cases were assessed using Cook's distance. The maximum Cook's distance was 0.197, which was well below the conventional threshold of 1.0. These results indicate that no serious outliers or highly influential cases were detected in the regression analysis.

The normality of residuals was examined using a histogram and normal P–P plot of standardized residuals. Both plots suggested no substantial departure from normality. Taken together, these diagnostic results suggest that no serious violation of the main assumptions of multiple regression analysis was detected. However, given the exploratory nature of the study and the small sample size, the regression results should be interpreted with caution.

5.5 Supplementary Analysis of Open-Ended Responses

The questionnaire included an open-ended question, yielding 20 valid responses. These responses were analyzed using exploratory content analysis to complement the quantitative results. The analysis examined whether themes corresponding to the three extracted factors appeared in respondents' narratives and also identified additional themes not fully captured by the structured scales.

The analysis revealed supplementary concerns related to AI-based HR systems, including anxiety about model updates and dependence on prompts. These findings provide additional insights into how employees interpret and make sense of AI-based HR practices beyond quantitative measures. A mapping of emergent themes from the open-ended responses to the three extracted factors is provided in Appendix B.

6. RESULTS

6.1 Factor Structure

Exploratory factor analysis identified three factors underlying perceptions of AI-based HR systems. The first factor (F1) reflected psychological acceptance / low resistance, capturing emotional aspects such as perceived warmth, low reluctance, and the absence of strong resistance toward AI-based HR systems. The second factor (F2) represented explainability–fairness-based trust, indicating confidence in transparent, understandable, and fair AI decision-making. The third factor (F3) captured ethics and governance perceptions, including responsibility, redress mechanisms, data handling, and transparency.

Table 2 reports the pattern matrix from the exploratory factor analysis and shows the final empirical item composition of the three composite variables used in the subsequent analyses. The item codes in Table 2 correspond to the full questionnaire items listed in Appendix A. Items with the prefix "RQ" indicate reverse-coded variables. After the factor structure was identified, the items loading on each factor were averaged to construct the corresponding composite scores: psychological acceptance / low resistance (F1), explainability–fairness-based trust (F2), and ethics and governance perceptions (F3). Behavioral intention (BI) was calculated separately as the mean of the three BI items used as the dependent variable.

6.2 Reliability

Internal consistency was assessed using Cronbach's α coefficients. Reliability was high for psychological acceptance / low resistance (F1; $\alpha = .872$) and explainability–

fairness-based trust (F2; $\alpha = .813$), and acceptable for behavioral intention (BI; $\alpha = .745$). Reliability for ethics and governance perceptions (F3; $\alpha = .658$) was lower but remained within an acceptable range for exploratory research.

6.3 Descriptive Statistics and Correlations

Table 4 presents the descriptive statistics and correlations for the main composite variables. The mean scores for psychological acceptance / low resistance (F1), explainability–fairness-based trust (F2), and behavioral intention (BI) were moderate to relatively high, whereas ethics and governance perceptions (F3) showed a comparatively lower mean score. Specifically, the mean score was 3.33 for F1, 3.60 for F2, 2.53 for F3, and 3.75 for BI. The standard deviations ranged from 0.69 to 0.78, indicating moderate variation across respondents.

Correlation analysis showed that behavioral intention was positively and significantly correlated with psychological acceptance / low resistance ($r = .637$, $p < .001$) and explainability–fairness-based trust ($r = .682$, $p < .001$). In contrast, the correlation between ethics and governance perceptions and behavioral intention was not statistically significant ($r = .165$). These results suggest that behavioral intention toward AI-based HR systems is more closely associated with psychological acceptance and explainability–fairness-based trust than with governance-related perceptions.

6.4 Regression Analysis

Multiple regression analysis indicated that the overall model was statistically significant ($R^2 = .613$, $p < .001$). Both explainability–fairness-based trust (F2; $\beta = .514$, $p < .001$) and psychological acceptance / low resistance (F1; $\beta = .442$, $p < .001$) positively predicted behavioral intention. In contrast, ethics and governance perceptions (F3) did not show a significant effect.

Regression diagnostics indicated no serious violation of key assumptions. The Durbin–Watson statistic was 2.156, VIF values ranged from 1.138 to 1.324, standardized residuals ranged from -2.397 to 1.461, and the maximum Cook's distance was 0.197. These results suggest no serious autocorrelation, multicollinearity, outliers, or highly influential cases.

6.5 Supplementary Findings from Open-Ended Responses

Exploratory analysis of open-ended responses supported the quantitative findings. Many respondents emphasized the importance of human judgment, emotional consideration, and dignity in HR decisions, reflecting psychological resistance to fully automated evaluation. Frequent references were also made to explainability and rule clarity, as well as concerns regarding model updates and output instability.

These qualitative insights complement the quantitative results by highlighting the central role of psychological acceptance and cognitive trust in shaping acceptance of AI-based HR systems (see Appendix B).

7. DISCUSSION

These findings refine the application of TAM to AI-HR contexts. TAM remains useful because behavioral intention provides a core outcome variable for understanding acceptance. However, the results suggest that perceived usefulness and ease of use alone are insufficient when AI is used for evaluative and consequential HR decisions. Building on TAM-based acceptance research, algorithmic decision-making studies, and human-centered AI-HR literature, this study shows that behavioral intention toward AI-based HR systems is shaped by explainability–fairness-based trust and psychological acceptance. The significant effects of these factors indicate that employees evaluate AI-HR systems not only as technical tools, but also as organizational decision-making mechanisms that affect dignity, fairness, and relational recognition. Thus, AI-HR acceptance should be understood as a multidimensional process involving cognitive trust, emotional acceptance, and governance-related expectations.

Three major findings are noteworthy. First, explainability–fairness-based trust (F2) and psychological acceptance / low resistance (F1) significantly predicted behavioral intention (BI) to use AI-based HR systems, whereas ethics and governance perceptions (F3) did not directly affect behavioral intention. Second, the strong effect of F2 indicates that acceptance of AI in HR depends not only on instrumental evaluations such as efficiency or usability, but also on the perception that AI-based decisions are explainable, procedurally fair, and institutionally legitimate. Third, the independent effect of F1 suggests that emotional and relational factors are not merely secondary reactions to perceived usefulness, but constitute a central dimension of AI-HR acceptance.

The strong effect of explainability–fairness-based trust suggests that acceptance of AI in HR decisions depends not only on whether AI systems are technically efficient, but also on whether they are perceived as legitimate decision-making mechanisms. Employees are more likely to accept AI-based HR systems when they can understand why a decision is made, when the decision criteria appear fair, and when the process is perceived as institutionally justified. This finding is consistent with previous studies emphasizing the importance of explainability, procedural fairness, and trust in algorithmic decision-making (Binns et al., 2018; Lee, 2018; Shin, 2021a, 2021b).

Recent discussions further suggest that transparency alone is insufficient. In addition to understanding how decisions are made, users must also have the possibility to challenge or appeal those decisions. This concept of contestability has been identified as a key element in sustaining trust in algorithmic systems. Lyons, Velloso, and Miller (2021) demonstrate that transparency by itself does not guarantee accountability. Effective contestability requires institutional safeguards such as human review, independent oversight, and procedural rights (Birahim, 2025). The results of this study suggest that trust grounded in such institutional legitimacy plays a central role in the acceptance of AI-based HR systems.

The independent effect of psychological acceptance / low resistance highlights the importance of emotional and relational factors in AI adoption. Respondents emphasized dignity, human judgment, and emotional consideration. This suggests that AI-based HR systems are not merely technical tools but relational systems that shape how individuals feel they are treated within an organization. This perspective aligns with the concept of interactional justice, which emphasizes respect and interpersonal treatment alongside procedural fairness (Bankins et al., 2022; Lee, 2018; Tyler & Blader, 2003).

According to the group engagement model proposed by Tyler and Blader (2003), respect reflects how individuals perceive their status and recognition within a group. From this perspective, decision procedures communicate identity-relevant information about whether individuals are valued and acknowledged. Consequently, AI-based HR systems may be interpreted not simply as technological tools but as implicit social actors that signal how individuals are positioned within the organization. Lee (2018) similarly shows that negative reactions to algorithmic decision-making often arise not only from concerns about performance or fairness, but also from experiences of being treated dehumanizingly or of lacking social approval. In other words, individuals do not accept decisions simply because they are efficient or formally fair; rather, they are more willing to accept decisions when they feel respected and when the basis of the decision is understandable and legitimate.

This psychological and relational sensitivity may be particularly pronounced in Japanese organizational contexts, where interdependent self-construal and relational recognition are culturally salient. As Markus and Kitayama (1991) argue, individuals in Japanese contexts tend to define themselves in relation to others rather than as fully autonomous actors. In such contexts, evaluation and treatment may be interpreted not merely as assessments of individual performance, but also as signals of relational standing and organizational respect. As a result, AI-based HR systems may be perceived not merely as neutral evaluation mechanisms but as organizational practices that implicitly communicate how employees are valued and recognized.

The concept of "nattoku" helps interpret this finding. In the present study, nattoku should not be understood as a directly measured variable, but as a culturally grounded interpretive framework. In Japanese organizational settings, acceptance of decisions often depends not only on whether the outcome is formally correct or efficient, but also on whether the process is perceived as understandable, respectful, and relationally legitimate. From this perspective, explainability and fairness are not merely cognitive evaluation criteria; they also contribute to employees' sense that the decision can be accepted as reasonable and legitimate. The significant effects of psychological acceptance and explainability–fairness-based trust may therefore reflect the importance of relational recognition and perceived respect in the Japanese HR context.

It should also be noted that the present study does not provide empirical evidence for other Asian countries. Although relational norms, contextual understanding, and interdependent self-construal may be relevant in some other Asian organizational contexts, the present findings should not be generalized beyond Japan without caution. Future comparative studies are needed to examine whether similar mechanisms operate in other cultural settings.

In contrast, ethics and governance perceptions (F3) did not directly predict behavioral intention. This finding suggests that governance-related factors may function less as drivers of active acceptance and more as baseline conditions that are expected to be satisfied. When ethical standards and governance mechanisms are in place, they do not necessarily increase the willingness to use AI systems. However, once they are perceived as absent, trust may decline rapidly.

This interpretation is consistent with previous studies on algorithmic governance (Mittelstadt et al., 2016; Shin & Park, 2019) and also aligns with Herzberg's concept of hygiene factors in organizational behavior. Ethics and governance do not necessarily enhance acceptance, but their absence becomes highly salient and undermines trust. In this sense, governance mechanisms may operate as "governance-by-default" requirements, whereas explainability–fairness-based trust and psychological acceptance function more directly as "trust-by-design" mechanisms that shape behavioral intention.

Taken together, the results indicate that acceptance of AI-based HR systems is primarily shaped by whether the system is perceived as trustworthy and psychologically acceptable. Governance mechanisms are necessary but not sufficient for acceptance. By distinguishing among cognitive trust, psychological acceptance, and governance-related baseline conditions, this study offers a more refined theoretical perspective on the acceptance of AI in organizational decision-making. This theoretical extension helps bridge technology acceptance research and human-centered AI governance in HRM.

These findings also have implications for HR marketing. If AI-based HR systems are understood as internal services that employees must accept, organizations need to communicate not only their technical efficiency but also their fairness, explainability, human oversight, and respect for employee dignity. In this sense, HR marketing is not limited to external employer branding or recruitment communication. It also includes internal communication and legitimacy-building processes through which employees come to understand why AI is being introduced, how it will be used, what safeguards are in place, and how human judgment remains involved.

The significant effects of explainability–fairness-based trust and psychological acceptance suggest that employees do not evaluate AI-HR systems only as technical tools. Rather, they interpret them as organizational practices that signal how employees are recognized, evaluated, and respected. Therefore, HR marketing can play an important role in framing AI-HR implementation as a fair, explainable, and human-centered organizational change, rather than as a purely efficiency-driven automation project.

8. CONCLUSION

This study explored acceptance of AI-based HR systems among working professionals in Japan and identified key cognitive and psychological dimensions underlying behavioral intention. The findings indicate that explainability–fairness-based trust and psychological acceptance / low resistance are significant predictors of acceptance, while ethics and governance perceptions appear to function more as foundational conditions than as direct motivators.

By emphasizing users' psychological perceptions rather than formal institutional distinctions alone, this study reframes AI-based HR systems as internal services that must be accepted by employees. This perspective provides a bridge between AI governance research and HR marketing. From an HR marketing perspective, the implementation of AI-HR systems requires more than technical deployment; it requires internal communication that explains the value, fairness, transparency, safeguards, and human-centered design of the system. Organizations seeking to introduce AI into HR should therefore communicate not only what AI can do, but also why it is legitimate, how it respects employee dignity, and how human judgment remains involved in consequential decisions.

Given the exploratory nature and limited sample size of this study, the findings should be interpreted with caution. Although the regression diagnostics did not indicate serious violations of the main assumptions, the sample size was relatively small, and the factor structure identified in this study should be regarded as provisional. Future research should examine the robustness of these findings using larger and more diverse samples, apply confirmatory factor analysis or structural equation modeling, examine indirect effects of governance factors through trust, and operationalize "nattoku," self-construal, and cultural moderators more directly. Cross-cultural comparative research would also be valuable for determining whether the mechanisms identified in the Japanese context apply to other Asian or non-Asian organizational settings.

ACKNOWLEDGMENT

This work was partially supported by JSPS KAKENHI Grant Number JP26K05161.

REFERENCES

Acquisti, A., Brandimarte, L., & Loewenstein, G. (2015). Privacy and human behavior in the age of information. *Science*, *347*(6221), 509–514. DOI: 10.1126/science.aaa1465 PMID: 25635091

Ahn, D., Almaatouq, A., Gulabani, M., & Hosanagar, K. (2021). Will we trust what we don't understand? Impact of model interpretability and outcome feedback on trust in AI. *arXiv*. https://arxiv.org/abs/2111.08222

Ali, A., & Rafi, N. (2024). Enhancing human resource management through advanced decision-making strategies: Harnessing the power of artificial intelligence for strategic, data-driven, and judicious choices. *Migration Letters : An International Journal of Migration Studies*, *21*(S8), 881–889. DOI: 10.59670/ml.v21iS8.9488

Araujo, T., Helberger, N., Kruikemeier, S., & de Vreese, C. H. (2020). In AI we trust? Perceptions about automated decision-making by artificial intelligence. *AI & Society*, *35*(3), 611–623. DOI: 10.1007/s00146-019-00931-w

Bankins, S., Formosa, P., Griep, Y., & Richards, D. (2022). AI decision making with dignity? Contrasting workers' justice perceptions of human and AI decision making in a human resource management context. *Information Systems Frontiers*, *24*(3), 857–875. DOI: 10.1007/s10796-021-10223-8

Bedemariam, R., & Wessel, J. L. (2023). The roles of outcome and race on applicant reactions to AI systems. *Computers in Human Behavior*, *148*, 107869. DOI: 10.1016/j.chb.2023.107869

Benabou, A., & Touhami, F. (2025). Artificial intelligence in human resource management: A PRISMA-based systematic review. *Acta Informatica Pragensia*, *14*(3), 489–505. DOI: 10.18267/j.aip.264

Binns, R., Van Kleek, M., Veale, M., Lyngs, U., Zhao, J., & Shadbolt, N. (2018). "It's reducing a human being to a percentage": Perceptions of justice in algorithmic decisions. In *Proceedings of the 2018 CHI Conference on Human Factors in Computing Systems* (pp. 1–14). Association for Computing Machinery. DOI: 10.1145/3173574.3173951

Birahim, S. A. (2025). Contesting the algorithm: Advancing a right to challenge AI decisions under the GDPR for algorithmic fairness. *Transforming Government: People. Process and Policy*, *19*(4), 895–913. doi:10.1108/TG-05-2025-0148

Biswas, M. I., Talukder, M. S., & Khan, A. R. (2024). Who do you choose? Employees' perceptions of artificial intelligence versus humans in performance feedback. *China Accounting and Finance Review*, *26*(4), 512–532. DOI: 10.1108/CAFR-08-2023-0095

Bouzerda, K., Hani, S., Rahmani, H., Hebaz, A., Dibi, A., & Mharzi, H. (2025). The rise of AI in human resource management: A systematic review of task automation through PRISMA. *Human Resources Management and Services*, *7*(4). Advance online publication. DOI: 10.18282/hrms4595

Calluso, C., & Devetag, M. G. (2025). The impact of technology acceptance and personality traits on the willingness to use AI-assisted hiring practices. *The International Journal of Organizational Analysis*, *33*(5), 1368–1385. DOI: 10.1108/IJOA-06-2024-4562

Cao, G. (2025). Domain expertise and AI adoption: Insights into HR managers' unified perspectives across roles and contexts. In *Proceedings of the 27th International Conference on Enterprise Information Systems (ICEIS 2025)* (Vol. 1, pp. 732–739). DOI: 10.5220/0013232200003929

Chheda, K., Thakur, U., Das, G. P., Parashar, M. K., & Reddy, K. (2025). AI-powered human resource management for enhancing employee recruitment efficiency and talent retention in organizations. *Management (Montevideo)*, *3*, 165. DOI: 10.62486/agma2025165

Davis, F. D. (1989). Perceived usefulness, perceived ease of use, and user acceptance of information technology. *Management Information Systems Quarterly*, *13*(3), 319–340. DOI: 10.2307/249008

Egea, J. M. O., & González, M. V. R. (2011). Explaining physicians' acceptance of EHCR systems: An extension of TAM with trust and risk factors. *Computers in Human Behavior*, *27*(1), 319–332. DOI: 10.1016/j.chb.2010.08.010

Fabeyo, S. (2025). Explainable AI in employment decision-making: A systematic review of transparency methods in hiring algorithms. *Issues in Information Systems*, *26*(3) 127–135. doi:10.48009/3_iis_2025_2025_110.

Fragouli, E. (2025). Workplace digital empathy: Reimagining employee well-being through AI. *The Business & Management Review*, *16*(2), 240–248. DOI: 10.24052/BMR/V16NU02/ART-22

Heffernan, M., & Dundon, T. (2016). Cross-level effects of high-performance work systems (HPWS) and employee well-being: The mediating effect of organisational justice. *Human Resource Management Journal*, *26*(2), 211–231. DOI: 10.1111/1748-8583.12095

Herzberg, F. (1966). *Work and the nature of man*. World Publishing.

Ismatullaev, U. V. U., & Kim, S.-H. (2024). Review of the factors affecting acceptance of AI-infused systems. *Human Factors*, *66*(1), 126–144. DOI: 10.1177/00187208211064707 PMID: 35344676

Kartikeya, A. (2022). Examining correlation between trust and transparency with explainable artificial intelligence. In *Science and Information Conference* (pp. 353–358). Springer. DOI: 10.1007/978-3-031-10464-0_23

Khalid, M. A., Sohail, M., Baig, M. M. B., Yusaf, S., Iqbal, A., & Syed, M. I. (2025). The human-centric paradox of AI in HRM: How technostress and digital literacy co-determine employee productivity in smart work environments. *Inverge Journal of Social Sciences*, *4*(4), 214–227. DOI: 10.63544/ijss.v4i4.191

Köchling, A., & Wehner, M. C. (2020). Discriminated by an algorithm: A systematic review of discrimination and fairness by algorithmic decision-making in the context of HR recruitment and HR development. *Business Research*, *13*(3), 795–848. DOI: 10.1007/s40685-020-00134-w

Köchling, A., Wehner, M. C., & Warkocz, J. (2023). Can I show my skills? Affective responses to artificial intelligence in the recruitment process. *Review of Managerial Science*, *17*(6), 2109–2138. DOI: 10.1007/s11846-021-00514-4

Laurim, V., Arpaci, S., Prommegger, B., & Krcmar, H. (2021). Computer, whom should I hire? Acceptance criteria for artificial intelligence in the recruitment process. In *Proceedings of the 54th Hawaii International Conference on System Sciences* (pp. 5494–5504). DOI: 10.24251/HICSS.2021.668

Lee, M. K. (2018). Understanding perception of algorithmic decisions: Fairness, trust, and emotion in response to algorithmic management. *Big Data & Society*, *5*(1), 1–16. DOI: 10.1177/2053951718756684

Lemons, M. A., & Jones, C. A. (2001). Procedural justice in promotion decisions: Using perceptions of fairness to build employee commitment. *Journal of Managerial Psychology*, *16*(4), 268–280. DOI: 10.1108/02683940110391517

Lepri, B., Oliver, N., Letouzé, E., Pentland, A., & Vinck, P. (2018). Fair, transparent, and accountable algorithmic decision-making processes: The premise, the proposed solutions, and the open challenges. *Philosophy & Technology*, *31*(4), 611–627. DOI: 10.1007/s13347-017-0279-x

Lyons, H., Velloso, E., & Miller, T. (2021). Fair and responsible AI: A focus on the ability to contest. *arXiv*. https://arxiv.org/abs/2102.10787

Mantello, P., Ho, M.-T., Nguyen, M.-H., & Vuong, Q.-H. (2023). Bosses without a heart: Socio-demographic and cross-cultural determinants of attitude toward emotional AI in the workplace. *AI & Society*, *38*(1), 97–119. DOI: 10.1007/s00146-021-01290-1 PMID: 34776651

Markus, H. R., & Kitayama, S. (1991). Culture and the self: Implications for cognition, emotion, and motivation. *Psychological Review*, *98*(2), 224–253. DOI: 10.1037/0033-295X.98.2.224

Mittelstadt, B. D., Allo, P., Taddeo, M., Wachter, S., & Floridi, L. (2016). The ethics of algorithms: Mapping the debate. *Big Data & Society*, *3*(2), 1–21. DOI: 10.1177/2053951716679679

Nakano, C., Yamada, T., Fukunaga, A., & Nomura, C. (2009). The fifth survey study of the institutionalization of ethics in Japanese corporations. [in Japanese]. *Journal of Japan Society for Business Ethics Study*, *16*, 151–163.

Park, H., Ahn, D., Hosanagar, K., & Lee, J. (2021). Human–AI interaction in human resource management: Understanding why employees resist algorithmic evaluation at workplaces and how to mitigate burdens. In *Proceedings of the 2021 CHI Conference on Human Factors in Computing Systems* (pp. 1–15). Association for Computing Machinery. DOI: 10.1145/3411764.3445304

Pavlou, P. A. (2003). Consumer acceptance of electronic commerce: Integrating trust and risk with the technology acceptance model. *International Journal of Electronic Commerce*, *7*(3), 101–134. DOI: 10.1080/10864415.2003.11044275

Revillod, G. (2025a). Exploring the acceptability of artificial intelligence in human resources management: Insights from Swiss organizations. *Systems Research and Behavioral Science*, *42*(4), 1061–1084. DOI: 10.1002/sres.3140

Revillod, G. (2025b). Trust influence on AI HR tools perceived usefulness in Swiss HRM: The mediating roles of perceived fairness and privacy concerns. *AI & Society*, *40*(6), 1–34. DOI: 10.1007/s00146-025-02216-x

Sadeghi, S. (2024). Employee well-being in the age of AI: Perceptions, concerns, behaviors, and outcomes. *arXiv*. https://arxiv.org/abs/2412.04796

Setiawati, R., Kusmara, A., & Kuusk, T. (2025). Managing transparency, fairness, and accountability in AI for sustainable human resource management. In *2025 4th International Conference on Creative Communication and Innovative Technology (ICCIT)* (pp. 1–7). IEEE. DOI: 10.1109/ICCIT65724.2025.11166968

Shin, D. (2021a). The effects of explainability and causability on perception, trust, and acceptance: Implications for explainable AI. *International Journal of Human-Computer Studies*, *146*, 102551. DOI: 10.1016/j.ijhcs.2020.102551

Shin, D. (2021b). The effects of explainability and transparency on trust in and acceptance of AI. *Information Communication and Society*, *24*(9), 1223–1241. DOI: 10.1080/1369118X.2020.1776378

Shin, D., & Park, Y. J. (2019). Role of fairness, accountability, and transparency in algorithmic trust. *Telematics and Informatics*, *38*, 33–45. DOI: 10.1016/j.tele.2018.11.007

Suriyaa, S. (2024). Exploring an AI-based algorithmic framework for ethical decision-making in human resource management procedures. *Shanlax International Journal of Management, 11*(S1-Mar), 228–234. DOI: 10.34293/management.v11iS1-Mar.8110

Suseno, Y., Chang, C., Hudik, M., & Fang, E. S. (2022). Beliefs, anxiety and change readiness for artificial intelligence adoption among human resource managers: The moderating role of high-performance work systems. *International Journal of Human Resource Management*, *33*(6), 1209–1236. DOI: 10.1080/09585192.2021.1931408

Tyler, T. R., & Blader, S. L. (2003). The group engagement model: Procedural justice, social identity, and cooperative behavior. *Personality and Social Psychology Review*, *7*(4), 349–361. DOI: 10.1207/S15327957PSPR0704_07 PMID: 14633471

Venkatesh, V., & Davis, F. D. (2000). A theoretical extension of the technology acceptance model: Four longitudinal field studies. *Management Science*, *46*(2), 186–204. DOI: 10.1287/mnsc.46.2.186.11926

Vorm, E. S., & Combs, D. J. (2022). Integrating transparency, trust, and acceptance: The intelligent systems technology acceptance model (ISTAM). *International Journal of Human-Computer Interaction*, *38*(18–20), 1828–1845. DOI: 10.1080/10447318.2022.2070107

Wang, Y., Kim, S., Rafferty, A., & Sanders, K. (2020). Employee perceptions of HR practices: A critical review and future directions. *International Journal of Human Resource Management*, *31*(1), 128–173. DOI: 10.1080/09585192.2019.1674360

Wolfe, D., Price, M., Choe, A., Kidd, F., & Wagner, H. (2025). Revisiting UTAUT for the age of AI: Understanding employees' AI adoption and usage patterns through an extended UTAUT framework. *arXiv*. https://arxiv.org/abs/2510.15142

Yamada, T., Nakano, C., & Fukunaga, A. (2020). The effects of organizational ethical climate on unethical conduct: An empirical study in Japanese firms. [in Japanese]. *Journal of Business Ethics Studies*, *27*, 187–203.

Yanamala, K. K. R. (2023). Transparency, privacy, and accountability in AI-enhanced HR processes. *Journal of Advanced Computing Systems*, *3*(3), 10–18. DOI: 10.69987/JACS.2023.30302

Yang, M. M., Lu, Y., & Cooke, F. L. (2026). Demystifying AI for the workforce: The role of explainable AI in worker acceptance and management relations. *Journal of Management Studies*, *63*(2), 438–472. DOI: 10.1111/joms.70039

Zhang, L., & Amos, C. (2024). Dignity and use of algorithm in performance evaluation. *Behaviour & Information Technology*, *43*(2), 401–418. DOI: 10.1080/0144929X.2022.2164214

Zhu, C. (2025). The role of AI tools in optimizing human resource management practices. *Advances in Curriculum Design & Education*, *1*(2), 1–13. DOI: 10.63808/acde.v1i2.132

APPENDIX

Table 1. Respondent Characteristics (Gender, Age, and Position)

Variable	Category	n	%
Gender			
	Male	32	72.7
	Female	12	27.3
Job level			
	Non-manager	22	50.0
	Manager	18	40.9
	Other	4	9.1
Age(N=43)			
	Mean(SD)	38.4(7.6)	
	Range	27-62	
20s (20-29)		4	9.3
30s (30-39)		22	51.2
40s (40-49)		14	32.6
50s (50-59)		2	4.7
60s (60-69)		1	2.3

Note. One age response is missing; valid N = 43.

Table 2. Pattern Matrix from Exploratory Factor Analysis (PAF with Direct Oblimin Rotation)

Construct (Factor)	Item	Short label	Loading
F1 Psychological Acceptance / Low Resistance	**RQ24**	Perceived lack of human warmth	**0.889**
	Q5	Supports person–job fit	**0.832**
	RQ25	Concern about constraining everyday behavior	**0.683**
	RQ21	Reluctance due to uncertainty	**0.679**
	RQ23	Concern about being unable to accept decisions	**0.506**
	RQ19	Desire to avoid involvement	**0.498**
	Q18	Perceived no major issues	**0.476**

continued on following page

Table 2. Continued

Construct (Factor)	Item	Short label	Loading
F2 Explainability–Fairness-Based Trust	**Q12**	Understanding of decision logic	**0.837**
	Q11	Explainable evaluation criteria	**0.700**
	Q7	Fairness of promotion decisions	**0.680**
	Q8	Reduced managerial subjectivity	**0.603**
	Q27	Perceived higher reliability	**0.520**
F3 Ethics & Governance Perceptions	**RQ15**	Difficulty fully understanding the system	**0.607**
	RQ29	Concern about unclear accountability	**0.554**
	RQ32	Lack of an appeal process is problematic	**0.538**
	RQ28	Concern about purposes of personal-data use	**0.506**
	RQ31	Perceived black-box opacity	**0.418**

Note. Extraction: Principal Axis Factoring. Rotation: Direct Oblimin (Kaiser normalized). Loadings < .40 suppressed. N = 44. The item codes correspond to the full questionnaire items listed in Appendix A. Reverse-coded items are indicated by the prefix "RQ." Items loading on each factor were averaged to construct the corresponding composite score.

Table 3. Scale Reliability (Cronbach's α) and Composite Score Construction

Scale	Items (k)	Cronbach's α
F1 Psychological Acceptance / Low Resistance	7	0.872
F2 Explainability–Fairness-Based Trust	5	0.813
F3 Ethics & Governance Perceptions	5	0.658
BI Behavioral Intention	3	0.745

Table 4. Descriptive Statistics (Means and Standard Deviations) and Correlations

Variable	Mean	SD	1	2	3	4
1. Psychological Acceptance (F1)	3.3312	0.7719	—			
2. Explainability–Fairness-Based Trust (F2)	3.5955	0.6988	.450**	—		
3. Ethics and Governance Perceptions (F3)	2.5318	0.6914	.318*	.269	—	
4. Behavioral Intention (BI)	3.75	0.7846	.637***	.682***	0.165	—

Note. Composite scores were calculated by averaging the items loading on each factor. BI was calculated as the mean of the three behavioral intention items. * p < .05, ** p < .01, *** p < .001.

Table 5. Multiple Regression Analysis Predicting Behavioral Intention

Predictor	B	SE	β	t	p	95% CI for B	VIF
Constant	0.506	0.463	—	1.092	0.282	[−0.431, 1.442]	—
Psychological Acceptance (F1)	0.450	0.115	0.442	3.911	< .001	[0.217, 0.682]	1.324
Explainability–Fairness-Based Trust (F2)	0.577	0.125	0.514	4.616	< .001	[0.324, 0.829]	1.282
Ethics & Governance Perceptions (F3)	−0.129	0.119	−.114	−1.087	0.284	[−0.370, 0.111]	1.138

Model fit: R = .783, R^2 = .613, Adjusted R^2 = .584, F(3, 40) = 21.163, p < .001, SEE = .506.

Table 6. Survey Items and Final Use in Analyses

Construct	Item code	Item wording	Reverse-coded (analysis var.)	Final use
PU	Q4	If AI is introduced into HR, the transparency of evaluations will increase.	No (Q4)	Excluded
PU	Q5	AI-based placement decisions help achieve the right person in the right job.	No (Q5)	F1
PU	Q6	Feedback based on AI analysis is helpful for my growth/development.	No (Q6)	Excluded
PU	Q7	AI-based HR evaluations make promotion decisions fairer.	No (Q7)	F2
PU	Q8	AI in HR reduces managers' subjectivity.	No (Q8)	F2
PU	Q9	For final HR decisions, subjective evaluations by humans are the most trustworthy.	Yes (RQ9)	Excluded
PEU	Q10	I feel it is easy to understand how AI evaluates me.	No (Q10)	Excluded
PEU	Q11	I think AI evaluation criteria are explainable to employees.	No (Q11)	F2
PEU	Q12	I can understand the logic behind AI-based decisions.	No (Q12)	F2
PEU	Q13	AI systems are too complex to understand.	Yes (RQ13)	Excluded
PEU	Q14	Information about the AI HR system is appropriately disclosed to employees.	No (Q14)	Excluded
PEU	Q15	It is difficult to fully understand how AI-based evaluations work.	Yes (RQ15)	F3
BI	Q16	If there were an AI-based evaluation system, I would like to use it.	No (Q16)	BI
BI	Q17	If an AI interview tool were introduced, I would actively use it.	No (Q17)	BI
BI	Q18	I think there is no particular problem with AI-based HR evaluations.	No (Q18)	F1

continued on following page

Table 6. Continued

Construct	Item code	Item wording	Reverse-coded (analysis var.)	Final use
BI	Q19	I would rather not be involved with AI in HR.	Yes (RQ19)	F1
BI	Q20	I am positive about AI becoming central to HR in the future.	No (Q20)	BI
BI	Q21	AI-based evaluation systems have many uncertainties, so I am reluctant to introduce them.	Yes (RQ21)	F1
RD	Q22	I feel uncomfortable in a workplace where AI monitors employees.	Yes (RQ22)	Excluded
RD	Q23	I think there will often be AI decisions that I cannot accept.	Yes (RQ23)	F1
RD	Q24	AI-based evaluations lack human warmth.	Yes (RQ24)	F1
RD	Q25	I think AI would unnecessarily constrain my day-to-day behavior.	Yes (RQ25)	F1
RD	Q26	There is an atmosphere that the introduction of AI in HR is welcomed.	No (Q26)	Excluded
RD	Q27	I feel AI is more reliable than humans because it is less influenced by emotions.	No (Q27)	F2
ECT	Q28	I am concerned about the purpose for which AI uses the personal data it collects.	Yes (RQ28)	F3
ECT	Q29	I feel uneasy that accountability is unclear even if AI's decision is wrong.	Yes (RQ29)	F3
ECT	Q30	Because AI cannot understand emotions or context, important decisions should be made by humans.	Yes (RQ30)	Excluded
ECT	Q31	I feel AI's decision process is a black box and opaque.	Yes (RQ31)	F3
ECT	Q32	I think it is a problem if employees cannot appeal AI-based evaluations.	Yes (RQ32)	F3
ECT	Q33	I think AI's decision criteria are clear and consistent.	No (Q33)	Excluded

1. Labels in parentheses indicate the intended construct (PU, PEU, BI, RD, ECT).
2. Items marked as reverse-coded were reverse-scored prior to analysis; the reverse-coded variables are denoted as RQxx.
3. "Final use" indicates whether the item was included in the final composite scores. Items not included are marked as "Excluded."
4. The questionnaire was administered in Japanese; the English wordings below are provided as author translations for reference.

Table 7. Themes Identified from Open-Ended Responses (n = 20)

Theme	Link to factors	n	%	Representative excerpts (short examples)
1. Human warmth, dignity, and relational legitimacy (psychological acceptance)	F1	5	25%	"Attune to people's feelings." / "Consider the person's 'heart'."
2. Explainability, rules, and acceptability (wanting to know reasons)	F2	4	20%	"Clear rules are necessary." / "I worry whether I can know the reason."
3. Usefulness, growing trust, and low resistance	BI / F1 / F2	6	30%	"I don't see any issues." / "Convenient (already used for self-analysis)."
4. Concerns about consistency and stability (model updates / prompt dependence)	Candidate extension of F2	2	10%	"If the model changes, the output changes." / "Results change depending on the prompt."
5. Data handling, leakage, and input-related risks (governance)	F3	3	15%	"Risk of data leakage." / "Humans are the ones who enter the data."
6. Bias, neutrality, and customization needs (fairness concerns)	F2 / F3	3	15%	"Bias caused by AI." / "Decisions differ by company → customization is needed."

Note. Percentages are calculated using *n = 20* open-ended responses as the denominator. Because a single response may include multiple themes, counts/percentages may overlap.

Chapter 7
Artificial Intelligence and Human Resource Management:
The Case of the Agricultural Credit Bank of Morocco

Adil El-Ouali
http://orcid.org/0009-0008-6615-1828
Sidi Mohamed Ben Abdellah University, Morocco

Ahmed El Hammoumi
Faculty of Legal, Economic, and Social Sciences, Dhar Mehrez, Fès, Morocco

ABSTRACT

The main objective of this study is to examine how artificial intelligence (AI) contributes to improving human resource management (HRM) in the case of the Agricultural Credit Bank of Morocco. In this context, the objective is to study and evaluate the impact of AI on the performance and productivity of human resources in a rapidly changing banking sector. The study is based on a quantitative methodology, conducted with a sample of 377 employees working at Banque Agricole du Crédit du Maroc, in order to achieve the objective of testing the dimension of artificial intelligence, taking into consideration the factors of human resources and technological tools. The analysis of the results was conducted using SPSS software, which allowed us to explore the link between the use of AI tools and its impact on HRM.

DOI: 10.4018/979-8-2600-2303-7.ch007

1. INTRODUCTION TO THE STUDY

1.1 Introduction

This chapter examines the influence of the digital revolution on the banking sector, focusing on the lack of empirical data related to the use of artificial intelligence through the case study of the Agricultural Credit Bank of Morocco. It highlights a major problem: the gap between significant technological investments and the inadequacy of human process dynamics as a consequence of rigid organizational structures. The study suggests an in-house competency assessment model and emphasizes the critical importance of human resources management (HRM) for transformation success. In addition, it offers professionals diagnostic tools to face the challenges related to the integration of new technologies such as artificial intelligence (AI), thus contributing to improving agility and updating human resources.

Banks face a growing challenge today to adapt to new technologies to survive and thrive in a competitive environment (Vives, 2019). For this, they must be technologically superior to their rivals (Puschmann, 2017), which leads many banks to use AI, especially in HR practices (Marques & Ferreira, 2020). AI aims to improve performance, decision quality, and operational efficiency (El Hammoumi & El-Ouali, 2025). The HRM have access to modern tools, such as digital technologies and robotics, which allow them to optimize their daily operations. These innovations stimulate creativity and agility within organizations and modernize HR processes, thus improving the overall performance of the company (El Hammoumi, Seghyar, El Hammoumi & El-Ouali, 2024). Recent literature specifies that new AI technologies contribute to organisational learning and managerial innovation, as well as strategic talent management through the automation of certain tasks and skills development (El-Ouali & Jellouli, 2025), thereby contributing to the competitiveness and resilience of the company, particularly in the post-Covid-19 era, where HRM must be able to adapt (El-Ouali & Jellouli, 2024).

Banks must face a continuous challenge of technological evolution that is currently becoming increasingly important, as they must constantly adapt to new technologies (Vives, 2019). Currently, to stay alive and grow, banks and neo-banks must be technologically advanced enough compared to their competitors (Puschmann, 2017). This requirement is notably what explains why many banks with large databases use artificial intelligence technologies, particularly in the field of HRM (Marques & Ferreira, 2020). They improve through performance, the quality of their decisions, and work efficiency (Arner et al., 2020).

HRM is seen as the fundamental basis of banking institutions, as it oversees the most valuable asset, namely human capital (Mahato, 2023). It is responsible for all activities related to human resources, ranging from the hiring, interviewing, and recruitment process to training and feedback collection, in order to identify the necessary skills based on the resources it has available (Amir et al., 2024). The optimal performance of all HR functions reflects the achievement of its goals, thus providing banks with a competitive advantage that sets them apart from their rivals (Alzghoul & Khaddam, 2024). It is precisely in this context that the present study is situated, which aims to define the role played by AI in optimising HRM in the banking sector, specifically in the case of the Agricultural Credit Bank of Morocco.

1.2 Previous Studies

1.2.1 Studies Related to Artificial Intelligence

According to some research, the integration of AI is transforming human resource management methods in companies. According to Tambe and his team (2019), although artificial intelligence facilitates automation and data analysis for HR managers, its integration faces challenges such as algorithmic biases and social adherence. Furthermore, Gélinas et al. (2022) emphasize that AI, now omnipresent in all aspects of HRM, from recruitment to performance evaluation, raises ethical and legal questions requiring appropriate governance.

For Ncube, Sishi, and Skinner (2025), AI perfects HRM by reducing human errors and refining procedures, but it depends on company preparation, employee training, and process clarity. According to Edralin (2010), human resource management approaches have promoted entrepreneurship in large Filipino companies, highlighting the paramount importance of staff-company interactions, training, development, and recruitment to achieve operational excellence.

What is important is that the study by Vlachos (2019) highlighted the role of HR practices in business growth and their link with performance. Chen and Huang (2009) demonstrated that knowledge management strengthens this link, highlighting a positive correlation between HR strategies, knowledge management, and creative performance. These studies highlight the benefits of AI technologies for HR, provided they are effective and promote employee involvement.

1.2.2 Studies Related to Human Resource Management (HRM)

Several studies show that the integration of AI-based technologies in HRM has a major impact on the transformation of practices within the organisation. Thus, according to Tambe, Cappelli, and Yakubovich (2019), while AI allows for efficient automation while better orchestrating data processing to inform HR decision-makers, the adoption of the technology remains significantly constrained by major obstacles such as algorithmic biases, the limitations of internal data processed, or even social acceptability. At the same time, Gélinas et al. (2022) show, through a systematic review, that AI is now involved in the entire HR lifecycle - from recruitment to performance management - establishing itself as a source of value, but also as an ethical, even legal, issue to be regulated by governance bodies. For Ncube, Sishi, and Skinner (2025), while AI has the potential to make human resource management more efficient, for example by reducing the number of human errors or by streamlining various processes, its positive effect largely revolves around organisational preparation, employee training, and adherence to the principles of transparency and fairness.

Edralin's study (2010) aimed to determine the extent to which HRM practices aid entrepreneurship and also to identify the HRM functions that are most entrepreneurship-oriented in large Philippine companies. One of the major findings of this study is that the companies in the group apply many human resource management practices, that these practices are related to HR functions, and that employee relations, training and development, recruitment, and selection almost equally help achieve operational excellence in these companies. While Vlachos's (2019) study aimed to highlight the extent to which HR practices can contribute to the company's growth, as well as to reveal the link that may exist between human resource management practices and the company's performance.

While Chen and Huang's (2009) study aimed to examine the impact of knowledge management on the link between human resource practices and creative performance. One of the major findings of the research reveals a positive correlation between human resource strategies, knowledge management, and creative performance.

Ultimately, the writings showed us that for HR, AI technologies have virtues to mobilise, provided they are effective from the standpoint of human resources and employee engagement.

1.2.3 Commentary on Previous Studies

By reviewing previous studies, the gaps between these studies and the present study can be identified as follows:

- Previous studies have varied in their determination of sample size, ranging from small to large samples of workers surveyed. However, this study was based on a sample of 294 employees of the bank under study, which made it easier for the researcher to obtain results for statistical analysis and recommendations to contribute to its development.
- The methodology of previous studies varied, with some studies using a descriptive and analytical approach and others using an empirical approach. This study uses a descriptive and analytical approach, which involves study-

ing the phenomenon under investigation as it occurs in reality, describing it accurately and expressing it qualitatively by explaining its characteristics, as well as quantitatively by providing a description that specifies the scope or size of the phenomenon and its degree of correlation with other phenomena, insofar as this corresponds to the subject of the study and its objectives.

- This study is consistent with several previous studies in that it relies on a survey to collect the data necessary for the study from respondents.
- Previous literature has informed this study in its approach to the literature and theoretical foundations of artificial intelligence, its dimensions and determinants, and human resource management. It has also helped this study to define the optimal methodology for measuring the study variables.

1.3 Research Question

Moroccan banks face obstacles in using modern technologies in human resource management. Studies show that there are organizational and administrative barriers that limit the optimal use of these technologies. Many employees do not possess the necessary technical skills and lack the motivation to use them. This underscores the importance of focusing on artificial intelligence in human resource management. The main problem is the weakness of HR functions at the bank in our case study due to the inadequacy of the artificial intelligence systems. That is why the issue of our study lies in diagnosing the human resources functions within the Crédit Agricole Bank of Morocco and their alignment with the implemented artificial intelligence systems.

1.4 Objectives of the Study

This study aims to analyze the role of artificial intelligence in improving human resources management within the bank Crédit Agricole du Maroc. This objective is achieved through the following areas: Analysis of the impact of human skills on the application of AI to improve human resources management within the Crédit Agricole bank in Morocco. highlighting the link between the concrete possibilities for applying AI and improving HRM within the Crédit Agricole bank of Morocco, analysis of the impact of artistic techniques for applying artificial intelligence on improving human resources management within the Crédit Agricole bank in Morocco, and the formulation of recommendations based on the results of this study.

1.5 Significance of the Study

This study derives its importance from the following factors:

a. The study presents a scientific analysis showing the impact of artificial intelligence on improving human resources management at the Agricultural Credit Bank of Morocco.
b. The internal problems faced by human resource management at the bank under review highlight the importance of adopting artificial intelligence programmes, as it is no longer possible to address these problems by increasing the number of employees, intensifying their training and increasing their capabilities.
c. Lack of research and studies on the impact of artificial intelligence on improving human resource management.
d. Importance of the sector of application (Agricultural Credit Bank of Morocco) This reinforces the importance of accessing results and recommendations that help management improve the bank's human resources management, considered to be the oldest bank operating in the banking sector.

1.6 Hypotheses of the Study

This study aims to test the following hypotheses:

Hypothesis n° 1: *there is a statistically significant relationship between the human potential for applying artificial intelligence and the improvement of human resources management within the Agricultural Credit Bank of Morocco.*

Hypothesis n° 2: *There is a statistically significant relationship between the material possibilities for applying artificial intelligence and the improvement of human resources management within Agricultural Credit Bank of Morocco.*

Hypothesis n° 3: *There is a statistically significant relationship between the technical dimension of artificial intelligence application technologies and improved human resource management at Agricultural Credit Bank of Morocco.*

1.7 Study Methodology

This study is based on a descriptive and analytical approach that involves examining and analysing all aspects of the entry. This approach is applied to the bank under study, enabling the following points to be determined:

1.7.1 Population and Samples Studied

The study population consisted of employees of Agricultural Credit Bank of Morocco. From this population, a sample was selected from different hierarchical levels, namely senior management, middle management and executive management. The study was based on a stratified random sample due to the relative homogeneity between the elements of its vocabulary and those of the population studied. This population comprised 12479 elements, while the research sample was constructed using a simple random sampling method, due to the relative homogeneity between the elements and units of this population, which allows this sample to represent the population studied to a large extent. This sample comprised 294 elements.

1.7.2 Data Collection Tools

For the Theoretical Study

The theoretical framework of this study is based on a set of scientific resources in French and English related to the subject under investigation, derived from the following sources: books and references, periodicals and research published on the Internet, conference proceedings related to the subject of our study, published scientific theses, and conference proceedings and scientific journals.

Regarding the Field Work

The data was collected using questionnaires developed on the basis of the theoretical study. These questionnaires were distributed to a sample of bankers working in the banks studied, and individual interviews were also conducted with some of them.

1.7.3 Data Processing Methods

We used a statistical software specialized in social sciences and statistical techniques tailored to the study's objectives to analyze the collected data. The methods used include the Cronbach alpha test to evaluate the consistency of the measurement tool, the survey reliability coefficient, the arithmetic means to judge the relevance of the responses from the examined sample in relation to the aspects of the study, the standard deviation to measure the level of dispersion of the participants' responses to each question on the studied variables and each main axis in relation to their arithmetic mean, and the coefficient of variation between the responses, as well as the simple linear regression test to analyze the correlation coefficient between the studied variables and establish the strength of their link.

1.8 Limitations of the Study

The limitations of this study are outlined in three main points: first, the temporal limitations that restrict the research to the period 2024-2025, dedicated to preparation. Next, the spatial limitations, focusing the analysis on the Agricultural Credit Bank of Morocco, increase the number of targeted community members and facilitate interactions with them. Finally, the objective limits, where the study focuses on the impact of the bank's adoption of artificial intelligence technologies on the improvement of human resource management, are clear.

2. THEORETICAL FRAMEWORK OF THE STUDY

2.1 Artificial Intelligence

Artificial intelligence encompasses computer systems and software that attempt to mimic human behaviour. Yufik (2019) asserts that these are the most intelligent programmes in computers, as they comprise two trends: the first is to increase the scope of information processing, and the second is to increase the degree of information comprehension. In other words, artificial intelligence comprises computer systems and software that attempt to mimic human behaviour. Jordan and Mitchell (2015) assert that these are the most intelligent programmes in computers, as they comprise two trends: the first is to increase the scope of information processing, and the second is to increase the degree of understanding of information. So, artificial intelligence allows companies to improve their processes, reduce their costs, and increase their efficiency, with employees increasingly relying on it to facilitate their decision-making and simplify the execution of their tasks (Jarrahi, 2018; Huang and Rust, 2018).

Given that this technology is relatively new and is used in various sectors of the organisation, most scientific advances in this field have occurred recently. It is with this in mind that, despite AI's image as an effective tool in human resource management, academic literature on the subject remains insufficient (Pan et al., 2022).

2.1.1 The Concept of Artificial Intelligence

Defining AI is a bit complicated because there is no single definition (Villani et al., 2018). Perceptions vary among people, from researchers to the general public. Although interest in AI has increased, there is no recognized definition in the academic literature, making the concept difficult to understand (Mikalef and Gupta, 2021).

The definition of AI raises debates, particularly around the term 'intelligence,' often compared to human intelligence. This semantic confusion reflects the ambitions of AI, which aim to establish links, in line with the Latin definition of intelligence. Modern algorithms are inspired by a 'naturalistic' model of the brain, seeking to imitate the processes and objectives of human intelligence (Blons, 2023).

AI is defined by specialists as the attempt to endow computers with the ability to think and create conscious devices capable of making choices and solving problems. It is also considered the science that develops machines capable of performing tasks requiring human intelligence, while studying intelligent behaviors for an application in computing.

One can therefore clearly perceive AI from two perspectives: the scientific perspective that studies the processes of human intelligence by using the computer as a tool to simulate humans and test theories and the technical perspective that strives to equip the computer with mental faculties comparable to those of humans, without seeking to faithfully reproduce human data processing.

2.1.2 Types of Artificial Intelligence

In banking, AI has transformed organizational structures and emphasizes the importance of effective HRM, thus promoting automation and skill improvement. Otherwise, this technology is indispensable for the adjustment and ethical regulation of algorithms, promoting clarity and credibility. Techniques such as expert systems, neural networks, evolutionary algorithms, and intelligent agents are beginning to integrate into the field of AI.

a. **Expert systems:** Knowledge-based systems are designed to replicate expert reasoning in order to solve complex problems using knowledge bases and reasoning rules. Recent advancements have integrated artificial intelligence techniques, such as natural language processing and deep learning, thereby enhancing their adaptability and real-time information processing capabilities (Santos et al., 2025).
b. **Artificial neural networks:** Neural networks, inspired by the brain, are composed of interconnected artificial neurons and are essential to deep learning, facilitating notable advances in fields such as image recognition, natural language understanding, and time series prediction. A recent study highlights the advanced architectures and applications of neural networks, particularly convolutional networks and hybrid architectures, in the field of artificial intelligence (Mienye & Swart, 2024).
c. **Genetic algorithms:** These are optimization and evolutionary algorithms that handle populations of solutions using operators such as selection, crossover, and mutation to reach an optimal solution. They are suited for complex optimization problems and are often combined with other AI techniques to optimize network architectures or adjust hyperparameters (Taha et al., 2025).
d. **Intelligent agents:** Autonomous agents are independent entities capable of perceiving, reasoning, and making decisions to achieve specific goals. They are characterized by their independence, reactivity, and ability to collaborate in decentralized systems, with applications in multi-agent environments and

intelligent information systems, while adapting to environmental changes (Wooldridge, 2021).

2.1.3 Characteristics of Artificial Intelligence

AI stands out for its ability to learn and adapt from complex data. This allows systems to modify their behavior based on recent information and changes in their environment. In other words, AI stands out for its ability to learn and adapt from complex data, which allows systems to modify their behavior based on new information and changes in the environment (Li et al., 2025). It is distinguished by the automation of tasks, which reduces the need for human intervention while boosting operational efficiency in various sectors (Wang et al., 2024). Another important feature is the dynamic customization of processes, as seen with adaptive learning platforms that automatically modify content based on user profiles (Tan et al., 2025). AI also relies on the analysis of large data sets to anticipate trends and aid strategic decision-making (Alherimi et al., 2025).

Among other characteristics of AI is that it facilitates real-time decision-making through rapid and predictive information processing (Wang et al., 2024). In addition, artificial intelligence has pattern recognition capabilities, which enable it to identify anomalies and automatically classify information. What makes it distinctive is its multimodal interaction capability, offering the ability to communicate through text, images, or voice commands. Recent advances also highlight the importance of ethics and responsible governance to ensure transparency, fairness, and security in socio-technical applications (Younas et al., 2025).

From our point of view, we believe that artificial intelligence is making considerable progress in all areas where it is currently experiencing rapid development and should be integrated into all functions and professions.

2.2 Human Resources Management (HRM)

2.2.1 Definition of HRM and its Objectives

2.2.1.1 Definition and Evolution of the Concept of HRM

Human resource management includes strategies and methods aimed at influencing employee performance and behavior, transcending mere administrative management to embrace a strategic perspective. It represents a fundamental philosophy of managers that aims to enhance human capital and create a competitive advantage (Kaufman, 2020). This method considers employees as strategic resources, rather than expenses to be reduced. Recent research highlights the importance of human resource management for human capital and organizational skills, considered an investment in employee abilities and engagement, thus generating distinctive assets for companies (Ployhart et al., 2021). This management of knowledge and talent is essential for value creation.

Currently, the digital era has profoundly transformed human resource management, leading to the emergence of "electronic HRM." This progression requires the use of analytical tools to guide data-driven decisions, process automation, and the emergence of new working methods (Bondarouk and Brewster, 2021). Noting also in other literature that technology optimizes administrative efficiency and enriches the employee experience, it is essential to emphasize the importance of ethical and responsible human resource management. This encompasses the valuing of diversity, equity, and inclusion; support for the mental and physical health of workers; as well as the incorporation of sustainable development goals into the company's social policies (De Stefano et al., 2023).

2.2.1.2 The Objectives of HRM

One of the primary objectives of human resource management is to align HR practices with the fundamental goals of the company, which allows it the opportunity to improve its efficiency and competitiveness. Moreover, human resource management strategies must encourage performance, efficiency, and innovation. In other words, human resource management aims to orchestrate human resources to mobilize them and contribute to the organization's results. (Arokiasamy et al., 2024). Another essential objective of HRM is to improve human capital through continuous training, talent management, and employee engagement.

According to Siraj et al. (2025), initiatives such as training and performance evaluation increase employe satisfaction and engagement, thereby improving overall performance. The HR function aims to retain talent while balancing ethics and responsibility with economic efficiency and employe well-being, with the goal of ensuring sustainable performance (Christina et al., 2025).

2.2.2 The Main Tasks of HRM

Management science specialists agree that HRM is an orderly system that mobilises a set of practices to align human resources with the organisation's strategy, thereby impacting organisational performance, competitiveness and sustainable value creation (Boxall & Macky, 2009). They also indicate that HRM practices can be classified into three broad categories, namely:

2..2.1 Specialised Practices

Specialised HRM practices represent all the practices carried out by human resources departments to manage the organisation's human capital in line with the company's strategy. The HR function manages a set of interdependent processes ranging from job analysis to career management, including job descriptions, workforce planning, recruitment, selection, training, compensation/benefits, etc (Arokiasamy et al., 2024). The most important of these practices are analysing, describing, classifying and evaluating posts, recruiting competent people, working on capacity development and establishing rules to ensure the proper use of human resources.

2.2.2 Administrative Practices

Human resources administrative practices cover tasks that are essential to the life of the company, such as HR planning, work organisation and performance monitoring. Planning allows the company's staffing needs to be assessed and organises positions and working relationships, while monitoring ensures that objectives are achieved through control and monitoring mechanisms. These three functions are important for the economic and social life of the company (Hoque & Atheef, 2024). These are therefore the practices that HRM needs to accomplish its specialised tasks and functions, the most important of which are human resources planning and organisation, guidance, and control.

2.2.3 Consultative Practices

HR advisory practices are associated with the strategic dimension of the HR function as a partner of leaders. It is to shed light on issues such as organisational change, conflict management, the impact and use of human resources technologies, guidance, and support on transformation themes. There are also activities to support managers on decision-making issues in HRM, led by the prism of corporate social responsibility and organisational agility (Clauss et al., 2025). This requires that the human resources management be more in contact and closer to other departments of the organisation, that it be better informed of their problems, and that it cooperates and understand their various activities better in order to be able to fulfil its advisory role as it should.

2.2.3 Operational Practices in HRM

There are a number of mechanisms for which HR management is accountable and which enable it to achieve its objectives, the most important of which are:

2.2.3.1 Attractiveness and Recruitment

The attractiveness of organisations and recruitment are crucial to attract the best candidates in a competitive job market. This influences employer branding and reputation, playing a key role in the decision of candidates to apply, due to a perceived attractive work environment (Elbendary et al., 2023). Today's recruitment methods incorporate elements such as communication on social media, candidate experience, and alignment between the organisation's values and candidates' expectations. All this contributes to making recruitment campaigns much more effective. (Kilson, 2025). In addition, organisations adopt strategies that rely on the analysis of organisational characteristics and their reputation to enhance their image of attractiveness and encourage a greater number of quality applications (Siem et al., 2025). The combination of a strong employer brand and effective recruitment processes is essential for improving the quality of recruitment and attracting international talent, according to recent research. The evolution of new generations' preferences and the strategic use of digital technologies reinforce the impact of these practices on the attractiveness and choices of candidates (Ghorbanzadeh, 2025).

2.2.3.2 Training and Development

Training and development are key tools to strengthen employees' skills, improve their performance, and help organisations adapt in an ever-changing world. Studies show that these practices have a positive impact on performance, both at the individual and organisational levels, especially when programmes are well designed, meet real needs, and are integrated into the overall strategy of the company (Keltu, 2024). Knowing that the research of Mampuru et al. (2024) emphasises that staff training and development significantly increase job satisfaction, loyalty, and talent retention. In addition, more extensive research shows that investing in skills development stimulates innovation, strengthens competitiveness and helps organisations adapt to market changes (Uddin & Ahmed, 2024).

Recent studies clearly show that training and development have a positive impact on the willingness to transfer learning in the professional environment and on the adoption of new technologies (Al-Mughairi, 2024). Furthermore, the international literature has highlighted the need to include in training and development programmes digital and sustainable approaches if one wants to have a positive impact on HRM practices.

2.2.3.3 Performance Evaluation

Most researchers agree that performance evaluation is a periodic process that aims to measure the strengths and weaknesses of an individual's efforts and behaviours at a given time in order to achieve a specific goal previously. defined by the organisation. Performance evaluation is an essential practice in HRM. Its objective is to measure, analyse and improve the contribution of employees to the objectives of the organisation. This approach allows for constructive feedback, identifying strengths and areas to be developed, while ensuring that individual behaviours are aligned with the organisation's strategic priorities (Murphy, 2025). Recent works focus on the perception of fairness and quality of feedback during performance evaluations have a positive impact on employees' engagement, their behavior beyond defined tasks and their job satisfaction (Van den Broek et al., 2024). Moreover, the adoption of more comprehensive evaluation systems, combining organisational objectives and individual indicators, strengthens the effectiveness of human resources management processes and facilitates strategic decision-making (Li, 2023).

Recent research shows that well-designed evaluation processes can not only improve talent retention but also encourage skill development and reduce initial reluctance (Oschman & Matjie, 2025).

2.3 The Relationship Between AI Applications and HRM Practices

AI is transforming HRM by shifting it towards an analytical and strategic role, rather than simply an administrative one. It enables large amounts of data to be processed, complex patterns to be identified, decision-making quality to be improved, human bias to be reduced, and processes to be optimised throughout the employee lifecycle (Naoum, & Balogh, 2026). As regards recruitment and candidate selection activities, AI algorithms allow, on the one hand, the analysis of CVs, the prediction of suitability, and the selection of profiles, on the other hand, the reduction of recruitment process time, as well as a greater objectivity in the choice of candidates (Mahat, 2024). In terms of employee development and training practices, the use of AI allows for adapting training programs to the individual's skills and performance, which promotes continuous learning, engagement, and talent retention (Sundari, & Riswan, 2025).

Regarding performance evaluation, intelligent systems provide continuous monitoring, provide personalized feedback and analyze behaviors to improve performance, while ensuring transparency and fairness (Úbeda García et al., 2025). In summary, AI greatly simplifies compensation management and employee support. It does this by analysing performance and labour market data and using chatbots to quickly answer human resources questions (Benabou & Touhami, 2025). In other words, AI is positioned as an essential strategic lever and tool for human resources management, as it improves the efficiency, accuracy and personalisation of HR practices. The ultimate goal is to ensure ethical and humane oversight to avoid bias and maintain employee trust (Naoum et al., 2026).

3. FRAMEWORK OF THE STUDY

3.1 Methodology and Description of the Sample Studied

The population studied in our case study has been precisely defined in order to target all employees of the Agricultural Credit Bank of Morocco. It includes senior managers, human resources managers, middle managers and supervisory staff, reflecting the diversity of functions within the institution. The objective was to ensure that all professional views were represented and taken into account in the analysis. This approach allows a thorough knowledge of the internal dynamics and practices of the organization, like banks. In total, the enumerated population of our case study included 12479 individuals at the beginning of the study, which constitutes a rich and significant sample. Compliance with this precise definition guarantees the relevance and reliability of the study results.

3.2 Study Sample

The study sample was determined using the following equation: $n = \frac{pq}{\left[\frac{\mathbf{E}}{\frac{\mathbf{Z}a}{2}}\right]2 + \frac{pq}{N}}$

$$n = \frac{0.50 * 0.50}{\left[\frac{0.5}{1.96}\right]2 + \frac{0.50 + 0.50}{12479}}$$

$$n = 294$$

$$n = \frac{0.25}{0.006700337}$$

$$n = 294$$

Where **N** is the studied population (number of employees 12479) of individuals.
n: Sample size.

z: 1.96% with a 95% confidence level (known value from normal distribution table).

p: Percentage of the characteristic present in society, which the researcher estimated at 50% in order to obtain a sample of maximum size. **q**: Inverse proportion (no description). **n** = 294

According to the sample size equation, 294 questionnaires were distributed, of which 294 were retrieved, a rate of 98.1%, which is sufficient for statistical analysis and dissemination of field study results.

3.3 Field Study Tool

In accordance with the methodology and objectives of the study, the survey was used as the main field study tool to obtain data for testing the hypotheses of the study and identifying variables to be measured by adopting a procedural concept for artificial intelligence and the management of human resources in the studied bank, depending on the studied problem and the study's objectives, in light of the literature associated with this subject, while developing this tool to adapt it to the procedural concepts of the variables in the study. The survey focused on the following themes:

3.3.1 Artificial Intelligence

Given that the objective of the study is to identify the impact of artificial intelligence on improving human resources management in the studied bank, emphasis was placed on the following elements to measure the dimensions of this axis, as shown in the table below:

Table 1. Elements for measuring the dimensions of artificial intelligence

Items	The sentences of the questionnaire that measure each dimension
Human capacity dimension	Statements 1 to 5
Financial capacity dimension	Statements 6 to 10
Dimension of artistic techniques	Statements 11 to 15

Source: Prepared by researchers

3.3.2 Human Resources Management

Emphasis was placed on the following elements to measure the human resources management axis in accordance with the following table:

Table 2. Human resource management measurement elements

Items	The sentences in the questionnaire that measure each dimension
Human resources management	Statements 16 to 25

Source: Prepared by researchers

After the survey took its final form, it was applied to the study sample, which showed an increase in validation rates for artificial intelligence and the human resource management scale, indicating the authenticity of the study tool, as shown in the following table:

Table 3. Validity coefficients of the study tool

Themes of the survey	**Number of forms**	**Number of sentences**	**Fidelity coefficient (r)**
The first focus area (artificial intelligence)	370	15	0.984
The second focus area (Human Resource Management)	370	10	0.871
The general focus of the survey	**370**	**25**	**0.989**

Source: Prepared by researchers

Statistical analysis showed an increase in stability coefficients for the artificial intelligence scale and the human resource management scale, which means that they are relevant to the research objectives and can therefore be used to measure what they were designed for. They also allow the results of the field study to be generalised, as shown in the following table:

Table 4. Stability coefficients of the study instrument

Themes of the survey	**Number of forms**	**Number of sentences**	**Fidelity coefficient (r)**
The first axis (artificial intelligence)	370	10	0.968
The second axis (Human resources management)	370	10	0.758
The general axis of the survey	**370**	**25**	**0.978**

Source: Prepared by researchers

3.4 Analysis and Interpretation of the Results of the Field Study and Hypothesis Testing

The study thus aims to present and analyse the results of the field study and hypothesis testing in light of the data obtained from the responses of the studied sample, which will allow the impact of artificial intelligence and human resources management to be analysed according to the following criteria:

3.4.1 Analysis and Interpretation of the Results of the First Axis of the Administrative Reform

The study measured the dimensions of artificial intelligence using sentences from (1) to (15). The following table shows the responses of the study sample to sentences indicating these dimensions, as follows:

Table 5. Responses of study sample keywords for sentences indicating artificial intelligence dimensions

Rank	Statement of the sentence	(X̄)	(σ)	(CV)
1	The bank is interested in training employees on different AI technologies.	2.16	1.18442	54%
2	The bank offers training programs for employees in various areas of AI.	1.71	0.67437	35.43%
3	There is in the bank a sufficient number of qualified employees to develop the network infrastructure.	1.98	0.79761	40.28%
4	There is a great conviction among most of the bank's employees regarding the strategic vision of AI in the different banking areas.	2.04	0.9142	44.81%
5	There are information technology specialists at the bank.	3.79	1.09203	28.81%
Human capabilities		**2.83**	**0.33781**	**11%**
6	The bank has a technological infrastructure that enables the application of AI.	2.14	1.1069	51.72%
7	The bank has a technological infrastructure that enables it to leverage its accumulated knowledge.	3.68	1.0142	27.56%
8	The bank has the necessary funds to purchase the equipment needed for AI applications.	1.92	1.02943	53.61%
9	The bank has the necessary financial allocations to purchase the infrastructure equipment needed for AI applications.	1.92	1.14724	59.75%
10	There is a budget allocated to the application of AI at the bank.	1.72	0.82476	47.95%
Financial resources		**2.13**	**0.56287**	**26.42%**
11	Systems and programs necessary for the application of AI are available.	3.98	1.16258	29.21%
12	An electronic feedback system is available.	1.88	0.96258	51.20%
13	An electronic system is available to receive all suggestions for improvement.	4.18	0.92891	22.22%
14	Data is exchanged between senior management and the various departments using modern, secure technologies.	1.69	0.92882	54.96%
15	There is an active website for the bank on the Internet.	3.78	124768	70%
Artistic techniques		**2.38**	**0.65327**	**27.45%**
Artificial intelligence		**2.45**	**0.36172**	**14.76%**

Source: prepared by researchers based on results from the SPSS V.26 program.

Table 5 presents descriptive statistics regarding the paragraphs related to the dimensions of artificial intelligence, based on arithmetic averages. The opinions of respondents show a significant variation, with coefficients of variation between 47.95% and 54%, indicating a high dispersion and a lack of consensus. For example, the second paragraph shows a coefficient of variation of approximately 47.95%, indicating low dispersion within this element. About human abilities, the average opinion is 2.83 with a standard deviation of 0.33781 and a coefficient of variation of 11%, indicating relatively homogeneous agreement. Responses vary widely, with averages ranging from 1.71 to 3.79, corresponding to respondents' perception in a low category of dissatisfaction regarding these abilities. For the financial resource's axis, the average opinion is 2.23, with a standard deviation of 0.56287 and a coefficient of variation of 15%, showing some cohesion of opinion but remaining in a low range with means of key expressions from 1.72 to 3.68. For artistic skills related to artificial intelligence, the average is 27.45 with a standard deviation of 0.65327. The coefficient of variation being 27.45% suggests a limited dispersion while reflecting a general feeling of artistic inadequacy with grades ranging from 1.69 to 4.18 and an average of 2.38, which also reflects an unfavorable appreciation. In sum, the sample seems to perceive deficits in several dimensions of artificial intelligence within the studied bank.

3.4.2 Analysis and Interpretation of the Results of the Second Axis Relating to HRM

The study used statements (16 to 25) to measure the human resource management dimension. The following table presents the responses of the sample studied to the statements relating to this dimension, as follows:

Table 6. Study participants' responses to expressions related to HRM

Rank	Statement of the sentence	(X)	(σ)	(CV)
16	HRM is based on determining human resource requirements based on the results of job analysis (job description and incumbent profile).	1.78	1.173	65.89%
17	HRM relies on effective information systems that facilitate the human resource planning process.	3.82	1.2428	31.78%
18	Sometimes, human resources management uses financial incentives to attract highly qualified individuals to fill important positions within the bank.	2.12	1.10778	52.25%
19	Sometimes, HR management uses moral incentives to attract people with financial skills to fill important positions within the bank.	1.79	1.05295	58.82%
20	The determination of employee training programmes depends on the results of their annual performance appraisal.	2.11	1.01285	48%
21	The incentive scheme implemented by the HR department is transparent and known to all employees.	2.04	1.12108	54.95%

continued on following page

Table 6. Continued

Rank	Statement of the sentence	(X)	(σ)	(CV)
22	The HR department constantly strives to align salaries and bonuses with inflation rates and current living conditions.	2.08	1.13056	54.35%
23	The end-of-service compensation system applied by the HR department is fair and impartial.	2.08	1.12405	54.04%
24	Employee performance is assessed by the line manager without discrimination or favouritism.	1.79	1.04324	58.28%
25	The HR department transfers the employee to another position that matches their abilities, based on the results of their performance evaluation in their current position.	1.91	0.8586	44.95%
Human resources management		**1.92**	**0.69382**	**36.13%**

Source: prepared by researchers based on results from SPSS V.26 programme

The table above presents certain descriptive statistical measures for the paragraphs relating to human resource management. The arithmetic means show that the opinions of respondents tend towards weakness in most paragraphs and towards strength in the case of paragraph 17. Furthermore, the values of the coefficients of variation vary between (44.95% and 65.89%), thus exceeding the percentage of (44.95%), which indicates a clear dispersion of opinions among the sample members and a lack of consensus on these paragraphs.

It turned out that the average opinion of the sample members was (1.92) with a standard deviation of (0.69382). The coefficient of variation was (36.13%), which is a good level of variation and indicates a limited difference between the members of the sample in their agreement on this axis, highlighting the weakness of human resource management in the bank studied.

3.5 Hypothesis Testing

Statistical hypothesis testing is used to decide whether to accept or reject these hypotheses. To verify the validity of a hypothesis, a random sample is taken from the population under study, and the necessary analysis is performed to estimate the value of the indicator covered by the hypothesis under study. This estimated value is then compared to the assumed value in order to make the appropriate decision. In light of this, the study seeks to test the following hypotheses:

Hypothesis 1: *There is a statistically significant relationship between the extent of human capabilities in applying artificial intelligence and improvements in HRM at Agricultural Credit Bank of Morocco.*

To verify the validity of this hypothesis, the following table illustrates the relationship between human potential for the application of artificial intelligence and improved human resource management at Agricultural Credit Bank of Morocco, as follows:

Table 7. Estimates from the simple regression model of the impact of human capacity on the application of AI to improve HRM at Agricultural Credit Bank of Morocco

Independent variable	Dependent variable	Correlation coefficient (R)	Coefficient of determination (R^2)	F	Significance
Human capacity to apply artificial intelligence	Human resources management	0.672	0.451	72.815	0.00^b

Source: prepared by the researchers based on the results of the SPSS program V.26 (statistically significant at the signification level of 0.05).

Table 7 shows that there is a positive correlation relationship between the size of material capabilities for the application of artificial intelligence and the improvement of human resources management, where the value of the correlation coefficient is (0.672). The data in the table also shows the stability of the validity of the model to test this hypothesis, based on the value (F) of (138.414), which is statistically significant at the level of significance (0.05). It is also clear from the same table that the dimension of material capacities for the application of artificial intelligence in this model explains about 45.1% of sustainable development, where the value of the coefficient of determination (R) is 0.451. Noting that the probability value (p = 0.000 < a = 0.05), it appears that there is a statistically significant effect of the independent variable on the dependent, and that the hypothesis according to which there is a statistically significant relationship between the dimension of material capacities for the application of artificial intelligence and the improvement of human resources management at the Agricultural Credit Bank of Morocco is accepted.

Hypothesis 2: *There is a statistically significant relationship between the extent of financial capacity for the application of artificial intelligence and improved human resource management within Agricultural Credit Bank of Morocco.*

To verify the validity of this hypothesis, the following table illustrates the model of the relationship between the financial capacity to apply artificial intelligence and the improvement of human resource management at Agricultural Credit Bank of Morocco as follows:

Table 8. Estimates from the simple regression model of the impact of the financial dimensions of AI implementation on HRM improvement at Agricultural Credit Bank of Morocco

Independent variable	Dependent variable	Correlation coefficient (R)	Coefficient of determination (R^2)	F	Significance
Dimension of financial capabilities to apply artificial intelligence	Human resources management	0.798	0.636	0.798	0.00[b]

Source: prepared by researchers based on the results of the SPSS V.26 program (statistically significant at a significance level of 0.05).

It appears from table N. (8) that there is a positive correlation relationship between the dimension of financial resources for the application of artificial intelligence and the improvement of human resource management, where the value of the correlation coefficient is (148.25). The data in the table shows the stability of the validity of the model to test this hypothesis, based on the value (F) of (148.25), which is statistically significant at the level of significance (0.05). It is also clear from the same table that the dimension of financial resources for the application of artificial intelligence in this model explains approximately (63.32%) of sustainable development, where the value of the coefficient of determination (R^2) is 0.6332. Noting that the probability value ($p = 0.000 < a = 0.05$), it appears that there is a statistically significant effect of the independent variable on the dependent variable and the acceptance of the hypothesis that there is a statistically significant relationship between the dimension of financial resources for the application of artificial intelligence and the improvement of human resource management at the Agricultural Credit Bank of Morocco.

Hypothesis 3: *There is a statistically significant relationship between the extent of artistic techniques for applying artificial intelligence and improvements in human resources management at Agricultural Credit Bank of Morocco.*

To verify the validity of this hypothesis, the following table illustrates the model of the relationship between the artistic technologies dimension of artificial intelligence application and improved human resources management at Agricultural Credit Bank of Morocco as follows:

Table 9. Estimates from the simple regression model of the impact of the scope of AI application techniques on improving HRM at Banque du Crédit Agricole du Maroc.

Independent variable	Dependent variable	Correlation coefficient (R)	Coefficient of determination (R^2)	F	Significance
Dimension of artistic techniques for applying artificial intelligence	Human resources management	0.819	0.6707	412.246	0.00[b]

Source: prepared by researchers based on the results of the SPSS V.26 program (statistically significant at a significance level of 0.05).

Table 9 shows that there is a positive correlation between the extent of artistic techniques in the application of artificial intelligence and improvements in human resource management, where the correlation coefficient is (0.819). The data in the table show the stability of the model's validity for testing this hypothesis, based on the value (F) of (412.329), which is statistically significant at the significance level (0.05). It is also clear from the same table that the dimension of artistic techniques in the application of artificial intelligence in this model explains approximately (67.07%) of sustainable development, where the value of the coefficient of determination (R^2) is (0.6707). Noting that the probability value ($p = 0.000 < a = 0.05$), it appears that there is a significant and statistically significant effect of the independent variable on the dependent variable, and acceptance of the hypothesis that there is a statistically significant relationship between the dimension of artistic techniques in the application of artificial intelligence and the improvement of human resource management at the Agricultural Credit Bank of Morocco.

4. THE RESULTS

4.1 Results Relating to the Study Assumptions

- There is a statistically significant relationship between the extent of human capabilities for the application of artificial intelligence and improved human resource management at Agricultural Credit Bank of Morocco.
- There is a statistically significant relationship between the scale of financial capacity for the application of artificial intelligence and improvements in human resources management at Agricultural Credit Bank of Morocco.
- There is a statistically significant relationship between the extent of artistic techniques in the application of artificial intelligence and improvements in human resources management at Agricultural Credit Bank of Morocco.

4.2 Results of the Field Study

The field study revealed the shortcomings of artificial intelligence applications and the weakness of human resources management practices in the studied bank, for the following reasons:

a. The bank shows a lack of interest in training its employees in AI, and it does not offer programs tailored to the sector. There is also an insufficient number of qualified employees to develop its network infrastructure. The opinions of employees reveal a disbelief in the strategic vision of AI and, despite these shortcomings, a strength emerges: the presence of employees specialized in information technology.
b. The implementation of AI in the bank is hindered by the low availability of technological infrastructures and necessary financial credits. The results of the sample highlight an insufficient budget for this integration, but also highlight an asset: the existence of a technological infrastructure capable of exploiting the accumulated knowledge.
c. The study highlights the weaknesses of the electronic feedback system, as well as the inadequacy of data exchanges between the different departments of the bank, despite the use of modern technologies. However, there are some positives that are emerging, such as high-performing websites for customers and systems in place for the application of artificial intelligence, including an electronic system for collecting improvement suggestions.
d. The bank's human resources management has several shortcomings, including a lack of identification of staff needs based on job analyses and annual employee evaluations. Training programmes are not aligned with these assessments, and the bonus system lacks transparency and fairness, ignoring inflation. Performance evaluation is considered imperfect, marked by favouritism, and the transfer of employees to positions in line with their skills is insufficient. Moreover, there are no incentives to attract qualified talents. Despite these weaknesses, a positive point was noted: the use of effective information systems that optimize human resources planning.

4.3 The Recommendations

To improve the integration of AI in the banking sector, the study suggests that the following main suggestions should be taken into consideration:

Prioritize the use of AI technologies in all banking operations, integrate AI into decision-making processes and improve HRM by adopting AI techniques within different departments.

It also advocates the development of appropriate infrastructure to support AI implementation, as well as improving staff awareness and understanding of these technologies, in order to dispel misconceptions. Employee training in financial technology and AI is considered essential to meet the changing needs of customers.

Finally, the study highlights the need to invest more in AI in order to improve banking services, particularly through digital applications and technologies.

5. GENERAL CONCLUSION

This study highlights the essential role of AI in human resources management methods within Agricultural Credit Bank of Morocco. The results show that, when AI is supported by adequate human, financial, and technical resources, a significant improvement in the performance and efficiency of human resource management processes can be observed.

The survey of 294 participants indicates that digitalization and automation facilitate more efficient decision-making and optimal allocation of resources while improving the working environment. However, obstacles such as insufficient training, limited budgets, and organizational deficiencies hinder the optimal use of AI.

These challenges require considerable commitment from people, a strategic perspective, constant learning, and HRM that is both transparent and fair. Artificial intelligence is perceived as an instrument of transformation that requires strong managerial commitment, constant investments, and gradual participation by employees. By opting for a structured digitalization strategy, the banking institution could optimize the efficiency of its human resources management and increase its competitiveness in an ever-changing banking environment.

Ultimately, successfully managing human resources thru AI at Crédit Agricole Bank of Morocco is not solely based on the technical complexity of the tool, but on the alignment between the decision-makers' vision and the available resources. Our results highlight that overcoming the identified obstacles, such as bias in evaluations and lack of transparency in incentives, requires an integration of AI that promotes fairness and data-driven decisions. This chapter reveals that the modernization of human resources goes far beyond the mere technological aspect. It is a true transformation, where technology serves as a tool for more human and strategic management.

REFERENCES

Al-Mughairi, A. M. (2024). The evaluation of training and development of employees: The case of a national oil and gas industry. *International Journal of Research in Human Resource Management*, *6*(2), 301–308. DOI: 10.33545/26633213.2024.v6.i2c.229

Alherimi, N., Abdulmaksoud, S., Ahmed, V., & Bahroun, Z. (2025). A systematic literature review of artificial intelligence advancements in green human resource management. *Sustainability (Basel)*, *17*(22), 10283. DOI: 10.3390/su172210283

Alzghoul, A., & Khaddam, A. (2024). Enhancing employee retention in banks: Analyzing the role of talent management, career development, and bank culture. *Banks and Bank Systems*, *19*(4), 96–111. DOI: 10.21511/bbs.19(4).2024.08

Amir, A., Zaman, S., & Tariq, M. I. (2024). Effect of Digital HRM on Employee Performance: The Role of Employee Trust and Organizational Identity in the Banking Sector of Pakistan. *Pakistan Journal of Humanities and Social Sciences*, *12*(1), 207–223. DOI: 10.52131/pjhss.2024.v12i1.1985

Arner, D. W., Barberis, J., & Buckley, R. P. (2020). The Evolution of Fintech: A New Post-Crisis Paradigm? *SSRN*, *47*(4), 1271–1319. DOI: 10.2139/ssrn.2676553

Arokiasamy, L., Fujikawa, T., Piaralal, S. K., & Arumugam, T. (2024). Role of HRM practices in organization performance. *International Journal of Sociotechnology and Knowledge Development*, *16*(1), 1–32. Advance online publication. DOI: 10.4018/IJSKD.334555

Benabou, A., & Touhami, F. (2025). Empowering human resource management through artificial intelligence: A systematic literature review and bibliometric analysis. *International Journal of Production Management and Engineering*, *13*(1), 59–76. Advance online publication. DOI: 10.4995/ijpme.2025.21900

Blons, E. (2023). *L'IA au cœur de l'entreprise: Une alliée pour votre stratégie RH*. Questions de Société. EMS Éditions.

Bondarouk, T., & Brewster, C. (2021). Conceptualising the future of HRM and technology research. *International Journal of Human Resource Management*, *32*(12), 2543–2568. DOI: 10.1080/09585192.2021.1925325

Boxall, P., & Macky, K. (2009). Research and theory on high-performance work systems. *Human Resource Management Journal*, *19*(1), 3–23. DOI: 10.1111/j.1748-8583.2008.00082.x

Chen, C.-J., & Huang, J.-W. (2009). Strategic human resource practices and innovation performance: The mediating role of knowledge management capacity. *Journal of Business Research*, *62*(1), 104–114. DOI: 10.1016/j.jbusres.2007.11.016

Christina, J. L., Alamelu, R., & Nigama, K. (2025). Synthesizing the impact of sustainable human resource management on corporate sustainability through multi method evidence. *Discover Sustainability*, *6*(1), 666. Advance online publication. DOI: 10.1007/s43621-025-01557-3

Clauss, C. B., de Frutos Belizón, J., & García Carbonell, N. (2025). Employee perceptions of HRM practices and beyond: A bibliometric analysis of theoretical perspectives and research foci. *Journal of Management & Organization*, *31*(5), 2317–2340. DOI: 10.1017/jmo.2025.10015

De Stefano, F., Bagdadli, S., & Camuffo, A. (2023). The HR role in corporate social responsibility and sustainability: A systematic review. *Human Resource Management Review*, *33*(1), 100926. DOI: 10.1016/j.hrmr.2022.100926

Edralin, D. M. (2010). Human resource management practices: Drivers for stimulating corporate entrepreneurship in large companies in the Philippines. *DLSU Business and Economics Review*, *19*(2), 25–41. DOI: 10.3860/ber.v19i2.1471

El Hammoumi, A., & El-Ouali, A. (2025). Impact of knowledge management on human resource performance: Case of the company Maroc Télécom. In *Evolving Strategies for Organizational Management and Performance Evaluation* (pp. 291–312). IGI Global., DOI: 10.4018/979-8-3373-0149-5.ch014

El Hammoumi, A., Seghyar, N., El Hammoumi, A. M., & El Ouali, A. (2024). The impact of artificial intelligence on employee adaptability to remote work. In 2024 3rd International Conference on Embedded Systems and Artificial Intelligence (ESAI) (pp. 1-5). IEEE. https://doi.org/DOI: 10.1109/ESAI62891.2024.10913897

El-Ouali, A., & Jellouli, T. (2024). L'avenir de la gestion des ressources humaines après la crise de la pandémie de Corona (COVID-19). Revue internationale d'études économiques et de gestion (IJESM), 4(1), 142-159. https://doi.org/DOI: 10.5281/zenodo.10698984

El-Ouali, A., & Jellouli, T. (2025). Training and development as effective strategies for human resource development in Moroccan companies. In *Innovative Recruitment and Retention for Employee Empowerment*. IGI Global., DOI: 10.4018/979-8-3693-6602-8.ch013

Elbendary, I., Elsetouhi, A. M., Marie, M., & Aljafari, A. M. (2023). Employment preferences of job applicants: Unfolding employer branding determinants. *Personnel Review*, *52*(5), 1244–1268. DOI: 10.1108/PR-03-2021-0188

Gélinas, D., Sadreddin, A., & Vahidov, R. (2022). Artificial Intelligence in Human Resources Management: A Review and Research Agenda. *Pacific Asia Journal of the Association for Information Systems*, *14*(6), 1–42. Advance online publication. DOI: 10.17705/1pais.14601

Ghorbanzadeh, D. (2025). Enhancing intentions to apply for job through social media characteristics. *Asia-Pacific Journal of Business Administration*, *16*(1), 151–169. DOI: 10.1108/APJBA-11-2024-0619

Hoque, K. E., & Atheef, M. (2024). A review of human resource management practices and their impact on school performance (2012–2022). *Human Resources Management and Services*, *6*(1), 3392. Advance online publication. DOI: 10.18282/hrms.v6i1.3392

Huang, M. H., & Rust, R. T. (2018). Artificial intelligence in service. *Journal of Service Research*, *21*(2), 155–172. DOI: 10.1177/1094670517752459

Jarrahi, M. H. (2018). Artificial intelligence and the future of work: Human-AI symbiosis in organizational decision making. *Business Horizons*, *61*(4), 577–586. DOI: 10.1016/j.bushor.2018.03.007

Jordan, M. I., & Mitchell, T. M. (2015). Machine learning: Trends, perspectives, and prospects. *Science*, *349*(6245), 255–260. DOI: 10.1126/science.aaa8415 PMID: 26185243

Kaufman, B. E. (2020). The evolution of strategic HRM as seen through two founding books: A 30th anniversary perspective on development of the field. *Human Resource Management*, *59*(5), 491–502. DOI: 10.1002/hrm.22007

Keltu, T. T. (2024). The effect of human resource development practice on employee performance with the mediating role of job satisfaction among Mizan Tepi University's academic staff. *Heliyon*, *10*(8), e29821. DOI: 10.1016/j.heliyon.2024.e29821 PMID: 38699710

Kilson, G. A. (2025). Optimizing employee attraction and retention in hospitality and tourism: A systematic review of employer branding research. *Administrative Sciences*, *15*(5), 153. DOI: 10.3390/admsci15050153

Li, J., Yan, Y., & Zeng, X. (2025). Exploring artificial intelligence in inclusive education: A systematic review of empirical studies. *Applied Sciences (Basel, Switzerland)*, *15*(23), 12624. DOI: 10.3390/app152312624

Li, Z. (2023). *Research on innovation of employee performance management appraisal system*. Academic Journal of Business & Management., DOI: 10.25236/AJBM.2023.051819

Mahat, D. (2024). Artificial intelligence in human resource management: Bibliometric analysis comparing Pre and Post COVID 19 literatures. *Formosa Journal of Multidisciplinary Research*, *3*(7), 2509–2530. Advance online publication. DOI: 10.55927/fjmr.v3i7.9875

Mahato, S. (2023). Talent Management Practices and Organizational Performance in Nepalese Private Banks. *KIC International Journal of Social Science and Management*, *2*(1), 129–151. DOI: 10.3126/kicijssm.v2i1.62472

Mampuru, M. P., Mokoena, B. A., & Isabirye, A. K. (2024). Training and development impact on job satisfaction, loyalty and retention among academics. SA Journal of Human Resource Management/SA Tydskrif vir Menslikehulpbronbestuur, 22, a2420. https://doi.org/DOI: 10.4102/sajhrm.v22i0.2420

Marques, A. I., & Ferreira, F. A. F. (2020). Artificial intelligence in banking: A systematic literature review. *Journal of Business Research*, *124*, 389–409. DOI: 10.1016/j.jbusres.2020.01.034

Mienye, I. D., & Swart, T. G. (2024). A comprehensive review of deep learning: Architectures, recent advances, and applications. *Information (Basel)*, *15*(12), 755. DOI: 10.3390/info15120755

Mikalef, P., & Gupta, M. (2021). Artificial intelligence capability: Conceptualization, measurement calibration, and empirical study on its impact on organizational creativity and firm performance. *Information & Management*, *58*(3), 103434. DOI: 10.1016/j.im.2021.103434

Murphy, K. R. (2025). The illusion of performance management. *Human Resource Management*. Advance online publication. DOI: 10.1002/hrm.70016

Naoum, R. F., Szakadáti, T., & Balogh, G. (2026). *Artificial Intelligence (AI) in human resource management (HRM): A systematic review of its dual impact on diversity, equity, and inclusion (DEI)*. Management Review Quarterly., DOI: 10.1007/s11301-025-00580-y

Ncube, T. R., Sishi, K. K., & Skinner, J. P. (2025). The impact of artificial intelligence on human resource management practices: An investigation. *SA Journal of Human Resource Management*, *23*, a2960. Advance online publication. DOI: 10.4102/sajhrm.v23i0.2960

Oschman, B., & Matjie, M. A. (2025). Exploring employees' experiences with performance appraisals at the South African Air Force. *SA Journal of Human Resource Management*, *23*(0), a2925. DOI: 10.4102/sajhrm.v23i0.2925

Pan, Y., Froese, F., Liu, N., Hu, Y., & Ye, M. (2022). The adoption of artificial intelligence in employee recruitment: The influence of contextual factors. *International Journal of Human Resource Management*, *33*(6), 1125–1147. DOI: 10.1080/09585192.2021.1879206

Ployhart, R. E. (2021). Human capital and the resource-based view: Advancing research on strategic human capital resources. *Journal of Management*, *47*(6), 1448–1471. DOI: 10.1177/01492063211003137

Puschmann, T. (2017). Fintech. *Business & Information Systems Engineering*, *59*(1), 69–76. DOI: 10.1007/s12599-017-0464-6

Santos, J. K. S., Siqueira, L. S., Faria, E. M. B., Bispo, K. A., Silva, G. J. F., & Soares, M. S. (2025). Methodological advances in expert systems with artificial intelligence. In *Anais do XXI Simpósio Brasileiro de Sistemas de Informação* (pp. 703–712). Sociedade Brasileira de Computação., DOI: 10.5753/sbsi.2025.246618

Siem, T. T., Nguyen, H. T. T., To, A. T., & Phong, T. K. (2025). Exploring trends in employer attractiveness research: A bibliometric coupling approach. *Acta Psychologica*, *227*, 105220. DOI: 10.1016/j.actpsy.2025.105220 PMID: 40570583

Siraj, R. (2025). Strategic human resource management and employee outcomes: A comprehensive literature review on the impact of SHRM practices on job satisfaction and organizational commitment. *The Critical Review of Social Sciences Studies*, *3*(1), 3154–3164. DOI: 10.59075/gh4rzd88

Sundari, M. H., Matheshkanna, L., & Riswan, M. (2025). Artificial intelligence in human resource management: A systematic literature review and human centered framework. [IRJAEM]. *International Research Journal on Advanced Engineering and Management*, *3*(10), 3010–3022. Advance online publication. DOI: 10.47392/IRJAEM.2025.0478

Taha, M. A., Saafan, M. M., & Ayyad, S. M. (2025). Revisiting natural selection: Evolving dynamic neural networks using genetic algorithms for complex control tasks. *Artificial Intelligence Review*, *58*(11), 366. DOI: 10.1007/s10462-025-11382-9

Tambe, P., Cappelli, P., & Yakubovich, V. (2019). Artificial intelligence in human resources management: Challenges and a path forward. *California Management Review*, *61*(4), 15–42. DOI: 10.1177/0008125619867910

Tan, L. Y., Hu, S., Yeo, D. J., & Cheong, K. H. (2025). Artificial intelligence-enabled adaptive learning platforms: A review. *Computers and Education: Artificial Intelligence*, *9*, 100429. DOI: 10.1016/j.caeai.2025.100429

Úbeda García, M., Marco Lajara, B., Zaragoza Sáez, P. C., & Poveda Pareja, E. (2025). Artificial intelligence, knowledge and human resource management: A systematic literature review of theoretical tensions and strategic implications. Journal of Innovation & Knowledge. https://doi.org/DOI: 10.1016/j.jik.2025.100809

Uddin, S. F., & Ahmed, B. (2024). Exploring the importance of employee training and development in achieving sustainable development goals. *International Journal of Research in Human Resource Management*, *6*(1), 145–148. DOI: 10.33545/26633213.2024.v6.i1b.184

Van den Broek, A. (2024). Human resource management and performance: A review and research agenda. *Human Resource Management*. Advance online publication. DOI: 10.1002/hrm.20315

Villani, C., Schoenauer, M., Bonnet, Y., Berthet, C., Cornut, A.-C., Levin, F., & Rondepierre, B. « Donner un sens à l'intelligence artificielle: pour une stratégie na-tionale et européenne », Rapport public, mars 2018 (https://www.vie-publique.fr/rapport/37225-donner-un-sens-lintelligence-artificielle-pour-une-strategie-nation)

Vives, X. (2019). Digital disruption in banking. *Annual Review of Financial Economics*, *11*(1), 243–272. DOI: 10.1146/annurev-financial-100719-120854

Vlachos, I. P. (2009). The effects of human resource practices on firm growth. *International Journal of Business Science and Applied Management*, *4*(2), 17–34. DOI: 10.69864/ijbsam.4-2.40

Wang, S., Wang, F., Zhu, Z., Tran, T., & Du, Z. (2024). Artificial intelligence in education: A systematic literature review. *Expert Systems with Applications*, *214*, 124167. DOI: 10.1016/j.eswa.2024.124167

Wooldridge, M. (2021). *Foundations of multiagent systems*. MIT Press., DOI: 10.7551/mitpress/14268.001.0001

Yawar, M. E., & Hakimi, M. Q. (2025). The impact of artificial intelligence technology on human resources performance in organizations. *EuroGlobal Journal of Linguistics and Language Education*, *2*(1), 96–108. DOI: 10.69760/egjlle.2500013

Younas, M., Ismayil, I., El-Dakhs, D. A. S., & Anwar, B. (2025). The impact of artificial intelligence-based learning tools in academic innovation: A review of Deep Seek, GPT, and Gemini (2020–2025). *Frontiers in Education*, *10*, 1689205. DOI: 10.3389/feduc.2025.1689205

Yufik, Y. M. (2019). The Understanding Capacity and Information Dynamics in the Human Brain. *Entropy (Basel, Switzerland)*, *21*(3), 308. Advance online publication. DOI: 10.3390/e21030308 PMID: 33267023

Chapter 8
Navigating Economic Uncertainty Through Strategic Human Resource Management:
Safeguarding Employee Well-Being – A Case Study of Indian Banks

Navneet Ranjan
http://orcid.org/0009-0000-2048-0513
Medhavi Skills University, India

Atanu Bhattacharya
http://orcid.org/0000-0003-2856-031X
ITM Vocational University, Vadodara, India

Uday Pratap Singh
http://orcid.org/0000-0003-0632-9934
Amity University, Jaipur, India

Manidipa Mukherjee
http://orcid.org/0009-0009-5182-2390
International School of Hospitality Management, India

Sanjit Cletus Gomes
http://orcid.org/0009-0000-3180-953X
International School of Hospitality Management, India

DOI: 10.4018/979-8-2600-2303-7.ch008

ABSTRACT

Drawing on social exchange theory and street-level bureaucracy perspectives, this study explores how Indian public banks strategically manage frontline staff to sustain performance amid economic instability. The research identifies three factor categories: job-related (e.g., staff discretion, role nature and recruitment of qualified talent), learning-related (e.g., continuous development, rise of MBA programs, workforce resilience) and context-related (e.g., career advancement opportunities, enhanced incentives during turbulence). Together, these factors explain how employees maintain stable performance despite national challenges. The study recommends continued investment in training particularly in crisis management, customer relations, well-being and urges other public sector bodies to replicate banking best practices. It further suggests that global financial actors integrate HRM strategies into reform proposals for India's public sector, contributing to limited empirical work on HRM and economic uncertainty in Asia.

INTRODUCTION

In the contemporary world, societies are facing a continuous series of unpredictable challenges, ranging from climate change and global health crises to political turmoil in developing regions, escalating terrorist threats and violent armed conflicts (Kwong et al., 2021) (Mousa & Abdelgaffar, 2023). These issues have contributed significantly to economic instability across nations (Arslan et al., 2022). Scholars widely agree that for banks of all kinds, establishing a strategic human resource management (SHRM) framework is crucial for ensuring a reliable workforce, maintaining adaptability in volatile circumstances and sustaining competitive advantage (Kabalina et al., 2019) (Wright & Snell, 1998). SHRM was described as "the pattern of planned human resource deployment and activities intended to enable an organization to achieve its goals" (Wright & McMahan, 1992). SHRM involves examining HRM systems and their connections with broader organizational structures, both internal and external, as well as recognizing the diverse actors who shape HR practices and the stakeholders who assess organizational performance and long-term viability (Jackson et al., 2014).

SHRM emphasizes aligning HR systems such as employee competencies, knowledge and behaviour with the organizational environment in which they operate (Cooke et al., 2021) (Delery & Gupta, 2016) (Sikora et al., 2016). This alignment explains why HR frameworks created in Western contexts may not always be suitable for developing countries (Mousa & Samara, 2022). From the perspective of neo-institutional theory (DiMaggio & Powell, 1991), organizations must adapt to their external environment and address the diverse expectations of stakeholders, which requires organizational members to demonstrate flexibility and adaptability (Zucker, 1991). Since organizations fundamentally depend on their workforce for survival (Kwong et al., 2021) resilience during turbulent times or extreme events becomes essential (Mousa, 2024a) (Mousa, 2024b). Nonetheless, many employees struggle to perform effectively in uncertain conditions (Reade, 2009), often due to elevated stress and burnout (Ererdi et al., 2022). In some cases, staff even resort to sick leave during crises (Howie, 2007). Conversely, employees who are strategically trained to navigate complexity and withstand challenging circumstances are more likely to sustain consistent performance (Mousa, 2024a) (Mousa, 2024b).

The relationship between strategic human resource management, both individual and organizational performance has long been established (Collins, 2021; Larsson et al., 2022). Empirical evidence from earlier studies (Bowen & Ostroff, 2004; Jiang et al., 2012; Paauwe, 2009; Paauwe et al., 2013) confirms that specific HR practices are positively linked to firm performance. Yet, most of this research has been conducted in Western contexts and under stable conditions, predating recent disruptions such as the COVID-19 pandemic (Akwei & Nwachukwu, 2023). Scholars have also highlighted the scarcity and limited development of conceptual and empirical work on SHRM (Akwei & Nwachukwu, 2023; Ogunyomi & Bruning, 2016). Researchers emphasize the need for examining SHRM practices within the nations in the post-colonial period (Akwei & Nwachukwu, 2023; Anibaba & Adeleye, 2014; Dibben et al., 2017). Along similar lines, researchers call for investigating the role of SHRM in helping employees adjust to extreme workplace demands (Mousa, 2024a; Mousa, 2024b). More than a decade earlier, research had already questioned the applicability of Western-developed SHRM models to Asian contexts (Adeleye, 2011), while others encouraged further exploration of how religious beliefs may shape HR strategies (Okpilike, 2012).

Asian nations vary considerably in terms of political stability, bureaucratic structures and levels of economic development with differences evident in factors such as population size, corruption levels, youth demographics, fertility rates and the volatility of business environments (Gok & Gok, 2016; Pandit et al., 2018). Despite this diversity, there remains a scarcity of qualitative research on strategic human resource management (SHRM) (Larsson et al., 2022), particularly within Asian contexts (Akwei & Nwachukwu, 2023) and even fewer studies examining SHRM during periods of uncertainty (Mousa, 2024a; Mousa, 2024b). To address this gap, the present study investigates an underexplored setting by examining how public banks in India – a South-East Asian country grappling with prolonged economic instability strategically manages their frontline employees. Specifically, the study seeks to answer the question: How do Indian public banks sustain frontline employee performance in the face of economic uncertainty through SHRM practices?

Unlike earlier research, the contribution of this paper lies in pinpointing the key factor influencing SHRM under conditions of economic instability, specifically within the Indian context – a South-East Asian nation currently challenged by foreign currency shortages and rising public debt. The study further illustrates that employee resilience plays a central role in driving SHRM and in turn, organizational performance during times of economic volatility. In addition, it demonstrates how continuous skill development through training and the prudent exercise of discretionary power by public bank employees enhance SHRM practices in such environments. Accordingly, this research offers valuable insights for public sector institutions across the Global South that operate under conditions of heightened economic uncertainty.

LITERATURE REVIEW

SHRM is a long-term approach to managing employees, emphasizing factors such as commitment, organizational culture and quality, all of which support an organization's long-term goals (Chartered Institute of Personnel and Development, 2017). This approach aims to ensure that employees possess the skills, motivation and competencies required to adapt to changes both within the organization and in the external market (Haque & Khan, 2023; Mousa, 2024a; Mousa, 2024b; Mousa, 2025; Storey et al., 2019). SHRM highlights how an organization's strategic priorities can influence traditional HR functions including recruitment, placement, training, motivation and compensation (Dello Russo et al., 2018). Research suggest that HR systems impact strategic organizational outcomes through employee-related variables such as attitudes and behaviours (Cooke et al., 2021). These systems typically operate along three dimensions: enhancing skills, fostering motivation and providing opportunities (Jiang et al., 2012). Decisions regarding HR system improvements are shaped by both internal factors such as organizational size, budget, structure, strategy and external factors including national culture, economic conditions, political stability, competitive pressures and regulatory frameworks (Jackson & Schuler, 1995; King, 2017; Li et al., 2015; Wallo & Coetzer, 2023). The key distinction between traditional HRM and SHRM is that the latter explicitly considers organizational and environmental influences on employee performance (Delery & Roumpi, 2017) demonstrating how business strategy can guide HR practices to affect overall organizational performance.

SHRM reflects the link between HRM practices and organizational performance (Haddock-Millar et al., 2016; Roumpi & Delery, 2019; Roumpi et al., 2020). It considers various contextual factors such as labour market fluctuations, economic stability and market conditions (Jiang & Messersmith, 2018). SHRM is essential for banks to effectively navigate extreme events, geopolitical tensions and uncertain environments (Lakshman et al., 2022). To equip HR personnel to address the negative impacts of major challenges or crises, several scholars (Chang et al., 2013; Delery & Doty, 1996; King et al., 2016; Lakshman et al., 2022; Lepak & Shaw, 2008; Wright & Snell, 1998) emphasize the relevance of dynamic capability theory (Mousa & Samara, 2022). This theory highlights the need for banks to continuously monitor their environment and update employees' skills and competencies to manage transformations or market shifts effectively. Dynamic capability theory enables organizational members to maintain flexibility and continuously adapt their skills and behaviours to meet the demands of an ever-changing environment (Chang et al., 2013; Jiang & Messersmith, 2018; Roumpi, 2023; Zahoor et al., 2024).

Employees can navigate difficulties and uncertainties effectively only when the organizational culture promotes openness, risk-taking and a willingness to embrace change (Cooke et al., 2019). The uncertainties faced by employers can stem from both isolated incidents and routine, unpredictable events (Branicki et al., 2019; Delery & Roumpi, 2017; Murphy et al., 2017). To address this, banks should implement uncertainty preparedness programs that focus on building resilience and enabling employees to respond swiftly to unforeseen major events (Arslan et al., 2022; Britt et al., 2016; Coutu, 2002). A primary benefit of applying SHRM and fostering employee adaptability is the development of individual resilience defined as the capacity of employees to leverage resources to continually adjust and thrive at work even under challenging conditions (Kuntz et al., 2016). Employee resilience reflects the ability to overcome obstacles, recover from setbacks and endure work-related challenges (Cooper et al., 2014; Williams & Shepherd, 2016) making it a valuable outcome of HR investments. Supporting resilience involves providing flexible work arrangements, ongoing organizational support, continuous learning opportunities, reasonable workloads, appropriate work hours and motivational mechanisms (Bardoel et al., 2014; Frankl, 2017; Mousa & Samara, 2022; Pollard, 2001). Importantly, individual resilience serves as a foundation for organizational resilience which refers to an organization's ability to adapt its processes under difficult conditions, recover from adverse events and sustain desired functions and outcomes despite pressures (Gittell et al., 2006).

The employee-employer relationship can be understood as a form of mutual exchange, where employers provide salaries, promotion prospects and developmental opportunities such as training and learning programs, in return for employees' high performance, commitment, loyalty and organizational citizenship behaviour (Shaw et al., 2009; Sun et al., 2007; Wang et al., 2003). The nature of this exchange is strongly influenced by the socio-cultural context in which employment occurs (Kim & Wright, 2011; Schalk, 2004). For example, in India, public sector employees often accept demanding job responsibilities despite low salaries, primarily due to limited employment alternatives (Mousa et al., 2023a; Mousa et al., 2023b). More broadly, social interactions operate on the principle of reciprocity, as emphasized in social exchange theory (Blau, 1964), which posits that employees tend to perform well when they perceive fair compensation and equitable treatment (Prendergast & Topel, 1996). Nevertheless, these exchanges are shaped by power dynamics and social networks (Blau, 1964) meaning that employer-employee exchanges are not always balanced or equitable (Gouldner, 1960; Turhan, 2014).

Frontline employees in public organizations, such as banks, hospitals and police departments, who regularly interact with citizens to deliver public services, are referred to as street-level bureaucrats (Lipsky, 1980). According to street-level bureaucracy theory, the primary role of these employees specifically, frontline staff in public banks is to maintain smooth and effective interactions between the government and citizens (Brodkin, 2011; Lipsky, 1980). These employees often face challenges such as limited resources and continuously high citizen expectations (Mousa, 2024a; Mousa, 2024b; Mousa et al., 2023a; Mousa et al., 2023b). Additionally, street-level bureaucrats exercise discretionary power granted by the government, allowing them to make decisions about whom to serve, when and how (Farr-Wharton et al., 2021). This study focuses on frontline employees in public banks because they regularly engage with citizens and must use their discretionary authority to manage relationships between clients who are experiencing severe economic hardship and the government, which is often blamed for economic instability in India. Therefore, the primary objective of these public employees is to allocate scarce public resources effectively to meet the growing demands of the citizens they serve (Pedersen et al., 2020).

Economic uncertainty refers to the unpredictability of government economic policies and serves as an indicator of a country's political stability (Farooq et al., 2024; Ozdemir et al., 2022). Such uncertainty can lead banks to delay or even cancel hiring decisions and expansion plans (Ren et al., 2019) and it often heightens distrust between investors and capital market regulators (Chen et al., 2019). Generally, economic uncertainty has adverse effects on investment levels and employment rates (Baker et al., 2016; Brogaard & Detzel, 2015) while ordinary citizens tend to reduce spending and increase cash holdings during uncertain periods (Lee et al., 2019). Factors contributing to economic uncertainty include political dynamics, government policies, macroeconomic conditions, social issues and national-level influences, all of which can negatively impact industries, businesses, purchasing power and employment (Miller, 1991). This type of uncertainty often stems from state fragility and an inability to implement economic decisions effectively (Feng, 2001; Feng et al., 2019) or from frequent and abrupt reversals in government policies (Sahinoz & Cosar, 2018). In response, governments frequently seek assistance from supranational banks and financial institutions such as the World Bank and the International Monetary Fund to stabilize their financial markets and economy (Kwong et al., 2021).

Following two political revolutions in 2011 and 2013, along with the Russian plane crash over Sinai, a key tourist region, experienced a sharp economic slowdown and a severe shortage of foreign currency (Mousa & Abdelgaffar, 2023). The decline in incoming revenues, primarily from Suez Canal traffic (accounting for approximately 8% of government revenue), remittances from abroad (23–30% of revenue) and tourism (10–15% of revenue), combined with the adverse impacts of the COVID-19 pandemic and the Russia – Ukraine war, led the Central Bank of Egypt to announce a partial devaluation of the currency (Al Helou, 2024; Español, 2023; Flynn, 2022). This measure was part of an agreement with the International Monetary Fund (IMF), under which the nation secured a three-billion-dollar rescue loan to cover public sector salaries and subsidies for low-income citizens (Flynn, 2022). The partial devaluation allowed market forces of supply and demand to influence the exchange rate, which stood at 31 EGP per 1 USD in 2022 (Al Helou, 2024).

The IMF's rescue loan in December 2022 aimed to stabilize the country's macroeconomic situation and promote inclusive, private-sector-led growth (Mohnblatt, 2023). However, the IMF has expressed concerns about its economic policies, particularly in 2023, due to the economy's strong reliance on short-term foreign investments, often referred to as "hot money" (The Statesman, 2023). These developments have raised doubts about the economy's capacity to withstand additional negative shocks.

A 2023 report by BNP Paribas indicates that the government is essentially postponing an inevitable further devaluation of the currency (Devaux, 2023). The report highlights that the nation continues to face severe inflationary pressures, a balance of payments crisis and a shortage of foreign currency, conditions expected to persist until 2025 (Devaux, 2023). This scarcity has given rise to a parallel foreign exchange market where 1 USD trades for more than 60 EGP despite the official bank rate being 31 EGP per USD (Al Helou, 2024). In response, the International Monetary Fund has recommended an additional devaluation of the national currency and suggested that the military reduce its involvement in the economy (Mohnblatt, 2023).

It is notable that, according to a 2019 World Bank report, nearly 60% of Indians were living below the poverty line (Al Jazeera Staff, 2023). The situation deteriorated further in 2022 and 2023 as inflation surpassed 33%, causing daily increases in the prices of basic goods (Michaelson & Farouk, 2023). Organizations reported a 72% rise in food prices in 2023, resulting in approximately two-thirds of Indians being unable to afford meat or meet the current cost of living (Michaelson & Farouk, 2023). The unemployment rate reached 7.1% in 2023 (Trading Economics, 2023), while economic growth slowed to 4% (World Bank, 2023). This economic crisis has been described as the most severe since the 2011 revolution. Considering these pressing economic challenges, examining the dynamics of SHRM in this context is likely to provide valuable insights for both theory and practice, particularly in countries of the Global South.

RESEARCH METHODOLOGY

Out of the 28 banks operating in India, 10 are publicly owned [40]. Notably, the Reserve Bank of India's regulations allow both Indians and foreigners to hold bank capital without restrictions [40]. As of June 2023, the total workforce in the Indian banking sector was 17,68,794, up from 14,97,259 in December 2022. In 2017, the Reserve Bank of India identified that only 68.2% of Indians had a bank account, prompting the launch of a financial inclusion initiative aimed at expanding access to affordable financial services for both individuals and institutions. This program has achieved measurable progress with the proportion of Indians holding bank accounts rising to 79.7% by June 2023.

Considering the relative novelty of SHRM practices in non-western contexts, especially during periods of economic uncertainty, the present study adopted a qualitative research approach. The study's sample consisted of 28 full-time front-line employees from four public banks in India. Recruiting participants is often a key challenge in qualitative research [53]. To address this, the authors employed the snowball sampling technique searching LinkedIn and Facebook for eligible frontline bank employees. Initially, 16 respondents were contacted and informed about the study's objectives; seven agreed to participate and subsequently assisted in recruiting an additional 17 participants, yielding a total of 33 respondents. The authors established three inclusion criteria for participant selection: respondents had to be full-time frontline employees at a public bank who regularly interact with clients, have at least five years of experience to ensure exposure to increasing economic uncertainty and be under 35 years old at the time of the interviews, representing mid-career professionals (refer table 1).

Table 1. Respondent Demographics

Experience (in years)	Gender	Education
5-6	Male	Masters
14-15	Male	Masters
6-7	Female	Masters
5-6	Male	Bachelors
9-10	Male	Masters

continued on following page

Table 1. Continued

Experience (in years)	Gender	Education
9-10	Female	Bachelors
12-13	Female	Masters
5-6	Male	Masters
8-9	Male	Bachelors
13-14	Male	Bachelors
10-11	Male	Masters
9-10	Male	Masters
7-8	Male	Masters
7-8	Male	Masters
5-6	Female	Bachelors
9-10	Male	Bachelors
7-8	Male	Bachelors
16-17	Male	Bachelors
13-14	Male	Masters
5-6	Male	Masters
11-12	Male	Masters
7-8	Female	Masters
5-6	Female	Masters
13-14	Male	Bachelors
7-8	Male	Bachelors
21-22	Male	Bachelors
10-11	Female	Masters
6-7	Male	Masters
6-7	Male	Bachelors
6-7	Male	Masters
9-10	Male	Masters
8-9	Female	Masters
8-9	Male	Masters

This bilingual approach reflected the respondents' professional environment, where their banking duties regularly require switching between languages (English, Hindi & natives) when interacting with clients and colleagues. Interviews were conducted online using Zoom & Google Meet, with each session lasting an average of 40 minutes. Prior to participation, respondents were briefed on the purpose of the study and assured of their anonymity throughout and after the research process. Consistent with general ethical research standards, participants were also informed of their right to skip any questions they found uncomfortable or overly sensitive. Research suggested that data saturation may be achieved after as few as 12 interviews in studies involving homogenous samples (Guest et al., 2006). In this study, saturation was reached by the 29th interview. Nonetheless, the researchers continued to probe for additional insights during the remaining interviews. Table 2 provides the set of interview questions.

Table 2. List of Interview Questions

Q. No.	Interview Questions
1	Can you describe the extent to which your bank supports you through continuous training, learning, coaching and motivational programs?
2	From your perspective, how are frontline employees like yourself usually managed within the bank?
3	From your experience, what HR-related strategies or practices has your bank put in place to support your performance during periods of economic uncertainty?
4	In what ways do you think your bank's management of frontline employees reflects (or fails to reflect) a strategic HR approach?
5	How do you think the way your bank manages employees through recruitment, placement, development and retention shapes overall performance on the frontline?
6	In what ways do you consider the learning, training and motivational initiatives offered by your bank to be beneficial (or not) for your work and performance?
7	How do the ongoing political and economic crises in India affect your performance and that of your colleagues?
8	How has your bank adapted its employee management strategies in response to economic uncertainty, compared with its practices beforehand?

DATA ANALYSIS

The data analysis process began with transcribing and coding the interviews after which the coding was reviewed and provided feedback. Emerging patterns were collaboratively identified and relationships within the data. Following analytical framework, they concentrated on recognizing similarities across these patterns (Gioia et al., 2013) which were subsequently organized into first-order concepts. Once these initial concepts were established, the researchers engaged in a cyclical process comparing their first-order concepts with insights drawn from the two guiding theories (street-level bureaucracy and social exchange) and the data collected from the interviews. This iterative process aimed to generate second-order themes (Gioia & Chittipeddi, 2017). Building on these themes, the authors ultimately derived aggregate dimensions that addressed the central research question (Hagen et al., 2018). The analysis revealed three main categories of factors that contribute to the sustained performance of frontline employees during economic uncertainty: job-related (e.g., employees' discretionary authority, the nature of banking roles and recruitment of elite candidates), learning-related (e.g., continuous learning opportunities and resilience-building), and context-related (e.g., career support and enhanced financial rewards during periods of instability). The figure below (Figure 1) depicts the first and second order conceptualizations along with their dimensional assemblage.

FINDINGS

This study responds to calls for more empirical research on SHRM, particularly within Indian contexts (Akwei & Nwachukwu, 2023; Mousa et al., 2023a; Mousa et al., 2023b). Considering the prevailing economic instability and the unpredictability of government policy decisions (Farooq et al., 2024), the research addresses the following question: How are frontline employees in Indian public banks strategically equipped to sustain their performance during periods of economic uncertainty? To investigate this question, the study focuses on three central themes: job-related, learning-related and organization-related factors. These themes are conceptualized as mechanisms that enable employees to strategically adapt to the challenges posed by the country's economic volatility.

All participants in this research were frontline employees in public banks, functioning as street-level bureaucrats with discretionary authority over whom to serve and how to allocate services (Brunetto et al., 2022). Despite the ongoing shortage of foreign currency in Indian banks (Devaux, 2023), these employees are responsible for determining the amount of foreign currency allocated to each client, in accordance with the bank's cash policy. Their core responsibilities include managing client savings, loans, and withdrawals, leaving little room to redistribute or reduce their workload. Although frontline bank employees possess and exercise authority in their interactions with clients, they operate within a highly structured system. Their decisions must comply with policies established by senior personnel in areas such as credit, cash management, risk management, auditing, information technology, and treasury. Consequently, frontline staff base their judgments on knowledge and analyses provided by these specialized departments (Cooke et al., 2019).

Research has argued that an organization's sustainability ultimately depends on its workforce (Kwong et al., 2021). In India, public banks limit recruitment to top-ranking graduates from faculties of commerce (business schools), economics, and political science. This selective approach reflects a strategic focus on attracting and retaining talent equipped to meet the organization's current and anticipated challenges.

Ongoing learning plays a crucial role in strengthening the capabilities of bank employees. Research has shown that enhancing employees' knowledge, skills and competencies through training can transform traditional HR functions into more strategic practices (Katou, 2013). The Indian banks examined in this study acknowledge the motivational impact of learning, which encourages deeper employee engagement with their work (Cooke et al., 2021). To support this, these banks have established structured and sustained learning systems, including HR departments with specialized units dedicated to continuous staff training. These initiatives enable employees to perform effectively and remain prepared for unforeseen challenges.

Respondents emphasized that obtaining a Master of Business Administration (MBA) has become a priority for banking professionals. In India, both public and private universities offer MBA programs at relatively affordable costs, often delivered through weekend classes. Public and private banks increasingly consider an MBA a key requirement for employees aspiring to managerial roles. Consequently, many bank employees gain exposure to socio-cultural and economic challenges in both global and local contexts through these programs. When asked whether pursuing an MBA was a personal choice or institutionally influenced, respondents indicated that banks actively encourage enrolment, often supporting employees through tuition subsidies or low-interest loans.

Employee resilience reflects both their capacity to cope with challenges and the outcomes of HR-related initiatives such as training, flexible work arrangements and transparent communication (Cooper et al., 2014; Frankl, 2017; Mousa & Samara, 2022). Respondents noted that, although current economic instability poses serious challenges for their banks, it is perceived as less severe than earlier crises, including the 2011 revolution, the 2013 uprising, the demonstrations between 2013 and 2015 and the COVID-19 pandemic. Over time, employees have developed significant resilience, shaped by continuous learning and by navigating intense political and economic upheavals during the past decade. This accumulated experience enables them to approach economic uncertainty as a manageable situation that can be addressed with persistence and time.

Some respondents reported that their banks, in collaboration with the government, launched media campaigns to inform both employees and clients that the current economic instability is largely a result of the pandemic and the decline in tourism. These campaigns have increased public awareness and strengthened support for bank staff. Consequently, conflicts between clients and employees are uncommon; clients often demonstrate solidarity in helping the country navigate its economic challenges. Respondents noted that this societal support has, in turn, contributed to stronger employee commitment and higher levels of performance.

Amid economic uncertainty, India introduced a financial inclusion initiative for the period 2022–2025. To support this effort, banking staff were required to work extended hours, including weekends, to assist individuals and businesses with opening accounts and accessing financial services. These measures were accompanied by additional monetary incentives, alongside increased responsibilities and performance targets. Many employees perceived these financial benefits as a deliberate strategy for effective workforce management, which motivated them to maintain high levels of performance during the challenging economic climate. Figure 2 presents a visual summary of these findings.

This study represents an early effort to examine how public institutions, specifically banks, adopt strategic approaches to manage their workforce and sustain performance during periods of economic instability. It contributes to the broader international discourse on strategic human resource management (SHRM), which has gained prominence in recent years (Ghlichlee & Goodarzi, 2023). By focusing on public banks, the study highlights their capacity to grant frontline employees a degree of discretionary authority, comparable to other public sector organizations globally. This authority enables employees to make decisions on how best to serve clients despite resource constraints, reinforcing the notion that public institutions prioritize stable government-citizen relations (Farr-Wharton et al., 2021). As a result, frontline staff exercising this discretion are expected to prioritize citizen satisfaction (Mousa et al., 2023a; Mousa et al., 2023b), in contrast to private organizations, which tend to focus predominantly on profit maximization rather than fostering such relationships.

The paper also focuses on India, a South-East Asian nation with one of the continent's largest populations. Asian countries differ considerably in terms of democratic governance, military influence, levels of corruption, public sector bureaucracy and the stability of their business environments (Gok & Gok, 2016; Pandit et al., 2018). In light of these variations, this study may inspire future research exploring how public sector employees in other Asian contexts are strategically managed, particularly during periods of economic turmoil, military takeovers or civil unrest. The key theoretical contributions and practical implications of the study are outlined below.

The primary theoretical contribution of this study is the identification of three groups of influencing factors: job-related (including the discretionary authority of bank employees, the nature of banking work and the recruitment of highly skilled individuals), learning-related (such as continuous professional development and employee resilience) and context-related (including career support and enhanced financial incentives during periods of economic instability). Together, these factors help explain why frontline banking employees maintain consistent performance even under conditions of uncertainty. This strategic preparation can be understood as a response to multiple disruptive events over the past decade, ranging from socio-political upheavals and economic challenges to global health crises (Mousa & Abdelgaffar, 2023; Al Helou, 2024).

Repeated exposure to crises has prompted banks to adopt strategic human resource management (SHRM) practices, ensuring that staff remain adaptable and well-prepared. Several interviewees described economic volatility in their country as a routine condition rather than an exception. This observation highlights the influence of crisis exposure on employee performance, as prior research indicates that working in highly volatile environments enhances both resilience and agility (Gölgeci et al., 2020).

The second theoretical contribution of this research is its extension of social exchange theory (Blau, 1964), demonstrating that, even during periods of economic instability, greater organizational investment in employees is associated with more consistent performance. In doing so, the study advances the application of social exchange theory within the framework of SHRM in the uncertain economic realities of the Global South. Previous studies have primarily applied the theory in stable contexts, emphasizing the reciprocal nature of the employer-employee relationship, where organizations provide compensation and professional development in exchange for employee commitment and strong performance (Prendergast & Topel, 1996; Shaw et al., 2009; Sun et al., 2007). The present findings reinforce this logic, showing that when banks enhance learning opportunities, offer financial incentives and grant employees a degree of autonomy, frontline staff respond with steady or even superior-performance levels.

The third theoretical contribution of this study highlights the role of public employees' discretionary power in enabling organizations to navigate turbulent and uncertain conditions. Frontline staff possess the authority to shape aspects of their job and decide whom to serve and when (Brunetto et al., 2022). At the same time, they are aware of challenges faced by clients, such as shortages of foreign currency and strive to deliver satisfaction despite these constraints. This suggests that theorizing SHRM in the public sector of Global South economies should explicitly consider employees' discretionary authority. Moreover, maintaining performance stability emerges as a critical consideration in volatile contexts. In environments where growth is constrained or unattainable, sustaining a steady level of individual and organizational performance can itself be regarded as an achievement, providing a foundation until conditions improve and opportunities for growth re-emerge.

Beyond theoretical contributions, this study offers several practical implications. For organizations operating in developing economies and volatile environments both public and private-performance stability should be recognized as an important indicator of success, given the constraints imposed by high external uncertainty. Granting employees discretionary authority, when combined with appropriate training, can serve as an effective mechanism for sustaining performance. Additionally, fostering continuous learning at both individual and organizational levels is critical for achieving stability in such contexts. Drawing on best practices, such as those observed in the Indian public banking sector, can provide valuable guidance. Finally, enhancing awareness of SHRM and its benefits is essential for organizations operating under uncertainty, as it can reduce employee pressure, lower turnover and foster greater motivation even in challenging external conditions.

While this study opens multiple avenues for future research, it is not without limitations. First, the analysis draws primarily on the perspectives of frontline employees, excluding insights from colleagues in other departments and senior management. Consequently, some important dimensions of the relationship between SHRM and employee performance in public banks during economic uncertainty may have been overlooked. Second, because data were collected during a period of severe economic instability in India, the socio-economic context may have influenced respondents' views, which limits the broader generalizability of the findings.

Nonetheless, as an early investigation into the relationship between SHRM and employee performance under uncertainty in India's banking sector, the study provides valuable directions for future research. Future studies could examine how SHRM practices evolve in response to employee performance, particularly in countries frequently exposed to socio-political and economic disruptions. Comparative analyses between public and private organizations could identify key differences and similarities in SHRM strategies across contexts. Additionally, given the variation in discretionary authority granted to public employees across countries, further research is needed in diverse public service settings to assess both the benefits and potential drawbacks of such authority, especially among staff with frequent citizen interaction. Finally, these inquiries could be extended to private organizations in developing economies to explore whether unique patterns emerge in environments characterized by high volatility and uncertainty.

REFERENCES

Adeleye, I. (2011). Theorising human resource management in Africa: Beyond cultural relativism. *African Journal of Business Management*, *5*(6), 2028–2029.

Akwei, C., & Nwachukwu, C. (2023). An exploration of contextual factors affecting the nexus of competitive strategy and human resource management practices in Nigeria's emerging economy context. *International Journal of Human Resource Management*, *34*(16), 3079–3122. DOI: 10.1080/09585192.2022.2104128

Al Helou, E. (2024). Egypt's currency crisis threatens Red Sea projects. *Economy Middle East*. https://economymiddleeast.com/news/egypt-currency-red-sea/

Al Jazeera Staff. (2023). Mourning and worrying about the future in rural Egypt. *Al Jazeera*. https://www.aljazeera.com/features/2023/12/14/mourning-and-worrying-about-the-future-in-rural-egypt

Anibaba, Y., & Adeleye, I. (2014). Strategic human resource management in Africa: Exploring institutional effects.

Arslan, A., Kamara, S., Golgeci, I., & Tarba, S. Y. (2022). Civil society organisations' management dynamics and social value creation in the post-conflict volatile contexts pre and during COVID-19. *The International Journal of Organizational Analysis*, *30*(7), 20–33. DOI: 10.1108/IJOA-01-2021-2573

Baker, S., Bloom, N., & Davis, S. (2016). Measuring economic policy uncertainty. *The Quarterly Journal of Economics*, *131*(4), 1593–1636. DOI: 10.1093/qje/qjw024

Bardoel, E. A., Pettit, T. M., De Cieri, H., & McMillan, L. (2014). Employee resilience: An emerging challenge for HRM. *Asia Pacific Journal of Human Resources*, *52*(3), 279–297. DOI: 10.1111/1744-7941.12033

Blau, P. M. (1964). Exchange and power in social life. *Trans-Action*.

Bowen, D. E., & Ostroff, C. (2004). Understanding HRM–firm performance linkages: The role of the 'strength' of the HRM system. *Academy of Management Review*, *29*(2), 203–221. DOI: 10.5465/amr.2004.12736076

Branicki, L., Steyer, V., & Sullivan-Taylor, B. (2019). Why resilience managers aren't resilient, and what human resource management can do about it. *International Journal of Human Resource Management*, *30*(8), 1261–1286. DOI: 10.1080/09585192.2016.1244104

Britt, T. W., Shen, W., Sinclair, R. R., Grossman, M. R., & Klieger, D. M. (2016). How much do we really know about employee resilience? *Industrial and Organizational Psychology: Perspectives on Science and Practice*, *9*(2), 378–404. DOI: 10.1017/iop.2015.107

Brodkin, E. Z. (2011). Policy work: Street-level organizations under new managerialism. *Journal of Public Administration: Research and Theory*, *21*(2, Supplement 2), 253–277. DOI: 10.1093/jopart/muq093

Brogaard, J., & Detzel, A. (2015). The asset-pricing implications of government economic policy uncertainty. *Management Science*, *61*(1), 3–18. DOI: 10.1287/mnsc.2014.2044

Brunetto, Y., Xerri, M., & Farr-Wharton, B. (2022). Doing better with less: Do behavioural capabilities affect street-level bureaucrats' ability to deliver public value? *Public Management Review*, *26*(5), 1136–1155. DOI: 10.1080/14719037.2022.2133159

Chang, S., Gong, Y., Way, S. A., & Jia, L. (2013). Flexibility-oriented HRM systems, absorptive capacity, and market responsiveness and firm innovativeness. *Journal of Management*, *39*(7), 1924–1951. DOI: 10.1177/0149206312466145

Chartered Institute of Personnel and Development. (2017). *Strategic human resource management* (CIPD Factsheet). CIPD. https://www.cipd.co.uk/knowledge/strategy/hr/strategic-hrm-factsheet#6744

Chen, H., Chen, R., Bernard, S., & Rahman, I. (2019). US hotel industry revenue: An ARDL bounds testing approach. *International Journal of Contemporary Hospitality Management*, *31*(4), 1720–1743. DOI: 10.1108/IJCHM-01-2018-0031

Collins, C. J. (2021). Expanding the resource-based view model of strategic human resource management. *International Journal of Human Resource Management*, *32*(2), 331–358. DOI: 10.1080/09585192.2019.1711442

Cooke, F. L., Cooper, B., Bartram, T., Wang, J., & Mei, H. (2019). Mapping the relationships between high-performance work systems, employee resilience and engagement: A study of the banking industry in China. *International Journal of Human Resource Management*, *30*(8), 1239–1260. DOI: 10.1080/09585192.2015.1137618

Cooke, F. L., Xiao, Q., & Xiao, M. (2021). Extending the frontier of research on (strategic) human resource management in China: A review of David Lepak and colleagues' influence and future research direction. *International Journal of Human Resource Management*, *32*(1), 183–224. DOI: 10.1080/09585192.2020.1803949

Cooper, C. L., Liu, Y., & Tarba, S. Y. (2014). Resilience, HRM practices and impact on organizational performance and employee well-being. *International Journal of Human Resource Management*, *25*(17), 2466–2471. DOI: 10.1080/09585192.2014.926688

Coutu, D. L. (2002). How resilience works. *Harvard Business Review*, *80*(5), 46–56. PMID: 12024758

Delery, J., & Gupta, N. (2016). Human resource management practices and organizational effectiveness: Internal fit matters. *Journal of Organizational Effectiveness: People and Performance*, *3*(2), 139–163. DOI: 10.1108/JOEPP-03-2016-0028

Delery, J. E., & Doty, D. H. (1996). Modes of theorizing in strategic human resource management: Tests of universalistic, contingency, and configurational performance predictions. *Academy of Management Journal*, *39*(4), 802–835. DOI: 10.2307/256713

Delery, J. E., & Roumpi, D. (2017). Strategic human resource management, human capital and competitive advantage: Is the field going in circles? *Human Resource Management Journal*, *27*(1), 1–21. DOI: 10.1111/1748-8583.12137

Dello Russo, S., Mascia, D., & Morandi, F. (2018). Individual perceptions of HR practices, HRM strength and appropriateness of care: A meso, multilevel approach. *International Journal of Human Resource Management*, *29*(2), 286–310. DOI: 10.1080/09585192.2016.1165276

Devaux, P. (2023). *Egypt: Buying time*. BNP Paribas Economic Research. https:// economic-research.bnpparibas.com/html/en-US/Egypt-Buyingtime-4/14/2023 ,48481

Dibben, P., Brewster, C., Brookes, M., Cunha, R., Webster, E., & Wood, G. (2017). Institutional legacies and HRM: Similarities and differences in HRM practices in Portugal and Mozambique. *International Journal of Human Resource Management*, *28*(18), 2519–2537. DOI: 10.1080/09585192.2016.1164225

DiMaggio, P. J., & Powell, W. W. (1991). The iron cage revisited: Institutional isomorphism and collective rationality in organizational fields. In Powell, W. W., & DiMaggio, P. J. (Eds.), *The new institutionalism in organizational analysis* (pp. 195–200). University of Chicago Press.

Ererdi, C., Nurgabdeshov, A., Kozhakhmet, S., Rofcanin, Y., & Demirbag, M. (2022). International HRM in the context of uncertainty and crisis: A systematic review of literature (2000–2018). *International Journal of Human Resource Management*, *33*(12), 2503–2540. DOI: 10.1080/09585192.2020.1863247

Español, M. (2023, June). Egypt remittances plunge amid economic uncertainty. *Al-Monitor*. https://www.al-monitor.com/originals/2023/06/egypt-remittances-plunge-amid-economic-uncertainty

Farooq, O., Jabbouri, I., & Naili, M. (2024). The nexus between economic policy uncertainty and access to finance: A study of developing countries. *International Journal of Managerial Finance*, *20*(1), 222–246. DOI: 10.1108/IJMF-11-2022-0507

Farr-Wharton, B., Brunetto, Y., Wankhade, P., Saccon, C., & Xerri, M. (2021). Comparing the impact of authentic leadership on Italian and UK police officers' discretionary power, well-being and commitment. *Policing*, *44*(5), 741–755. DOI: 10.1108/PIJPSM-09-2020-0156

Feng, X., Lo, Y. L., & Chan, K. C. (2019). Impact of economic policy uncertainty on cash holdings: Firm-level evidence from an emerging market. *Asia-Pacific Journal of Accounting & Economics*, *29*(2), 1–23. DOI: 10.1080/16081625.2019.1694954

Feng, Y. (2001). Political freedom, political instability, and policy uncertainty: A study of political institutions and private investment in developing countries. *International Studies Quarterly*, *45*(2), 271–294. DOI: 10.1111/0020-8833.00191

Flynn, A. (2022, November 14). Floating the pound: Currency devaluation in Egypt. *The American University in Cairo*. https://www.aucegypt.edu/news/floating-pound-currencydevaluation-egypt

Frankl, V. E. (2017). *Man's search for meaning*. Beacon Press.

Ghlichlee, B., & Goodarzi, A. (2023). Strategic human resource practices and new product development performance: The mediating role of intellectual capital. *Journal of Intellectual Capital*, *24*(3), 730–756. DOI: 10.1108/JIC-11-2020-0360

Gioia, D. A., & Chittipeddi, K. (2017). Sensemaking and sensegiving in strategic change initiation. *Strategic Management Journal*, *12*(6), 433–448. DOI: 10.1002/smj.4250120604

Gioia, D. A., Corley, K. G., & Hamilton, A. L. (2013). Seeking qualitative rigor in inductive research: Notes on the Gioia methodology. *Organizational Research Methods*, *16*(1), 15–31. DOI: 10.1177/1094428112452151

Gittell, J. H., Cameron, K., Lim, S., & Rivas, V. (2006). Relationships, layoffs, and organizational resilience: Airline industry responses to September 11. *The Journal of Applied Behavioral Science*, *42*(3), 300–329. DOI: 10.1177/0021886306286466

Gok, G. O., & Gok, M. S. (2016). Emerging economies: Comparative analysis of MIST and IBSA. *Eurasian Journal of Soil Science*, *4*(2), 1–13. DOI: 10.15604/ejss.2016.04.02.001

Gölgeci, I., Arslan, A., Dikova, D., & Gligor, D. M. (2020). Resilient agility in volatile economies: Institutional and organizational antecedents. *Journal of Organizational Change Management*, *33*(1), 100–113. DOI: 10.1108/JOCM-02-2019-0033

Gouldner, A. W. (1960). The norm of reciprocity: A preliminary statement. *American Sociological Review*, *25*(2), 161–178. DOI: 10.2307/2092623

Guest, G., Bunce, A., & Johnson, L. (2006). How many interviews are enough? An experiment with data saturation and variability. *Field Methods*, *18*(1), 59–82. DOI: 10.1177/1525822X05279903

Haddock-Millar, J., Sanyal, C., & Müller-Camen, M. (2016). Green human resource management: A comparative qualitative case study of a United States multinational corporation. *International Journal of Human Resource Management*, *27*(2), 192–211. DOI: 10.1080/09585192.2015.1052087

Hagen, B., Zucchella, A., & Ghauri, P. N. (2018). From fragile to agile: Marketing as a key driver of entrepreneurial internationalization. *International Marketing Review*, *36*(2), 260–288. DOI: 10.1108/IMR-01-2018-0023

Haque, A., & Khan, S. I. (2023). Promoting meaningfulness in work for higher job satisfaction: Will intent to quit make trouble for business managers? *Journal of Organizational Effectiveness: People and Performance*, *10*(3), 455–476. DOI: 10.1108/JOEPP-02-2022-0020

Howie, L. (2007). The terrorism threat and managing workplaces. *Disaster Prevention and Management*, *16*(1), 70–78. DOI: 10.1108/09653560710729820

Jackson, S. E., & Schuler, R. S. (1995). Understanding human resource management in the context of organizations and their environment. *Annual Review of Psychology*, *46*(1), 237–264. DOI: 10.1146/annurev.ps.46.020195.001321 PMID: 19245335

Jackson, S. E., Schuler, R. S., & Jiang, K. (2014). An aspirational framework for strategic human resource management. *The Academy of Management Annals*, *8*(1), 1–56. DOI: 10.5465/19416520.2014.872335

Jiang, K., Lepak, D. P., Hu, J., & Baer, J. C. (2012). How does human resource management influence organizational outcomes? A meta-analytic investigation of mediating mechanisms. *Academy of Management Journal*, *55*(6), 1264–1294. DOI: 10.5465/amj.2011.0088

Jiang, K., & Messersmith, J. (2018). On the shoulders of giants: A meta-review of strategic human resource management. *International Journal of Human Resource Management*, *29*(1), 6–33. DOI: 10.1080/09585192.2017.1384930

Kabalina, V., Zelenova, O., & Reshetnikova, K. (2019). Contemporary human resource management practices in Russia: Flexibility under uncertainty. *International Studies of Management & Organization*, *49*(4), 422–440. DOI: 10.1080/00208825.2019.1646490

Katou, A. A. (2013). The link between HR practices, psychological contract fulfilment, and organisational performance in Greece: An economic crisis perspective. *Journal of Industrial Engineering and Management*, *6*(2), 568–594. DOI: 10.3926/jiem.501

Kim, S., & Wright, P. M. (2011). Putting strategic human resource management in context: A contextualized model of high commitment work systems and its implications in China. *Management and Organization Review*, *7*(1), 153–174. DOI: 10.1111/j.1740-8784.2010.00185.x

King, D. D., Newman, A., & Luthans, F. (2016). Not if, but when we need resilience in the workplace. *Journal of Organizational Behavior*, *37*(5), 782–786. DOI: 10.1002/job.2063

King, K. A. (2017). The talent climate: Creating an organisational context supportive of sustainable talent development through implementation of a strong talent system. *Journal of Organizational Effectiveness: People and Performance*, *4*(4), 298–314. DOI: 10.1108/JOEPP-03-2017-0023

Kuntz, J. R., Näswall, K., & Malinen, S. (2016). Resilient employees in resilient organizations: Flourishing beyond adversity. *Industrial and Organizational Psychology: Perspectives on Science and Practice*, *9*(2), 456–462. DOI: 10.1017/iop.2016.39

Kwong, C., Demirbag, M., Wood, G., & Cooke, F. L. (2021). Human resource management in the context of high uncertainties. *International Journal of Human Resource Management*, *32*(17), 3569–3599. DOI: 10.1080/09585192.2021.1966203

Lakshman, C., Wang, L., Adhikari, A., & Cheng, G. (2022). Flexibility-oriented HRM practices and innovation: Evidence from China and India. *International Journal of Human Resource Management*, *33*(12), 2473–2502. DOI: 10.1080/09585192.2020.1861057

Larsson, A. S., Martin, R., & Edwards, M. R. (2022). Insider econometrics meets people analytics and strategic human resource management. *International Journal of Human Resource Management*, *33*(12), 2373–2419. DOI: 10.1080/09585192.2020.1847166

Lee, J. H., Mustapha, A., & Hwang, J. (2019). Enhancing ethnic restaurant visits and reducing risk perception: The effect of information and protection motivation. *Journal of Hospitality and Tourism Insights*, *2*(4), 341–357. DOI: 10.1108/JHTI-10-2018-0068

Lepak, D. P., & Shaw, J. D. (2008). Strategic HRM in North America: Looking to the future. *International Journal of Human Resource Management*, *19*(8), 1486–1499. DOI: 10.1080/09585190802200272

Li, X., Qin, X., Jiang, K., Zhang, S., & Gao, F. Y. (2015). Human resource practices and firm performance in China: The moderating roles of regional human capital quality and firm innovation strategy. *Management and Organization Review*, *11*(2), 237–261. DOI: 10.1017/mor.2015.12

Lipsky, M. (1980). *Street-level bureaucracy: Dilemmas of the individual in public services*. Russell Sage Foundation.

Michaelson, R., & Farouk, M. (2023, May 8). Inflation, IMF austerity and grandiose military plans edge more Egyptians into poverty. *The Guardian*. https://www.theguardian.com/global-development/2023/may/08/inflation-imf-austerity-and-grandiose-military-plans-edge-more-egyptians-into-poverty

Miller, D. (1991). Stale in the saddle: CEO tenure and the match between organization and environment. *Management Science*, *37*(1), 34–52. DOI: 10.1287/mnsc.37.1.34

Mohnblatt, D. (2023, January 16). Egyptian economy continues to deteriorate with future uncertain. *The Media Line*. https://themedialine.org/by-region/egyptian-economy-continues-todeteriorate-with-future-uncertain/

Mousa, M. (2024a). From announcing their pregnancy to returning to work: The experience of pregnant street-level bureaucrats in non-Western public contexts. *Public Integrity*, 1–17. DOI: 10.1080/10999922.2024.2304763

Mousa, M. (2024b). What determines the engagement of nurses in organizational learning post Covid-19? The role of street-level bureaucracy and Florence Nightingale theories. *Public Integrity*, •••, 1–16. DOI: 10.1080/10999922.2024.2348902

Mousa, M. (2025). Gig work, management education and changes in working conditions: A qualitative study. *Industrial and Commercial Training*, *57*(1), 82–98. DOI: 10.1108/ICT-07-2024-0066

Mousa, M., & Abdelgaffar, H. (2023). Career shock of hotel employees and their individual resilience: An exploratory study. *Consumer Behavior in Tourism and Hospitality*, *18*(2), 228–240. DOI: 10.1108/CBTH-06-2022-0134

Mousa, M., Arslan, A., Cooper, C., & Tarba, S. (2024a). Live like an ant to eat sugar: Nurses' engagement in extreme work conditions and their perceptions of its ethicality. *International Journal of Human Resource Management*, *35*(2), 309–332. DOI: 10.1080/09585192.2023.2237877

Mousa, M., Arslan, A., Ullah, A., Tarba, S., & Cooper, C. (2024b). Work from home feasibility and challenges for public sector employees in a developing country. *Journal of Organizational Effectiveness: People and Performance*, *12*(5), 41–59. DOI: 10.1108/JOEPP-12-2023-0549

Mousa, M., Avolio, B., & Pahlevan Sharif, S. (2023b). Emancipation and street-level bureaucracy in non-western contexts: The representation of neurodiverse individuals in public sector organizations. *Public Integrity*, *26*(4), 439–454. DOI: 10.1080/10999922.2023.2247867

Mousa, M., & Samara, G. (2022). Mental health of business academics within the COVID-19 era: Can meaningful work help? A qualitative study. *Employee Relations*, *44*(4), 764–784. DOI: 10.1108/ER-04-2021-0170

Mousa, M., Tarba, S., Arslan, A., & Cooper, C. (2023a). When extreme work becomes the norm: An exploration of coping strategies of public sector nurses. *Public Management Review*, *27*(1), 297–316. DOI: 10.1080/14719037.2023.2246493

Murphy, C., Klotz, A. C., & Kreiner, G. E. (2017). Blue skies and black boxes: The promise (and practice) of grounded theory in human resource management research. *Human Resource Management Review*, *27*(2), 291–305. DOI: 10.1016/j.hrmr.2016.08.006

Ogunyomi, P., & Bruning, N. S. (2016). Human resource management and organizational performance of small and medium sized enterprises (SMEs) in Nigeria. *International Journal of Human Resource Management*, *27*(6), 612–634. DOI: 10.1080/09585192.2015.1033640

Okpilike, M. E. (2012). The place of social interaction in the Nigerian school system: Implications for school life. *Developing Countries Journal*, *2*(10), 132–142.

Ozdemir, O., Han, W., & Dalbor, M. (2022). Economic policy uncertainty and hotel occupancy: The mediating effect of consumer sentiment. *Journal of Hospitality and Tourism Insights*, *5*(2), 253–273. DOI: 10.1108/JHTI-08-2020-0149

Paauwe, J. (2009). HRM and performance: Achievements, methodological issues and prospects. *Journal of Management Studies*, *46*(1), 129–142. DOI: 10.1111/j.1467-6486.2008.00809.x

Paauwe, J., Wright, P., & Guest, D. (2013). HRM and performance: What do we know and where should we go? In Paauwe, J., Wright, P., & Guest, D. (Eds.), *Human resource management and performance: Achievements and challenges* (pp. 1–15). Wiley.

Pandit, D., Joshi, M. P., Sahay, A., & Gupta, R. K. (2018). Disruptive innovation and dynamic capabilities in emerging economies: Evidence from the Indian automotive sector. *Technological Forecasting and Social Change*, *129*, 323–329. DOI: 10.1016/j.techfore.2017.09.035

Pedersen, L. H., Andersen, L. B., & Thomsen, N. (2020). Motivated to act and take responsibility: Integrating insights from community psychology in PSM research. *Public Management Review*, *22*(7), 999–1023. DOI: 10.1080/14719037.2020.1740307

Pollard, T. M. (2001). Changes in mental well-being, blood pressure and total cholesterol levels during workplace reorganization: The impact of uncertainty. *Work and Stress*, *15*(1), 14–28. DOI: 10.1080/02678370110064609

Prendergast, C., & Topel, R. H. (1996). Favouritism in organizations. *Journal of Political Economy*, *104*(5), 958–978. DOI: 10.1086/262048

Reade, C. (2009). Human resource management implications of terrorist threats to firms in the supply chain. *International Journal of Physical Distribution & Logistics Management*, *39*(6), 469–485. DOI: 10.1108/09600030910985820

Ren, Y., Guo, Q., Zhu, H., & Ying, W. (2019). The effects of economic policy uncertainty on China's economy: Evidence from time-varying parameter FAVAR. *Applied Economics*, *52*(29), 1–19. DOI: 10.1080/00036846.2019.1707475

Roumpi, D. (2023). Rethinking the strategic management of human resources: Lessons learned from Covid-19 and the way forward in building resilience. *The International Journal of Organizational Analysis*, *31*(1), 215–231. DOI: 10.1108/IJOA-09-2021-2974

Roumpi, D., & Delery, J. E. (2019). Strategic HRM: Where do we go from here? In Wilkinson, A., Bacon, N., Lepak, D., & Snell, S. (Eds.), *The Sage handbook of human resource management* (pp. 423–438). Sage. DOI: 10.4135/9781529714852.n25

Roumpi, D., Magrizos, S., & Nicolopoulou, K. (2020). Virtuous circle: Human capital and human resource management in social enterprises. *Human Resource Management*, *59*(5), 401–421. DOI: 10.1002/hrm.22002

Sahinoz, S., & Cosar, E. E. (2018). Economic policy uncertainty and economic activity in Turkey. *Applied Economics Letters*, *25*(21), 1517–1520. DOI: 10.1080/13504851.2018.1430321

Schalk, R. (2004). Changes in the employment relationship across time. In Coyle-Shapiro, J., Shore, L. M., Taylor, S., & Tetrick, L. E. (Eds.), *The employment relationship: Examining psychological and contextual perspectives* (pp. 284–311). Oxford University Press. DOI: 10.1093/oso/9780199269136.003.0013

Shaw, J. D., Dineen, B. R., Fang, R., & Vellella, R. F. (2009). Employee–organization exchange relationships, HRM practices, and quit rates of good and poor performers. *Academy of Management Journal*, *52*(5), 1016–1033. DOI: 10.5465/amj.2009.44635525

Sikora, D. M., Thompson, K. W., Russell, Z. A., & Ferris, G. R. (2016). Reimagining overqualified human resources to promote organizational effectiveness and competitive advantage. *Journal of Organizational Effectiveness: People and Performance*, *3*(1), 23–42. DOI: 10.1108/JOEPP-03-2015-0012

Storey, J., Ulrich, D., & Wright, P. M. (2019). *Strategic human resource management: A research overview*. Routledge. DOI: 10.4324/9780429490217

Sun, L. Y., Aryee, S., & Law, K. S. (2007). High-performance human resource practices, citizenship behavior, and organizational performance: A relational perspective. *Academy of Management Journal*, *50*(3), 558–577. DOI: 10.5465/amj.2007.25525821

The Statesman. (2023), available at: https://www.thestatesman.com/opinion/egypts-downturn-1503244320.html

Trading economics (2023), available at: https://tradingeconomics.com/egypt/unemployment-rate

Turhan, M. (2014). Organizational cronyism: A scale development and validation from the perspective of teachers. *Journal of Business Ethics*, *123*(2), 295–308. DOI: 10.1007/s10551-013-1839-3

Wallo, A., & Coetzer, A. (2023). Understanding and conceptualising the daily work of human resource practitioners. *Journal of Organizational Effectiveness: People and Performance*, *10*(2), 180–198. DOI: 10.1108/JOEPP-01-2022-0013

Wang, D., Tsui, A. S., Zhang, Y., & Ma, L. (2003). Employment relationships and firm performance: Evidence from an emerging economy. *Journal of Organizational Behavior*, *24*(5), 511–535. DOI: 10.1002/job.213

Williams, T. A., & Shepherd, D. A. (2016). Building resilience or providing sustenance: Different paths of emergent ventures in the aftermath of Haiti earthquake. *Academy of Management Journal*, *59*(6), 2069–2102. DOI: 10.5465/amj.2015.0682

World Bank. (2023). https://documents.worldbank.org/en/publication/documents-reports/documentdetail/099624304122329292/idu07c72dd550d99104e560a5fd0e79e14053665

Wright, P., & McMahan, G. (1992). Theoretical perspectives for strategic human resource management. *Journal of Management*, *18*(2), 295–322. DOI: 10.1177/014920639201800205

Wright, P. M., & Snell, S. A. (1998). Toward a unifying framework for exploring fit and flexibility in strategic human resource management. *Academy of Management Review*, *23*(4), 756–772. DOI: 10.2307/259061

Zahoor, N., Roumpi, D., Tarba, S., Arslan, A., & Golgeci, I. (2024). The role of digitalization and inclusive climate in building a resilient workforce: An ability–motivation–opportunity approach. *Journal of Organizational Behavior*, *45*(9), 1431–1459. DOI: 10.1002/job.2800

Zucker, L. G. (1991). The role of institutionalization in cultural persistence. In Powell, W. W., & DiMaggio, P. J. (Eds.), *The new institutionalism in organizational analysis* (pp. xx–xx). University of Chicago Press.

Compilation of References

Abuhantash, A. (2023). The future of HR management: Exploring the potential of e-HRM for improving employee experience and organizational outcomes. *World Journal of Advanced Research and Reviews*, *18*(2), 647–651. DOI: 10.30574/wjarr.2023.18.2.0883

Acquisti, A., Brandimarte, L., & Loewenstein, G. (2015). Privacy and human behavior in the age of information. *Science*, *347*(6221), 509–514. DOI: 10.1126/science.aaa1465 PMID: 25635091

Adeleye, I. (2011). Theorising human resource management in Africa: Beyond cultural relativism. *African Journal of Business Management*, *5*(6), 2028–2029.

Ahn, D., Almaatouq, A., Gulabani, M., & Hosanagar, K. (2021). Will we trust what we don't understand? Impact of model interpretability and outcome feedback on trust in AI. *arXiv*. https://arxiv.org/abs/2111.08222

Akram, S., Buono, P., & Lanzilotti, R. (2024). Recruitment chatbot acceptance in a company: A mixed method study on human-centered technology acceptance model. *Personal and Ubiquitous Computing*, *28*(6), 961–984. Advance online publication. DOI: 10.1007/s00779-024-01826-4

Akwei, C., & Nwachukwu, C. (2023). An exploration of contextual factors affecting the nexus of competitive strategy and human resource management practices in Nigeria's emerging economy context. *International Journal of Human Resource Management*, *34*(16), 3079–3122. DOI: 10.1080/09585192.2022.2104128

Al Helou, E. (2024). Egypt's currency crisis threatens Red Sea projects. *Economy Middle East*. https://economymiddleeast.com/news/egypt-currency-red-sea/

Al Jazeera Staff. (2023). Mourning and worrying about the future in rural Egypt. *Al Jazeera*. https://www.aljazeera.com/features/2023/12/14/mourning-and-worrying-about-the-future-in-rural-egypt

Al-Ali, W., Ameen, A., Issac, O., Nusari, M., & Alrajawi, I. (2018). The impact of job happiness on job performance in the oil and gas industry in UAE. 2nd International Conference on Healthcare and Allied Sciences (ICHAS), Shah Alam, Malaysia. https://www.researchgate.net/publication/328307095

Alanka, D. (2024). Content analysis as a qualitative research method: A theoretical framework. Kronotop Journal of Communication, 1(1), 64-84. Retrieved November 25, 2025, from https://dergipark.org.tr/tr/pub/kronotop/issue/82784/1405579

Albaqami, A. (2016). Determinants of turnover intention among faculty members in Saudi public universities (PhD thesis). University of Salford. https://salforrepository.worktribe.com/preview/1493456/Final%20Turnover%20Thesis%20-Adi%20 Albaqami%201-11-2016%20.pdf%202.pdf

Alherimi, N., Abdulmaksoud, S., Ahmed, V., & Bahroun, Z. (2025). A systematic literature review of artificial intelligence advancements in green human resource management. *Sustainability (Basel)*, *17*(22), 10283. DOI: 10.3390/su172210283

Ali, A., & Rafi, N. (2024). Enhancing human resource management through advanced decision-making strategies: Harnessing the power of artificial intelligence for strategic, data-driven, and judicious choices. *Migration Letters : An International Journal of Migration Studies*, *21*(S8), 881–889. DOI: 10.59670/ml.v21iS8.9488

Al-Mughairi, A. M. (2024). The evaluation of training and development of employees: The case of a national oil and gas industry. *International Journal of Research in Human Resource Management*, *6*(2), 301–308. DOI: 10.33545/26633213.2024.v6.i2c.229

Alrawahi, S., Sellgren, S. F., Altouby, S., Alwahaibi, N., & Brommels, M. (2020). The application of Herzberg's two-factor theory of motivation to job satisfaction in clinical laboratories in Omani hospitals. *Heliyon*, *6*(9), e04829. DOI: 10.1016/j.heliyon.2020.e04829 PMID: 32954029

Alshatti Schmidt, D., Alboloushi, B., Thomas, A., & Magalhaes, R. (2025). Integrating artificial intelligence in higher education: Perceptions, challenges, and strategies for academic innovation. *Computers and Education Open*, *9*, 100274. DOI: 10.1016/j.caeo.2025.100274

Altoobi, S., & Awashreh, R. (2025). Workplace bullying framework for organizational health and employee well-being. In B. Alareeni (Ed.), *Big data in finance: Transforming the financial landscape* (Vol. 164, pp. [insert page range if known]). Springer. https://doi.org/DOI: 10.1007/978-3-031-75095-3_33

Alzghoul, A., & Khaddam, A. (2024). Enhancing employee retention in banks: Analyzing the role of talent management, career development, and bank culture. *Banks and Bank Systems*, *19*(4), 96–111. DOI: 10.21511/bbs.19(4).2024.08

American Civil Liberties Union. (2024). ACLU complaint to the FTC regarding Aon Consulting, Inc. Retrieved November 25, 2025, from https://www.aclu.org/press-releases/aclu-files-ftc-complaint-against-major-hiring-technology-vendor-for-deceptively-marketing-online-hiring-tests-as-bias-free

Amir, A., Zaman, S., & Tariq, M. I. (2024). Effect of Digital HRM on Employee Performance: The Role of Employee Trust and Organizational Identity in the Banking Sector of Pakistan. *Pakistan Journal of Humanities and Social Sciences*, *12*(1), 207–223. DOI: 10.52131/pjhss.2024.v12i1.1985

Amnesty International Türkiye. (n.d.). Discrimination. Retrieved November 25, 2025, from https://www.amnesty.org.tr/

Angkasirisan, T. (2024). Naturalistic multimodal emotion data with deep learning can advance the theoretical understanding of emotion. *Psychological Research*, *89*(1), 36. DOI: 10.1007/s00426-024-02068-y PMID: 39708231

Anibaba, Y., & Adeleye, I. (2014). Strategic human resource management in Africa: Exploring institutional effects.

An, J., Huang, D., Lin, C., & Tai, M. (2025). Measuring gender and racial biases in big language models: Intersectional evidence from automated résumé evaluation. *PNAS Nexus*, *4*(3), 1–14. DOI: 10.1093/pnasnexus/pgaf089 PMID: 40144775

Araujo, T., Helberger, N., Kruikemeier, S., & de Vreese, C. H. (2020). In AI we trust? Perceptions about automated decision-making by artificial intelligence. *AI & Society*, *35*(3), 611–623. DOI: 10.1007/s00146-019-00931-w

Arion, F. H., Harutyunyan, G., Aleksanyan, V., Muradyan, M., Asatryan, H., & Manucharyan, M. (2024). Determining digitalization issues (ICT adoption, digital literacy, and the digital divide) in rural areas by using sample surveys: The case of Armenia. *Agriculture*, *14*(2), 249. DOI: 10.3390/agriculture14020249

Arner, D. W., Barberis, J., & Buckley, R. P. (2020). The Evolution of Fintech: A New Post-Crisis Paradigm? *SSRN*, *47*(4), 1271–1319. DOI: 10.2139/ssrn.2676553

Arokiasamy, L., Fujikawa, T., Piaralal, S. K., & Arumugam, T. (2024). Role of HRM practices in organization performance. *International Journal of Sociotechnology and Knowledge Development*, *16*(1), 1–32. Advance online publication. DOI: 10.4018/IJSKD.334555

Arslan, A., Cooper, C. L., Khan, Z., Gölgeci, İ., & Ali, I. (2021). Artificial intelligence and human workers interaction at team level: A conceptual assessment of the challenges and potential HRM strategies. *International Journal of Manpower*, *43*(1), 75–88. DOI: 10.1108/IJM-01-2021-0052

Arslan, A., Kamara, S., Golgeci, I., & Tarba, S. Y. (2022). Civil society organisations' management dynamics and social value creation in the post-conflict volatile contexts pre and during COVID-19. *The International Journal of Organizational Analysis*, *30*(7), 20–33. DOI: 10.1108/IJOA-01-2021-2573

Ateeq, A., Al-refaei, A.-A., Alzoraiki, M., Milhem, M., & Ali, S. A. (2024). Digitalization and its impact on HRM: Leveraging ICT for efficient workforce management. In *Springer Proceedings in Business and Economics* (Vol. 524, pp. 551–558). Springer., DOI: 10.1007/978-3-031-54379-1_48

Awashreh, R. A., & Omri, I. (2024). Factors determinant of career happiness in Oman banking sector. *SA Journal of Human Resource Management*, *22*(0), a2384. DOI: 10.4102/sajhrm.v22i0.2384

Awashreh, R., & Al Ghunaimi, H. (2024). Navigating burnout in the public sector: Strategies for enhancing employee well-being and organizational performance. *Evolutionary Studies in Imaginative Culture*, *8*(3), 212–225. DOI: 10.70082/esiculture.vi.1855

Awashreh, R., & Al Toobi, S. (2025). Workplace bullying and its effects on job performance: Evidence from the health sector. *Journal of Applied Social Science*, *19*(3), 275–291. DOI: 10.1177/19367244251324916

Awashreh, R., Al-Ghunaimi, H., Saleh, R., & Al-Bahri, M. N. (2024). The impact of leadership roles and strategies on employees' job satisfaction in Oman. *Pakistan Journal of Life and Social Sciences*, *22*(2), 1724–1736. DOI: 10.57239/PJLSS-2024-22.2.00120

Awashreh, R., & Hamid, A. A. (2025). The role of entrepreneurial leadership in driving employee innovation: The mediating effect of knowledge sharing. *Cogent Business & Management*, *12*(1), 2466812. Advance online publication. DOI: 10.1080/23311975.2025.2466812

Awashreh, R., & Khademizadeh, S. (2025). Navigating the Ethical Frontier: Privacy, Bias, and Regulation in AI Development. *Arab Journal of Administrative Sciences*, *31*(3), 563–591. DOI: 10.34120/ajas.v31i3.1273

Baker, S., Bloom, N., & Davis, S. (2016). Measuring economic policy uncertainty. *The Quarterly Journal of Economics*, *131*(4), 1593–1636. DOI: 10.1093/qje/qjw024

Bandara, N., & Katukurunda, K. G. W. K. (2025). Exploring happiness: Integrating philosophical theories and psychological models among university students. *Indonesian Journal of Educational Research and Technology*, *5*(2), 163–178.

Bankins, S., Formosa, P., Griep, Y., & Richards, D. (2022). AI decision making with dignity? Contrasting workers' justice perceptions of human and AI decision making in a human resource management context. *Information Systems Frontiers*, *24*(3), 857–875. DOI: 10.1007/s10796-021-10223-8

Bardoel, E. A., Pettit, T. M., De Cieri, H., & McMillan, L. (2014). Employee resilience: An emerging challenge for HRM. *Asia Pacific Journal of Human Resources*, *52*(3), 279–297. DOI: 10.1111/1744-7941.12033

Barocas, S., & Selbst, A. D. (2016). Big data's disparate impact. *California Law Review*, *104*(3), 671–732. DOI: 10.15779/Z38BG31

Bayana, E. (2025). *Bias in AI recruitment tools: Impacted groups, legal risks, historical foundations, and next steps*. Research Archive of Rising Scholars., DOI: 10.58445/rars.2177

BBC News. (2021). *California sues Activision Blizzard over alleged harassment.* Retrieved November 25, 2025, from https://www.bbc.com/news/technology-57929543

Bedemariam, R., & Wessel, J. L. (2023). The roles of outcome and race on applicant reactions to AI systems. *Computers in Human Behavior*, *148*, 107869. DOI: 10.1016/j.chb.2023.107869

Benabou, A., & Touhami, F. (2025). Artificial intelligence in human resource management: A PRISMA-based systematic review. *Acta Informatica Pragensia*, *14*(3), 489–505. DOI: 10.18267/j.aip.264

Benabou, A., & Touhami, F. (2025). Empowering human resource management through artificial intelligence: A systematic literature review and bibliometric analysis. *International Journal of Production Management and Engineering*, *13*(1), 59–76. Advance online publication. DOI: 10.4995/ijpme.2025.21900

Bertrand, M., & Mullainathan, S. (2004). Are Emily and Greg more employable than Lakisha and Jamal? A field experiment on labor market discrimination. *The American Economic Review*, *94*(4), 991–1013. DOI: 10.1257/0002828042002561

Bhatti, S. A. N., Faqirah, M. R., & Ullah, M. F. (2025). The Future of HR: Exploring the Benefits and Challenges of Digital Transformation. *International Journal of Engineering Business Management*, *9*(1), 67–80. DOI: 10.22161/ijebm.9.1.6

Binns, R., Van Kleek, M., Veale, M., Lyngs, U., Zhao, J., & Shadbolt, N. (2018). "It's reducing a human being to a percentage": Perceptions of justice in algorithmic decisions. In *Proceedings of the 2018 CHI Conference on Human Factors in Computing Systems* (pp. 1–14). Association for Computing Machinery. DOI: 10.1145/3173574.3173951

Birahim, S. A. (2025). Contesting the algorithm: Advancing a right to challenge AI decisions under the GDPR for algorithmic fairness. *Transforming Government: People. Process and Policy*, *19*(4), 895–913. doi:10.1108/TG-05-2025-0148

Biswas, M. I., Talukder, M. S., & Khan, A. R. (2024). Who do you choose? Employees' perceptions of artificial intelligence versus humans in performance feedback. *China Accounting and Finance Review*, *26*(4), 512–532. DOI: 10.1108/CAFR-08-2023-0095

Black, J. S., & Van Esch, P. (2021). AI-enabled recruiting in the war for talent. *Business Horizons*, *64*(4), 513–524. DOI: 10.1016/j.bushor.2021.02.015

Blau, P. M. (1964). Exchange and power in social life. *Trans-Action*.

Blons, E. (2023). *L'IA au cœur de l'entreprise: Une alliée pour votre stratégie RH*. Questions de Société. EMS Éditions.

Boateng, G. O., Neilands, T. B., Frongillo, E. A., Melgar-Quiñonez, H. R., & Young, S. L. (2018). Best practices for developing and validating scales for health, social, and behavioral research: A primer. *Frontiers in Public Health*, *6*, 149. DOI: 10.3389/fpubh.2018.00149 PMID: 29942800

Böhmer, N., & Schinnenburg, H. (2023). Critical exploration of AI-driven HRM to build up organizational capabilities. *Employee Relations*, *45*(5), 1057–1082. DOI: 10.1108/ER-04-2022-0202

Bondarouk, T., & Brewster, C. (2021). Conceptualising the future of HRM and technology research. *International Journal of Human Resource Management*, *32*(12), 2543–2568. DOI: 10.1080/09585192.2021.1925325

Bositkhanova, N., & Dadaboyev, S. M. U. (2025). Revolutionizing workforce planning: The strategic function of AI in HR strategy. *Discover Global Society*, *3*(1), 100. Advance online publication. DOI: 10.1007/s44282-025-00252-y

Bourezg, M., Khassawneh, O., Singh, S., Mohammad, T., Melhem, M. J., & Darwish, T. K. (2024). Exploring the path to job satisfaction among women in the Middle East: A contextual perspective. Gender in Management, ahead-of-print. https://doi.org/DOI: 10.1108/GM-11-2023-0411

Bouzerda, K., Hani, S., Rahmani, H., Hebaz, A., Dibi, A., & Mharzi, H. (2025). The rise of AI in human resource management: A systematic review of task automation through PRISMA. *Human Resources Management and Services*, *7*(4). Advance online publication. DOI: 10.18282/hrms4595

Bowen, D. E., & Ostroff, C. (2004). Understanding HRM–firm performance linkages: The role of the 'strength' of the HRM system. *Academy of Management Review*, *29*(2), 203–221. DOI: 10.5465/amr.2004.12736076

Boxall, P., & Huo, Y. (2022). HRM practices and employee satisfaction: A comparative study. *Journal of Management*, *53*(1), 40–55.

Boxall, P., & Macky, K. (2009). Research and theory on high-performance work systems. *Human Resource Management Journal*, *19*(1), 3–23. DOI: 10.1111/j.1748-8583.2008.00082.x

Bozkurt Gümrükçüoğlu, Y., & Yakacak, G. A. (2024). The use of artificial intelligence in recruitment processes and algorithmic discrimination. *Ankara University Faculty of Law Journal, 72*(4), 1701-1757. Retrieved November 25, 2025, from DOI: 10.33629/auhfd.1403311

Branicki, L., Steyer, V., & Sullivan-Taylor, B. (2019). Why resilience managers aren't resilient, and what human resource management can do about it. *International Journal of Human Resource Management*, *30*(8), 1261–1286. DOI: 10.1080/09585192.2016.1244104

Britt, T. W., Shen, W., Sinclair, R. R., Grossman, M. R., & Klieger, D. M. (2016). How much do we really know about employee resilience? *Industrial and Organizational Psychology: Perspectives on Science and Practice*, *9*(2), 378–404. DOI: 10.1017/iop.2015.107

Brodkin, E. Z. (2011). Policy work: Street-level organizations under new managerialism. *Journal of Public Administration: Research and Theory*, *21*(2, Supplement 2), 253–277. DOI: 10.1093/jopart/muq093

Brogaard, J., & Detzel, A. (2015). The asset-pricing implications of government economic policy uncertainty. *Management Science*, *61*(1), 3–18. DOI: 10.1287/mnsc.2014.2044

Brunetto, Y., Xerri, M., & Farr-Wharton, B. (2022). Doing better with less: Do behavioural capabilities affect street-level bureaucrats' ability to deliver public value? *Public Management Review*, *26*(5), 1136–1155. DOI: 10.1080/14719037.2022.2133159

Calluso, C., & Devetag, M. G. (2025). The impact of technology acceptance and personality traits on the willingness to use AI-assisted hiring practices. *The International Journal of Organizational Analysis*, *33*(5), 1368–1385. DOI: 10.1108/IJOA-06-2024-4562

Cao, G. (2025). Domain expertise and AI adoption: Insights into HR managers' unified perspectives across roles and contexts. In *Proceedings of the 27th International Conference on Enterprise Information Systems (ICEIS 2025)* (Vol. 1, pp. 732–739). DOI: 10.5220/0013232200003929

Cardillo, A. (2025). *How many countries use AI? (New 2025 data).* Retrieved November 25, 2025, from https://explodingtopics.com/blog/companies-using-ai

Căvescu, A. M., & Popescu, N. (2025). Predictive analytics in human resources management: Evaluating AIHR's role in talent retention. *AppliedMath*, *5*(3), 99. DOI: 10.3390/appliedmath5030099

Chang, S., Gong, Y., Way, S. A., & Jia, L. (2013). Flexibility-oriented HRM systems, absorptive capacity, and market responsiveness and firm innovativeness. *Journal of Management*, *39*(7), 1924–1951. DOI: 10.1177/0149206312466145

Chartered Institute of Personnel and Development. (2017). *Strategic human resource management* (CIPD Factsheet). CIPD. https://www.cipd.co.uk/knowledge/strategy/hr/strategic-hrm-factsheet#6744

Chen, C.-J., & Huang, J.-W. (2009). Strategic human resource practices and innovation performance: The mediating role of knowledge management capacity. *Journal of Business Research*, *62*(1), 104–114. DOI: 10.1016/j.jbusres.2007.11.016

Chen, H., Chen, R., Bernard, S., & Rahman, I. (2019). US hotel industry revenue: An ARDL bounds testing approach. *International Journal of Contemporary Hospitality Management*, *31*(4), 1720–1743. DOI: 10.1108/IJCHM-01-2018-0031

Chen, Z. (2023). Ethics and discrimination in artificial intelligence-enabled recruitment practices. *Humanities & Social Sciences Communications*, *10*(1), 567. DOI: 10.1057/s41599-023-02079-x

Chheda, K., Thakur, U., Das, G. P., Parashar, M. K., & Reddy, K. (2025). AI-powered human resource management for enhancing employee recruitment efficiency and talent retention in organizations. *Management (Montevideo)*, *3*, 165. DOI: 10.62486/agma2025165

Choi, Y. (2021). A study of employee acceptance of artificial intelligence technology. *European Journal of Management and Business Economics*, *30*(3), 318–330. DOI: 10.1108/EJMBE-06-2020-0158

Christina, J. L., Alamelu, R., & Nigama, K. (2025). Synthesizing the impact of sustainable human resource management on corporate sustainability through multi method evidence. *Discover Sustainability*, *6*(1), 666. Advance online publication. DOI: 10.1007/s43621-025-01557-3

Clauss, C. B., de Frutos Belizón, J., & García Carbonell, N. (2025). Employee perceptions of HRM practices and beyond: A bibliometric analysis of theoretical perspectives and research foci. *Journal of Management & Organization*, *31*(5), 2317–2340. DOI: 10.1017/jmo.2025.10015

Collins, C. J. (2021). Expanding the resource-based view model of strategic human resource management. *International Journal of Human Resource Management*, *32*(2), 331–358. DOI: 10.1080/09585192.2019.1711442

Columbia Engineering. (2025). *AI vs. machine learning*. Retrieved November 25, 2025, from https://ai.engineering.columbia.edu/ai-vs-machine-learning/

Cooke, F. L., Cooper, B., Bartram, T., Wang, J., & Mei, H. (2019). Mapping the relationships between high-performance work systems, employee resilience and engagement: A study of the banking industry in China. *International Journal of Human Resource Management*, *30*(8), 1239–1260. DOI: 10.1080/09585192.2015.1137618

Cooke, F. L., Xiao, Q., & Xiao, M. (2021). Extending the frontier of research on (strategic) human resource management in China: A review of David Lepak and colleagues' influence and future research direction. *International Journal of Human Resource Management*, *32*(1), 183–224. DOI: 10.1080/09585192.2020.1803949

Cooper, C. L., Liu, Y., & Tarba, S. Y. (2014). Resilience, HRM practices and impact on organizational performance and employee well-being. *International Journal of Human Resource Management*, *25*(17), 2466–2471. DOI: 10.1080/09585192.2014.926688

Cordeiro, D., Lopezosa, C., & Guallar, J. (2025). A methodological framework for AI-driven textual data analysis in digital media. *Future Internet*, *17*(2), 59. DOI: 10.3390/fi17020059

Coutu, D. L. (2002). How resilience works. *Harvard Business Review*, *80*(5), 46–56. PMID: 12024758

Crist, C. (2024). AI tools are biased in ranking job candidates' resumes, study shows. *HR Dive*. Retrieved November 25, 2025, from https://www.hrdive.com/news/ai-tools-are-biased-in-ranking-job-applicants-resumes/732134/

Dalimunthe, H. H. B., Sutisna, A., Karnadi, K., Retnowati, E., & Tijari, A. (2021). Social entrepreneurship empowerment in the Indonesian archipelagic communities. *Indonesian Journal of Business and Entrepreneurship*, *7*(2), 103. DOI: 10.17358/ijbe.7.2.103

Dargan, M. (2023). Model act for algorithmic models: A regulatory solution for AI used in recruitment decisions. *University of Houston Law Center Review*. Retrieved November 25, 2025, from https://houstonlawreview.org/article/74110/stats/30/downloads

Dastin, J. (2018). Amazon scraps secret AI recruiting tool that showed bias against women. *Reuters*. Retrieved November 25, 2025, from https://www.reuters.com/article/us-amazon-com-jobs-automation-idUSKCN1MK08G

Davis, F. D. (1989). Perceived usefulness, perceived ease of use, and user acceptance of information technology. *Management Information Systems Quarterly*, *13*(3), 319–340. DOI: 10.2307/249008

De Stefano, F., Bagdadli, S., & Camuffo, A. (2023). The HR role in corporate social responsibility and sustainability: A systematic review. *Human Resource Management Review*, *33*(1), 100926. DOI: 10.1016/j.hrmr.2022.100926

Deep, P. D., Ghosh, N., & Chen, Y. (2025). Faculty burnout in higher education: Effects on student engagement, learning outcomes, and artificial intelligence-driven institutional responses. *Journal of Educational and Developmental Psychology*, *15*(1), 29–45. DOI: 10.5539/jedp.v15n1p29

Delery, J. E., & Doty, D. H. (1996). Modes of theorizing in strategic human resource management: Tests of universalistic, contingency, and configurational performance predictions. *Academy of Management Journal*, *39*(4), 802–835. DOI: 10.2307/256713

Delery, J. E., & Roumpi, D. (2017). Strategic human resource management, human capital and competitive advantage: Is the field going in circles? *Human Resource Management Journal*, *27*(1), 1–21. DOI: 10.1111/1748-8583.12137

Delery, J., & Gupta, N. (2016). Human resource management practices and organizational effectiveness: Internal fit matters. *Journal of Organizational Effectiveness: People and Performance*, *3*(2), 139–163. DOI: 10.1108/JOEPP-03-2016-0028

Dello Russo, S., Mascia, D., & Morandi, F. (2018). Individual perceptions of HR practices, HRM strength and appropriateness of care: A meso, multilevel approach. *International Journal of Human Resource Management*, *29*(2), 286–310. DOI: 10.1080/09585192.2016.1165276

Devaux, P. (2023). *Egypt: Buying time*. BNP Paribas Economic Research. https://economic-research.bnpparibas.com/html/en-US/Egypt-Buyingtime-4/14/2023,48481

Dibben, P., Brewster, C., Brookes, M., Cunha, R., Webster, E., & Wood, G. (2017). Institutional legacies and HRM: Similarities and differences in HRM practices in Portugal and Mozambique. *International Journal of Human Resource Management, 28*(18), 2519–2537. DOI: 10.1080/09585192.2016.1164225

DiMaggio, P. J., & Powell, W. W. (1991). The iron cage revisited: Institutional isomorphism and collective rationality in organizational fields. In Powell, W. W., & DiMaggio, P. J. (Eds.), *The new institutionalism in organizational analysis* (pp. 195–200). University of Chicago Press.

Dima, J., Gilbert, M., Dextras-Gauthier, J., & Giraud, L. (2024). The effects of artificial intelligence on human resource activities and the functions of the human resource triad: Opportunities and challenges. *Frontiers in Psychology, 15*, 1360401. Advance online publication. DOI: 10.3389/fpsyg.2024.1360401 PMID: 38903456

Dušková, M. V., & Vita, M. (2022). Automated information retrieval from the bibliographic metadata: A way to facilitate the systematic literature review. *4th International Conference on Advanced Research Methods and Analytics (CARMA 2022)*. https://doi.org/DOI: 10.4995/CARMA2022.2022.15104

Edralin, D. M. (2010). Human resource management practices: Drivers for stimulating corporate entrepreneurship in large companies in the Philippines. *DLSU Business and Economics Review, 19*(2), 25–41. DOI: 10.3860/ber.v19i2.1471

Egea, J. M. O., & González, M. V. R. (2011). Explaining physicians' acceptance of EHCR systems: An extension of TAM with trust and risk factors. *Computers in Human Behavior, 27*(1), 319–332. DOI: 10.1016/j.chb.2010.08.010

El Hammoumi, A., Seghyar, N., El Hammoumi, A. M., & El Ouali, A. (2024). The impact of artificial intelligence on employee adaptability to remote work. In 2024 3rd International Conference on Embedded Systems and Artificial Intelligence (ESAI) (pp. 1-5). IEEE. https://doi.org/DOI: 10.1109/ESAI62891.2024.10913897

El Hammoumi, A., & El-Ouali, A. (2025). Impact of knowledge management on human resource performance: Case of the company Maroc Télécom. In *Evolving Strategies for Organizational Management and Performance Evaluation* (pp. 291–312). IGI Global., DOI: 10.4018/979-8-3373-0149-5.ch014

Elbendary, I., Elsetouhi, A. M., Marie, M., & Aljafari, A. M. (2023). Employment preferences of job applicants: Unfolding employer branding determinants. *Personnel Review*, *52*(5), 1244–1268. DOI: 10.1108/PR-03-2021-0188

Electronic Privacy Information Center. (2019). *Federal Trade Commission: Complaint and request for investigation, injunction, and other relief.* Retrieved November 25, 2025, from https://epic.org/wp-content/uploads/privacy/ftc/hirevue/EPIC_FTC_HireVue_Complaint.pdf

El-Ouali, A., & Jellouli, T. (2024). L'avenir de la gestion des ressources humaines après la crise de la pandémie de Corona (COVID-19). Revue internationale d'études économiques et de gestion (IJESM), 4(1), 142-159. https://doi.org/DOI: 10.5281/zenodo.10698984

El-Ouali, A., & Jellouli, T. (2025). Training and development as effective strategies for human resource development in Moroccan companies. In *Innovative Recruitment and Retention for Employee Empowerment*. IGI Global., DOI: 10.4018/979-8-3693-6602-8.ch013

El-Said, O., & Aziz, H. (2022). Job satisfaction and potential opportunities for career growth among hotel employees: The case of Oman. *Tourism and Hospitality Research*, *22*(4), 488–507. DOI: 10.1177/14673584221074925

ENAR - European Network Against Racism. (2020). *Equal@Work: Algorithmic discrimination in employment* (Equal@Work Toolkit). Retrieved November 25, 2025, from https://www.enar-eu.org/wp-content/uploads/2020_equal_work_algoritmic_discrimination_1_.pdf

Ererdi, C., Nurgabdeshov, A., Kozhakhmet, S., Rofcanin, Y., & Demirbag, M. (2022). International HRM in the context of uncertainty and crisis: A systematic review of literature (2000–2018). *International Journal of Human Resource Management*, *33*(12), 2503–2540. DOI: 10.1080/09585192.2020.1863247

Español, M. (2023, June). Egypt remittances plunge amid economic uncertainty. *Al-Monitor*. https://www.al-monitor.com/originals/2023/06/egypt-remittances-plunge-amid-economic-uncertainty

European Parliament and Council of the European Union. (2024). Regulation (EU) 2024/1689 of the European Parliament and of the Council of 13 June 2024 laying down harmonised rules on artificial intelligence and amending Regulations (EC) No 300/2008, (EU) No 167/2013, (EU) No 168/2013, (EU) 2018/858, (EU) 2018/1139 and (EU) 2019/2144 and Directives 2014/90/EU, (EU) 2016/797 and (EU) 2020/1828 (Artificial Intelligence Act). Official Journal of the European Union. Retrieved April 27, 2026, from https://eur-lex.europa.eu/eli/reg/2024/1689/oj/eng

Fabeyo, S. (2025). Explainable AI in employment decision-making: A systematic review of transparency methods in hiring algorithms. *Issues in Information Systems*, *26*(3) 127–135. doi:10.48009/3_iis_2025_2025_110.

Faedlulloh, D., Meutia, I. F., Yulianti, D., & Karmilasari, V. (2021). Gotong royong digital: Praktik baru solidaritas warga di era pandemi. *Jantra*, *16*(1), 1–14. DOI: 10.52829/jantra.v16i1.118

Farooq, O., Jabbouri, I., & Naili, M. (2024). The nexus between economic policy uncertainty and access to finance: A study of developing countries. *International Journal of Managerial Finance*, *20*(1), 222–246. DOI: 10.1108/IJMF-11-2022-0507

Farr-Wharton, B., Brunetto, Y., Wankhade, P., Saccon, C., & Xerri, M. (2021). Comparing the impact of authentic leadership on Italian and UK police officers' discretionary power, well-being and commitment. *Policing*, *44*(5), 741–755. DOI: 10.1108/PIJPSM-09-2020-0156

Feng, J., Yu, B., Tan, W. H., Dai, Z., & Li, Z. (2025). Key factors influencing educational technology adoption in higher education: A systematic review [Review of *Key factors influencing educational technology adoption in higher education: A systematic review*]. *PLOS Digital Health, 4*(4). Public Library of Science. DOI: 10.1371/journal.pdig.0000764

Feng, X., Lo, Y. L., & Chan, K. C. (2019). Impact of economic policy uncertainty on cash holdings: Firm-level evidence from an emerging market. *Asia-Pacific Journal of Accounting & Economics*, *29*(2), 1–23. DOI: 10.1080/16081625.2019.1694954

Feng, Y. (2001). Political freedom, political instability, and policy uncertainty: A study of political institutions and private investment in developing countries. *International Studies Quarterly*, *45*(2), 271–294. DOI: 10.1111/0020-8833.00191

Fitzpatrick, J., Basu, K., & Klar, R. (2024). AI hiring tools risk discrimination, watchdog tells Congress. *Bloomberg Law*. Retrieved November 25, 2025, from https://news.bgov.com/bloomberg-government-news/ai-hiring-tools-risk-discrimination-watchdog-tells-congress

Fletcher, J. R. (2024). An ontological turn in the sociology of personal life: Tracing facet methodology's connective ontology. *The Sociological Review*, *72*(3), 475–492. DOI: 10.1177/00380261231212099 PMID: 41908731

Flynn, A. (2022, November 14). Floating the pound: Currency devaluation in Egypt. *The American University in Cairo*. https://www.aucegypt.edu/news/floating-pound-currencydevaluation-egypt

Fragouli, E. (2025). Workplace digital empathy: Reimagining employee well-being through AI. *The Business & Management Review*, *16*(2), 240–248. DOI: 10.24052/BMR/V16NU02/ART-22

Frankl, V. E. (2017). *Man's search for meaning*. Beacon Press.

Freitas, J. D., Agarwal, S., Schmitt, B. H., & Haslam, N. (2023). Psychological factors underlying attitudes toward AI tools [Review of *Psychological factors underlying attitudes toward AI tools*]. *Nature Human Behaviour, 7*(11), 1845. Nature Portfolio. DOI: 10.1038/s41562-023-01734-2

Gallegos, I. O., Rossi, R. A., Barrow, J., Tanjim, M. M., Kim, S., Dernoncourt, F., Yu, T., Zhang, R., & Ahmed, N. K. (2024). Bias and fairness in large language models: A survey. *Computational Linguistics*, *50*(3), 1097–1179. DOI: 10.1162/coli_a_00524

Gélinas, D., Sadreddin, A., & Vahidov, R. (2022). Artificial Intelligence in Human Resources Management: A Review and Research Agenda. *Pacific Asia Journal of the Association for Information Systems*, *14*(6), 1–42. Advance online publication. DOI: 10.17705/1pais.14601

Gencoglu, B., Helms-Lorenz, M., Maulana, R., Jansen, E. P. W. A., & Gencoglu, O. (2023). Machine and expert judgments of student perceptions of teaching behavior in secondary education: Added value of topic modeling with big data. *Computers & Education*, *193*, 104682. DOI: 10.1016/j.compedu.2022.104682

George Reyes, C. E., & Glasserman, L. (2020). Research competencies mediated by technologies: A systematic review of the literature in Scopus. *Preprints*. https://doi.org/DOI: 10.20944/preprints202007.0125.v1

Gerards, J., & Xenidis, R. (2021). *Algorithmic Discrimination in Europe: Challenges and Opportunities for Gender Equality and Non-Discrimination Law*. European Commission. Retrieved November 25, 2025, from https://op.europa.eu/en/publication-detail/-/publication/082f1dbc-821d-11eb-9ac9-01aa75ed71a1

Ghadi, M. Y., & Almanaga, M. (2020). The impact of employee happiness on organizational performance. *Journal of Organizational Behavior*, *41*(5), 500–520.

Ghlichlee, B., & Goodarzi, A. (2023). Strategic human resource practices and new product development performance: The mediating role of intellectual capital. *Journal of Intellectual Capital*, *24*(3), 730–756. DOI: 10.1108/JIC-11-2020-0360

Ghorbanzadeh, D. (2025). Enhancing intentions to apply for job through social media characteristics. *Asia-Pacific Journal of Business Administration*, *16*(1), 151–169. DOI: 10.1108/APJBA-11-2024-0619

Ghosh, O., & Kumar, B. (2025). Reimagining community resilience and engagement through the digital innovation. In *Fostering Resilience and Quality of Life Through Sustainable Urban Evolution* (pp. 233–262). IGI Global., DOI: 10.4018/979-8-3373-0390-1.ch008

Gillespie, T. (2014). The relevance of algorithms. In Gillespie, T., Boczkowski, P. J., & Foot, K. A. (Eds.), *Media Technologies: Essays on Communication, Materiality, and Society*. MIT Press Scholarship Online., DOI: 10.7551/mitpress/9042.003.0013

Gillmore, T. (2024). California bill to regulate artificial intelligence heats up AI debate. *The Epoch* Times. Retrieved November 25, 2025, from https://www.theepochtimes.com/us/california-bill-to-regulate-artificial-intelligence-heats-up-ai-debate-5706662

Gioia, D. A., & Chittipeddi, K. (2017). Sensemaking and sensegiving in strategic change initiation. *Strategic Management Journal*, *12*(6), 433–448. DOI: 10.1002/smj.4250120604

Gioia, D. A., Corley, K. G., & Hamilton, A. L. (2013). Seeking qualitative rigor in inductive research: Notes on the Gioia methodology. *Organizational Research Methods*, *16*(1), 15–31. DOI: 10.1177/1094428112452151

Gittell, J. H., Cameron, K., Lim, S., & Rivas, V. (2006). Relationships, layoffs, and organizational resilience: Airline industry responses to September 11. *The Journal of Applied Behavioral Science*, *42*(3), 300–329. DOI: 10.1177/0021886306286466

Gligorea, I., Cioca, M., Oancea, R., Gorski, A.-T., Gorski, H., & Tudorache, P. (2023). Adaptive learning using artificial intelligence in e-learning: A literature review. *Education Sciences*, *13*(12), 1216. DOI: 10.3390/educsci13121216

Gok, G. O., & Gok, M. S. (2016). Emerging economies: Comparative analysis of MIST and IBSA. *Eurasian Journal of Soil Science*, *4*(2), 1–13. DOI: 10.15604/ejss.2016.04.02.001

Gölgeci, I., Arslan, A., Dikova, D., & Gligor, D. M. (2020). Resilient agility in volatile economies: Institutional and organizational antecedents. *Journal of Organizational Change Management*, *33*(1), 100–113. DOI: 10.1108/JOCM-02-2019-0033

Gouldner, A. W. (1960). The norm of reciprocity: A preliminary statement. *American Sociological Review*, *25*(2), 161–178. DOI: 10.2307/2092623

Greiner, L. (2025). Open-source AI recruitment models are weighted toward male candidates, study finds. *Computerworld.* Retrieved November 25, 2025, from https://www.computerworld.com/article/3977889/open-source-ai-hiring-models-are-weighted-toward-male-candidates-study-finds.html

Guest, G., Bunce, A., & Johnson, L. (2006). How many interviews are enough? An experiment with data saturation and variability. *Field Methods, 18*(1), 59–82. DOI: 10.1177/1525822X05279903

Haddock-Millar, J., Sanyal, C., & Müller-Camen, M. (2016). Green human resource management: A comparative qualitative case study of a United States multinational corporation. *International Journal of Human Resource Management, 27*(2), 192–211. DOI: 10.1080/09585192.2015.1052087

Hagen, B., Zucchella, A., & Ghauri, P. N. (2018). From fragile to agile: Marketing as a key driver of entrepreneurial internationalization. *International Marketing Review, 36*(2), 260–288. DOI: 10.1108/IMR-01-2018-0023

Hajian, M., & Kashani, S. J. (2021). Evolution of the concept of sustainability: From Brundtland Report to sustainable development goals. *Sustainable Resource Management: Modern Approaches and Contexts*, 1–24. https://doi.org/DOI: 10.1016/B978-0-12-824342-8.00018-3

Haque, A., & Khan, S. I. (2023). Promoting meaningfulness in work for higher job satisfaction: Will intent to quit make trouble for business managers? *Journal of Organizational Effectiveness: People and Performance, 10*(3), 455–476. DOI: 10.1108/JOEPP-02-2022-0020

Hasan, M. M., & Mishra, V. (2025). Impact of Herzberg's Two-Factor Theory and its influence on employee retention: A sectoral comparative study in Bangladesh. *Kelaniya Journal of Human Resource Management, 20*(1), 40–72. DOI: 10.4038/kjhrm.v20i1.152

Heffernan, M., & Dundon, T. (2016). Cross-level effects of high-performance work systems (HPWS) and employee well-being: The mediating effect of organisational justice. *Human Resource Management Journal, 26*(2), 211–231. DOI: 10.1111/1748-8583.12095

Herschel, R., & Miori, V. M. (2017). Ethics & big data. *Technology in Society, 49*, 31–36. DOI: 10.1016/j.techsoc.2017.03.003

Herzberg, F. (1966). *Work and the nature of man*. World Publishing.

Ho, A. K., Sidanius, J., Pratto, F., Levin, S., Thomsen, L., Kteily, N., & Sheehy-Skeffington, J. (2012). Social dominance orientation: Revisiting the structure and function of a variable predicting social and political attitudes. *Personality and Social Psychology Bulletin, 38*(5), 583–606. DOI: 10.1177/0146167211432765 PMID: 22215697

Hoque, K. E., & Atheef, M. (2024). A review of human resource management practices and their impact on school performance (2012–2022). *Human Resources Management and Services*, *6*(1), 3392. Advance online publication. DOI: 10.18282/hrms.v6i1.3392

Howie, L. (2007). The terrorism threat and managing workplaces. *Disaster Prevention and Management*, *16*(1), 70–78. DOI: 10.1108/09653560710729820

Huang, M. H., & Rust, R. T. (2018). Artificial intelligence in service. *Journal of Service Research*, *21*(2), 155–172. DOI: 10.1177/1094670517752459

Hunter, D. J. (2024). Artificial intelligence & the capacity for discrimination: The imperative need for frameworks, various teams & human liability. *IgMin Research*, *10*(2), 801–806. DOI: 10.61927/igmin250

IBM. (2023). *Global AI Adoption Index – Enterprise Report.* Retrieved November 25, 2025, from https://share.google/Qj2lhnTj3lSCAPYOW

IBM. (2025). *Enterprise AI development: Obstacles & opportunities.* Retrieved November 25, 2025, from https://filecache.mediaroom.com/mr5mr_ibmnewsroom/198591/Enterprise%20AI%20Development%20Survey.pdf

Iliadis, A., & Russo, F. (2016). Critical data studies: An introduction. *Big Data & Society*, *3*(2), 2053951716674238. Advance online publication. DOI: 10.1177/2053951716674238

Iqbal, N., Ahmad, M., & Allen, M. M. C. (2019). Unveiling the relationship between e-HRM, impersonal trust and employee productivity. *Management Research Review*, *42*(7), 879–899. DOI: 10.1108/MRR-02-2018-0094

Ismatullaev, U. V. U., & Kim, S.-H. (2024). Review of the factors affecting acceptance of AI-infused systems. *Human Factors*, *66*(1), 126–144. DOI: 10.1177/00187208211064707 PMID: 35344676

Issa, H., Qudeid, F., & Zaroukhy, F. (2020). Job burnout and its relationship to the performance of faculty members at the Faculty of Humanities and Social Sciences, Chlef University. *Al-Wahat Journal for Research and Studies*, *13*(2), 1055–1080.

Jackson, S. E., & Schuler, R. S. (1995). Understanding human resource management in the context of organizations and their environment. *Annual Review of Psychology*, *46*(1), 237–264. DOI: 10.1146/annurev.ps.46.020195.001321 PMID: 19245335

Jackson, S. E., Schuler, R. S., & Jiang, K. (2014). An aspirational framework for strategic human resource management. *The Academy of Management Annals*, *8*(1), 1–56. DOI: 10.5465/19416520.2014.872335

Jarrahi, M. H. (2018). Artificial intelligence and the future of work: Human-AI symbiosis in organizational decision making. *Business Horizons*, *61*(4), 577–586. DOI: 10.1016/j.bushor.2018.03.007

Jiang, K., Lepak, D. P., Hu, J., & Baer, J. C. (2012). How does human resource management influence organizational outcomes? A meta-analytic investigation of mediating mechanisms. *Academy of Management Journal*, *55*(6), 1264–1294. DOI: 10.5465/amj.2011.0088

Jiang, K., & Messersmith, J. (2018). On the shoulders of giants: A meta-review of strategic human resource management. *International Journal of Human Resource Management*, *29*(1), 6–33. DOI: 10.1080/09585192.2017.1384930

Joachimiak, M. P., Miller, M. A., Caufield, J. H., Ly, R., Harris, N. L., Tritt, A., Mungall, C. J., & Bouchard, K. E. (2024). The Artificial Intelligence Ontology: LLM-assisted construction of AI concept hierarchies. Lawrence Berkeley National Laboratory. https://doi.org//arXiv.2403.18074DOI: 10.48550

Joachimiak, M. P., Miller, M. A., Caufield, J. H., Ly, R., Harris, N. L., Tritt, A., Mungall, C. J., & Bouchard, K. E. (2025). The artificial intelligence ontology: LLM-assisted construction of AI concept hierarchies. *Applied Ontology*, *19*(4), 408–418. DOI: 10.1177/15705838241304103

Jordan, M. I., & Mitchell, T. M. (2015). Machine learning: Trends, perspectives, and prospects. *Science*, *349*(6245), 255–260. DOI: 10.1126/science.aaa8415 PMID: 26185243

Kabalina, V., Zelenova, O., & Reshetnikova, K. (2019). Contemporary human resource management practices in Russia: Flexibility under uncertainty. *International Studies of Management & Organization*, *49*(4), 422–440. DOI: 10.1080/00208825.2019.1646490

Karakoç Keskin, E., & Demirel, E. S. (2025). Turkish Adaptation of the Algorithmic Media Content Awareness Scale (AMCA-scale) and Analysis of the Relationships Between Scale Factors. *Akdeniz University Faculty of Communication Journal*, (48), 236–256. DOI: 10.31123/akil.1628894

Kartikeya, A. (2022). Examining correlation between trust and transparency with explainable artificial intelligence. In *Science and Information Conference* (pp. 353–358). Springer. DOI: 10.1007/978-3-031-10464-0_23

Katou, A. A. (2013). The link between HR practices, psychological contract fulfilment, and organisational performance in Greece: An economic crisis perspective. *Journal of Industrial Engineering and Management*, *6*(2), 568–594. DOI: 10.3926/jiem.501

Kaufman, B. E. (2020). The evolution of strategic HRM as seen through two founding books: A 30th anniversary perspective on development of the field. *Human Resource Management*, *59*(5), 491–502. DOI: 10.1002/hrm.22007

Keltu, T. T. (2024). The effect of human resource development practice on employee performance with the mediating role of job satisfaction among Mizan Tepi University's academic staff. *Heliyon*, *10*(8), e29821. DOI: 10.1016/j.heliyon.2024.e29821 PMID: 38699710

Khalid, M. A., Sohail, M., Baig, M. M. B., Yusaf, S., Iqbal, A., & Syed, M. I. (2025). The human-centric paradox of AI in HRM: How technostress and digital literacy co-determine employee productivity in smart work environments. *Inverge Journal of Social Sciences*, *4*(4), 214–227. DOI: 10.63544/ijss.v4i4.191

Khan, A. E., Hasan, M. J., Anjum, H., Mohammed, N., & Momen, S. (2024). Predicting life satisfaction using machine learning and explainable AI. *Heliyon*, *10*(10), e31158. DOI: 10.1016/j.heliyon.2024.e31158 PMID: 38818204

Khan, A., & Nasim, S. (2024). Mapping research on the subjective well-being of knowledge workers: A systematic enquiry deploying bibliometrics. *Management Review Quarterly*, *75*(1), 911–954. DOI: 10.1007/s11301-023-00399-5

Khan, S., Ullah, S., & Nobanee, H. (2024). ICT diffusion, e-governance, and sustainability in the digital era. *Sustainable Futures : An Applied Journal of Technology, Environment and Society*, *8*, 100272. DOI: 10.1016/j.sftr.2024.100272

Kilson, G. A. (2025). Optimizing employee attraction and retention in hospitality and tourism: A systematic review of employer branding research. *Administrative Sciences*, *15*(5), 153. DOI: 10.3390/admsci15050153

Kim, P. T. (2017). Auditing algorithms for discrimination. U. Pa. L. Rev. Online, 166, 189. Retrieved November 25, 2025, from https://scholarship.law.upenn.edu/cgi/viewcontent.cgi?article=1212&context=penn_law_review_online

Kim, B.-J., & Lee, J. (2025). Psychological consequences of artificial intelligence adoption: Job insecurity and depression in longitudinal perspective with corporate social responsibility as a moderator. *Journal of Innovation & Knowledge*, *10*, 100815. DOI: 10.1016/j.jik.2025.100815

Kim, S., & Wright, P. M. (2011). Putting strategic human resource management in context: A contextualized model of high commitment work systems and its implications in China. *Management and Organization Review*, *7*(1), 153–174. DOI: 10.1111/j.1740-8784.2010.00185.x

King, D. D., Newman, A., & Luthans, F. (2016). Not if, but when we need resilience in the workplace. *Journal of Organizational Behavior*, *37*(5), 782–786. DOI: 10.1002/job.2063

King, K. A. (2017). The talent climate: Creating an organisational context supportive of sustainable talent development through implementation of a strong talent system. *Journal of Organizational Effectiveness: People and Performance*, *4*(4), 298–314. DOI: 10.1108/JOEPP-03-2017-0023

Koçak, A., & Arun, Ö. (2006). The sampling issue in content analysis studies. *Selçuk Communication, 4*(3), 21–28. https://izlik.org/JA45WN28TT

Köchling, A., & Wehner, M. C. (2020). Discriminated by an algorithm: A systematic review of discrimination and fairness by algorithmic decision-making in the context of HR recruitment and HR development. *Business Research*, *13*(3), 795–848. DOI: 10.1007/s40685-020-00134-w

Köchling, A., Wehner, M. C., & Warkocz, J. (2023). Can I show my skills? Affective responses to artificial intelligence in the recruitment process. *Review of Managerial Science*, *17*(6), 2109–2138. DOI: 10.1007/s11846-021-00514-4

Kruahong, S., Tankumpuan, T., Kelly, K., Davidson, P. M., & Kuntajak, P. (2023). Community empowerment: A concept analysis. *Journal of Advanced Nursing*, *79*(8), 2845–2859. DOI: 10.1111/jan.15613 PMID: 36912456

Kumar, N. (2024). *AI recruitment statistics 2025 (Worldwide data).* Retrieved November 25, 2025, from https://www.demandsage.com/ai-recruitment-statistics/

Kumar, V., & Pansari, A. (2016). The construct, measurement, and impact of employee engagement: A marketing perspective. *Customer Needs and Solutions*, *1*(1), 52–67. DOI: 10.1007/s40547-013-0006-4

Kuntz, J. R., Näswall, K., & Malinen, S. (2016). Resilient employees in resilient organizations: Flourishing beyond adversity. *Industrial and Organizational Psychology: Perspectives on Science and Practice*, *9*(2), 456–462. DOI: 10.1017/iop.2016.39

Kwong, C., Demirbag, M., Wood, G., & Cooke, F. L. (2021). Human resource management in the context of high uncertainties. *International Journal of Human Resource Management*, *32*(17), 3569–3599. DOI: 10.1080/09585192.2021.1966203

Lakshman, C., Wang, L., Adhikari, A., & Cheng, G. (2022). Flexibility-oriented HRM practices and innovation: Evidence from China and India. *International Journal of Human Resource Management*, *33*(12), 2473–2502. DOI: 10.1080/09585192.2020.1861057

Lambrecht, A., & Tucker, C. (2019). Algorithmic bias? An empirical study of apparent gender-based discrimination in the display of STEM career ads. *Management Science*, *65*(7), 2966–2981. DOI: 10.1287/mnsc.2018.3093

Langenkamp, M., Costa, A., & Cheung, C. (2019). *Hiring Fairly in the Age of Algorithms*. Retrieved November 25, 2025, from https://ssrn.com/abstract=3723046 DOI: 10.2139/ssrn.3723046

Lansing, A. E., Romero, N. J., Siantz, E., Silva, V., Center, K., Casteel, D., & Gilmer, T. (2023). Building trust: Leadership reflections on community empowerment and engagement in a large urban initiative. *BMC Public Health*, *23*(1), 1252. DOI: 10.1186/s12889-023-15860-z PMID: 37380973

Larsson, A. S., Martin, R., & Edwards, M. R. (2022). Insider econometrics meets people analytics and strategic human resource management. *International Journal of Human Resource Management*, *33*(12), 2373–2419. DOI: 10.1080/09585192.2020.1847166

Laurim, V., Arpaci, S., Prommegger, B., & Krcmar, H. (2021). Computer, whom should I hire? Acceptance criteria for artificial intelligence in the recruitment process. In *Proceedings of the 54th Hawaii International Conference on System Sciences* (pp. 5494–5504). DOI: 10.24251/HICSS.2021.668

Leavitt, K., Barnes, C. M., & Shapiro, D. L. (2024). The Function of Human Managers within Algorithmic Performance Management Systems: A Process Model of Employee Trust in Managers through Reflexivity. *Academy of Management Review*, *50*(4), 745–767. DOI: 10.5465/amr.2022.0058

Lee, B., Lee, C., Choi, I., & Kim, J. (2022). Analyzing determinants of job satisfaction based on two-factor theory. *Sustainability (Basel)*, *14*(19), 12557. DOI: 10.3390/su141912557

Lee, J. H., Mustapha, A., & Hwang, J. (2019). Enhancing ethnic restaurant visits and reducing risk perception: The effect of information and protection motivation. *Journal of Hospitality and Tourism Insights*, *2*(4), 341–357. DOI: 10.1108/JHTI-10-2018-0068

Lee, K. (2018). *Artificial intelligence and the new world order: China's Silicon Valley*. Houghton Mifflin Harcourt.

Lee, M. K. (2018). Understanding perception of algorithmic decisions: Fairness, trust, and emotion in response to algorithmic management. *Big Data & Society*, *5*(1), 1–16. DOI: 10.1177/2053951718756684

Lemons, M. A., & Jones, C. A. (2001). Procedural justice in promotion decisions: Using perceptions of fairness to build employee commitment. *Journal of Managerial Psychology*, *16*(4), 268–280. DOI: 10.1108/02683940110391517

Lepak, D. P., & Shaw, J. D. (2008). Strategic HRM in North America: Looking to the future. *International Journal of Human Resource Management*, *19*(8), 1486–1499. DOI: 10.1080/09585190802200272

Lepri, B., Oliver, N., Letouzé, E., Pentland, A., & Vinck, P. (2018). Fair, transparent, and accountable algorithmic decision-making processes: The premise, the proposed solutions, and the open challenges. *Philosophy & Technology*, *31*(4), 611–627. DOI: 10.1007/s13347-017-0279-x

Li, J., Brar, A., & Roihan, N. (2021). The use of digital technology to enhance language and literacy skills for indigenous people: A systematic literature review. *Computers and Education Open*, *2*, 100035. DOI: 10.1016/j.caeo.2021.100035

Li, J., Yan, Y., & Zeng, X. (2025). Exploring artificial intelligence in inclusive education: A systematic review of empirical studies. *Applied Sciences (Basel, Switzerland)*, *15*(23), 12624. DOI: 10.3390/app152312624

Lipsky, M. (1980). *Street-level bureaucracy: Dilemmas of the individual in public services*. Russell Sage Foundation.

Li, X., Qin, X., Jiang, K., Zhang, S., & Gao, F. Y. (2015). Human resource practices and firm performance in China: The moderating roles of regional human capital quality and firm innovation strategy. *Management and Organization Review*, *11*(2), 237–261. DOI: 10.1017/mor.2015.12

Li, Z. (2023). *Research on innovation of employee performance management appraisal system*. Academic Journal of Business & Management., DOI: 10.25236/AJBM.2023.051819

Lyons, H., Velloso, E., & Miller, T. (2021). Fair and responsible AI: A focus on the ability to contest. *arXiv*. https://arxiv.org/abs/2102.10787

Madanchian, M. (2024). From Recruitment to Retention: AI Tools for Human Resource Decision-Making. *Applied Sciences (Basel, Switzerland)*, *14*(24), 11750. DOI: 10.3390/app142411750

Madanchian, M., & Taherdoost, H. (2025). Barriers and Enablers of AI Adoption in Human Resource Management: A Critical Analysis of Organizational and Technological Factors. *Information (Basel)*, *16*(1), 51. DOI: 10.3390/info16010051

Mahat, D. (2024). Artificial intelligence in human resource management: Bibliometric analysis comparing Pre and Post COVID 19 literatures. *Formosa Journal of Multidisciplinary Research*, *3*(7), 2509–2530. Advance online publication. DOI: 10.55927/fjmr.v3i7.9875

Mahato, S. (2023). Talent Management Practices and Organizational Performance in Nepalese Private Banks. *KIC International Journal of Social Science and Management*, *2*(1), 129–151. DOI: 10.3126/kicijssm.v2i1.62472

Mampuru, M. P., Mokoena, B. A., & Isabirye, A. K. (2024). Training and development impact on job satisfaction, loyalty and retention among academics. SA Journal of Human Resource Management/SA Tydskrif vir Menslikehulpbronbestuur, 22, a2420. https://doi.org/DOI: 10.4102/sajhrm.v22i0.2420

Mantello, P., Ho, M.-T., Nguyen, M.-H., & Vuong, Q.-H. (2023). Bosses without a heart: Socio-demographic and cross-cultural determinants of attitude toward emotional AI in the workplace. *AI & Society*, *38*(1), 97–119. DOI: 10.1007/s00146-021-01290-1 PMID: 34776651

Markus, H. R., & Kitayama, S. (1991). Culture and the self: Implications for cognition, emotion, and motivation. *Psychological Review*, *98*(2), 224–253. DOI: 10.1037/0033-295X.98.2.224

Marques, A. I., & Ferreira, F. A. F. (2020). Artificial intelligence in banking: A systematic literature review. *Journal of Business Research*, *124*, 389–409. DOI: 10.1016/j.jbusres.2020.01.034

Martínez-Bravo, M. C., Sádaba Chalezquer, C., & Serrano-Puche, J. (2022). Dimensions of digital literacy in the 21st century competency frameworks. *Sustainability (Basel)*, *14*(3), 1867. DOI: 10.3390/su14031867

McKinsey & Company. (2024). Superagency in the workplace: Empowering people to unlock AI's full potential at work. Retrieved November 25, 2025, from https://www.mckinsey.com/capabilities/tech-and-ai/our-insights/superagency-in-the-workplace-empowering-people-to-unlock-ais-full-potential-at-work#/

Mehrabi, N., Morstatter, F., Saxena, N., Lerman, K., & Galstyan, A. (2021). A survey on bias and fairness in machine learning. *ACM Computing Surveys*, *54*(6), 1–35. DOI: 10.1145/3457607

Met, İ., Erkoç, A., İpek, B., & Atakara Kızıldere, N. (2023). Being a game changer with happy workers: The Ziraat Bank example. *Heliyon*, *9*(7), e18027. DOI: 10.1016/j.heliyon.2023.e18027 PMID: 37519673

Metin, O., & Ünal, Ş. (2022). Content analysis technique: Its use in PhD theses in communication sciences and sociology. *Anadolu University Journal of Social Sciences*, *22*(2), 273–294. DOI: 10.18037/ausbd.1227356

Michaelson, R., & Farouk, M. (2023, May 8). Inflation, IMF austerity and grandiose military plans edge more Egyptians into poverty. *The Guardian*. https://www.theguardian.com/global-development/2023/may/08/inflation-imf-austerity-and-grandiose-military-plans-edge-more-egyptians-into-poverty

Mienye, I. D., & Swart, T. G. (2024). A comprehensive review of deep learning: Architectures, recent advances, and applications. *Information (Basel)*, *15*(12), 755. DOI: 10.3390/info15120755

Mikalef, P., & Gupta, M. (2021). Artificial intelligence capability: Conceptualization, measurement calibration, and empirical study on its impact on organizational creativity and firm performance. *Information & Management*, *58*(3), 103434. DOI: 10.1016/j.im.2021.103434

Miller, D. (1991). Stale in the saddle: CEO tenure and the match between organization and environment. *Management Science*, *37*(1), 34–52. DOI: 10.1287/mnsc.37.1.34

Milne, S. (2024). AI tools show biases in ranking job candidates' names according to perceived race and gender. *UW News*. Retrieved November 25, 2025, from https://www.washington.edu/news/2024/10/31/ai-bias-resume-screening-race-gender/

Mittelstadt, B. D., Allo, P., Taddeo, M., Wachter, S., & Floridi, L. (2016). The ethics of algorithms: Mapping the debate. *Big Data & Society*, *3*(2), 1–21. DOI: 10.1177/2053951716679679

Mohnblatt, D. (2023, January 16). Egyptian economy continues to deteriorate with future uncertain. *The Media Line*. https://themedialine.org/by-region/egyptian-economy-continues-todeteriorate-with-future-uncertain/

Moloantoa, M., & Dorasamy, N. (2017). Job satisfaction among academic employees in institutions of higher learning. Problems and Perspectives in Management, 15(3–1), 193–200. https://doi.org/DOI: 10.21511/ppm.15(3-1).2017.03

Mousa, M. (2024a). From announcing their pregnancy to returning to work: The experience of pregnant street-level bureaucrats in non-Western public contexts. *Public Integrity*, 1–17. DOI: 10.1080/10999922.2024.2304763

Mousa, M. (2024b). What determines the engagement of nurses in organizational learning post Covid-19? The role of street-level bureaucracy and Florence Nightingale theories. *Public Integrity*, •••, 1–16. DOI: 10.1080/10999922.2024.2348902

Mousa, M. (2025). Gig work, management education and changes in working conditions: A qualitative study. *Industrial and Commercial Training, 57*(1), 82–98. DOI: 10.1108/ICT-07-2024-0066

Mousa, M., & Abdelgaffar, H. (2023). Career shock of hotel employees and their individual resilience: An exploratory study. *Consumer Behavior in Tourism and Hospitality, 18*(2), 228–240. DOI: 10.1108/CBTH-06-2022-0134

Mousa, M., Arslan, A., Cooper, C., & Tarba, S. (2024a). Live like an ant to eat sugar: Nurses' engagement in extreme work conditions and their perceptions of its ethicality. *International Journal of Human Resource Management, 35*(2), 309–332. DOI: 10.1080/09585192.2023.2237877

Mousa, M., Arslan, A., Ullah, A., Tarba, S., & Cooper, C. (2024b). Work from home feasibility and challenges for public sector employees in a developing country. *Journal of Organizational Effectiveness: People and Performance, 12*(5), 41–59. DOI: 10.1108/JOEPP-12-2023-0549

Mousa, M., Avolio, B., & Pahlevan Sharif, S. (2023b). Emancipation and street-level bureaucracy in non-western contexts: The representation of neurodiverse individuals in public sector organizations. *Public Integrity, 26*(4), 439–454. DOI: 10.1080/10999922.2023.2247867

Mousa, M., & Samara, G. (2022). Mental health of business academics within the COVID-19 era: Can meaningful work help? A qualitative study. *Employee Relations, 44*(4), 764–784. DOI: 10.1108/ER-04-2021-0170

Mousa, M., Tarba, S., Arslan, A., & Cooper, C. (2023a). When extreme work becomes the norm: An exploration of coping strategies of public sector nurses. *Public Management Review, 27*(1), 297–316. DOI: 10.1080/14719037.2023.2246493

Murire, O. (2024). Artificial Intelligence and Its Function in Shaping Organizational Work Practices and Culture. *Administrative Sciences, 14*(12), 316. DOI: 10.3390/admsci14120316

Murphy, C., Klotz, A. C., & Kreiner, G. E. (2017). Blue skies and black boxes: The promise (and practice) of grounded theory in human resource management research. *Human Resource Management Review, 27*(2), 291–305. DOI: 10.1016/j.hrmr.2016.08.006

Murphy, K. R. (2025). The illusion of performance management. *Human Resource Management.* Advance online publication. DOI: 10.1002/hrm.70016

Muttaqijn, M. I., Effendi, Y., & Kusumawati, I. (2025). Integrating evidence-based management principles with green economy in Kampung Tematik. *International Journal of Sustainable Development and Planning*, *20*(4), 1731–1739. DOI: 10.18280/ijsdp.200434

Nakano, C., Yamada, T., Fukunaga, A., & Nomura, C. (2009). The fifth survey study of the institutionalization of ethics in Japanese corporations. [in Japanese]. *Journal of Japan Society for Business Ethics Study*, *16*, 151–163.

Naoum, R. F., Szakadáti, T., & Balogh, G. (2026). *Artificial Intelligence (AI) in human resource management (HRM): A systematic review of its dual impact on diversity, equity, and inclusion (DEI)*. Management Review Quarterly., DOI: 10.1007/s11301-025-00580-y

Nawaz, N., Arunachalam, H., Pathi, B. K., & Gajenderan, V. (2024). The adoption of artificial intelligence in human resources management practices. *International Journal of Information Management Data Insights*, *4*(1), 100208. DOI: 10.1016/j.jjimei.2023.100208

Ncube, T. R., Sishi, K. K., & Skinner, J. P. (2025). The impact of artificial intelligence on human resource management practices: An investigation. *SA Journal of Human Resource Management*, *23*, a2960. Advance online publication. DOI: 10.4102/sajhrm.v23i0.2960

Nigam, A. K.Abhishek Kumar Nigam. (2024). Digital divide and financially marginalized communities: Strategies for implementation of NEP 2020. *International Journal For Multidisciplinary Research*, *6*(2), 14909. Advance online publication. DOI: 10.36948/ijfmr.2024.v06i02.14909

NIST - National Institute of Standards and Technology. (2023). Artificial intelligence risk management framework (AI RMF 1.0) (NIST AI 100-1). U.S. Department of Commerce. Retrieved April 27, 2026, from https://nvlpubs.nist.gov/nistpubs/ai/NIST.AI.100-1.pdf

Noble, S. U. (2018). *Algorithms of Oppression: How Search Engines Reinforce Racism*. NYU Press., DOI: 10.18574/nyu/9781479833641.001.0001

O'Neil, C. (2016). *Weapons of math destruction: How big data increases inequality and threatens democracy*. Penguin Press.

Ogunyomi, P., & Bruning, N. S. (2016). Human resource management and organizational performance of small and medium sized enterprises (SMEs) in Nigeria. *International Journal of Human Resource Management*, *27*(6), 612–634. DOI: 10.1080/09585192.2015.1033640

Oğuz, Ö. (2024). Algorithmic discrimination in the workplace. *Süleyman Demirel University Faculty of Law Journal, 14*(2), 1851–1886. Retrieved November 25, 2025, from. DOI: 10.52273/sduhfd.1581436

Okpilike, M. E. (2012). The place of social interaction in the Nigerian school system: Implications for school life. *Developing Countries Journal*, *2*(10), 132–142.

Olutimehin, D. O., Ofodile, O. C., Ejibe, I., Odunaiya, O. G., & Soyombo, O. T. (2024). IMPLEMENTING AI IN BUSINESS MODELS: STRATEGIES FOR EFFICIENCY AND INNOVATION. *International Journal of Management & Entrepreneurship Research*, *6*(3), 863–877. DOI: 10.51594/ijmer.v6i3.940

Oschman, B., & Matjie, M. A. (2025). Exploring employees' experiences with performance appraisals at the South African Air Force. *SA Journal of Human Resource Management*, *23*(0), a2925. DOI: 10.4102/sajhrm.v23i0.2925

Ouakili, O. E. (2025). The impact of Artificial Intelligence (AI) on Recruitment Process. *Open Journal of Business and Management*, *13*(2), 749–762. DOI: 10.4236/ojbm.2025.132039

Outakoski, H., Cocq, C., & Steggo, P. (2018). Strengthening indigenous languages in the digital age: Social media–supported learning in Sápmi. *Media International Australia, Incorporating Culture & Policy*, *169*(1), 21–31. DOI: 10.1177/1329878X18803700

Ozdemir, O., Han, W., & Dalbor, M. (2022). Economic policy uncertainty and hotel occupancy: The mediating effect of consumer sentiment. *Journal of Hospitality and Tourism Insights*, *5*(2), 253–273. DOI: 10.1108/JHTI-08-2020-0149

Paauwe, J. (2009). HRM and performance: Achievements, methodological issues and prospects. *Journal of Management Studies*, *46*(1), 129–142. DOI: 10.1111/j.1467-6486.2008.00809.x

Paauwe, J., Wright, P., & Guest, D. (2013). HRM and performance: What do we know and where should we go? In Paauwe, J., Wright, P., & Guest, D. (Eds.), *Human resource management and performance: Achievements and challenges* (pp. 1–15). Wiley.

Pal, R., Shaikh, S., Satpute, S., & Bhagwat, S. (2022). Resume classification using various machine learning algorithms. *ITM Web of Conferences, 44*, 03011. DOI: 10.1051/itmconf/20224403011

Panda, G., Dash, M. K., Samadhiya, A., Kumar, A., & Mulat-Weldemeskel, E. (2023). Artificial intelligence as an enabler for achieving human resource resiliency: Past literature, expose debate and future research directions. *International Journal of Industrial Engineering and Operations Management*, *6*(4), 326–347. DOI: 10.1108/IJIEOM-05-2023-0047

Pandit, D., Joshi, M. P., Sahay, A., & Gupta, R. K. (2018). Disruptive innovation and dynamic capabilities in emerging economies: Evidence from the Indian automotive sector. *Technological Forecasting and Social Change*, *129*, 323–329. DOI: 10.1016/j.techfore.2017.09.035

Pan, Y., Froese, F., Liu, N., Hu, Y., & Ye, M. (2022). The adoption of artificial intelligence in employee recruitment: The influence of contextual factors. *International Journal of Human Resource Management*, *33*(6), 1125–1147. DOI: 10.1080/09585192.2021.1879206

Park, H., Ahn, D., Hosanagar, K., & Lee, J. (2021). Human–AI interaction in human resource management: Understanding why employees resist algorithmic evaluation at workplaces and how to mitigate burdens. In *Proceedings of the 2021 CHI Conference on Human Factors in Computing Systems* (pp. 1–15). Association for Computing Machinery. DOI: 10.1145/3411764.3445304

Pavlou, P. A. (2003). Consumer acceptance of electronic commerce: Integrating trust and risk with the technology acceptance model. *International Journal of Electronic Commerce*, *7*(3), 101–134. DOI: 10.1080/10864415.2003.11044275

Pedersen, L. H., Andersen, L. B., & Thomsen, N. (2020). Motivated to act and take responsibility: Integrating insights from community psychology in PSM research. *Public Management Review*, *22*(7), 999–1023. DOI: 10.1080/14719037.2020.1740307

Pew Research Center. (2023). *AI in hiring and employee evaluation: What Americans think*. Retrieved November 25, 2025, from https://www.pewresearch.org/internet/2023/04/20/ai-in-hiring-and-evaluating-workers-what-americans-think/

Pham, T. D. T., & Duong, N. T. (2024). Investigating learning burnout and academic performance among management students: A longitudinal study in English courses. *BMC Psychology*, *12*(1), 219. DOI: 10.1186/s40359-024-01725-6 PMID: 38650026

Ploγhart, R. E. (2021). Human capital and the resource-based view: Advancing research on strategic human capital resources. *Journal of Management*, *47*(6), 1448–1471. DOI: 10.1177/01492063211003137

Pollard, T. M. (2001). Changes in mental well-being, blood pressure and total cholesterol levels during workplace reorganization: The impact of uncertainty. *Work and Stress*, *15*(1), 14–28. DOI: 10.1080/02678370110064609

Polson, J. M., Khan, A. Y., & Wilson, E. G. (2024). AI workplace screener faces bias lawsuit: Five lessons for employers and five lessons for AI developers. Retrieved November 25, 2025, from https://www.jdsupra.com/legalnews/ai-workplace-screener-faces-bias-9455001/

Prasad, K., & De, T. (2024). Generative AI as a catalyst for HRM practices: Mediating effects of trust. *Humanities & Social Sciences Communications*, *11*(1), 1362. Advance online publication. DOI: 10.1057/s41599-024-03842-4

Prendergast, C., & Topel, R. H. (1996). Favouritism in organizations. *Journal of Political Economy*, *104*(5), 958–978. DOI: 10.1086/262048

Purcell, Z. A., & Bonnefon, J. F. (2023). Research on Artificial Intelligence is Reshaping Our Definition of Morality. *Psychological Inquiry*, *34*(2), 100–101. DOI: 10.1080/1047840X.2023.2248857

Puschmann, T. (2017). Fintech. *Business & Information Systems Engineering*, *59*(1), 69–76. DOI: 10.1007/s12599-017-0464-6

Qahtani, E. A., & Alsmairat, M. A. K. (2023). Assisting artificial intelligence adoption drivers in human resources management: A mediation model. *Acta Logistica*, *10*(1), 141–150. DOI: 10.22306/al.v10i1.371

Qasmi, F., & Fatima, S. K. (2024). Enhancing education and well-being through artificial intelligence: Opportunities and challenges. In *Breaking barriers with generative intelligence: Using GI to improve human education and well-being* (pp. 154–164). Springer Nature Switzerland., DOI: 10.1007/978-3-031-65996-6_13

Quesada, O., & Martínez de Lafuente, D. (2024). *Too old to work? A field experiment on age discrimination in the Spanish labor market.* Retrieved November 25, 2025, from https://ssrn.com/abstract=4704576 DOI: 10.2139/ssrn.4704576

Raghavan, M., Barocas, S., Kleinberg, J., & Levy, K. (2020). Mitigating bias in algorithmic recruitment: Evaluating claims and practices. *Proceedings of the ACM Conference on Fairness, Accountability, and Transparency*, 469–481. DOI: 10.1145/3351095.3372828

Rao, P. S., Venkatesan, L. N., Cherubini, M., & Jayagopi, D. B. (2025, October). Invisible Filters: Cultural Bias in Hiring Evaluations Using Large Language Models. In Proceedings of the AAAI/ACM Conference on AI, Ethics, and Society (Vol. 8, No. 3, pp. 2164-2176). Retrieved November 25, 2025, from https://arxiv.org/pdf/2508.16673

Raudenská, P. (2023). Single-item measures of happiness and life satisfaction: The issue of cross-country invariance of popular general well-being measures. *Humanities & Social Sciences Communications*, *10*(1), 861. DOI: 10.1057/s41599-023-02299-1

Reade, C. (2009). Human resource management implications of terrorist threats to firms in the supply chain. *International Journal of Physical Distribution & Logistics Management*, *39*(6), 469–485. DOI: 10.1108/09600030910985820

Ren, Y., Guo, Q., Zhu, H., & Ying, W. (2019). The effects of economic policy uncertainty on China's economy: Evidence from time-varying parameter FAVAR. *Applied Economics*, *52*(29), 1–19. DOI: 10.1080/00036846.2019.1707475

Revillod, G. (2025a). Exploring the acceptability of artificial intelligence in human resources management: Insights from Swiss organizations. *Systems Research and Behavioral Science*, *42*(4), 1061–1084. DOI: 10.1002/sres.3140

Revillod, G. (2025b). Trust influence on AI HR tools perceived usefulness in Swiss HRM: The mediating roles of perceived fairness and privacy concerns. *AI & Society*, *40*(6), 1–34. DOI: 10.1007/s00146-025-02216-x

Rieke, A., & Bogen, M. (2018). Help wanted: An examination of hiring algorithms, equity, and bias. *Upturn*. Retrieved April 27, 2026, from https://www.upturn.org/reports/2018/hiring-algorithms/

Rimbawati, P. (2023). Influence of COVID in digitizing and collective endeavor in Indonesia. *Medical Research Archives*, *11*(6). Advance online publication. DOI: 10.18103/mra.v11i6.3861

Roumpi, D. (2023). Rethinking the strategic management of human resources: Lessons learned from Covid-19 and the way forward in building resilience. *The International Journal of Organizational Analysis*, *31*(1), 215–231. DOI: 10.1108/IJOA-09-2021-2974

Roumpi, D., & Delery, J. E. (2019). Strategic HRM: Where do we go from here? In Wilkinson, A., Bacon, N., Lepak, D., & Snell, S. (Eds.), *The Sage handbook of human resource management* (pp. 423–438). Sage. DOI: 10.4135/9781529714852.n25

Roumpi, D., Magrizos, S., & Nicolopoulou, K. (2020). Virtuous circle: Human capital and human resource management in social enterprises. *Human Resource Management*, *59*(5), 401–421. DOI: 10.1002/hrm.22002

Rubinkam, M. (2024). Convenience store chain with hundreds of outlets in 6 states hit with discrimination lawsuit. *AP News*. Retrieved November 25, 2025, from https://apnews.com/article/sheetz-discrimination-suit-biden-campaign-visit-9cc14287564a8821a54acbc83ae3de83

Ruggerio, C. A. (2021). Sustainability and sustainable development: A review of principles and definitions. *The Science of the Total Environment*, *786*, 147481. DOI: 10.1016/j.scitotenv.2021.147481 PMID: 33965820

Ruggiano, N., & Perry, T. E. (2019). Conducting secondary analysis of qualitative data: Should we, can we, and how? *Qualitative Social Work: Research and Practice*, *18*(1), 81–97. DOI: 10.1177/1473325017700701 PMID: 30906228

Sadeghi, S. (2024). Employee well-being in the age of AI: Perceptions, concerns, behaviors, and outcomes. *arXiv*. https://arxiv.org/abs/2412.04796

Saeed, M., Maarouf, H. M., & Younis, R. A. A. (2025). The function of HRM-service quality in the relationship between electronic human resource management and perceived performance. *Future Business Journal*, *11*(1), 1. Advance online publication. DOI: 10.1186/s43093-024-00415-4

Sahinoz, S., & Cosar, E. E. (2018). Economic policy uncertainty and economic activity in Turkey. *Applied Economics Letters*, *25*(21), 1517–1520. DOI: 10.1080/13504851.2018.1430321

Sajja, R., Sermet, Y., Cikmaz, M., Cwiertny, D., & Demir, I. (2024). Artificial intelligence-enabled intelligent assistant for personalized and adaptive learning in higher education. *Information (Basel)*, *15*(10), 596. DOI: 10.3390/info15100596

Sakarji, S. R., Abdullah Thani, A. K., & Faris, N. (2022). Job satisfaction and individual happiness among employees: An empirical evidence at public higher education institution. *International Journal of Academic Research in Business & Social Sciences*, *12*(6), 128–140. DOI: 10.6007/IJARBSS/v12-i6/12877

Saleh, A., Adhani, A., & Mujahiddin, . (2022). Utilization of online social work education for community empowerment. *Advances in Social Science, Education and Humanities Research*. Advance online publication. DOI: 10.2991/978-2-494069-07-7_10 PMID: 36624497

Salim, M., & Rosyidi, Z. (2025). Digital literacy development towards Golden Indonesia 2045. *Journal of Practice Learning and Educational Development, 5*(3), 539–558. DOI: 10.58737/jpled.v5i3.539

Santos, J. K. S., Siqueira, L. S., Faria, E. M. B., Bispo, K. A., Silva, G. J. F., & Soares, M. S. (2025). Methodological advances in expert systems with artificial intelligence. In *Anais do XXI Simpósio Brasileiro de Sistemas de Informação* (pp. 703–712). Sociedade Brasileira de Computação., DOI: 10.5753/sbsi.2025.246618

Sarwar, N., Bung, P., Shaikh, M., & Grover, R. (2023). A study on factors influencing workplace happiness and its relationship with job satisfaction, employee retention, and work performance. *Journal of Informatics Education and Research, 3*(2). Advance online publication. DOI: 10.52783/jier.v3i2.556

Schalk, R. (2004). Changes in the employment relationship across time. In Coyle-Shapiro, J., Shore, L. M., Taylor, S., & Tetrick, L. E. (Eds.), *The employment relationship: Examining psychological and contextual perspectives* (pp. 284–311). Oxford University Press. DOI: 10.1093/oso/9780199269136.003.0013

Setiawati, R., Kusmara, A., & Kuusk, T. (2025). Managing transparency, fairness, and accountability in AI for sustainable human resource management. In *2025 4th International Conference on Creative Communication and Innovative Technology (ICCIT)* (pp. 1–7). IEEE. DOI: 10.1109/ICCIT65724.2025.11166968

Setiono, B. A., & Hidayat, S. (2022). Influence of Service Quality with the Dimensions of Reliability, Responsiveness, Assurance, Empathy and Tangibles on Customer Satisfaction. *International Journal of Economics Business and Management Research, 6*(9), 330–341. DOI: 10.51505/IJEBMR.2022.6924

Shaw, J. D., Dineen, B. R., Fang, R., & Vellella, R. F. (2009). Employee–organization exchange relationships, HRM practices, and quit rates of good and poor performers. *Academy of Management Journal, 52*(5), 1016–1033. DOI: 10.5465/amj.2009.44635525

Shen, P., Wan, D., & Zhu, A. Z. X. (2024). Investigating the effect of AI service quality on consumer well-being in retail context. *Service Business, 19*(1), 5. Advance online publication. DOI: 10.1007/s11628-024-00575-x

Shin, D. (2021a). The effects of explainability and causability on perception, trust, and acceptance: Implications for explainable AI. *International Journal of Human-Computer Studies, 146*, 102551. DOI: 10.1016/j.ijhcs.2020.102551

Shin, D. (2021b). The effects of explainability and transparency on trust in and acceptance of AI. *Information Communication and Society*, *24*(9), 1223–1241. DOI: 10.1080/1369118X.2020.1776378

Shin, D., & Park, Y. J. (2019). Role of fairness, accountability, and transparency in algorithmic trust. *Telematics and Informatics*, *38*, 33–45. DOI: 10.1016/j.tele.2018.11.007

Siem, T. T., Nguyen, H. T. T., To, A. T., & Phong, T. K. (2025). Exploring trends in employer attractiveness research: A bibliometric coupling approach. *Acta Psychologica*, *227*, 105220. DOI: 10.1016/j.actpsy.2025.105220 PMID: 40570583

Sikora, D. M., Thompson, K. W., Russell, Z. A., & Ferris, G. R. (2016). Reimagining overqualified human resources to promote organizational effectiveness and competitive advantage. *Journal of Organizational Effectiveness: People and Performance*, *3*(1), 23–42. DOI: 10.1108/JOEPP-03-2015-0012

Silalahi, H. T., Basyuni, M., Aritonang, E. Y., Slamet, B., Hartini, K. S., & Wee, A. K. S. (2024). Management of mangrove landscape and ecosystem for ecotourism. *Global Journal of Environmental Science and Management*, *10*(4), 1977–1992. DOI: 10.22034/GJESM.2024.04.29

SimanTov-Nachlieli, I. (2025, January). I. (2024). More to Lose: The Adverse Effect of High Performance Ranking on Employees' Preimplementation Attitudes Toward the Integration of Powerful AI Aids. *Organization Science*, *36*(1), 1–20. Advance online publication. DOI: 10.1287/orsc.2023.17515

Singh, A., & Banerji, R. (2022). Happiness at work, organizational citizenship behavior, and workplace diversity: A study on Indian private sector bank employees. *Industrial and Commercial Training*, *54*(3), 460–475. DOI: 10.1108/ICT-05-2021-0037

Siraj, R. (2025). Strategic human resource management and employee outcomes: A comprehensive literature review on the impact of SHRM practices on job satisfaction and organizational commitment. *The Critical Review of Social Sciences Studies*, *3*(1), 3154–3164. DOI: 10.59075/gh4rzd88

Sivakaminathan, S., & Musi, E. (2025). ChatGPT is a gender bias echo-chamber in HR recruitment: An NLP analysis and framework to uncover the language roots of bias. *AI & Society*. Advance online publication. DOI: 10.1007/s00146-025-02564-8

Sonderling, K., Bradford, J. K., & Casimir, L. (2022). The promise and the peril: Artificial intelligence and employment discrimination. *University of Miami Law Review*, *77*(1). Retrieved November 25, 2025, from https://repository.law.miami.edu/cgi/viewcontent.cgi?article=4692&context=umlr

Storey, J., Ulrich, D., & Wright, P. M. (2019). *Strategic human resource management: A research overview*. Routledge. DOI: 10.4324/9780429490217

Sumarmi, S., Untari, S., & Meiji, N. H. P. (2022). Desa Pancasila: The implementation of Gotong Royong values as social capital in Indonesia. *Komunitas*, *14*(2), 225–238. DOI: 10.15294/komunitas.v14i2.27789

Sundari, M. H., Matheshkanna, L., & Riswan, M. (2025). Artificial intelligence in human resource management: A systematic literature review and human centered framework. [IRJAEM]. *International Research Journal on Advanced Engineering and Management*, *3*(10), 3010–3022. Advance online publication. DOI: 10.47392/IRJAEM.2025.0478

Sun, L. Y., Aryee, S., & Law, K. S. (2007). High-performance human resource practices, citizenship behavior, and organizational performance: A relational perspective. *Academy of Management Journal*, *50*(3), 558–577. DOI: 10.5465/amj.2007.25525821

Suriyaa, S. (2024). Exploring an AI-based algorithmic framework for ethical decision-making in human resource management procedures. *Shanlax International Journal of Management, 11*(S1-Mar), 228–234. DOI: 10.34293/management.v11iS1-Mar.8110

Suseno, Y., Chang, C., Hudik, M., & Fang, E. S. (2022). Beliefs, anxiety and change readiness for artificial intelligence adoption among human resource managers: The moderating role of high-performance work systems. *International Journal of Human Resource Management*, *33*(6), 1209–1236. DOI: 10.1080/09585192.2021.1931408

Sweeeft (2025). *Applicant tracking system: What it is and how it could benefit HR professionals.* Retrieved November 25, 2025, from https://www.sweeeft.ai/en/articles/the-benefits-of-an-ai-powered-applicant-tracking-system-ats-for-hr-teams-88

Taha, M. A., Saafan, M. M., & Ayyad, S. M. (2025). Revisiting natural selection: Evolving dynamic neural networks using genetic algorithms for complex control tasks. *Artificial Intelligence Review*, *58*(11), 366. DOI: 10.1007/s10462-025-11382-9

Tambe, P., Cappelli, P., & Yakubovich, V. (2019). Artificial intelligence in human resources management: Challenges and a path forward. *California Management Review*, *61*(4), 15–42. DOI: 10.1177/0008125619867910

Tan, L. Y., Hu, S., Yeo, D. J., & Cheong, K. H. (2025). Artificial intelligence-enabled adaptive learning platforms: A review. *Computers and Education: Artificial Intelligence*, *9*, 100429. DOI: 10.1016/j.caeai.2025.100429

Tavşancıl, E., & Aslan, E. (2001). *Content analysis for verbal, written, and other materials with application examples.* Epsilon Publishing.

The People Space. (2020). *HR and AI ethics: How artificial intelligence in the workplace is changing the role of HR leaders.* Retrieved November 25, 2025, from https://www.thepeoplespace.com/sites/default/files/downloads/hr_and_ai_ethics_ebook_2020.pdf

The Statesman. (2023), available at: https://www.thestatesman.com/opinion/egypts-downturn-1503244320.html

Thijssen, L., Coenders, M., & Lancee, B. (2020). Ethnic discrimination in the Dutch labor market: Differences between ethnic minority groups and the role of personal information about job candidates. *Journal of International Migration and Integration*, *22*, 1125–1150. DOI: 10.1007/s12134-020-00795-w

Timis, D. (2025). *Jobs and the future of work: How "age-proofing" AI in the workplace can foster inclusivity.* World Economic Forum. Retrieved November 25, 2025, from https://www.weforum.org/stories/2025/03/how-age-proofing-ai-in-workplace-can-foster-inclusivity/

Todoli-Signes, A. (2019). Algorithms, artificial intelligence and automated decisions concerning workers and the risks of discrimination: The necessary collective governance of data protection. *Transfer: European Review of Labour and Research*, *25*(4), 465–481. DOI: 10.1177/1024258919876416

Tomasev, N., Maynard, J. L., & Gabriel, I. (2025). Manifestations of xenophobia in AI systems. *AI & Society*, *40*(2), 741–763. DOI: 10.1007/s00146-024-01893-4

Torralba, A., & Ali, H. (2024). Ethical considerations of artificial intelligence in human resources: Impact on job performance and organizational culture. Retrieved November 25, 2025, from https://www.researchgate.net/publication/382000437_Ethical_Considerations_of_Artificial_Intelligence_in_Human_Resources_Impact_on_Job_Performance_and_Organizational_Culture

Trading economics (2023), available at: https://tradingeconomics.com/egypt/unemployment-rate

Turhan, M. (2014). Organizational cronyism: A scale development and validation from the perspective of teachers. *Journal of Business Ethics*, *123*(2), 295–308. DOI: 10.1007/s10551-013-1839-3

Tyler, T. R., & Blader, S. L. (2003). The group engagement model: Procedural justice, social identity, and cooperative behavior. *Personality and Social Psychology Review*, *7*(4), 349–361. DOI: 10.1207/S15327957PSPR0704_07 PMID: 14633471

Úbeda García, M., Marco Lajara, B., Zaragoza Sáez, P. C., & Poveda Pareja, E. (2025). Artificial intelligence, knowledge and human resource management: A systematic literature review of theoretical tensions and strategic implications. Journal of Innovation & Knowledge. https://doi.org/DOI: 10.1016/j.jik.2025.100809

Uddin, S. F., & Ahmed, B. (2024). Exploring the importance of employee training and development in achieving sustainable development goals. *International Journal of Research in Human Resource Management*, *6*(1), 145–148. DOI: 10.33545/26633213.2024.v6.i1b.184

Valtonen, A., Saunila, M., Ukko, J., Treves, L., & Ritala, P. (2025). AI and employee wellbeing in the workplace: An empirical study. *Journal of Business Research*, *199*, 115584. DOI: 10.1016/j.jbusres.2025.115584

Van den Broek, A. (2024). Human resource management and performance: A review and research agenda. *Human Resource Management*. Advance online publication. DOI: 10.1002/hrm.20315

Venkatesh, V., & Davis, F. D. (2000). A theoretical extension of the technology acceptance model: Four longitudinal field studies. *Management Science*, *46*(2), 186–204. DOI: 10.1287/mnsc.46.2.186.11926

Verdonck, M., Gailly, F., de Cesare, S., & Poels, G. (2015). Ontology-driven conceptual modeling: A systematic literature mapping and review. *Applied Ontology*, *10*(3–4), 197–227. DOI: 10.3233/AO-150154

Villani, C., Schoenauer, M., Bonnet, Y., Berthet, C., Cornut, A.-C., Levin, F., & Rondepierre, B. « Donner un sens à l'intelligence artificielle: pour une stratégie na-tionale et européenne », Rapport public, mars 2018 (https://www.vie-publique.fr/rapport/37225-donner-un-sens-lintelligence-artificielle-pour-une-strategie-nation)

Vives, X. (2019). Digital disruption in banking. *Annual Review of Financial Economics*, *11*(1), 243–272. DOI: 10.1146/annurev-financial-100719-120854

Vlachos, I. P. (2009). The effects of human resource practices on firm growth. *International Journal of Business Science and Applied Management*, *4*(2), 17–34. DOI: 10.69864/ijbsam.4-2.40

Vorm, E. S., & Combs, D. J. (2022). Integrating transparency, trust, and acceptance: The intelligent systems technology acceptance model (ISTAM). *International Journal of Human-Computer Interaction*, *38*(18–20), 1828–1845. DOI: 10.1080/10447318.2022.2070107

Wahyudi, L., Panjaitan, H. P., & Junaedi, A. T. (2023). Leadership style, motivation, and work environment on job satisfaction and employee performance at the Environment and Hygiene Department of Pekanbaru City. *Journal of Applied Business and Technology*, *4*(1), 55–66. DOI: 10.35145/jabt.v4i1.119

Wallo, A., & Coetzer, A. (2023). Understanding and conceptualising the daily work of human resource practitioners. *Journal of Organizational Effectiveness: People and Performance*, *10*(2), 180–198. DOI: 10.1108/JOEPP-01-2022-0013

Walsh, A., Gallagher, D., & McCarthy, A. (2017). Does happiness promote career success? Revisiting the evidence. *Journal of Career Assessment*, *26*(2), 199–219. DOI: 10.1177/1069072717751441

Wang, D., Tsui, A. S., Zhang, Y., & Ma, L. (2003). Employment relationships and firm performance: Evidence from an emerging economy. *Journal of Organizational Behavior*, *24*(5), 511–535. DOI: 10.1002/job.213

Wang, S., Wang, F., Zhu, Z., Tran, T., & Du, Z. (2024). Artificial intelligence in education: A systematic literature review. *Expert Systems with Applications*, *214*, 124167. DOI: 10.1016/j.eswa.2024.124167

Wang, Y., Kim, S., Rafferty, A., & Sanders, K. (2020). Employee perceptions of HR practices: A critical review and future directions. *International Journal of Human Resource Management*, *31*(1), 128–173. DOI: 10.1080/09585192.2019.1674360

Wang, Y., & Kosinski, M. (2018). Deep neural networks are more accurate than humans at detecting sexual orientation from facial images. *Journal of Personality and Social Psychology*, *114*(2), 246–257. DOI: 10.1037/pspa0000098 PMID: 29389215

Wassan, S. (2021). How Artificial Intelligence Transforms the Experience of Employees. *Türk Bilgisayar ve Matematik Eğitimi Dergisi*, *12*(10), 7116. DOI: 10.17762/turcomat.v12i10.5603

Williams, T. A., & Shepherd, D. A. (2016). Building resilience or providing sustenance: Different paths of emergent ventures in the aftermath of Haiti earthquake. *Academy of Management Journal*, *59*(6), 2069–2102. DOI: 10.5465/amj.2015.0682

Wolfe, D., Price, M., Choe, A., Kidd, F., & Wagner, H. (2025). Revisiting UTAUT for the age of AI: Understanding employees' AI adoption and usage patterns through an extended UTAUT framework. *arXiv*. https://arxiv.org/abs/2510.15142

Wooldridge, M. (2021). *Foundations of multiagent systems*. MIT Press., DOI: 10.7551/mitpress/14268.001.0001

World Bank. (2023). https://documents.worldbank.org/en/publication/documents-reports/documentdetail/099624304122329292/idu07c72dd550d99104e560a5fd0e79e14053665

Wright, P. M., & Snell, S. A. (1998). Toward a unifying framework for exploring fit and flexibility in strategic human resource management. *Academy of Management Review*, *23*(4), 756–772. DOI: 10.2307/259061

Wright, P., & McMahan, G. (1992). Theoretical perspectives for strategic human resource management. *Journal of Management*, *18*(2), 295–322. DOI: 10.1177/014920639201800205

Yamada, T., Nakano, C., & Fukunaga, A. (2020). The effects of organizational ethical climate on unethical conduct: An empirical study in Japanese firms. [in Japanese]. *Journal of Business Ethics Studies*, *27*, 187–203.

Yanamala, K. K. R. (2023). Transparency, privacy, and accountability in AI-enhanced HR processes. *Journal of Advanced Computing Systems*, *3*(3), 10–18. DOI: 10.69987/JACS.2023.30302

Yang, M. M., Lu, Y., & Cooke, F. L. (2026). Demystifying AI for the workforce: The role of explainable AI in worker acceptance and management relations. *Journal of Management Studies*, *63*(2), 438–472. DOI: 10.1111/joms.70039

Yawar, M. E., & Hakimi, M. Q. (2025). The impact of artificial intelligence technology on human resources performance in organizations. *EuroGlobal Journal of Linguistics and Language Education*, *2*(1), 96–108. DOI: 10.69760/egjlle.2500013

Yin, L., Alba, D., & Nicoletti, L. (2024). OpenAI's GPT is a recruiter's dream tool: Tests show there's racial bias. *Bloomberg Technology*. Retrieved November 25, 2025,from https://www.bloomberg.com/graphics/2024-openai-gpt-hiring-racial-discrimination/?embedded-checkout=true

Younas, M., Ismayil, I., El-Dakhs, D. A. S., & Anwar, B. (2025). The impact of artificial intelligence-based learning tools in academic innovation: A review of Deep Seek, GPT, and Gemini (2020–2025). *Frontiers in Education*, *10*, 1689205. DOI: 10.3389/feduc.2025.1689205

Yousuf, M., & Saqib, N. (2021). Impact of job satisfaction on employee turnover intention at Bank Al-Habib. *Journal of Entrepreneurship, Management, and Innovation*, *3*(1), 1–26. DOI: 10.52633/jemi.v3i1.49

Yufik, Y. M. (2019). The Understanding Capacity and Information Dynamics in the Human Brain. *Entropy (Basel, Switzerland)*, *21*(3), 308. Advance online publication. DOI: 10.3390/e21030308 PMID: 33267023

Yu, L., Li, Y., & Fan, F. (2023). Employees' Appraisals and Trust of Artificial Intelligences' Transparency and Opacity. *Behavioral Sciences (Basel, Switzerland)*, *13*(4), 344. DOI: 10.3390/bs13040344 PMID: 37102857

Zahoor, N., Roumpi, D., Tarba, S., Arslan, A., & Golgeci, I. (2024). The role of digitalization and inclusive climate in building a resilient workforce: An ability–motivation–opportunity approach. *Journal of Organizational Behavior*, *45*(9), 1431–1459. DOI: 10.1002/job.2800

Zhang, L., & Amos, C. (2024). Dignity and use of algorithm in performance evaluation. *Behaviour & Information Technology*, *43*(2), 401–418. DOI: 10.1080/0144929X.2022.2164214

Zhang, P. (2024). Application of Artificial Intelligence (AI) in Recruitment and Selection: The Case of Company A and Company B. *Journal of Business and Management Studies*, *6*(3), 224. DOI: 10.32996/jbms.2024.6.3.18

Zhu, C. (2025). The role of AI tools in optimizing human resource management practices. *Advances in Curriculum Design & Education*, *1*(2), 1–13. DOI: 10.63808/acde.v1i2.132

Zwitter, A. (2014). Big data ethics. *Big Data & Society*, *1*(2), 2053951714559253. Advance online publication. DOI: 10.1177/2053951714559253

About the Contributors

Henning Tirrel is affiliated with the Ostfalia University of Applied Sciences in Wolfsburg (Germany) as a Professor for Business Administration with a major on Human Resource Management at the Faculty of Business. He holds a PhD in Business Administration from the University of Nicosia (Cyprus, EU). Henning does research in strategic and digital human resource management, the role of AI in HRM, (digital) employer branding, workplace flexibility practices and leadership, which has been published in peer reviewed scientific journals and books. On a regularly basis, Henning presents his research in international conferences. He is also a Fellow of the EuroMed Academy.

Hans Rüdiger Kaufmann is Full Professor in Management at the University of Nicosia in Cyprus since 2006 until today. Since 2016, he is affiliated with the University of Applied Management Studies Mannheim as Professor for International Sales Management. He was/is the Chair of 3 programs: B.A Management & Leadership, B.A. Management & Leadership (Professional Vocational University) and M.A. Business Management/M.A. Business Management & Digital Leadership (international). Consumerism and Management related topics are the core of his well cited research reflected in many book publications (including Handbooks), book contributions, journal publications, editorial engagement, key notes, and international conference publications/organization. In particular, his interests revolve around consumerism related themes such as branding, luxury, identity and new trends, i.e. sustainability, digitalization and AI. Prof. Kaufmann is Editor-in-Chief of the journal Progress in Industrial Ecology. He has been a launching member and President/Vice President of the following research networks: American Marketing Association (AMA) Global Marketing SIG, EuroMed Research Business Institute, CIRCLE International, Consumer Brand Relationship Institute.

***

Raed Atef is an Assistant Professor of Management Studies. He has served as a faculty member, researcher, and consultant across diverse academic and professional settings. Dr. Atef is actively engaged in consulting, research, and training initiatives with government agencies, non-governmental organizations, and the private sector. He has collaborated with several universities and has published numerous scholarly research papers and studies in his areas of expertise.

Emrah Ayhan graduated from Middle East Rechnical University, Political Science and Public Administration program (English) in 2010 and completed his master's degree in 2013 at the Berlin School of Economics and Law. He earned his PhD at Ankara Yıldırım Beyazıt University in 2019 with a dissertation on the organizational performance of civil society organizations. His research focuses on digital public administration, artificial intelligence, smart cities, governance, civil society, comparative politics, migration, and organizational theory. Since 2021, he has served as an Associate Professor at Anadolu University, teaching at undergraduate, master's, and PhD levels in both Turkish and English, including courses at Sungkyunkwan University in South Korea. He has published widely, contributed to national and international projects, and received continuous academic incentive awards since 2016. His recent SCIE-Q1 studies in 2024 and 2025 highlight his interdisciplinary contributions to public administration, AI, and governance.

Atanu Bhattacharya has started the career in Front Office with Radisson Hotels in 2010 and served till the position of Lobby Manager. He joined the academics in 2014 and has been in association with some reputed colleges all over India such as Golden Regency Institute, AIMS College of Hotel Management, Regal College of Hotel Management & Tourism, Om Sterling Global University and is currently working as Head of the Department, Medhavi Skills University. He has 13 International Research Papers under his belt. He has also secured publishing authority for 6 Indian Patents under Intellectual Property Rights.

Müjde Ertürk completed her first bachelor's degree in International Relations at the Faculty of Political Sciences, Ankara University, in 2011. She later earned a second bachelor's degree in Economics from Anadolu University in 2015. In June 2025, she completed her master's degree in the Department of Political Science and Public Administration, specializing in Human Rights. Ertürk worked for 8 years in the finance section of a private company in Ankara, Türkiye, where she gained extensive experience in administrative and financial operations. For the past year, she has been serving in the company's human resources department, focusing on personnel processes and organizational support. Fluent in English and French, she has a growing academic and professional interest in artificial intelligence, human rights, labor rights, public administration, and human resources. Through her interdisciplinary background, she brings a unique perspective to the study of rights-based governance and emerging technologies.

Sanjit Gomes serves as the Dean of Studies at the International School of Hospitality Management (ISHM), Kolkata. With extensive academic and administrative experience, he plays a pivotal role in shaping the institution's academic framework, ensuring quality education, and fostering a culture of excellence.

Hendry Hartono, SE., MM., currently serves as a lecturer in the Binus Business School Undergraduate Program at Bina Nusantara University. He holds a Bachelor of Economics and a Master of Management from Atma Jaya University, Jakarta, and a Doctoral degree in Management from Bina Nusantara University. His professional non-academic certifications include Certified International Research Reviewer (CIRR), Certified Leadership Management Associate (CLMA), and Certified Supply Chain Management Professional (CSCMP). Dr. Hendry has extensive experience in business consulting, specializing in strategic management, innovation, and entrepreneurship. As an active researcher in management, he has published numerous articles in Scopus- and WoS-indexed proceedings and scientific journals.

Mitsunori Hirogaki is an Associate Professor at the Faculty of Economics, Kyushu University, Japan. He received his PhD in Commerce from Kobe University. His research focuses on consumer behavior, international marketing, and marketing strategies in mature societies, with particular attention to cross-cultural perspectives. He has also been involved in big data analysis projects at the Center for the Study of the Creative Economy, Doshisha University, developing systems to identify seeds of innovation. Dr. Hirogaki is a member of the Japan Society of Marketing and Distribution, the Japan Association for Consumer Studies, and the Japanese Economic Association.

Zoya Khan is a PhD Candidate in the School of Human Resources Management at York University. Her research examines issues of equity, inclusion, and belonging among digital nomads in host countries, with an emphasis on cross-cultural adaptation and integration experiences. She is particularly interested in how mobile professionals navigate legal, social, and organizational boundaries in the context of globalized, remote work.

Ian Mizuki is a PhD Candidate in the School of Human Resources Management at York University. He also teaches at the University of Toronto. His research centers on the future of work, examining how artificial intelligence (AI) is transforming human behavior, decision-making, and organizational dynamics. He explores the strategic, organizational, ethical, and governance implications of AI integration across diverse workplace settings, with a focus on how individuals adapt to, resist, and collaborate with intelligent systems.

Manidipa Mukherjee is an Assistant Professor at the International School of Hospitality Management (ISHM), Kolkata. With academic expertise in Hospital Management, she actively mentors undergraduate and postgraduate students, bridging the gap between theoretical knowledge and industry practice.

Danang Prihandoko is an active lecturer at BINUS University. His research interests focus on MSME performance, particularly digital transformation and digital capability, drawing on the Technology–Organization–Environment (TOE) framework, Resource-Based View (RBV), and Dynamic Capabilities theory. He is currently pursuing doctoral studies with a research focus on MSME business performance in the digital era. His work has been published in several international conferences and primarily addresses issues related to digital business.

Navneet Ranjan is the Head of Department – Hospitality & Tourism at Medhavi Skills University. He has been instrumental in developing industry-relevant curricula, mentoring students, and promoting experiential learning across academic programs. His research interests include vocational education models, competency-based training, and industry-academia collaboration. Navneet has led multiple initiatives that align academic learning with real-world applications in the hospitality sector. He is known for fostering innovation, enhancing student engagement, and building strong industry partnerships. This publication reflects his commitment to advancing research-driven education and professional excellence in hospitality and tourism.

Rapeeporn Rungsithong, Ph.D. is an Associate Professor of Global Strategy and International Business at Chulalongkorn Business School, Chulalongkorn University, Thailand. Her research focuses on multinational enterprises (MNEs), particularly the internationalization of emerging market firms and outward foreign direct investment (OFDI). She examines how emerging market multinational enterprises develop competitive advantages and expand into global markets. Her research has been published in international peer-reviewed journals, including Industrial Marketing Management and the Journal of Industrial Marketing Management. She is also the author of the book International Business Management: Case Studies in Southeast Asia (2025), which presents practical case studies on multinational corporations operating in Southeast Asia.

Tagor Sigiro, CPA, is an esteemed financial expert and senior Assurance Partner who exemplifies the highest standards of professionalism in the Indonesian accounting landscape through his dual mastery of complex auditing and strategic regulatory compliance. Holding elite micro-credentials and official licenses from the Indonesian Financial Services Authority (OJK) for both the Banking and Capital Market sectors, he has established an impeccable track record in safeguarding the financial integrity of major publicly listed corporations. Beyond his executive practice, Sigiro is a prominent contributor to the advancement of accounting science, frequently serving as an expert lecturer at prestigious institutions such as Universitas Gadjah Mada (UGM) and Universitas Katolik Parahyangan (UNPAR). By bridging the gap between sophisticated theoretical frameworks and real-world industry demands, he actively shapes the future of the profession through his insights on digital transformation and ethical governance, solidifying his role as a pivotal figure in Indonesia's professional and academic communities as of 2026.

Uday Singh has twelve years of experience in hospitality with nine years in education and three years of experience in industry in front office. He is currently working in Amity University Rajasthan as Assistant professor concerned with subjects of front office and tourism. He published research papers and patents in the field of hospitality.

Index

A

B

C

D

E

H

I

J

L

M

O

P

Q

S

W

www.ingramcontent.com/pod-product-compliance
Lightning Source LLC
LaVergne TN
LVHW081524300926
849161LV00006B/1294
9798260023037